CLOCKWORK WORLDS

Contributions to the Study
of Science Fiction and Fantasy
Series Editor: Marshall Tymn

The Mechanical God: Machines in Science Fiction
Thomas P. Dunn and Richard D. Erlich, editors

Comic Tones in Science Fiction: The Art of Compromise
with Nature
Donald M. Hassler

Formula Fiction? An Anatomy of American Science Fiction,
1930-1940
Frank Cioffi

H. P. Lovecraft: A Critical Study
Donald R. Burleson

A Literary Symbiosis: Science Fiction/Fantasy Mystery
Hazel Beasley Pierce

The Intersection of Science Fiction and Philosophy:
Critical Studies
Robert E. Myers, editor

CLOCKWORK WORLDS

Mechanized Environments in SF

Edited by
Richard D. Erlich and Thomas P. Dunn

Contributions to the Study of Science Fiction and Fantasy, Number 7

Greenwood Press
Westport, Connecticut • London, England

Library of Congress Cataloging in Publication Data

Main entry under title:

Clockwork worlds, mechanized environments in SF.

(Contributions to the study of science fiction and
fantasy, ISSN 0193-6875 ; no. 7)
  "Companion volume to . . . The mechanical god, machines
in science fiction"—Pref.
  Bibliography: p.
  Includes index.
  1. Science fiction—History and criticism.
2. Dystopias in literature. I. Erlich, Richard D.
II. Dunn, Thomas P. III. Series.
PN3433.6.C56 1983   809.3'876   83-1718
ISBN 0-313-23026-9 (lib. bdg.)

Library of Congress Catalog Card Number: 83-1718
ISBN: 0-313-23026-9
ISSN: 0193-6875

First published in 1983

Greenwood Press
A division of Congressional Information Service, Inc.
88 Post Road West
Westport, Connecticut 06881

Printed in the United States of America

10 9 8 7 6 5 4 3 2 1

cf. P. K. Dick

We were nervous and we didn't know we could do it. Those machines had kept going as long as we could remember. When we finally pulled the switch and there was some quiet, I finally remembered something . . . that I was a human being, that I could stop those machines, that I was *better* than those machines anytime.

—Sit-down striker, Akron, Ohio (1936)

And did the Countenance Divine
Shine forth upon our clouded hills?
And was Jerusalem builded here
Among these dark Satanic Mills?

—William Blake, Preface to *Milton* (1804-1808)

CONTENTS

PREFACE

This anthology is about mechanized environments in SF and is a companion volume to our anthology of critical essays, *The Mechanical God: Machines in Science Fiction* (Greenwood Press, 1982). In *The Mechanical God* we insisted, usually, on limiting discussion to quite literal machines in what most critics regard as straight science fiction. In *Clockwork Worlds*, we have allowed for metaphorical "mechanization" and have encouraged contributors to deal with "SF": speculative fiction (to appropriate Robert A. Heinlein's phrase)—a broad literary category that includes science fiction, utopias and dystopias, and related genres.[1]

Because this is a complex subject, we have tried in organizing this volume to provide coverage of it in several different ways. First, Arthur O. Lewis, a lifelong student of literary motifs and emblems, gives a comprehensive overview of clockwork worlds, defining the term further and setting it in political and literary historical context. Next a series of five essays beginning with Merritt Abrash's consideration of Dante's *Inferno* shows something of the development of the motif in classic pieces of dystopian fiction. A second group of essays deals directly with the motif as treated by some of the major figures of modern science fiction, including Harlan Ellison and Robert A. Heinlein, R. A. Lafferty, Philip K. Dick, and Kurt Vonnegut, Jr. The four essays in the third, or "Special Topics," section study mechanized environments from a variety of viewpoints, methodological approaches, and special interests.[2]

We also have provided a List of Works Useful for the Study of Mechanized Environments in SF. This List has its own introduction, so we will comment here only upon its place in what we can call the economy of *Clockwork Worlds*.[3] It is in the traditional location at the end of the volume, just before the back matter, and it performs the traditional functions of such lists: placing this volume in its context in the canon of criticism, and providing suggestions for further study. Knowledge of that context will greatly aid readers in studying, and evaluating, the essays in *Clockwork Worlds*. Testing the theses and hypotheses and applying the insights of these essays to additional works should improve our understanding of SF.

ACKNOWLEDGMENTS

We wish now to thank several people for their generous assistance in compiling this volume. First to Albert J. Rudnickas, and (later) Daniel J. Giancola, our editorial assistants for this volume and for its companion, *The Mechanical God,* our continued gratitude for the many hours of digging, ferreting, and correcting. And thanks also to our series editor Marshall B. Tymn for his help with our annotated list; to Becky Zartner, research librarian at the Hamilton Campus of Miami University, for locating primary and secondary works; and finally to our proofreaders John M. Tritica and Sally Joyce Cross, and to the secretarial staff of Miami University's English Department, in particular Donna Shackelford, whose patient and careful attention made a book of our palimpsest of strikeovers, carets, and hen-scratching. To these we say, "More is thy due than more than all can pay."

NOTES

1. "Utopia" is a New Latin coinage by Sir Thomas More (1516), from the Greek *ou* 'not, no' plus *topos* 'place'. There is a pun, however: Utopia, No Place, is also *eutopia*, a—or *the*—Good Place. Inversely, "dystopia" means a Bad Place, with no puns or hesitations about whether or not such places can exist. To be quite exact (as Gorman Beauchamp and others have noted), we also should speak of "euchronia" and "dyschronia," that is, Good Time(s) and Bad Time(s), since many relevant myths and stories deal much less with where their worlds are located than with when. (The Golden Age was, and the Last Days will be, worldwide phenomena; Oceania in *1984* is certainly a bad place, but there's little indication that the other countries of the world of 1984 are any better—and Orwell's title is clearly a year, not a location. And so forth.) We have not attempted to be that exact. In general, we and the other contributors to *Clockwork Worlds* limit ourselves to "utopia," retaining More's pun, and "dystopia"; where exactness is advisable, we may also use "eutopia."

2. We have attempted to ensure that the essays in this volume are easily readable by a wide variety of students of the theme of mechanized environments, and we think we have succeeded in doing so. The only essay that may prove occasionally difficult is that by Daniel W. Ingersoll, Jr., who presents some highly technical concerns in anthropology. If you have difficulty understanding an essay in *Clockwork Worlds*, you might return to it after a look at some of the relevant items cited in the "List."

3. During our hours of conferring, we were forced to the shorter alternative, "clockworlds" in preference to our somewhat tongue-twisting title. But we want to keep the title, not only for its obvious allusion to Anthony Burgess' novel, *A Clockwork Orange*, but also for the onomatopoetic whirling sound of the phrase. It suggests the antithesis of the Music of the Spheres: the buzzing of the hive, the hum of E. M. Forster's Machine, and the sound of John W. Campbell's Twilight City—the steady, gentle beat of perfect, deathless machines.

CLOCKWORK WORLDS

Arthur O. Lewis

INTRODUCTION

Although generalizations about human history and human behavior are always dangerous and seldom accurate, there is something to be said for describing human activity over the millennia as an attempt—though unconscious—to repeal the second law of thermodynamics; that is, to create order in an ever more entropic universe. Philosophers and scientists alike have proposed that even the concepts of time and space are merely attempts of the human mind to organize the chaos around it. Historically, man's most effective way of imposing order upon his surroundings has been to come together in social groups and, through the use of tools and machines, to provide an environment more suited, more orderly, in which human beings can live. Such activity seems to fulfill a basic human need, but it is this very activity that has led to what the editors of this volume call *clockwork worlds*.

The term is pejorative. It implies that such planned, orderly, and unchanging worlds are not what mankind really wants or perhaps deserves. It reflects a common view that we have already given up too much of our individuality and are in the process of giving up more in order to attain both the material comfort of things and the spiritual uplift of belonging. It is not a new view, but certainly today more people are writing about it more vigorously, and indeed more persuasively, than at any other time in human history. The crux of the argument now, as in earlier times, involves a double question: What does it mean to be human; and, How much of being human must one give up to attain the desired order? The first question is a major concern of this work's companion volume, *The Mechanical God*. The second is quite rightly a major concern of this volume. Again, if one may generalize, the answer of an earlier day to the second question was, A great deal of our humanity must be sacrificed for order—but the sacrifice is worth it. At the present time, it would appear to be, Even a little loss of humanity is too much. Thus worlds, clockwork or otherwise, that a hundred years ago were regarded as utopian are today clearly regarded as dystopian.[1]

Few thinkers have laid so heavy a debt on subsequent political and social thought as did Jean Jacques Rousseau, and his ideas for bettering human life will serve to place our subject in context. The solution to the problem of inequality among men, Rousseau wrote in *The Social Contract* (1762), is "To find a form of association which may defend and protect with the whole force of the community the person and property of every associate, and by means of which each, coalescing with all, may nevertheless obey only himself, and remain as free as before."[2] In such association, "Each of us puts in common his person and his whole power under the supreme direction of the general will; and in return we receive every member as an indivisible part of the whole."[3] The loss of natural liberty and an unlimited right to take what we want is balanced by gaining civil liberty and the right to what we already possess. It is the rights of this "moral and collective body" as opposed to those of the "individual members" that concern many of the writers discussed in this volume.[4] When the collective takes too much away from the individual, in some cases even denying that there is such a thing as an individual, what is left may not be human. Rousseau's arguments—and those of his predecessors as far back as Plato and Aristotle—for the desirability of achieving a common, reciprocal view of our dependence on each other have become, if not less valid, less acceptable in the light of recent history.

Nevertheless we continue to move toward, and to believe in, social— that is, collective—decisions. There is, as William H. Whyte, Jr., puts it, a "contemporary body of thought which makes morally legitimate the pressures of society against the individual. Its major propositions are three: a belief in the group as the source of creativity; a belief in 'belongingness' as the ultimate need of the individual; and a belief in the application of science to achieve the belongingness."[5] This is, as Whyte points out, essentially a utopian faith. It is also, with some modification, the faith of a great many thinkers with whom one would never associate the concept of a clockwork world. It is behind most of those calls for a one-world, planet-wide brotherhood of man. ("Mankind as a whole has always striven to organize a universal state.")[6] In science fiction it is behind those stories of galaxies-wide organizations of intelligent beings who have solved the problems of war, pollution, and fettered minds. And when there are protests that such organization and such belonging make human beings somehow less human, it is behind the response that only education and living in such an environment are needed to make us somehow more human or, even better, suprahuman beings. There are those who, like Whyte, believe that we have already reached the first level of such a clockwork world.

Rousseau began his arguments for organization of societies with the premise that such comings together are a necessity of survival; this premise is even more overwhelming in our day than in his. It is not only that war may destroy such a world as we have, but also that only by sharing equitably can Earth's resources sustain us. We are menaced by war and famine, and too often our response to these menaces is as grim as that implied by Fyodor Dostoevsky a century ago in the pessimistic "Grand Inquisitor" section of *The Brothers Karamazov*: "They will understand themselves, at last, that freedom and bread enough for all are inconceivable together, for they will never, never be able to share among themselves."[7] As the probability of such understanding grows, the clockwork worlds of fiction seem less and less distinguishable from the real world.

Such convergence of the real and the fictional can be better understood by examining several metaphors that have frequently been used to describe human social organizations: the human body, the hive, the machine. For Rousseau, following Plato and Aristotle among others, human society is best described as "the collective *moi*," "the public person," and, especially among political thinkers, this analogy with the human body has been often used.[8] But as seventeenth- and eighteenth-century thinkers absorbed the new science, with its new evidence about the universe, their concept of the human body changed: "Let us then conclude boldly that man is a machine, and that in a whole universe there is but a single substance differently modified."[9] The human body is a watch or an automaton: "man is but an animal, or a collection of springs which wind each other up. . . ."[10] Given this mechanistic view not only of the universe, but of men, it is easy to understand why some later planners have found it easy to accept individuals as mere cogs in a greater, social machine.

A second analogy, used less often as metaphor than as homily, is that of the hive. When highly organized, human society closely resembles the stratified, unchanging beehive, wasp nest, and anthill. And, not surprisingly, very early in history such insect societies were held up as models for the ideal social—and sometimes religious—commonwealth. Thus, in ancient Greece bees were symbols of work and obedience. In Egyptian hieroglyphics the sign of the bee designated royalty, "partly by analogy with the monarchic organization of the insects, but more especially because of the ideas of industry, creative activity and wealth which are associated with the production of honey."[11] The *Hieroglyphica* of Horapollo, first printed in 1505 but existing in manuscript at least a century earlier, had a profound influence on Renaissance political thought: "How to represent a people obedient to their king? They depict a BEE, for of all animals bees alone have a king, whom the crowd of bees follow, and to whom as to a king they yield obedience. It is intimated also, as well from the remarkable usefulness of honey as from the force which the animal has in its sting, that

a king is both useful and powerful for carrying on their affairs."[12] Geoffrey
Whitney's emblem of a hive of bees depicts the ideal state:

A Common-wealthe, by this, is right expreste;
Bothe him that rules, and those, that doe abaye:
Or suche, as are the heads above the rest,
Whome here, the Lorde in highe estate dothe staye:
　　By whose supporte, the meaner sorte doe live,
　　And unto them all reverence dulie give.[13]

As late as the nineteenth century, in *The Revolt of the Bees* (1830), John
Minter Morgan introduced his concept of the perfect state with a lengthy
narrative of the woes that befall a colony of bees that replaces the traditional cooperative system with a humanlike system of competition. The bees
learn their lesson, and in the final pages there is a vision of mankind when
"Wealth, which had before laid in masses, was not beneficially diffused and
greatly increased."[14]

Lewis Thomas reflects a more contemporary attitude—while explaining
why the hive analogy is so effective—when he draws attention to the
behavior of weaver ants: "What makes us more uncomfortable is that they,
and the bees and termites and social wasps, seem to live two kinds of lives:
they are individuals, going about the day's business without much evidence
of thought for tomorrow, and they are at the same time component parts,
cellular elements, in the huge, writhing, ruminating organism of the Hill,
the nest, the hive. It is because of this aspect, I think, that we most wish for
them to be something foreign. We do not like the notion that there can be
collective societies with the capacity to behave like organisms. If such things
exist, they can have nothing to do with us."[15] But he goes on to point out
that men "are by all odds the most social of all social animals—more inter-
dependent, more attached to each other, more inseparable in our behavior
than bees. . . ."[16]

In a sense the third analogy for human organization, the machine, grows
out of the first two. The machine used thus is usually not a *literal* great
mechanical device but a *figurative* political device. It is the planned society
carried to its logical conclusion, based on the mechanistic view of mankind
and the hive concept of fitting individuals into appropriate niches.[17] In
recent fiction the most common such device is the city.

"The earliest of all societies, and the only natural one, is the family,"[18]
said Rousseau, but neither he nor any influential social planner before or
after believed that civilization could be built on this primitive association
alone. The way to a more perfect organization of society has been almost
without exception to create a larger unit. For Auguste Comte and a few
utopians like Sir Thomas More, combining families and their strength

served as the basis for the larger unit. More often the proposal has been either to eliminate the family altogether or to so subordinate it as to make it almost nonexistent. In such societies the individual becomes the basic unit, with carefully defined functions and duties and little or no freedom, as in the case of the social insect.

Whatever the basic unit, the most common larger unit has been the city—a machine, Lewis Mumford suggests, from its inception: ". . . it is at the very beginning of urban civilization that one encounters not only the archetypal form of the city as utopia but also another co-ordinate utopian institution essential to any system of communal regimentation: the machine."[19] But what might well have been a utopia soon became a dystopia, "For the city that first impressed the image of utopia upon the mind was made possible only by another daring invention of kingship: the collective human machine, the platonic model of all later machines."[20] The great collective machine could do work that individuals singly could not do, but it incorporated "most of the dehumanized routines of our later machine technology."[21] Human beings could, it was discovered, alter the conditions of their lives. One way, as in the early city, was through "total submission to a central authority, forced labor, lifetime specialization, inflexible regimentation, one-way communication, and readiness for war."[22] Later utopian writers have believed that "similar results could be attained by voluntary effort and free association and mutual aid, rather than by military compulsion, royal or platonic."[23] It is this technological, centralized, regimented, and ugly "invisible machine" that has most often defined what we mean by clockwork worlds. Most planned societies, technologically oriented or not, are designed for the good life; most, unfortunately, quite soon develop dystopian aspects.

Not all clockwork worlds involve high technology; some make no mention of machines, mechanical or metaphorical. Nevertheless, "Ours is a society in which machines are one of man's ways of adapting to his environment,"[24] and clockwork worlds are only a reflection of those aspects of modern society that cause us to speak with familiarity not only of the computer and the assembly line but also of the political machine and the war machine. This political organization and use of human beings to accomplish a greater, or at least a larger, purpose than individuals could is a modern version of the archetypal city machine. At its worst it treats human beings as pieces of the machine that can be placed or recast at will to fit the general purposes of society.

Changing the individual to fit society's needs is seldom the result of deliberately evil intent. One might accept the view "that there is a kind of 'basic man' which is ultimately a machine, to which circumstances, life in society, institutions have added in the course of time certain extras which turned this simple mechanism into a complex, selfish, incalculable and passion-filled being.''[25] In that case, education, persuasion, and coercion are all possible means for changing him to something "better."

A little-known but interesting example of the potential for such "improvements" may be found in "Sarragalla—The Mechanized Island," in Alexander Moszkowski's *The Isles of Wisdom* (1924). Sarragalla is an experiment "which is directed towards specific practical objects, the utilization of power, the saving of time, and similar fine things."[26] Sarragalla has solved the problem of nuclear fission, using "inexhaustible deposits of the minerals thorium and uran" from a neighboring island.[27] This unlimited power has made possible concentration on the principle of mechanical perfection.

Sarragalla has—among other mechanical marvels—movable roadways, a single-track railroad (trains pass over each other on mobile rails), communication by wrist radio, and "telurgie" (medical treatment at a distance); but the most important concern is to use the energy of human beings more effectively to save time. One method is by speaking compressed language. There is, however, no question of free time: "Another fallacy. 'Free time,' strictly speaking is an absurdity. The mechanized man hasn't any, does not need it, and if he had it, would endeavour to occupy it in labour. Man is the sum total of his physical phenomena, and the latter know nothing of free time. The breath, the circulation of the blood, the renewal of the tissue, digestion; they are the most ideal workers; they know no pauses, and no evening respites. Man has in himself the mechanical prototypes. Why should he not imitate them?" The response to the visitor's demur, "Because he gets tired and must recuperate" is scornful: "The more he mechanizes himself, the less tired he becomes. The works of a clock do not need to be sent away for a holiday; they are technically perfect. . . . To a genuine worker amusement offers nothing more than crystalized, glittering tedium.''[28] On Sarragalla everyone agrees: workers became discontent when an eight-hour day was introduced, have asked for a twelve-hour day, and are expected later to demand twenty hours: "The dominant idea in the mechanized state is to transform the *nonchalant* worker into the *willing* worker.''[29]

The true nature of the Sarragallans is shown when the leader of the neighboring island refuses to provide necessary uran and thorium; telurgie is used to murder him by inflicting a stroke. The Sarragallans see no ethical problem: "There is one human being less, who had long had his day. It is not worth mentioning in comparison with the number of those whose survival is assured.''[30] Nevertheless, Moszkowski's view is a gentle one compared to those of many recent writers.

Not only the human spirit, for some of these more pessimistic writers, but also the human body must be remolded in order to create a completely ordered society. Thus, the hero of David M. Parry's *Scarlet Empire* (1906), rescued from drowning by a citizen of the Empire (Atlantis, which has survived at the bottom of the sea), is told that "the Scarlet Empire is a social democracy, the most advanced form of government in history";[31] but on his first day there he witnesses the arrest of a young man for "one of the most serious crimes known in Atlantis—that of seeking to obtain more than one's just portion of food."[32] He discovers how serious that crime is when he realizes why the people of Atlantis are so much smaller than those of his own world, and that they are solving the problem of limited resources "Simply by lessening the amount of food essential for life . . . a few grains of weight being clipped off the daily allowance for each person each year. Who can say but that in a few generations the amount of food required will be so small as to reduce labor to a minimum?"[33] Atlantis has most of the other attributes of the planned society: strict enforcement of laws, occupations chosen for the individual by the state, marriage to suit the state's needs, and even the lethe weed (shades of Aldous Huxley's soma!) to keep everyone happy. Most importantly, all is done in the name of Democracy, of majority rule: "The individual is merely one atom of the whole. The majority knows what is good for all, and when it speaks the individual must yield his opinion."[34]

In some works the human beings who serve the great machine are themselves machine-like. In Thea von Harbou's novel *Metropolis* (1926), the changing of shifts is described thus:

Along the street it came, along its own street which never crossed with other people's streets. It rolled on, a broad, an endless stream. The stream was twelve files deep. They walked in even step. Men, men, men—all in the same uniform, from throat to ankle in dark blue linen, bare feet in the same hard shoes, hair tightly pressed down by the same black caps.

And they all had the same faces. And they all appeared to be of the same age. They held themselves straightened up, but not straight. They did not raise their heads, they pushed them forward. They planted their feet forward, but they did not walk. The open gates of the New Tower of Babel, the machine center of Metropolis gulped the masses down.[35]

The stage directions in Eugene O'Neill's *Hairy Ape* (1922) are most revealing: The stokers (though often compared to animals in a cage) "jump up mechanically,"[36] and "shovel with a rhythmic motion, swinging as on a pivot. . . . But there is order in it, rhythm, a mechanical regulated recurrence, a tempo."[37] They often speak in chorus, and "The chorused word has a brazen metallic quality as if their throats were phonograph horns."[38] In a scene ashore: "The crowd from church enter from the right, sauntering slowly and affectedly, their heads held stiffly up. . . . A procession of gaudy marionettes, yet with something of the relentless horror of Frankensteins in their detached, mechanical unawareness."[39]

There is, of course, much more to Herman Melville's "Tartarus of Maids" (1855) than mere criticism of working conditions in a paper mill, but such passages as the following are certainly a severe commentary on the impact of the machine on its human servants. "Not a syllable was breathed. Nothing was heard but the low, steady overruling hum of the iron animals. The human voice was banished from the spot. Machinery—that vaunted slave of humanity—here stood menially served by human beings, who served mutely and cringingly as the slave serves the Sultan. The girls did not so much seem accessory wheels to the general machinery as mere cogs to the wheels."[40] Nor is it an accident that early in Karel Čapek's *R. U. R.* the heroine is unable to distinguish a robot from a man,[41] and the later discovery that human beings have lost the final feature that distinguishes them from robots—the ability to reproduce—comes as no surprise: "people are becoming superfluous."[42] It is Čapek's way of symbolizing the destruction of human beings through their becoming too much a part of a machine civilization.

Extrapolation from trends of our own society can be most productive in describing what happens when the things that individuals want can be attained only by the destruction of some for the benefit of others. In William Earls's science fiction story "Traffic Problem" (1970), there is no malice, only a desire to get the job done—to keep the traffic flowing so that individuals can get to work and back. That proper performance by the traffic manager means risk for a comparative few is unimportant. Thus he keeps traffic moving by periodic increases in the speed limit, more efficient removal of the frequent wrecks, elimination of obstacles that cause congestion and accidents (the Empire State Building, for example, forces traffic traveling at a hundred miles an hour to take too sharp a curve), and by replacing open space with parking lots. In such a situation people simply do not count and even the leaders are mere cogs. When the director dies, the ex-traffic manager, now director, moves upstairs, where his first important order is to get rid of what had been his chief problem as traffic manager. He orders the Empire State Building torn down: "Later that day he looked south from the roof. . . . The flow [of traffic] was good and he smiled. He couldn't remember doing anything so necessary before."[43]

In these clockwork worlds it is difficult to find evidence of deliberate malice. Greed, stupidity, misplaced trust, *yes*; evil, *no*. Service of mankind is the goal. Only in the most obvious exceptions—George Orwell's *Nineteen Eighty-Four* (1949), for example—is destruction of men other than an unexpected byproduct of the desire to improve their lives.

In this respect many social machines differ little from the more traditional view of machines as Frankenstein-monsters that turn against their makers. Even here the intent of the machine's builders is almost always to benefit mankind, but inevitably the machine mangles mankind. The mangling may be so subtle as to be almost unnoticeable, as in Isaac Asimov's "Evitable Conflict" (1950), where robots control the world for the benefit of mankind but only by "shaking the boat . . . just enough to shake loose those few which cling to the side for purposes the Machines consider harmful to Humanity."[44] It may be as obvious as the rebellious, man-eating machines of Stephen Vincent Benét's "Nightmare Number Three" (1935). It may even be the old story of the machine in the hands of the mad scientist, as in the case of the almost unknown (and rightfully so) "Aunt Edie" of A. A. Glynn's *Plan for Conquest* (1963), the "story of a man-made thing that got too clever."[45] Like Samuel Butler in *Erewhon* (1872), Glynn warns of "man becoming a victim of his own achievements, man becoming a victim of his own cleverness, *man ultimately becoming dominated by his own machines.*"[46] Or, as a minor character in the book puts it, "Machines! Those things will ruin mankind! They are taking over, I tell you. . . . The machines are taking over!"[47]

In 1911, observing the "patient" efforts of several small machines to move heavy loads, W. A. Dwiggins speculated: "Suppose that all these mechanical slaves serving mankind got sick of their jobs . . . suppose that they managed to . . . get in touch with one another and pool their grudges. . . . Suppose that the higher orders of the machine fraternity, already raised to almost human levels in point of automatic functioning, should take the next step in evolution and emerge as *personalities*, with faculties of judgment, selection, purpose, organization, and individual action. . . . What, then, would be the position of humankind upon Earth?"[48] Erewhonian society had of course banned all mechanical devices to prevent just such a development as Dwiggins suggests. Nevertheless, many of the works discussed in *Clockwork Worlds* pay tribute to this continuing fear. The symbol of masses of workers marching into the mouth of the hungry machine in *Metropolis* is one of the most powerful in fiction or film,[49] but it is only an extreme example of a very common view of the fate of humankind in a machine-dominated world.[50]

E. M. Forster's "The Machine Stops" (1909), is an excellent example of what goes wrong when people place too much reliance on their technological creations: "We created the Machine, to do our will, but we cannot make it do our will now."[51] Thomas Dunn and Richard Erlich are quite right in regarding this work as the prime example of the twentieth-century dystopian literature, embodying "two symbols for individual human helplessness and triviality: the beehive and the machine."[52] But the Machine did not start out that way, and there are many well-known stories about great machines that continue to benefit mankind.

John W. Campbell, Jr., under the name of Don A. Stuart, wrote several stories that might be regarded as follow-ups to "The Machine Stops." In "Twilight" (1934), men of the distant future know less about the machines that keep them alive than do the characters in Forster's story. They are "Little, hopeless, wondering men amid vast unknowing, blind machines that started three million years before—and just never knew how to stop. They are dead—and can't die and be still."[53] The machines are benevolent, but they have destroyed mankind. In "The Machine" (1935), Campbell-Stuart explores another possibility. In the short space of 150 years, Gaht, the thinking machine from another star, has brought humanity to a care-free, beautiful life. But, as was the case with Gaht's creators, human beings now want all play and no work; "the lesson of helpful destruction" must be applied again. By withdrawing its assistance the machine forces men back to a more primitive way of life, so that a few survive to make a less pleasant but more human world. Two succeeding stories published in 1935, "The Invaders," and "The Rebellion," continue the hopeful saga through invasion and enslavement by, to mankind's ultimate victory over, alien beings. The benevolent machine, programmed to help and protect the race it serves even at the cost of individual lives, had done its job.[54]

A victory for humanity may be found in Frederik Pohl's tongue-in-cheek "Midas Plague" (1954), in which the necessity of molding human beings to consume goods (so important a part of the economy in *Brave New World* [1932]) is met by the hero's inspired proposal to let the machines consume: "No longer was mankind hampered by inadequate supply or drowned by overproduction. What mankind needed was there. What the race did not require passed into the insatiable—and adjustable—robot maw. Nothing was wasted. For a pipeline has two ends."[55] Presumably this machine-made utopia, the ultimate in recycling, will continue until the resources of Earth are exhausted, and its inhabitants will become like those subhuman creatures in "Twilight," or the Eloi of H.G. Wells's *Time Machine* (1895).

Finally, there are writers who have envisioned machines as the faithful servant of man, even beyond the life of man, as in Clifford Simak's *City* (1952), where they serve man's successors, the Dogs, or Ray Bradbury's poignant story of postnuclear times, "There Will Come Soft Rains" (1950).[56] A few stories also assure us that despite an ability to destroy civilization through machines, man can once more resume control. Thus in Brian Aldiss' "But Who Can Replace a Man?" (1958) the quarreling hier-archy of thinking machines will, we know, come to an end when that "abject figure" sees the fleeing machines: " 'Get me food,' he croaked. 'Yes, Master,' said the machines. 'Immediately!' "[57]

As has been noted several times, many clockwork worlds are uninten-tional. This is especially so in the case of utopias. The utopian impulse has always been to improve the life of human beings. Those aspects that we find unacceptable frequently come about because the means necessary to attain the desired ends remove too much of our humanity. In one sense, utopia is the utopian writer's escape from those things he finds reprehensible in his own society. Thus, if Plato's *Republic* is accepted as a utopian proposal—which in its broadest sense it is—one must remember that this ideal society grew out of a discussion of the nature of justice and how it can be achieved. Francis Bacon's Bensalem, a clockwork world if ever there was one, is controlled by Salomon's House, which claims its mission to be "the knowledge of causes, and secret motions of things; and the enlarging of the bounds of human empire, to the effecting of all things possible."[58] Edward Bellamy believed that in his utopian society human effort would "be directed to the general advancement and elevation of the human type."[59] B. F. Skinner proposes to build a better world "with available principles of 'behavioral engineering.' "[60] And numerous attempts to live in harmony with nature and/or God have appeared even in the twentieth century: for example, James Hilton's *Lost Horizon* (1933), and Ernest Callenbach's *Ecotopia* (1975). Acceptance of these possibly better worlds depends upon how far one wishes to go in subordinating the individual to the common good. The yoke is heavier in some such societies than in others, but in some the additional weight of law or custom is not much greater than in our own. The problem is less a matter of accepting restrictions on one's activities— for we all do so daily—than of balancing such restrictions against the greater good they bring.

In our own world the rules multiply, even when only good is intended. Even worse, as Phyllis J. Day points out in her contribution to this volume, the human beings who need society's help frequently become mere objects to be treated only according to rules, the benevolent intent of which have long since been forgotten. If we could somehow maintain that benevolent intent, would it be a better world? Not according to a very large number of contemporary thinkers.

Despite initial benevolence, machines both literal and metaphorical are seldom shown as unambiguously good. Even when no physical destruction is foreseen, no suspicions of a desire to alter human mentality, an important argument maintains that man was not meant to live in a state that completely satisfies all his needs and desires. It is in portrayals and criticism of the social machine—the benign clockwork world—that this point of view is most often expressed. Thus the most significant rebuttals to Bellamy's *Looking Backward: 2000-1887* (1888), were not those that objected to the impossibility of building such a society but those that regarded its logical development as the creation of citizens who would no longer live up to their full human potential. Other utopian proposals are similarly criticized. An argument often made in opposition to even the best of utopian communities is that mere satisfaction of all human physical needs would make us into something less than human by removing what is described variously as curiosity, ambition, or simply individual control of one's destiny. Thus in

Robert Sheckley's "Street of Dreams, Feet of Clay" (1968) the ideal, planned, utopian city of Bellwether is too all-encompassing, too sure of what is good and bad for the individual, for the prospective citizen to accept it—probably precisely because, as the city screams at the departing, disillusioned Carmody: "All of you humans are disagreeable animals, and you're never really satisfied with anything."[61]

What these critics are saying, and what the dystopian writers are demonstrating, is that man is not a machine to be tempered and squeezed and set into place as part of some collective enterprise—utopia, the state, society. Men are individuals and even the promise of the radical improvement of human life through such conformity raises horrifying possibilities. However such improvements may be brought about—through the big lie of Plato's myth of the metals, the happy association of Charles Fourier, the brainwashing of David Karp, Orwell, and Skinner, the preconditioning of *Brave New World*, the scientific omniscience of *New Atlantis* and *The Shape of Things to Come*, or even the common-good politics of *Ecotopia* or the religious fervor of *Lost Horizon*—these improvements are all what Dostoevsky called "golden dreams." He is eloquent on their results:

Oh, tell me, who first declared, who first proclaimed that man only does nasty things because he does not know his real interests; and that if he were enlightened, if his eyes were opened to his real normal interests, man would at once cease to do nasty things, would at once become good and noble because, being enlightened and understanding his real advantage, he would see his own advantage in the good and nothing else, and we all know that not a single man can knowingly act to his own disadvantage. Consequently, so to say, he would begin doing good through necessity.[62]

But, continues Dostoevsky, this is not so: man "everywhere and always, whoever he may be, has preferred to act as he wished and not in the least as his reason and advantage dictated. . . . What a man needs is simply *independent* choice, whatever that independence may cost and wherever it may lead."[63] Man, that is to say, is irrational and must remain so. Such at least is a highly prevalent view among the modern intellectuals who invent clockwork dystopias.

The authors of the essays in this volume come to varying conclusions about the impact and importance of clockwork worlds, but it is the consideration of the problems raised by such societies—not agreement—that is important. Certainly few studies can be more revealing of contemporary attitudes about human society than those that concern themselves with such matters. Despite the almost ubiquitous suggestions for alternatives to an ever more machinelike existence, there seems little possibility, barring a major catastrophe either natural or man-made, of turning off the track down which mankind started so many years ago, when he first began to use tools of one kind or another to extend the capacities of his own body and discovered that by joining with others he could accomplish more. Norbert Wiener has suggested that "in connection with machines . . . there is no reason why they may not resemble human beings in representing pockets of decreasing entropy in a framework in which the large entropy tends to increase." While he goes on to deny "that the specific physical, chemical, and spiritual processes of life as we ordinarily know it are the same as those of life-imitating machines,"[64] his juxtaposition of human beings and machines—and his finding significant similarities between men and machines—is typical of contemporary thought. We do find it necessary to compare human life both individual and collective with the "life" of our machines. We think that way and perhaps we even feel that way.

Wiener may be right in drawing attention to the entropy-decreasing aspects of both machines and human beings. As I noted at the beginning of this Introduction, there is much to be said for an unconscious human drive to repeal the second law of thermodynamics. When we consider that final death of all things, we struggle to prevent it. Thus far, the most common approach has been to organize the things of nature and ourselves for more efficient use of those physical and social forces that make up our world. Most of the writers and filmmakers discussed in this book appear to believe that this is the wrong approach: we don't know enough to do it right. Further, as a society we appear to believe that, as Dostoevsky put it, beginning his argument *against* the Crystal Palace, the planned society, "we have only to discover these laws of nature, and man will no longer be responsible for his actions and life will become exceedingly easy for him."[65] But Dostoevsky did not provide a workable solution to the problem he described; nor do the artists considered in this volume. Nevertheless, their examination of what we give up in our attempt to gain order is necessary if we are to avoid a dystopian future and reach a better one—clockwork or otherwise.

NOTES

1. Throughout this Introduction, I shall often equate clockwork worlds with utopia or dystopia. This is, of course, an oversimplification, for the equation is not universal. Although many clockwork worlds are obviously dystopias—bad places —there are many dystopias that are not necessarily clockwork worlds. Similarly, not all utopias—good places—become clockwork worlds. There is however a tendency, because utopias are by their very nature planned societies, for utopian writers to propose those collective, stratified societies which may be called clockwork worlds.

2. Jean Jacques Rousseau, *The Social Contract and Discourse on the Origin of Inequality*, ed. and with introd. Lester G. Crocker (New York: Washington Square/ Pocket Books, 1967), bk. I, ch. 6, pp. 17-18.

3. Ibid., pp. 18-19.

4. Ibid., p. 19.

5. William H. Whyte, Jr., *The Organization Man* (1956; rpt. Garden City, NY: Doubleday, Anchor, n.d.), p. 7.

6. Fyodor Dostoevsky, "The Grand Inquisitor" [*The Brothers Karamazov,* bk. V, ch. 5], in *Notes from Underground and the Grand Inquisitor,* trans. and with introd. Ralph E. Matlaw (New York: E. P. Dutton, 1960), p. 133.

7. Ibid., p. 127.

8. See Giuseppa Saccaro-Battisti, "Changing Metaphors of Political Structures," *Journal of the History of Ideas,* 44 (January-March 1983), 31-54.

9. Julien Offray de la Mettrie, *Man A Machine* (1748), trans. Gertrude C. Bussey et al. (LaSalle, IL: Open Court Publishing, 1961), p. 148.

10. Ibid., p. 135.

11. J. E. Cirlot, *A Dictionary of Symbols,* trans. Jack Sage (New York: Philosophical Library, 1962), pp. 22-23.

12. Henry Green, *Shakespeare and the Emblem Writers* (London: Trübner & Co., 1870), p. 359; see also *The Hieroglyphics of Horapollo,* trans. George Boas, The Bollingen Series XXIII (New York: Pantheon Books, 1950), bk. 1, no. 62, p. 84. Obviously, only men could possibly rule, even in a beehive! A frequent later use of the beehive was to represent the obstacles and pain involved in obtaining the honey—the good things of life; see, for example, Francis Quarles, Emblem 3, in *Emblems Divine and Moral* (1635; rpt. London: William Tegg, 1865), pp. 10-12.

13. Geoffrey Whitney, *A Choice of Emblemes* (Leyden, Netherlands: Christopher Plantin, 1586), pp. 200-201. Whitney's hive is drawn from Alciati's Emblem 148, which used wasps as a model for the ideal state.

14. John Minter Morgan, *The Revolt of the Bees* (London: Hurst, Chance, and Co., 1830), p. 271.

15. Lewis Thomas, *The Lives of a Cell: Notes of a Biology Watcher* (New York: Viking Press, 1974), p. 12.

16. Ibid., p. 14.

17. See Thomas P. Dunn and Richard D. Erlich, "A Vision of Dystopia: Bee Hives and Mechanization," *Journal of General Education,* 33 (Spring 1981), 45-58.

18. Rousseau, *Social Contract,* bk. I, ch. 2, p. 8.

19. Lewis Mumford, "Utopia, The City and The Machine," in *Utopias and Utopian Thought,* ed. Frank E. Manuel (Cambridge and Boston: Houghton Mifflin, 1966), p. 11.

20. Ibid., p. 15.

21. Ibid., p. 17.

22. Ibid.

23. Ibid., p. 19.

24. A. O. Lewis, Jr., ed., *Of Men and Machines* (New York: E. P. Dutton, 1963), p. xxxi.

25. Thomas Molnar, "The Essence of Modernity," *Modern Age,* 24 (Fall 1980), 381.

26. Alexander Moszkowski, "Sarragalla—The Mechanized Island," in *The Isles of Wisdom,* trans. H. J. Stenning (London: George Routledge and Sons, 1924), pp. 313-14.

27. Ibid., p. 150.

28. Ibid., pp. 161-62.

29. Ibid., p. 169.

30. Ibid., p. 203.

31. David M. Parry, *The Scarlet Empire* (Indianapolis: Bobbs-Merrill, 1906), p. 9.

32. Ibid., p. 26.

33. Ibid., pp. 148-49.

34. Ibid., pp. 17-18.

35. Thea von Harbou, *Metropolis* (1926; rpt. New York: Ace Books, 1963), ch. 1, p. 18. Von Harbou's work was the basis for Fritz Lang's film, *Metropolis*, script by Lang and von Harbou.

36. Eugene O'Neill, *The Hairy Ape*, in *Nine Plays* (New York: Modern Library, 1959), p. 49 (stage direction in Yank's penultimate speech at the end of sc. 1).

37. Ibid., p. 55 (stage direction beginning sc. 3).

38. Ibid., p. 42, p. 60, etc. (stage directions with the "Think!" gag, sc. 1, shortly after Paddy's whiskey song, and beginning of sc. 4).

39. Ibid., p. 69 (stage direction near middle of sc. 5).

40. Herman Melville, "The Paradise of Bachelors and the Tartarus of Maids," in *Shorter Works of Hawthorne and Melville*, ed. Hershel Parker (Columbus, OH: Charles F. Merrill, 1972), p. 286.

41. Karel Čapek, *R. U. R.*, Act I, rpt. in Lewis, ed., *Of Men and Machines*, pp. 10-13.

42. Ibid., Act II, p. 32.

43. William Earls, "Traffic Problem," in *The City: 2000 A.D., Urban Life through Science Fiction*, ed. Ralph Clem, Martin Harry Greenberg, and Joseph Olander (Greenwich, CT: Fawcett, 1976), p. 252.

44. Isaac Asimov, "The Evitable Conflict," in *I, Robot* (New York: New American Library, 1956), p. 190; Stephen Vincent Benét, "Nightmare Number Three," rpt. in Lewis, *Of Men and Machines*.

45. A. A. Glynn, *Plan for Conquest* (New York: Arcadia House, 1969), p. 190.

46. Ibid., p. 26.

47. Ibid., p. 55.

48. William A. Dwiggins, *Millennium I* (New York: Alfred A. Knopf, 1945), p. [vii]; in the play, "homogrub" eventually subdues the great machines which have sought to exterminate these "larvae" while awaiting the return of the creator, Man.

49. Von Harbou, *Metropolis*, ch. 1, p. 17.

50. There are, of course, hundreds of novels and stories about malevolent, human-dominating machines, some of which expect mankind's worship if not his flesh. In addition to several Chapters in *Clockwork Worlds* and *The Mechanical God*, excellent discussions about dangerous machines may be found in three recent books: Harold L. Berger, *Science Fiction and the New Dark Age* (1976), Patricia S. Warrick, *The Cybernetic Imagination in Science Fiction* (1980), and Gary K. Wolfe, *The Known and the Unknown: The Iconography of Science Fiction* (1979); see section IV, Literary Criticism, of *Clockwork World's* List for full citations and brief annotations.

51. E. M. Forster, "The Machine Stops," in Lewis, *Of Men and Machines*, p. 279.

52. Dunn and Erlich, "Vision of Dystopia," p. 46.

53. Don A. Stuart (pseud. of John W. Campbell Jr.), "Twilight," in *The Best of John W. Campbell*, ed. Lester del Rey (Garden City, New York: Doubleday, 1976), p. 42.

54. John W. Campbell, "The Machine," in *Best of John W. Campbell*, p. 52, for the quotation; "The Invaders" and "The Rebellion" both collected in *Best of John W. Campbell*.

55. Frederik Pohl, "The Midas Plague" (*Galaxy*, April 1954), collected in *The Best of Frederik Pohl,* ed. Lester del Rey (Garden City, NY: Doubleday, 1975), p. 160.

56. Clifford Simak, *City* (New York: Gnome Press, 1952); Ray Bradbury, "There Will Come Soft Rains," *Colliers*, 6 May 1950.

57. Brian Aldiss, "But Who Can Replace a Man?," in Lewis, *Of Men and Machines*, p. 343.

58. Francis Bacon, "New Atlantis" (1626), rpt. in *Famous Utopias of the Renaissance*, ed. Frederic R. White (Chicago: Packard and Company, 1946), p. 240.

59. Quoted by John L. Thomas from Edward Bellamy's unpublished Notebooks, in Introduction to Bellamy, *Looking Backward: 2000-1887,* ed. John L. Thomas (Cambridge, MA: Harvard University Press, 1967), p. 48.

60. B. F. Skinner, *Walden Two* (New York: Macmillan, 1948), p. 9.

61. Robert Sheckley, "Street of Dreams, Feet of Clay" (*Galaxy*, Feb. 1968) rpt. in *The City*, ed. Clem, Greenberg, and Olander, p. 78.

62. Fyodor Dostoevsky, "Notes from Underground," in *Notes from Underground*, pt. 1, ch. 7, p. 18.

63. Ibid., p. 23.

64. Norbert Wiener, *The Human Use of Human Beings: Cybernetics and Society* (Garden City, NY: Doubleday, Anchor, 1954), p. 32.

65. Dostoevsky, "Notes from Underground," p. 22.

PART I

ARCHETYPE AND PROTOTYPE

1

DANTE'S HELL AS AN IDEAL
MECHANICAL ENVIRONMENT

Between the First and Second Circles of Hell in Dante's *Divine Comedy* sits
Minos, the judge of the damned. He has no role to play in the First
Circle—Limbo, the nonpunitive abode of virtuous pagans and unbaptized
children of the Christian era—but assigns all other damned souls to their
appropriate places:

At the threshold Minos examines their guilt, he judges, and according to his girdings
he sends them on their way. I mean when a soul whose misfortune it has been to be
born comes before him, he confesses everything; and Minos, that expert in the
nature of sins, sees what place in hell fits the sinner. Minos girds himself with his tail
as many times as there are levels in hell he wishes the sinner to be placed beneath.[1]

In other words, Minos receives data, processes it, and provides output in
accordance with his programming. The data is complete ("Minos who
apprehends everyone"),[2] the programming flawless ("Minos to whom
it is not granted to err"),[3] and the output appears as a form of "display,"
the number of turns in the tail indicating the circle to which the soul is condemned. The analogy between Minos and a computer is obvious in the
1980s, but only pure intuition could have led Dante to such a concept in the
early fourteenth century.

At the other end of Hell, Satan stands frozen in the ice of Lake Cocytus,
in the midst of those condemned for treachery. The lake remains intensely
frozen because of the icy winds produced by the beating of Satan's wings.
He is bound to keep beating them since he is desperate to escape, so the lake
is kept frozen by what amounts to an automatic mechanism. Once the
arrangement is operative—and notice the foresight with which Satan, alone
of those in the Ninth Circle, is allowed to have his upper body free of the
ice—it keeps working without outside intervention or control.

Between these two analogues to machines lies a gigantic hive which, although it contains no machines in the literal sense, is pervaded by characteristics such as endless repetition and standardized operation usually associated with the idea of the mechanical. Like a perfectly functioning hive, it is enclosed, organized in every aspect to fulfill an overriding purpose, and composed of units each of which is singlemindedly absorbed in playing its assigned role. There are no loose ends and no wasted motion.

The purpose of Dante's Hell is the fulfillment of justice (as it applies to the damned—the other souls find their justice in Purgatory and Paradise). The sufferings imposed are not merely retribution, but retribution as part of the divine plan. The damned are subjected to torment not for its own sake, but because it is the justice they have earned (and, apparently, sought).[4] Since it is inherent in Dante's concept of Hell that the consequences of justice be predictable, appropriate, eternal, and unchanging, Hell must be organized like a giant machine which, once set in motion, goes on running forever without further divine initiative. Once the whirlwind in the Second Circle is started up, the shades of the carnal are flung about like leaves for all eternity. Once the tombs are superheated by the flames in the Sixth Circle, the heretics are fated to lie suffering in them endlessly. Once the various agents of torture in the Eighth Circle are in action, the fraudulent undergo their assorted agonies forevermore.

Dante goes to considerable lengths to vary punishments, as between different types of sin and different intensities of the same sin, so Hell does not become monotonous to the reader in its lack of variety as a theological concept. Only great imaginative and literary skill could maintain interest in thousands of lines describing one-sided violence—hapless souls subjected to repetitious torments which allow no possibility of resistance, evasion, or termination. The mechanical essence which Dante often found it desirable to embellish and enliven stands revealed in a case where his invention is relatively weak. In one of the rings in the Eighth Circle, the sowers of discord are revoltingly hacked apart by a single devil, as Dante learns from one of the mutilated damned staggering around the ring:

There is a devil here within who adorns us in a most cruel way: when we have turned the bend in our sorrowful circuit, he sets each one of our band back on our way with a hack of his sword, since our wounds have healed before others pass before him again.[5]

It is hard to know in what way this devil, performing the same actions over and over and programmed so that each of the damned suffers precisely in accordance to his or her sins, can be differentiated from a machine. In the absence of any further characterization, it might as well be a clockwork devil, which certainly detracts from true devilish quality. Elsewhere, Dante takes great pains to give the warders of Hell touches of personality, most strikingly by providing vivid names and individualized behavior to the

Demons who skewer and shred grafters trying to lift themselves out of the boiling pitch in which they are immersed in the Eighth Circle. Although punishment is exacted by these Demons with the same inevitability as everywhere else in Hell, their characterization, and the fact that two of them begin brawling after being duped by one of the grafters, diffuses the monotonous notion of implacable mechanical operation.[6]

The mechanical shows through in a more complex way in one ring of the Seventh Circle, where souls damned for violence against others stand, each at a depth appropriate to his or her particular sin, in a river of boiling blood. The punishment is enforced by Centaurs, who patrol the banks ready to shoot arrows into any of the damned who try to rise further than decreed out of the blood.

The functioning of this arrangement is interesting. The Centaurs are in Hell because of their semibestial nature (which seems a bit unfair to hold against them, since they are, after all, semibeasts), most apparent in their savage hunting. Therefore, at the same time as divine justice is applied to the Centaurs by placing them deep in Hell, their special talents are put to use in enforcing the just fate of others of the damned. Since the Centaurs, as savage hunters, can be relied upon to put arrows through any of the damned who try to evade punishment, the system has an automatic quality similar to the perpetual freezing of Lake Cocytus by Satan's wings. The damned will inevitably attempt to ease their pains; the Centaurs will just as inevitably force them with great violence (which these damned, while alive, had exercised against others) to endure their fated torment. Such an interaction, occurring over and over without variation throughout eternity, should be characterized, even in the absence of machines, as mechanical.[7]

However, the Centaurs, along with the Demons who ride herd on the grafters, are wholly unnecessary to Dante's overall conception of Hell. The violent-against-others could be kept submerged in the boiling blood by the same unspecified power that keeps the heretics in their white-hot tombs (which have open lids), or the sullen in the Fifth Circle buried in the slime. As a general rule, the damned are forced to submit to their punishments by sheer divine decree rather than by objectified compulsion. There is, of course, no necessary correlation between the source of punishment and its mechanical quality, but infliction of distress by visible authority is obviously closer to human experience, and Dante's few examples of enforcement by guards are among the most unpleasant episodes in Hell. Part of their horror lies in the sense that the agents of retribution operate automatically and are impervious to any form of appeal. Readers can be moved by the idea of the application of divine force only in proportion to their belief in such force's reality but have less choice about reacting to descriptions of physical torture inflicted by creatures partly human at best and functioning with the inevitablity, regularity, and impersonality of machines.

Oddly enough, these warders (or even the disembodied divine forces that they manifest) are no more significant in the overall operation of Hell than are the damned themselves. Each of the latter is as necessary to the proper functioning of the Hell-hive as worker bees are to a beehive. Such bees are needed to carry out practical tasks, since the objective of the beehive is survival; the sufferings of the damned are no less essential in Hell, since there the objective is fulfillment of justice.

Although Hell ultimately is kept running by divine power, on a day-to-day basis it maintains itself on its own steam, so to speak. Neither escape nor change in individual condition is possible, and hence there is no chance of disruption from within. Change, prohibited in any case by divine will, is not even practical. The warders have nothing to gain from upsetting the status quo, since they cannot ever leave their work areas, much less Hell itself. As for the damned, they are not only physically helpless but have lost the very possibility of hope.[8]

The notion of Hell as *purely* mechanical, however, would have been as unacceptable to Dante as the notion of a mechanical Paradise. No room would be left for the freedom of human will which is indispensable to his whole cosmological scheme. Free will is subsumed in abstruse theological doctrine in Paradise, but in Hell is manifested in defiance by the damned. The Rebellious Angels refuse to let Dante and Virgil enter lower Hell; Capaneus, in the Seventh Circle as punishment for blasphemy, continues to blaspheme; the thief Vanni Fucci makes an obscene gesture toward God. Individual acts of defiance merely trigger more intense suffering, and the Rebellious Angels are dealt with through outside intervention in the form of a messenger dispatched from Paradise to overawe them. The fact that the creator of the machinery of Hell found it necessary to intervene to keep it running properly might seem a flaw in the concept of Hell as a mechanical environment, but since Dante is the first person ever to enter Hell in a corporeal state (excepting Christ's descent to Limbo), his visit may be thought of as a block of one kind of material fed into a machine designed to stamp products out of another kind. Dante occasions a number of unprecedented events in Hell, but everything he observes and hears that does not directly concern his presence bespeaks unfailing mechanical efficiency.

The acts of defiance, ineffective though they are, nevertheless serve to reveal Hell not as a *perfect* mechanical environment—which would not be interesting in reference to human beings—but as an *ideal* one, given the necessity of free will in the universe. It is unmistakably a hive, but a hive of humans, not of bees; it functions with maximum efficiency, but its human components retain awareness and individuality. In spite of the absolute and undisguised determinism which governs Hell throughout eternity, the damned bear no resemblance to robots, zombies, or other varieties of mechanized or dehumanized beings. Dante succeeds where so many later writers failed in portraying a pervasively mechanized environment in the round without falsifying or trivializing the humanity of its inhabitants.

The Divine Comedy endures because of its combination of literary genius and intellectual power, but it is also an astonishing work on the less exalted level of science fiction concepts and insights. Dante's detailed and internally consistent description of a complete, dystopian society within the Earth, centuries before any other writer attempted such a presentation, is a stunning feat of imagination. His choice of a hive existence as the organizational principle of an ultimate Hell for human beings is a stroke of intuition. Finally, his appreciation of the characteristics of a mechanical environment long before any existed in fact or fiction is the achievement of an extraordinary intellect. In the course of his magisterial exploration of the human soul, Dante illuminates aspects of human organization almost beyond imagination in his time and the subject of few comparable insights even in ours.

NOTES

1. Dante Alighieri, *La Divina Commedia,* ed. Natalino Sapegno (Milano: Riccardo Ricciardi, Editore, n.d.), canto V, 11. 5-12. Trans. from the Italian by John Romano, Miami University, Oxford, Ohio.

2. Ibid., canto XX, 1. 35.

3. Ibid., canto XXIX, 1. 120.

4. Ibid., canto III, 11. 121-23.

"My son," said my courteous teacher, "All who die in the wrath of God come together here from every land, and they are eager to cross over the stream because divine justice so spurs them on that in them fear of Hell becomes desire for it."

5. Ibid., canto XXVIII, 11. 37-42.

6. The fact that one of the damned successfully dupes the Demons cannot be considered a flaw in the inevitability of punishment. His "success" consists of diverting the Demons so that he can jump back into the boiling pitch before they are able to tear him to pieces (which would, of course, not be "fatal"). Some triumph!

7. A mechanical environment without literal machines has the singular advantage that there is nothing to wear out or be wrecked or to require necessarily finite sources of energy. Even the most amazing science fictional machines, like Arthur C. Clarke's Diaspar, can have and grant only "virtual eternity," lasting as long as our universe but no longer (Clarke, *The City and the Stars* [1956; rpt. New York: New American Library, 1957], ch. 10, p. 73). Dante's Hell, of course, *will* survive the end of the universe as we know it, a feat beyond even O'Brien's claim, in George Orwell's *Nineteen Eighty-Four*, of immortality and omnipotence for those who merge themselves with the Party (Orwell, *Nineteen Eighty-Four* [1949; rpt. as *1984*, New York: New American Library, 1961], pt. 3, sect. III, pp. 218, 220).

8. Even the virtuous pagans in Limbo, Hell's most desirable neighborhood, suffer eternal depression because, as Virgil explains, without hope the damned live on in desire (Dante Alighieri, *La Divina Commedia*, canto IV, 1. 42).

Reimer Jehmlich

2

COG-WORK: THE ORGANIZATION OF LABOR
IN EDWARD BELLAMY'S *LOOKING BACKWARD*
AND IN LATER UTOPIAN FICTION

It is not only mechanized environments—Disneylands of all types and sizes —that threaten to cripple modern man and alienate him from both his fellow man and nature. A more immediate threat, so it seems, is contained in the means and methods by which such artifacts are being made—"advanced machinery" and "progressive" methods of human engineering. These threaten to dehumanize man by totally mechanizing his work.

The problems which arise here are as old as the industrial revolution and have increased rather than diminished since the eighteenth and nineteenth centuries. Their discussion should be of particular interest to science fiction writers, for these problems are just the stuff that science fiction is allegedly made of, namely, human problems engendered by technological progress and thus epitomizing the mixed blessings of modern civilization.

In truth, however, there is little explicit extrapolation and discussion of labor problems in science fiction. They are referred to indirectly if at all and, as a rule, greatly simplified or misrepresented; the problems of theoretical labor and flesh-and-blood workers are, in most science fiction, not rationally examined but only emotionally commented upon.[1] One has to turn to the parent genre of science fiction—utopian fiction—to find more comprehensive and unambiguous responses. Though often derided as dully old-fashioned, utopias seem in fact more genuinely contemporary and prophetic in dealing with labor issues than their modern offspring.

The following study examines this contention with reference to two classical nineteenth-century utopias, Edward Bellamy's *Looking Backward: 2000-1887* (1888), and William Morris's *News from Nowhere* (1890); and three more recent texts: B. F. Skinner's *Walden Two* (1948), Ivan Yefremov's *Andromeda* (1954), and Aldous Huxley's *Island* (1962).[2] I will investigate which aspects of modern working life the individual author thinks most detrimental and what alternatives he suggests; whether or not his diagnosis and therapy reflect attitudes toward work common to his time; and whether it is possible to discern marked shifts of emphasis in turning from older to more recent, from English to American, and from "Western" to "Eastern" utopias.

These questions, of course, cannot be discussed comprehensively. This applies in particular to the question of extraliterary influences, including the large body of theoretical literature which cannot possibly be given full consideration.[3] We must rest content with casting a glance at what seems the most important background material in this field, Karl Marx's classical analysis of working conditions in modern industry. A brief outline of Marx's chief axioms and arguments provides the starting point and frame of reference.

With the rise of capitalism—so goes Marx's well-known line of argumentation—work has become more and more dehumanized. It has been reduced to a mere commodity and thus has lost its creative and emancipatory potential. This is due to the profit motive that dominates capitalist economies. To remain competitive, the capitalist employer must keep the costs of production as low as possible. He does so in two ways, by badly paying his workers and by introducing labor-saving machines. This means that the workers are not only exploited and impoverished, but also are degraded to machine operators forced to do dull and unsatisfactory work. The result is frustration and alienation; the only remedy a revolutionary change. Once the number of capitalists has been drastically reduced by a continuous process of concentration, the workers are to disown them, take over the control of the economy and production and thus, eventually, to rehumanize labor.

Of particular relevance here is what Marx says about the manner of work in pre- and post-revolutionary society. In *Capital* (1887) he gives a very lucid and suggestive description of machine production in capitalist industry, a description that is in part truly prophetic, since it focuses on problems that were to fully materialize only much later.

In manufacture the workmen are parts of a living mechanism. In the factory we have a lifeless mechanism independent of the workman, who becomes its mere living appendage. . . . The lightening of the labour, even, becomes a sort of torture, since the machine does not free the labourer from work, but deprives the work of all interest. . . . The technical subordination of the workmen to the uniform motion of the instruments of labour, and the peculiar composition of the body of workpeople . . . give rise to a barrack discipline, which is elaborated into a complete system in the factory . . . dividing the workpeople into operatives and overlookers, into private soldiers and sergeants of an industrial army.[4]

Even more vividly suggestive, though less detailed and concrete, is Marx's description of liberated labor:

In communist society, where nobody has one exclusive sphere of activity but each can become accomplished in any branch he wishes, society regulates the general production and thus makes it possible for me to do one thing today and another tomorrow, to hunt in the morning, to fish in the afternoon, rear cattle in the evening, criticise after dinner, just as I have in mind, without ever becoming, fisherman, shepherd or critic.[5]

This may sound rather nostalgic and Arcadian. In *Capital*, however, Marx leaves little doubt that there is to be a continuation, even intensification, of industrial production. As he points out, mechanization is not bad in itself, but has, on the contrary, a revolutionary, liberating potential:

Modern Industry, by its very nature . . . necessitates variation of labour, fluency of function, universal mobility of the labourer. . . . It compels society, under penalty of death, to replace the detail-worker of to-day, crippled by life-long repetition of one and the same trivial operation, and thus reduced to the mere fragment of a man, by the fully developed individual, fit for a variety of labours, ready to face any change of production, and to whom the social functions he performs are but so many modes of giving free scope to his own natural and acquired powers.[6]

Whether this transformation will come more or less automatically or whether it will have to be enforced by the workers is not clearly said here. Nor does Marx specify his contention that, once freed from the fetters of capitalism, mechanized work will cease to be frustrating and alienating and become interesting, satisfactory, and creative instead. There are other unfinished lines in Marx's sketch of the future; for such omissions, however, he cannot and should not be blamed, for he is on foreign ground here, infringing on the domain of the utopian writer. It is in fact the utopian writer's task to imaginatively complement and make tangible what critics such as Marx have only outlined, to colorfully transform sketches of the future into detailed maps of Futuria.[7]

Edward Bellamy's utopian *Looking Backward* is certainly no fictionalized version of *Capital* but, nevertheless, shows striking parallels to Marx's analyses: it too is chiefly concerned with contemporary labor problems and arrives at similar insights, at least as far as the anatomy of capitalist economy is concerned.

Freelance writer and amateur economist Bellamy, the son of a clergyman, has his protagonist, Julian West, awake in the Boston of the year 2000 after 113 years of deep sleep. One of the first questions West asks his host, Dr. Leete, is, "What solution, if any, have you found for the labor question?"[8] He explains that it had been "the Sphinx's riddle of the nineteenth century, and . . . was threatening to devour society, because the answer was not forthcoming."[9] He remembers that there was ruthless competition among innumerable small capitalists, which led to an equally ruthless exploitation of the laborers and meant, furthermore, a shameful waste of labor potential and raw materials. There was a strong trend toward concentration which, as he learns from Dr. Leete, reached its climax at the turn of the century, when the new conglomerations of firms threatened to totally enslave the workers: "They believed that the great corporations were preparing for them the yoke of a baser servitude than had ever been imposed on the race, servitude not to men but to soulless machines incapable of any motive but insatiable greed."[10] Accordingly the workers organized to resist the trusts and threatened to cripple the whole economy by continuous strikes. What is sketched here seems, in fact, like a scenario based on Marx's theories and predictions. A direct influence is rather improbable, however, and Bellamy seems to have arrived more or less independently at his analysis—by critically reacting to the contemporary American labor scene.[11] This scene was very likely to induce such criticism, for it was characterized by a rapid and uncontrolled growth of capitalism and a concomitant process of equally rapid concentration. Both set in after the military triumph of the industrialized North in the Civil War, progressed faster and more unexpectedly than in Europe, and, as a consequence, produced harsher social injustice and fiercer opposition from the workers.[12]

What Bellamy makes Julian West say about the "Sphinx" threatening "to devour society" is thus not an anticipation of things to come, but of fairly close description of the American situation in the late 1880s, and the way people reacted to it.

Bellamy's answer to the "Sphinx's riddle" seems both pleasant and simple. There had to be no class warfare, as Dr. Leete explains; people realized that it was much more beneficial and profitable for both workers and capitalists if they cooperated, and nationalized all industries. The process of concentration had revealed that big trusts were more efficient than small firms, and after the state had become the sole capitalist, this observation was fully verified: production became incomparably more efficient than before the "glorious evolution"; there was also an end to injustice, social inequality, and aggressive competition.

It was this idea of peaceful nationalization that made *Looking Backward* a bestseller and a cult book—as we would say today—in no time. It was translated into more than a dozen foreign languages and inspired the foundation of hundreds of Bellamy Clubs to promote "nationalism," as Bellamy's concept was then termed. Bellamy was not only hailed as "the Moses of today" for showing his contemporaries the "promised land,"[13] he was also compared and found superior to Marx for speaking more simply and effectively to the masses.[14]

Marxian critics have, as a rule, adopted a less enthusiastic attitude. They have, in particular, found fault with Bellamy's concept of a nonviolent revolution.[15] Such a revolution does seem un-Marxian, but on the whole this bloodless revolution is both less problematical and less objectionable than the bright post(r)evolutionary alternative that Bellamy presents: life in the America of the future is almost exclusively determined by a centrally directed, rigidly departmentalized economic system. The president and government which nominally still exist have economic tasks only, computing what will be needed and regulating industrial output accordingly. Their work is easy, however: "The machine which they direct [so Julian learns] is indeed a fast one, but so logical in its principles and direct and simple in its workings that it all but runs itself."[16] The comparison—even equation—with a machine seems very apt indeed, for although Bellamy says very little about actual machinery, his economic system has both the clockwork precision and effectiveness of mechanized production. Its reliability is in particular due to the existence of an "industrial army" in which all future Americans have to serve from age twenty-one to forty-five. They thus learn diligence and discipline and are offered the following enticing prospects:

First comes the unclassified grade of common laborers, men of all work, to which all recruits during their first three years belong. This grade is a sort of school and a very strict one, in which the young men are taught habits of obedience, subordination, and devotion to duty. . . . [A]ll who have passed through the unclassified grade without serious disgrace have an equal opportunity to choose the life employment they have most liking for. Having selected this, they enter upon it as apprentices. The length of the apprenticeship naturally differs in different occupations. At the end of it the apprentice becomes a full workman, and a member of his trade or guild.[17]

And it is then that the actual rat race begins, the competition for the better positions in the military hierarchy. There are periodical "regradings" at which the workers are either promoted or degraded according to their achievements. Those that have done well are publicly rewarded and mentioned in the papers. Needless to say there are various privileges for the higher ranks. "Officers" have, for instance, much more choice with regard to the branch and kind of work they want to go into than do "commoners," and they need no longer work, but only supervise the lower ranks.

Marx spoke of barrack discipline and a pseudomilitary hierarchy in modern industry as well, but denounced them as contemporary evils. That Bellamy should present them as utopian achievements seems very peculiar, indeed. This can be explained partly by the specifically American problems he reacts to in *Looking Backward*, but must, however, also be blamed on his rather limited critical and prophetic vision.

As has already been pointed out, the intensification of class antagonisms in the 1880s came rather unexpectedly to most Americans and deeply shocked them. They got the impression that both society and the economy were heading toward utter chaos and anarchy. There was thus a widespread yearning for order and stability, a yearning that was evidently shared by Bellamy. It made him shape his brave new militaristic world accordingly and explains the enthusiastic reception it found, particularly in America.

The urgent problem of how to better organize the economy and labor made Bellamy, on the other hand, consider too little the concomitant and even more urgent problem of how to humanize them. Significantly enough, he neither makes his protagonist reflect on the concrete implications of mechanized production in the nineteenth century, nor sends him into a future factory to watch industrial soldiers in action. This is not to say that his reformatory interest and zeal are exclusively focused on questions of economic planning and human engineering. He provides for the individual as well: everyone gets the same amount of credits just for being a person,[18] is consulted before being assigned a job, and is given all kinds of incitements and aids when required to do heavy or nasty work. But the industrial army nevertheless perpetuates competition and inequality and—what is more problematic—it exempts the individual from even the slightest possibility of codetermination. It is only as a consumer that he is granted some participation in the setting up of plans. As a laborer, he has no such rights. Efficiency comes first; it is the economic machinery of the state and its output that are most important, not the actual operators of that machinery. They have got to adapt to it, not vice versa.

Evidently, behind this accentuation lies a concept of labor different from that of Marx: work is considered a necessary evil with which man has to come to terms, not a potential means of self-realization. That Bellamy in fact subscribes to that harsher concept—which is, of course, part of the Puritan heritage[19]—is indicated by the following statement made by Dr. Leete:

. . . the labor we have to render as our part in securing for the nation the means of a comfortable physical existence is by no means regarded as the most important, the most interesting, or the most dignified employment of our powers. We look upon it as a necessary duty to be discharged before we can fully devote ourselves to the higher exercise of our faculties, the intellectual and spiritual enjoyments and pursuits which alone mean life.[20]

At the age of forty-five, Bellamy's future Americans can fully indulge in such "enjoyments and pursuits," for it is then that they are discharged from the industrial army to "first really attain . . . their majority and become enfranchised from discipline and control."[21]

Instead of a working and a leisure *class* Bellamy thus has a working and a leisure *generation*. That is an enticingly simple solution—as enticingly simple and naive indeed as his suggested reforms in the field of industrial production.

It would be unfair, however, to blame Bellamy too severely for his obvious shortsightedness. Even his severest critics have to admit that Bellamy devised his utopia with a genuine compassion for the underprivileged and that he was fully convinced of the practicability of his reform plans. Their problematic implications were, in fact, difficult to foresee at the time. Frederick W. Taylor and the "second industrial revolution" had not yet come nor was there, at least in America, much in the way of a fully developed, centralized bureaucracy. And, last but not least, there was not yet a leisure industry, catering to the idle: mass leisure was not yet a problem, but still a sweet utopian dream.[22]

This is not to say that reality had first to give the lie to Bellamy's hypotheses before the weak spots of his cog-work socialism could be detected. They were already evident to some of his more sensitive contemporaries. One of the harshest reviews came from William Morris, the British artist, writer, factory owner, and socialist, best known for his association with the Pre-Raphaelite brotherhood.

Morris' main objection to Bellamy was that his utopia neglected art and individuality and sacrificed people to machinery and to the "machine life" that Morris sees as "the best which Bellamy can imagine for us on all sides; it is not to be wondered at then that his only idea of making labour tolerable is to decrease the amount of it by means of fresh . . . developments of machinery."[23] He did not rest content with thus articulating his reservations. A year later he himself presented a utopia in *News from Nowhere*. In this "utopian romance . . . of an epoch of rest" (subtitle), it is again labor questions that play the most important part. Also as in *Looking Backward*, a utopian time traveler visits the bright future and gives a review of the "past" that amounts to a critique of capitalism. Morris does not, however, share Bellamy's belief in a peaceful transition to socialism, but insists—to the satisfaction of Marxist critics[24]—on the necessity of a bloody revolution. At the same time, and more importantly, he goes much farther than Bellamy in his therapy for the labor problem—and has thereby puzzled rather than delighted orthodox Marxians.

In Morris' future England there is hardly any regimentation of work and only the most inconspicuous remnants of mechanization. For Morris' people of the future have realized—after some initial errors—that it is not enough simply to socialize the means of production and then carry on as before. It became evident that a true emancipation from the old order presupposed a redefinition and reevaluation of human work.

Work had to become meaningful and creative again, not just quantitatively effective. To ensure this, mechanized production was gradually curtailed: "Machine after machine was quietly dropped under the excuse that the machines could not produce works of art, and that works of art were more and more called for."[25] Thus it was possible to concentrate on making well and shaping beautifully whatever objects were needed, and to derive "conscious sensuous pleasure" from creating and using them.[26] Since the common goal was the creation of a human, aesthetically pleasant environment, even work that formerly was considered dull and nasty assumed a pleasurable aspect.

The visitor from the nineteenth century encounters, in fact, happy and healthy people only—people who without the least external coercion serve, help, and support their neighbors whenever necessary (thus making civil servants and social workers superfluous). In addition, also voluntarily, they work in the fields or in small workshops, where they make beautiful things for their own pleasure and their neighbors' benefit.

The rediscovery of nonmechanized farm work and handicrafts has made possible a leisurely manner of work and life; it has put an end to—or at least almost made obsolete—the division of labor and, equally important, allowed the development of more satisfactory forms of social organization and communal life than existed in nineteenth-century England. The Futurians live in small, loosely structured and organized communities, practicing, if at all necessary, a form of basic democracy. For there is neither a central government nor large urban areas with a complicated infrastructure. England has been turned once again into "a garden, where nothing is wasted and nothing is spoilt, with the necessary dwellings, sheds, and workshops scattered up and down the country, all trim and neat and pretty."[27]

This is far removed from Bellamy's factory and city civilization indeed. It is also less dryly presented. Morris makes fuller use of the "utopian novel" medium than does Bellamy. He conjures up the beauty, grace, and freshness of the good new life by vivid description and gives his protagonist not only a guided-tour impression of the brave future world but allows him to actually encounter and experience it with his senses.

That Morris passionately rejects what Bellamy, with like passion, dreams of, is undoubtedly due in part to personal reasons, but seems also to reflect national idiosyncrasies. As an artist, craftsman, and employer, Morris had direct experiences in the sphere of industry, experiences that made him more sensitive to the labor situation and to problems of mechanized and standardized production. He took, moreover, an active part in the British socialist movement and thus gained further and deeper insights into the machinations of capitalism. And, last but not least, he was a citizen of the oldest industrial nation, a country that had suffered from the ill effects of industrialization much longer and, since it was more densely populated, suffered much more intensely than the United States. For this reason, there had been a stronger and longer opposition to industrialization in England than in the New World. Morris was not the first to formulate such criticism, nor is his therapy altogether original. That he chooses, as he explicitly says, fourteenth-century England as a prototype for his utopia links him with John Ruskin, Thomas Carlyle, and other nineteenth-century cultural critics who had similar dreams of a preindustrial future.[28]

Though he has been justly criticized for such regressive nostalgia, it should be noted that Morris does not blindly and radically condemn the use of machines. What has been achieved in Nowhere and is duly celebrated is not a total abolition of machinery, but its strict control. Morris' attitude toward mechanization is more fully explained in "The Society of the Future" (1887), a political lecture to fellow socialists which can be considered the theoretical concomitant of *News from Nowhere*. "Possibly the few more important machines will be very much improved, and the host of unimportant ones fall into disuse, and as to many or most of them, people will be able to use them or not as they fell inclined."[29]

Similarly, Morris does not call for an unqualified return to the past. The late Middle Ages provide important suggestions, but they are not used as a blueprint. And what is thought valuable is not created out of the blue, by a mere act of will, but rather is discovered after a long process of trial and error. The outcome is a collectively shaped, postrevolutionary and—as it seems—truly communist society. Orthodox Marxists who tend automatically to link social and technological progress have naturally been puzzled rather than delighted by Morris' utopian vision and have denounced it as sadly reactionary and regressive.[30] Such judgments seem too rash and dogmatic, however. For viewed in the light of "The German Ideology" and other early writings, *News from Nowhere* is quite in line with Marx's ideas about the future. It can very well be seen as an imaginative embodiment of the "realm of liberty" in which all opposition and tension between hand and brain work, labor and leisure, social and private activities have been suspended: where it is possible "to hunt in the morning, to fish in the afternoon, rear cattle in the evening, criticise after dinner."

Orthodox Marxism or not, *News from Nowhere* is certainly not a dead classic. According to James Redmond:

[It] points clearly to a crisis in European culture that seems as insoluble today as it seemed to Morris in 1890; for two centuries or so we have been living through a technological revolution of unprecedented scope and violence, so that the *trappings* of human life have changed much more than in the previous two thousand years, while the essential requirements of the individual personality have remained much the same.[31]

Nevertheless it was *Looking Backward* rather than *News from Nowhere* that set the pattern for utopian fiction in the following decades. In America over one hundred utopias were established between 1889 and 1900—most of them strongly influenced by Bellamy.[32] And Morris found no immediate

followers in England either. H. G. Wells, it is true, had very critically commented upon the effects of technological progress in his early "scientific
romances"—notably in *The Time Machine* (1895), *The Island of Dr.
Moreau* (1896), and *The First Men in the Moon* (1901)—but he later
changed his position and wrote utopian scenarios such as *A Modern Utopia*
(1905) and *The Shape of Things to Come* (1933) that are similar to *Looking
Backward* in their unqualified opting for progress and efficiency and reveal
a functional conception of work as well. It was only after the Russian
Revolution on the one hand and the so-called second industrial revolution
on the other that such utopias began to appear problematical, in spite
of—or rather because of—the fact that each revolution fulfilled part of
Bellamy's prophecies: the Russian Revolution actually led to a complete
nationalization of all industries; Russia's embryonic capitalist system was
replaced by a centrally directed and controlled economy, and the labor force
was reorganized in pseudomilitary fashion. But the good effects prophecied
by Bellamy did not really materialize. There was not much in the way of
universal equality and brotherhood, no drastic reduction of working time,
and certainly no rich variety of goods made available to everyone (as
Bellamy had forseen for his future America). The goals of efficient production and smooth distribution were, on the other hand, and ironically
enough, most perfectly attained in capitalist countries. It was there that
"refined" methods of organizing and rationalizing work—as foreseen by
both Bellamy and Marx—had been developed in the meantime and proven
in fact extremely efficient.[33] But the "second industrial revolution"—and
notably its most important constituent, the "Taylorization" of the labor
process—did not prove beneficial for laborers; it rather intensified their
frustration and alienation.

Thus the actual development of the labor situation in the second decade
of the twentieth century seemed to leave little room for optimistic extrapolation. There was no room for Morris' Nowhere, really. But there was
no reason for hopefully looking backward to Bellamy either. Bellamy's
dream evoked nightmares now—and was treated accordingly, at least in
Britain and other European countries. It was here that from now on a continuous line of dystopias—from Yevgeny Zamiatin's *We* (ca. 1920) to
George Orwell's *Nineteen Eighty-Four* (1949)—appeared, "negative" or
"inverted" utopias that vehemently denounced centralization, mechanization, and regimentation as the chief concomitant evils of industrial (and
socialist) progress.

In America, there were no dystopias, but for a long time, as in England,
no positive utopias either. It was only after the Second World War that
the utopian tradition was revived in both countries—notably in B. F.
Skinner's *Walden Two* and Aldous Huxley's *Island*. In both utopias the
reformation of work is still a major issue and is given almost as much atten-

tion as in *Looking Backward* and *News from Nowhere*. There are further and more surprising parallels, however; Skinner and Huxley seem to have retained basically the same preferences and prejudices as Bellamy and Morris, for they offer similar or, to be more exact, similarly different solutions.

Thus Walden Two, a utopian colony situated in contemporary America, is like Bellamy's America of the future: a planners' and bureaucrats' rather than a workers' paradise. For in spite of protestations to the contrary, its principal goal is to make work more efficient and productive, not more creative and satisfactory. Frazier, the cicerone and founding father of the colony, accordingly criticizes the waste of talent and energy in capitalist America:

Now [having handled the unemployed] what about those who are actually at work? Are they working to the best advantage? Have they been carefully selected for the work they are doing? Are they making the best use of labor-saving machines and methods? What percentage of the farms in America are mechanized as we are here? Do the workers welcome and improve upon labor-saving devices and methods? How many good workers are free to move on to more productive levels? How much education do workers receive to make them as efficient as possible?[34]

In *Walden Two*, a group of planners and managers who at the same time are the government—appointed, not elected—see to it that such deficiencies are avoided or competently counteracted. They decide on the introduction of "labor-saving devices," compute how many laborers will be needed in each branch of industry and agriculture, and "assign different credit values to different kinds of work, and adjust them from time to time on the basis of demand."[35] By thus canalizing and effectively employing the labor potential they do not aim at a steady increase in production, however. The colonists are, in an economic sense, no-growth fetishists. Their aim is, on the contrary—and here is one of the few points in *Walden Two* that reflects, even anticipates, topical reform issues[36]—to consume less than the average American and to avoid overproduction and affluence. When they nevertheless aim at an increase in productivity, it is in order to save labor; that is, to shorten the average working time, which has already been reduced to four hours a day and obviously is to be further curtailed in the future. For, as in *Looking Backward*, it is the "enjoyments and pursuits" of leisure time that are deemed the really important essence of life. Skinner does not devalue work as much as Bellamy; he attributes to it some internal value at least,[37] but he is as forbiddingly autocratic with regard to the workers. They have as little possibility of codetermination as the workers in *Looking Backward*. In both the political sphere and in questions of labor and economy all decisions are made by experts. Frazier/Skinner has a cynically naive explanation of why this should be so:

In Walden Two no one worries about the government except the few to whom that worry has been assigned. To suggest that everyone should take an interest would seem as fantastic as to suggest that everyone should become familiar with our Diesel engines. Even the constitutional rights of the members are seldom thought about, I'm sure. The only thing that matters is one's day-to-day happiness and a secure future.[38]

To ensure such day-to-day happiness and to confirm at the same time the social stability of Walden Two, Frazier has devised an educational program that epitomizes his contempt of the individual, a program based on "behavioral engineering." It is to teach the individual "positive behavior," and adapt him to the necessities of communal life. This is to be achieved by a system of rather crude and occasionally cruel rewards and punishments and, what seems more problematical, without any previous discussion of what constitutes socially desirable and satisfactory behavior.[39] Again it is the experts who alone can decide such questions. They have already "successfully" and atrociously experimented with children; their final aim is to completely control the adults as well. Such habit formation will, among other things, have very significant consequences for the organization of labor: there will no longer be any necessity to indulge in the "extravagance" of "a free choice of jobs";[40] people will be so conditioned as to want just the jobs that are available, and they will achieve "immeasurably increased efficiency, because they can stick to a job without suffering the aches and pains which soon beset most of us. They get new horizons, for they are spared the emotions characteristic of frustration and failure."[41]

The methods of behavioral control suggested by Skinner may be more refined than those outlined by Bellamy, but they are definitely more cynical and wicked: as a professional psychologist and twentieth-century man, Skinner knows well what mass manipulation and "benevolent" dictatorship imply. He cannot, one would suppose, brush aside both the evidence of recent history and the warnings of dystopian writers. The truly exasperating thing is that he does, and does so consciously: one visitor to the community compares Walden Two to *Brave New World* (1932), and Frazier to Hitler, only to have Frazier flatly and stubbornly deny that any such parallels exist. Having thus silenced all objections, Skinner shamelessly presents as utopian what is in fact only a redaction of *Brave New World* with Mustapha Mond as protagonist.

Skinner's obsession with "behavioral engineering" (his phrase) may be partly due to the moral disorientation of the postwar years and the need for an antidote to it. However, his mania can also be explained as the power fantasy of a frustrated psychologist.[42] In *Walden Two*, Skinner obviously stages in an imaginative context what was denied him in reality: a large-scale experiment with human beings as subjects. That he experiments with fictitious instead of real personalities is a blessing for the latter, of course, and a possible defense of his book. Even so, as a fictitious embodiment of a psychological theory *Walden Two* has serious flaws; the theory is neither convincingly defended nor embodied by Frazier, so that the conversion of Skinner's alter ego, the book's Narrator, comes as rather a surprise. More important, there is no obvious connection between the theoretical super-structure and practical life in the community. The people presented to the visitors as walking examples of utopian bliss seem happy indeed, but for very conventional reasons—not because they have been successfully con-ditioned, but because they enjoy the simple life and concrete work in a country commune. The communal movement in America seems in fact to have been Skinner's basic inspiration, which he then tried to adapt to his psychological ideas. But he failed to do so convincingly: a small community is simply no adequate testing ground for economic planners and behavioral engineers planning to rule the world—be they real or only fictitious.

Aldous Huxley's utopia has a more exotic setting than *Walden Two*. Placed on a fictitious Indonesian island called Pala, *Island* presents a more organic and, above all, more humane model of the good life. Through the cooperation of its native raja and a Scottish doctor, Pala has become a moderately modern state that makes use of Western technology to fight hunger, ignorance, and overpopulation; at the same time, Pala preserves a good many of its time-honored Eastern traditions and so avoids the defects and evils of industrial civilization. Pala is thus a well-balanced blend of "both worlds—the Oriental and the European, the ancient and the modern."[43] The "third alternative" to what the Savage in *Brave New World* had to choose from, Pala is neither as crude and primitive as the Reserva-tion nor as perversely mechanized and "refined" as the rest of the world. Rather it harbors a decentralized, cooperative society that uses "science and technology . . . as though, like the Sabbath, they had been made for men, not . . . as though men were to be adapted and enslaved to them."[44] As Dr. MacPhail, the cicerone, explains: "Pala's a federation of self-governing units, geographical units, professional units, economic units—so there's plenty of scope for small-scale initiative and democratic leaders, but no place for any kind of dictator at the head of a centralized government."[45]

There is also no place or necessity for an excessive division of labor and permanent specialization. Most people work alternately in the fields and forests and the medium-sized, local factories. Asked whether this system works well, Dr. MacPhail outlines the Palanese attitude toward work and efficiency:

It depends what you mean by "well." It doesn't result in maximum efficiency. But then in Pala maximum efficiency isn't the categorial imperative that it is with you. You think first of getting the biggest possible output in the shortest possible time.

We think of human beings and their satisfactions. Changing jobs doesn't make for the biggest output in the fewest days. But most people like it better than doing one kind of job all their lives. If it is a choice between mechanical efficiency and human satisfaction, we choose satisfaction.[46]

Though there are some debatable touches in the Palanese conception of work as well, particularly the view that physical work is good for character training and should therefore be prescribed for every adolescent, Huxley presents on the whole a much more pleasant alternative to contemporary working conditions than does Skinner. It appears the more striking when we compare it to the horrific vision he painted in *Brave New World*—the vision of innumerable "Bokanovsky Groups" toiling mechanically in fully automated factories.

Huxley had earlier presented a vehement and more straightforward criticism of the dangers inherent in mechanical and industrial progress. In *Point Counter Point* (1928), one of his early social satires, he denounces "overproduction . . . more specialization and standardization of work . . . and diminution of initiative and creativeness" as the most notorious evils.[47] He does not, however, devise as radical an alternative as he will in *Brave New World*. What he suggests in the way of a provisional solution is still in the tradition of Bellamy: "The first step [wrote Huxley in 1928] would be to make people live dualistically, in two compartments. In one compartment as industrial workers, in the other as human beings. As idiots and machines for eight hours out of every twenty-four and real human beings for the rest."[48] Though not explicitly stated, the next step must necessarily go beyond this "solution"; it must suspend the duality between labor and leisure, machine existence and full human life. The solution found in *Island* is thus at least indirectly prefigured in a novel written some thirty years earlier. And the ultimate model is, of course, Morris' still older *News from Nowhere*. That there should be closer parallels between *Island* and *News from Nowhere*—and *Walden Two* and *Looking Backward* respectively—than between *Island* and *Walden Two* can certainly not be accidental.

The existence of such similarities and differences suggests that utopias reflect national idiosyncrasies more clearly and more stubbornly than ordinary literature—that *Looking Backward* and *Walden Two* are "typically American" since they call for a pragmatic, quantitative, and technocratic approach to socioeconomic problems, whereas *News From Nowhere* and *Island* express the more "genuinely British" (and possibly European) concern with aesthetic and democratic values. The same national idiosyncrasies can be discerned in these books' antiutopian counterparts and complements: *The Time Machine*, "The Machine Stops," *Brave New World*, *Nineteen Eighty-Four*, and Aldous Huxley's *Ape and Essence* (1949).[49]

True and apt as such an interpretation may be with respect to the texts discussed, we should draw no hasty conclusions and undue generalizations without keeping in mind that the American utopian tradition is much richer than the literary utopias may suggest, for it comprises actual utopian experiments as well.[50] If these were taken into account, the evidence would be much more colorful and varied and would thus discourage any rash generalizations with regard to what is "typically American." Actually, it is such practical experiments (and this is a further point with which to modify too simplistic an interpretation) rather than sociological theories that seem to have inspired the more recent utopias. I have suggested such an influence already with respect to Skinner; it can also be postulated for Huxley. Both rest content with designing small communities that are fully embedded in the contemporary world rather than being spatially or temporally removed from it. And both of them try to steer clear of either socialism or capitalism and present a "third way," a good new world that is, above all, a practical alternative to "normal" society. Such modesty and sobriety (and perhaps also naiveté) is something that unites Skinner and Huxley in spite of all other differences. It expresses a common concern with growth fetishism in industry, business, and administration, a concern which, although not altogether new when *Walden Two* and *Island* were written, still found critical articulation much later in books like D. L. Meadows and D. H. Meadows' *The Limits to Growth* (1972), and E. F. Schumacher's *Small is Beautiful* (1973).[51] That *Walden Two* and *Island* likewise reflect and anticipate such critical tendencies makes them both *modern* utopias and indicates that there is a common line of development in British and American utopian fiction in spite of strongly enduring national idiosyncrasies. The utopian imagination in America and England has definitely lost much of its former scope and revolutionary impetus. It has become markedly more domesticated and concretely down-to-earth since the nineteenth century, when Bellamy and Morris designed utopias that were not small-scale at all, but were set in the future and implicitly comprised the whole world.

Such modesty, even resignation, is naturally no constituent of recent Eastern utopias, represented here by the well-known and very popular *Andromeda* of Ivan Yefremov, a paleontologist by training and one of the leading Russian writers of speculative fiction. *Andromeda* has no visitor from our world to discover the marvels of utopia. This may not be accidental, for such a visitor is traditionally the medium of topical criticism, which is a delicate issue in Soviet literature indeed. Anyway, the marvels of utopia are directly if a bit clumsily revealed in *Andromeda*, in lectures given by various characters or by straight description.

Yefremov's good new world is set in the distant future, in an age called the "Era of the Great Ring," because its dominant characteristic is an interstellar TV network which links an audience of truly cosmic scope. The network is mainly employed, of course, to transmit reports on terrestrial achievements. The peoples of the Earth, so a billionfold audience learns in a historical program, have almost completed a paradigmatic evolution for the better. They have overcome all of the national and, above all, social barriers that still separated them in the Age of Fission (the twentieth century). One nation, they have by a communal effort defeated hunger, poverty, and sickness.

At the beginning of this evolution stood a redefinition and reevaluation of labor. People "realized that all their strength, all the future of mankind, lay in labor, in the correlated efforts of millions of free people."[52] And they likewise realized that the ultimate goal could not be "man's gradual liberation from the necessity to work,"[53] as had been dreamed by early utopian writers. It became clear that, on the contrary:

man needed to work to the full measure of his strength but his labour had to be creative and in accordance with his natural talents and inclinations, and it had to be varied and changed from time to time. The development of cybernetics, the technique of automatic control, a comprehensive education and the development of intellectual abilities coupled with the finest physical training of each individual, made it possible for a person to change his profession frequently, learn another easily and bring endless variety into his work so that it becomes more and more satisfying.[54]

Yefremov does not specify what working conditions were like before, nor does he in any way make clear what has brought about this change. He has been duly criticized for such vagueness in the Soviet Union and by Marxist critics in other countries,[55] although his remarks with regard to "liberated" work have naturally been widely acclaimed. In this instance Yefremov remains very close to Marx—closer than he is to Bellamy, whose admiration for discipline he shares but not his conception of work; and closer than he is to Morris as well, because he does not attack machine production.

More interesting than Yefremov's theoretical position, however, is the way he tries to embody it imaginatively. He devises a man-made millenium which fascinates us with its gigantic scope and rational construction. Thanks to the communal efforts of mankind, the face of the Earth has been completely transformed. There has not only been a massive manipulation of the climate (by leveling mountains, melting the polar caps, and so forth), but, more daring still, a systematic and radical "redistribution of Earth's surface into dwelling and industrial zones."[56] So that they may enjoy the blessings of a warm and mild climate, most people have been lodged in an "unbroken chain of urban settlements" that lie between "thirty and forty degrees of North and South latitude," while foodstuffs, timber, and industrial goods are being produced in the adjoining zones.[57] To save energy and raw materials, there has been a concentration of allied lines of production in the agricultural and industrial belts and, moreover, a marked simplification and standardization of products. There were almost no problems in running the economy once all these changes were completed; one central council of economics suffices to control production for the whole world.

The question remains, of course, whether such a perfect system is, of necessity, bound to stifle rather than encourage individual initiative and creativity; whether it will not in the long run provide the very conditions for alienation and regimentation that dystopian writers have warned against. Yefremov naturally denies that such failure is inherent in utopia, but he fails to make his hypothesis convincing and tangible. His futurians indulge in interesting scientific projects but rarely ever talk about—let alone work a spell in—industrial or agricultural production. When one of the main characters eventually does decide "to work to the full measure of his strength" (to return to the programmatic statement quoted above), only after a considerable amount of red tape is he assigned a job. And what he finds there does not seem "creative and in accordance with his natural talents and inclinations" at all, for he is offered work in a fully automated diamond mine. The work comprises "watching the dials of the sorting machines . . . and keeping constant watch over the calculating machines that computed the ever-changing resistance of the rock, the pressure and expenditure of water, the depth of the shaft and the expulsion of solid matter."[58] Eventually he goes to a submarine titanium mine, to work that seems even less enticing: "He spent his daily tours of duty in semi-dark rooms, packed with indicator dials, where the pump of the air conditioning system could scarcely cope with the overwhelming heat made worse by the increased pressure due to the inevitable leakage of compressed air."[59] Brave new work, indeed!

Adolescents, at least, have more interesting tasks. They perform the "twelve labors of Hercules," hard, challenging pioneer and Boy Scout work like building roads in the mountains or watching out for sharks on a beach. It is work, however, that in a fully mechanized world seems far from necessary, even difficult to create at all. Yefremov does not seem to have been aware of such difficulties and inconsistencies in his work; and this is scarcely surprising, for he was naturally extrapolating from the economic and technological situation of the Soviet Union when he wrote *Andromeda*, a situation certainly not characterized by affluence and overautomation. Siberia enlarged and projected into distant centuries was thus the natural utopian paradise.

As has become evident, Western utopias also suffer from such limitations. They are likewise dependent on the prejudices and limited aspirations of their times. Nor can they constantly develop new ideas and alternatives with regard to concrete problems like that of work. The theoretical possibilities will soon be exhausted here; what seems possible and necessary is a stronger "fictionalization" of utopian literature, to transform ideas into imaginative experiences and thus make them more tangible. Actually and practically, this means a *rapprochement* of science fiction and utopia. For science fiction has the more powerful but at the same time more emotionally centered narrative strategies and symbols; utopian fiction the drier but more definitely enlightening methods of discussion and exposition.

NOTES

1. SF protagonists rarely engage in any sort of ordinary labor. Even if they have a fairly modest job, their work is, as a rule, presented as most glamorous and stimulating—a compensation devoutly to be wished, not a reflection of actual labor problems. Neither are labor problems sufficiently represented by the image or "icon" of robots. As personified machines, robots are closely linked with the problem field of mechanized labor; still, they are usually dissociated from the factory context and presented as emotionally charged, but rather unspecified, symbols of "mechanization as such." Though often given full human shape and almost full human faculties, robots are less humanoid workers than mere *aliens*, to be either befriended or destroyed. The problems that they embody are thus "solved" in a deceptively simple way.

2. I use and quote from the following editions: Edward Bellamy, *Looking Backward: 2000-1887* (New York: New American Library, 1960); William Morris, *News from Nowhere*, ed. James Redmond (London: Routledge & Kegan Paul, 1970); B. F. Skinner, *Walden Two* (1948; rpt. New York: Macmillan, 1976 [Quotations reprinted with permission of Macmillan Publishing Co., Inc. from *Walden Two* by B. F. Skinner. Copyright 1948, renewed 1976 by B. F. Skinner]); Ivan Yefremov, *Andromeda: A Space-Age Tale,* trans. George Hanna (Russian text 1957; trans. Moscow Foreign Language Publishing House, n.d.); Aldous Huxley, *Island* (1962; rpt. London: Panther, 1976).

[Pagination of the 1976 rpt. of *Walden Two* differs from that of the 1962 Macmillan edition, but not enough to cause serious difficulties. The editors will supply, in parentheses, page citations for the 1963 Bantam edition of *Island.*]

3. For a useful historical survey, see articles under "work" in Philip P. Wiener, ed., *Dictionary of the History of Ideas* (1973), and *"Arbeit"* in the standard German reference *Religion in Geschichte und Gegenwart* (*RGG*). For more recent trends in coping with labor problems, see Russell L. Ackoff, *Redesigning the Future: A Systems Approach to Societal Problems* (New York: John Wiley & Sons, 1974), esp. ch. 3.

4. Karl Marx, *Capital: A Critical Analysis of Capitalist Production*, trans. Samuel Moore and Edward Aveling, 3rd edn. (1887; rpt. London: Lawrence & Wishart, 1957), I, ch. 15, 422-23.

5. Karl Marx, "The German Ideology," quoted by Shlomo Avineri, *The Social and Political Thought of Karl Marx* (Cambridge, England: Cambridge University Press, 1968), p. 231. An English trans. of Marx's text was not available to me.

6. Marx, *Capital*, I, ch. 15, 493-94.

7. See Avineri, *Social and Political Thought,* pp. 202-31 and passim.

8. Bellamy, *Looking Backward*, ch. 5, p. 49.

9. Ibid.

10. Ibid., p. 52.

11. Hartmut Lück, *Fantastik, Science Fiction, Utopie: Das Realismusproblem der utopisch-fantastischen Literatur* (Giessen, Germany: Focus Verlag, 1977), p. 193.

12. Robert L. Shurter, *The Utopian Novel in America, 1865-1900* (New York: AMS Press, 1973), pp. 51-73.

13. Ibid., p. 169.

14. See Elizabeth Sadler, "One Book's Influence: Edward Bellamy's 'Looking Backward,' " *The New England Quarterly*, 17 (1944), 530-55, esp. 539.

15. Lück, *Fantastik*, p. 202.

16. Bellamy, *Looking Backward*, ch. 17, p. 128.

17. Ibid., ch. 12, p. 93.

18. There is no money in the America of the future; every citizen has a kind of credit card with which he "pays" until his yearly account is exhausted.

19. See articles cited above, n.3.

20. Bellamy, *Looking Backward*, ch. 18, p. 136.

21. Ibid., p. 137.

22. A sharp-sighted analysis of problems to come appeared a bit later, however: Thorstein Veblen, *Theory of the Leisure Class* (1899). Equally anticipatory is the depiction of the Eloi in H. G. Wells, *The Time Machine* (1895).

23. William Morris, *The Commonweal* (1889), quoted by Redmond, Introd., *News from Nowhere*, p. xxxvii.

24. See Lück, *Fantastik*, p. 208.

25. Morris, *News from Nowhere*, ch. 27, p. 155.

26. Ibid., ch. 15, p. 78.

27. Ibid., ch. 10, p. 61.

28. See Redmond, Introd., *News from Nowhere*, pp. xxviii-xxxiv.

29. William Morris, "The Society of the Future" (1887), in *Political Writings of William Morris*, ed. and introd. A. L. Morton (Berlin, GDR: Seven Seas Books, 1973), pp. 188-204, esp. 196. For Morris' concept of work, see also his lecture "Useful Work Versus Useless Toil," ibid., pp. 86-108.

30. See Lück, *Fantastik,* pp. 207-08.

31. Redmond, Introd., *News from Nowhere*, p. xxxviii.

32. See Sadler, "One Book's Influence," p. 542.

33. See *"Arbeit"* in *RGG* (see n.3 above).

34. Skinner, *Walden Two*, ch. 8, p. 54.

35. Ibid., p. 46. Frazier notes here that "Bellamy suggested the principle [of varying credit units] in *Looking Backward*."

36. In his foreword to the 1976 reissue of *Walden Two*, Skinner discusses the issues of bigness and growth and mentions E. F. Schumacher's book *Small is Beautiful* (1973).

37. Skinner points out that physical work is good for body and soul and has even his managers and planners do "big-muscle" labor (ch. 8).

38. Skinner, *Walden Two*, ch. 29, p. 254.

39. For a critical assessment of Skinner's muddled thinking with regard to means

and ends, see Ramakrishna Puligandla, *Fact and Fiction in B. F. Skinner's Science and Utopia* (St. Louis, MO: Warren H. Green, 1974).

40. Skinner, *Walden Two*, ch. 8, p. 54.

41. Ibid., ch. 14, p. 102.

42. See, for example, B. F. Skinner, *Reflections on Behaviorism and Society* (Englewood Cliffs, NJ: Prentice-Hall, 1978).

43. Huxley, *Island*, ch. 8, pp. 150-51 (130).

44. Aldous Huxley, *Brave New World* (1932; rpt. Harmondsworth, England: Penguin, 1950), Foreword, p. viii. The Foreword bears the copyright date of 1946.

45. Huxley, *Island*, ch. 9, p. 170 (149).

46. Ibid., pp. 173-74 (151).

47. Aldous Huxley, *Point Counter Point* (London: Chatto, 1928), ch. 23, pp. 416-17.

48. Ibid., p. 417.

49. See Lyman Tower Sargent, "English and American Utopias: Similarities and Differences," *Journal of General Education*, 28 (1976), 16-22.

50. For a useful survey, see Everett Webber, *Escape to Utopia: The Communal Movement in America* (New York: Hasting House Publishers, 1959).

51. See note 36.

52. Yefremov, *Andromeda*, ch. 2, p. 60.

53. Ibid, p. 61.

54. Ibid., p. 62.

55. See Lück, *Fantastik*, p. 308.

56. Yefremov, *Andromeda*, ch. 2, p. 63.

57. Ibid.

58. Ibid., ch. 7, p. 221.

59. Ibid., p. 233.

Charles Elkins **3**

E. M. FORSTER'S "THE MACHINE STOPS": LIBERAL-HUMANIST HOSTILITY TO TECHNOLOGY

> Intellectuals, in particular literary
> intellectuals, are natural Luddites.
>
> —C. P. Snow

First published in 1909 in the *Oxford and Cambridge Review*, when Edward Morgan Forster was scarcely thirty years old, "The Machine Stops" has been cited by critics as one of the first antitechnological dystopias, "and a remarkable story to have been written so early in this century."[1] However, so pervasive has been the development of the antitechnological bias within the dystopian tradition that, except for the artistry of the presentation, contemporary readers might find Forster's story quite *un*remarkable. Familiar with such novels as Aldous Huxley's *Brave New World* (1932), D. F. Jones's *Colossus* (1966), George Orwell's *Nineteen Eighty-Four* (1949), Kurt Vonnegut's *Player Piano* (1952), and Yevgeny Zamiatin's *We* (ca. 1920), many readers could view Forster's themes as commonplace if not trite.

Consequently, appreciating Forster's masterful achievement demands that the critic undertake several tasks. The first is to place the work in its historical and intellectual context. It is a truism that writers do not create in a vacuum; "The Machine Stops" is a strategic answer to a number of socio-psychological questions and tensions out of which it arose. The next task is to show where and how Forster goes beyond his contemporaries to dramatize and thus create attitudes toward technology which are at the heart of liberal reactions to technology; responses that transcend the sociopolitical fears of his contemporaries and go straight to the heart of the liberal's vision of a technological dystopia. The final effort is to critique Forster's work as a viable strategy for dealing with technology. The results of this investigation lead to three related theses: (1) "The Machine Stops" can be seen as one outcome of a general turning away by influential intellectuals and critics from science and technology, especially the perceived technological optimism of H. G. Wells; (2) Forster's work goes beyond the usual antitechnological themes by dramatizing the role of science and technology in the demystification of nature—a process intimately connected with the rise of science and capitalism; and (3) as an alienated writer, ill at ease in his own class and age, Forster could not extricate himself from the ideological constraints of his particular situation and, thus, could do little more than sound a warning to those who are overly optimistic about the future and man's relationship with his creations.

As England proceeded through her Industrial Revolution, there were two major negative responses to developing machine technology—the first from the working class, the second from the intellectuals. Up to and through most of the nineteenth century, most machines were created to increase production. From 1811 to 1816 groups of workingmen called Luddites fought against the encroachment of these machines, which they believed caused unemployment and low wages. The Luddites smashed cotton power looms and wool-shearing machines before being suppressed by the government. However, toward the end of the nineteenth century came machines intended more for consumer use and for personal benefit (for example, telephones, movie projectors, gramophones, bicycles, radios, washing machines, refrigerators, vacuum cleaners, and so forth). And it was this aspect of machine production that encouraged some of Forster's contemporaries, such as George Orwell, to observe that they were living in a civilization that was "air-conditioned, chromium-plated, [and] gadget ridden."[2] As one historian of technology writes: ". . . after 1918 the situation worsened. Unemployment and the inability to sell what could be produced become chronic features of the economy—so much so that some came to believe that too much was being produced (in spite of the fact that most people could not get the things they wanted). . . ."[3]

Yet, for the intellectual the antipathy toward science and technology went much deeper. In the nineteenth century the growth of technology increasingly enhanced science and its world view. This development

had . . . many destructive consequences for traditional cultural synthesis, particularly in the sphere of religion. . . . This led, in turn, to the split between science and humanistic culture. . . . *Homo faber* . . . has been fragmented. The active component of culture, altering nature and society, has been allocated to science and technology. The meaningful one, the human self-interpretation which alone could make sense of this activity has been ascribed to those devoid of any practical competence.[4]

This split was disastrous; as Martin Green observes: "In England the conjunction of the Industrial and Scientific Revolutions called forth a tradition of cultural criticism which—though perhaps this country's greatest intellectual achievement—was cripplingly on the defensive, setting literary, cultural, personal values in radical opposition to science and to modern life in general."[5]

This antagonism toward science and technology is registered in the works of practically all of the leading writers of the period. Samuel Hynes, in *The Edwardian Turn of Mind*, writes that George Bernard Shaw was disappointed that science "had not lived up to the hopes we formed of it in the 1860's," and that the interest in psychological and psychic research was a reaction against Victorian mechanism and science.[6] D. H. Lawrence's attack on science and technology was even more virulent than Shaw's. Lawrence was convinced that Western industrial culture debased man; it overemphasized the rational, analytic intelligence at the expense of man's synthetic, intuitive, natural instincts. Lawrence believed that "science, late Christianity and democracy developed more or less together and cooperated in maintaining the standardized culture he wished destroyed."[7] Science and technology's link with industrialism made them even more hateful, and Lawrence not only raises the issue of rationality versus intuition that concerned Forster, but he also confronts the issue of control, of autonomous technology, with the question: "After all, we are masters of our own inventions. Are we really so feeble and inane that we cannot get rid of the monsters we have brought forth?"[8]

Lawrence had an unlikely defender in the figure of George Orwell. While H. G. Wells scoffed at Lawrence's primitivism and his critique of progress, Orwell assailed Wells's naively optimistic conviction "that science can solve all the ills that humanity is heir to."[9] Orwell argued that "one must admit that whether Lawrence's view of life is true or whether it is perverted, it is at least an advance on the science worship of H. G. Wells or the shallow Fabian progressiveness of writers like Bernard Shaw."[10] As he clearly dramatized in *Nineteen Eighty-Four*, Orwell understood how science and technology could be perverted to become instruments not of human liberation, but of terror. As it was for Forster, the development of the airplane was for Orwell a symbol for the corruption of science and technology. Orwell observes that "the equation of science and common sense does not really hold good. The aeroplane, which was looked forward to as a civilizing influence but in practice has hardly been used except for dropping bombs, is a symbol of that fact."[11]

In 1903 a Frenchman, Henri Farmon, flew a heavier-than-air machine over a kilometer course. Forster observed that "It really *is* a new civilization. I have been born at the end of the age of peace and can't expect to feel anything but despair. Science, instead of freeing man . . . is enslaving him to machines."[12]

Furthermore, like Forster, Orwell understood the political implications of technology. Using the airplane again as the symbol of misguided technology, Orwell writes: "The processes involved in making, say, an aeroplane are so complex as to be only possible in a planned, centralized society, with all the repressive apparatus that that implies."[13] Likewise, Forster says, "Bureaucracy, in a technical age like ours, is inevitable. The advance of science means the growth of bureaucracy and the reign of the expert. And, as a result, society and the State will be the same thing."[14]

Like Orwell and Forster, Aldous Huxley also criticized H. G. Wells's technological optimism. And, like "The Machine Stops," Huxley's *Brave New World* began as Huxley's "having a little fun pulling the leg of H. G. Wells."[15] And, just as he reacted against Lawrence's work, Wells called *Brave New World* "defeatist."[16] Just as Lawrence had made an allusion to Mary Shelley's monster, Huxley observed: ". . . technology was made for man, not man for technology, but unfortunately [we have] created a world in which man seems to be made for technology. . . . We do have to start thinking how we can get control again of our inventions. This is a kind of Frankenstein monster problem."[17] Like Lawrence's and Forster's work, *Brave New World* showed man living in fear of direct, primitive experience; nature is mediated by technology. The Savage had no place in technologically sophisticated society. Furthermore, just as in "The Machine Stops," *Brave New World* depicted the devastating effects of technology on the family with the separation of mother from child.

Clearly, then, Forster is in the chorus with his contemporaries and singing the same tune. Still, it is not unimportant to recognize that "The Machine Stops" was one of the first works to voice this protest against technology. Twenty-three years before *Brave New World*, Forster wrote "The Machine Stops" as "a reaction against one of the earlier heavens of H. G. Wells."[18] It is, as Mark Hillegas observes, a "Wellsian scientific romance set in a Wellsian future," and it foreshadows many of the sociopolitical elements in the later dystopias of Zamiatin, Huxley, and Orwell.[19]

"The Machine Stops" depicts an underground, hivelike world, similar to the society in H. G. Wells's *When the Sleeper Wakes*. Individuals live, isolated, in cells; all of their needs are administered to and controlled by the Committee, which, in turn, acts as a liaison to the Machine. The plot involves the conflict between Vashti, a woman completely integrated into her world, and her son Kuno, a rebel against this society. Kuno desires to visit the surface of the Earth, ultimately a crime punishable by death. Through Vashti's eyes and her debates with Kuno, the reader is able to grasp the essential characteristics of this world. People live alone and communicate with each other via visionphones. Everyday life is regulated by the Book of the Machine, containing instructions "against every possible contingency." Individuals do nothing for themselves; they are seldom required to make even the minimal muscular effort to move from place to place or to pick up a fallen object. Muscles have atrophied because in the society of the Machine it is a "demerit" to have them, and infants who show signs of becoming strong adults are killed.[20] All aspects of life are mediated by technology; people do not touch; empirical, direct experience is denigrated; only secondhand and thirdhand ideas are valued. Despite their claim to have transcended the need for religion, people begin to worship the Machine and to treat the Book of the Machine as a sacred text.

In addition to adopting this new religion, people decide that respirators, those devices which make it possible to visit the Earth's surface, are to be abolished since anyone who wishes knowledge of the surface need only listen to a "gramophone" or look at a "cinematophote."[21] Vashti knew that Kuno was ultimately doomed; he could never agree to this new law. As for herself, in the years that followed Vashti was content with the routine of her life: "her life went peacefully forward until the final disaster."[22]

Beginning with insignificant but annoying mechanical malfunctions, the "final disaster" is precipitated by the mysterious but complete failure of the Machine. The uncomprehending population, degenerate and enfeebled by their total dependence on the Machine, cannot save themselves. They are totally annihilated. The narrator sums up the situation: "Man, the flower of all flesh, the noblest of all creatures visible, man who had once made God in his image, and had mirrored his strength in the constellations, beautiful naked man was dying, strangled in the garments he had woven. Century after century had he toiled, and here was his reward."[23] The "garment" is technology.

In passages such as this, one senses the heavy hand of the narrator, yet, for the most part, Forster handles his story with the artistry characteristic of his later work. He skillfully weaves his imagery, for example, into patterns which create a tightly knit whole. Whiteness and colorlessness become the symbols for this entire degenerate world. Vashti's face is "as white as a fungus."[24] The creatures that pull Kuno from the Earth's surface and back into the interior of the planet are described as "long white worm[s]."[25] The narrator observes that the people had physically degenerated "until the body was white pap."[26] Ultimately, the lack of direct, personal contact and the avoidance of firsthand ideas would produce "a generation absolutely colorless."[27]

So impressed is he by his mother's adventure in crossing the roof of the world to visit him, Kuno does not believe Vashti will be interested in his visit to the Earth's surface and his account of the "little . . . low colourless hills" he has seen; still, he tries to explain to her the impression made on his imagination by the living Earth, recalling the turf of the hills as "a skin, under which their muscles rippled."[28] He feels that people of the past must have responded deeply to the hills and loved them. Memory of a color then returns to him; the color of the mist between "his" hill and those in the distance, he says, was "a belt . . . the colour of pearl."[29] Finally, as they

die Kuno kisses his mother and, gasping, explains to her the significance of
their adventures: although they are dying they have won back some of the
sense of life as it was for Aelfrid when he defeated the Danes and as it still is
for those who live on the surface of the Earth and dwell in "the cloud that is
the colour of a pearl."[30] Here, nature's color and richness stand in stark
contrast to the diseased, "white" society of the Machine. Forster's imagery
works superbly to underscore the major themes of his narrative. Mark
Hillegas sums up Forster's achievement in "The Machine Stops."

Forster . . . gives expression to some of the most important humanist fears about
the machine—the fear that the machine will lead to the mechanization of human life
and finally to the control of human life; the fear that the machine will dwarf men
and take from them their self-respect, pride, and sense of uniqueness; the fear that
reliance on the machine will be not only psychologically and spiritually harmful, but
in the end physically destructive; and the fear that men may come to make the
machine a fake idol which they will worship.[31]

If one had to summarize Forster's fears, one could argue that "The
Machine Stops" expresses dramatically what has come to be almost an
obsession with modern, liberal humanists—the fear that technology is out
of control. In a recent book on the subject, Langdon Winner writes: "One
symptom of a profound stress that affects modern thought is the prevalence
of the idea of autonomous technology—the belief that somehow technology
has gotten out of control and follows its own course independent of human
direction."[32] Clearly, Forster's story incorporates this attitude. The people
in his society have little or no say in the management of their own lives. No
one knows how the Machine works. Directives come from the mysterious
Committee or are taken from the Book of the Machine. Mechanical break-
downs are reported to the Committee of the Mending Apparatus, but if
questions or complaints are "unmechanical," the Committee will not
respond. In the end, when the Machine begins to break down, people are
helpless; the idea that the Machine *could* break down is incomprehensible.
When Vashti tells one of her friends that Kuno has warned her that the
Machine is stopping, her friend replies: "The Machine is stopping? . . .
What does that mean? The phrase conveys nothing to me."[33] The society's
fate is entirely within the control of the Machine, which no one understands
or directs.

As Winner suggests, "Autonomous technology is ultimately nothing
more or less than the question of human autonomy held up to a different
light."[34] From the middle of the nineteenth century to the present, the question of human autonomy has come to the fore as a crucial issue in any discussion of the human situation. The theological questions concerning the
nature of God, determinism, and man's free will have not been entirely
abandoned. The secularization of the modern world put the concept of

human autonomy in some new contexts but did not diminish its force. Charles Darwin's theory of natural selection confronted thinkers with the possibility of environmental determinism. Karl Marx's concept of the modes of production determining the relations of production and, hence, man's consciousness, seemed to subtract from man's ability to determine his own destiny. And Sigmund Freud's theory that individual behavior was directed by unconscious forces over which one had no control dealt a devastating blow to any argument for human autonomy. Not only did forces external to man limit his freedom, but there were processes within his own mind that severely restricted his range of choices and modes of action. Thus, the fear of autonomous technology is one more theme in modern man's sense of his loss of mastery of himself and his world.

It is, however, a major theme in any discussion of man's place in the modern world. As Hannah Arendt argues, "Whatever touches or enters into a sustained relationship with human life immediately assumes the character of a condition of human existence."[35] In discussing work, she makes a distinction between tools and machines:

There never was any doubt about man's being adjusted or needing special adjustment to the tools he used; one might as well adjust him to his hands. The case of machines is entirely different. Unlike the tools of workmanship, which at every given moment in the work process remain the servants of the hand, the machines demand that the laborer serve them, that he adjust the natural rhythm of his body to their mechanical movement.[36]

Yet the fear of autonomous technology goes far beyond the question of technology's involvement in man's work. Since the late nineteenth century, thinkers have associated technology with a succession of changes in which the world is transformed and encapsulated by a growing scientific technology. This technology comprises a huge technical system which seems to function and expand by "a process of self-generation beyond human intervention. Within this system people are "dwarfed by the complex apparatus surrounding them, which they must employ if they are to survive."[37] In addition to these assumptions comes the realization that technology is *not* neutral; instead technologies "provide a positive content to the area of life in which they are applied, enhancing certain ends, denying or even destroying others."[38] People cannot employ technology in any way they wish; for technology to function, individuals must "see to it that the appropriate operating procedures and techniques are followed and that all the material conditions for operations are met. . . . of the meanings of autonomous technology . . . this is the most significant."[39] Finally, if Forster's dystopian world seems in the *totality* of its mechanistic organization a little far-fetched, one should note Winner's remarks: " . . . modern technology is a way of organizing the world . . . potentially, *there is no limit to the extent of this organization.* In the end, literally everything within human reach can or will be rebuilt, resynthesized, reconstructed, and incorporated into the system of technical instrumentality."[40]

The consequences of this fear of autonomous technology reverberated in the political realm as well. While some of Forster's contemporaries flirted with socialism of various hues, many were liberals, as was Forster himself. Yet the political conclusion derived from the assumptions of a technological society—namely, the need for a technocracy—is abhorrent to liberalism. From Francis Bacon's *New Atlantis* through the utopian writings of Claude Henri de Rouvroy Saint-Simon and the versions of R. Buckminster Fuller to the science fiction novels of Isaac Asimov and Robert Heinlein runs the argument that authority and power are a product of knowledge and that those who know should rule. The great mass of men must be excluded from positions of power and authority because they lack the specialized knowledge needed to govern a technological society. Technocrats must rule because only they can. Such a conclusion would surely disturb Forster who, while giving only "two cheers for democracy," nevertheless believed that it was the best form of government we could reasonably expect. As Winner puts it, premises of the technocratic position "are totally incompatible with a central notion that justifies the practice of liberal politics: the idea of responsible, responsive, representative government."[41] It should not be surprising, then, that for Forster and his liberal contemporaries the overwhelming success of science and its application as technology was seen with a good deal of ambivalence and anxiety.

However, Forster's concern with technology goes further than that of his contemporaries and relates to his basic humanism. Central to "The Machine Stops" is the theme of isolation. Technology intervenes, cutting people off from direct experience with each other and severing man from nature. Throughout his life, one of Forster's chief concerns was exploring obstacles to human communication and solidarity, be they class, as in *Howards End* (1910), or nationality, as in *A Passage to India* (1924). If there is one sentence which could stand as a symbol for everything in which Forster believed, it would be the epigraph beginning *Howards End*—"Only connect. . . ." This is what matters. In "The Machine Stops" people are isolated from one another. There are no families; mother love is destroyed; the Machine had decreed that "Parents, duties of, . . . cease at the moment of birth. P.422327483."[42] Because of the Machine it is no longer customary for people to touch one another. Such behavior has "become obsolete."[43] Vashti is outraged when an airline stewardess tries to steady her to keep her from falling. All human intercourse is mediated by technology. Kuno wants to see his mother, not view her through a visionphone. He tries to explain to Vashti that while the Machine is a great thing the ersatz experiences it provides are no true substitute for the real thing; that while he sees *something like* Vashti in the plate, he does not see *her*, not does he hear the real Vashti. In short, he wants her to come to him so that they can experience each other directly.[44] Vashti listens with uncomprehending disbelief.

Even more than isolating people from each other, technology has isolated man from nature; has come between man and nature. Vashti says that she "dislikes the stars." Flying over Earth in an airplane, she finds the stars distracting—"they seemed intolerable."[45] The landscape below the airplane provided "no ideas." As the narrator explains, man "had harnessed Leviathan. All the old literature, with its praise of Nature, and its fear of Nature, rang false as the prattle of a child."[46] Yet for Kuno (and Forster), nature is a living thing; landscapes take the shape of "prostrate" men; mountains are described as "breasts." The Earth is alive; Kuno feels it. The heavens, the stars in particular, are humanized by Kuno. He described one set of stars to Vashti:

> "I had an idea that they were like a man."
> "I do not understand."
> "The four big stars are the man's shoulders and his knees. The three stars in the middle are like the belts that men wore once, and the three stars hanging are like a sword."[47]

Again, Vashti does not understand. For Kuno, nature must be directly experienced and humanized; it excites *his* imagination and *he* responds to it directly. The Machine does not determine his reality; for Kuno, "Man is the measure. . . . Man's feet are the measure for distance, his hands are the measure for ownership, his body is the measure for all that is lovable and desirable and strong."[48] But for the rest of society, nature has lost her charm; mediated by technology, nature ceases to arouse man's imagination. With the development of technology, man ceases to trust his senses and his common sense. Hannah Arendt argues that

it was not reason but a man-made instrument, the telescope, which actually changed the physical world view; . . . *Homo faber* . . . as he arose from the great revolution of modernity, though he was to acquire an undreamed of ingenuity in devising instruments to measure the infinitely large and the infinitely small, was deprived of those permanent measures that precede and outlast the fabrication process and form an authentic and reliable absolute with respect to the fabricating activity.[49]

According to computer scientist Joseph Weizenbaum:

This rejection of direct experience was to become one of the principal characteristics of modern science. Gradually, then ever more rapidly and, it is fair to say more compulsively, experiences of reality had to be represented as numbers in order to appear legitimate in the eyes of the common wisdom. Today enormously intricate manipulations of often huge sets of numbers are thought capable of producing new sets of reality. These are validated by composing the newly derived numbers with pointer readings on still more instruments that mediate between man and nature, and which, of course, produce still more numbers.[50]

What has happened, argue Arendt and Weizenbaum—and this lies at the very center of Forster's thinking—is that as a result of his technology man is no longer at home in his world. He no longer trusts his senses because his environment is mediated by technology, by instruments of his own creation. One critic of that symbol of modern technology, the television, writes:

Natural environments have given way to human environments.

What we see, hear, touch, taste, smell, feel, and understand about the world has been processed for us. Our experiences of the world can no longer be called direct, or primary. They are secondary, mediated experiences. . . . living within artificial, reconstructed, arbitrary environments that are strictly the products of human conception, we have no way to be sure that we know what is true and what is not. We have lost context and perspective.[51]

In addition, and related to this loss of a personal, direct contact with the world as a consequence of technology, come the growth of bureaucracy and what might be called the rationalization of everyday life. Like Orwell, Forster believed that "bureaucracy in a technical age like ours, is inevitable."[52] In "The Machine Stops," all regulations are codified in the Book of the Machine; all directions come from and all requests must be addressed to the Committee of the Machine. No one knows who this committee is or how it functions; when it ceases to function, no explanations are given. The world of "The Machine Stops" is very similar to some of Franz Kafka's creations. The impersonal but powerful bureaucracy is organized around the model of the Machine.

The choice of the machine as a paradigm of organization is not accidental. . . . The growth of modern technology and the improvement of machine design . . . demanded . . . the development of appropriate social accommodations to insure their smooth and fruitful functioning. . . . In time, a profound symbiosis has arisen between man and machine in which the orderly operation, the sustained control, and the predictability necessary for the efficient functioning of the machine have inevitably been reflected in an ever greater measure of social order, systemization, and organization—affecting every aspect of human affairs.[53]

It is a world that leaves little room for the poetic, the irrational, and the fantastic.

That world is not congenial to the likes of Forster. Writing about Samuel Butler's *Erewhon* (1872), a Victorian novel satirizing society's dependence on machines, Forster says that he was influenced by Butler's style: "I liked that idea of fantasy, of muddling up the actual and impossible until the reader isn't sure which is which.''[54] In "The Machine Stops," Kuno's imagination and fantasies serve only to condemn him. A society controlled by the Machine has no place for the poet. It is a world regulated, systematized and, above all, rational. Its inhabitants scorn any romantic notions of nature and the very mention of religion. Even as they worship the Machine, the people avoid the label "religion" since the Machine protects them against superstition.[55]

In this calculating, rational world, magic has been eliminated. Irritated by any waste of his time, Vashti keeps scolding Kuno to "be quick." She herself is constantly engaged in meaningless activity. It is a world where, as Max Weber observes, "Waste of time is thus the first, and in principle the deadliest of sins.''[56] It is a society and culture built upon "the combination of rationalism and empiricism" described by Robert K. Merton, except that the empiricism has been abandoned as useless because everything is mediated by the Machine.[57] It is a culture dominated by the "process of spreading rationality" characterized by economist Joseph Schumpeter: "The capitalist process rationalizes behavior and ideas and by doing so chases from our minds, along with metaphysical belief, mystic and romantic ideas of all sorts . . . capitalistic [organization] is rationalistic and anti-heroic.''[58] In short, it is Forster's own world, taken to its logical conclusion. It is a world we recognize.

"The Machine Stops" provides its audience with a particular way of seeing the world, and it names that world in such a way as to communicate an attitude toward it. Moreover, that world is as much Edwardian England as it is the remote future. As the philosopher George Herbert Mead tells us in his *The Philosophy of the Present* (1959), we create images of the past and future in order to solve problems in the present.[59] For Forster as well as many of his contemporaries, one of the most pressing problems was how to deal with an emerging industrial technological society whose basic values and social organization appeared to be a clear threat to man's imaginative life and to intimate, personal human relationships. "The Machine Stops" does not suggest any solutions to these problems. As they are dying, Kuno tells Vashti that there are humans on the surface of the Earth who have escaped destruction and will rekindle civilization but will not repeat man's enslavement to the Machine. But Kuno is totally unconvincing.

Kuno assumes that man can control his technology and, hence, his destiny. However, at least from the narrative of "The Machine Stops," his position is unearned and unpersuasive. When Vashti says, "Oh, tomorrow —some fool will start the Machine again, tomorrow," the reader can just as easily believe her. Forster has certainly communicated an attitude toward this mechanized world, but since no compelling reasons are given as to *why* and *how* man lost control of his technology, there are no cogent justifications for believing that history will not repeat itself. The narrator explains: ". . . Humanity, in its desire for comfort, had over-reached itself. It had exploited the reaches of nature too far. Quietly and complacently, it was sinking into decadence, and progress had come to mean the progress of the Machine."[60] One is tempted to ask how all this happened. It is perhaps an unfair question. Forster is dramatizing the *effects* of a totally mechanized world rather than its causes and the events that lead up to it. The repulsion one has for this society works to create attitudes toward an overdependence on technology which may assist its readers in rethinking their priorities and restructuring their relationships to technology. In this way "The Machine Stops" links with other works by Forster's contemporaries to produce a cultural critique of Edwardian industrial-technological society.

At the same time, while "The Machine Stops" satirizes and rejects this mechanized hell, the satire and antipathy is mixed with a sense of resignation and futility. It is a curious mixture inasmuch as satire's goal is the improvement of man's institutions and the correction of his foibles. Yet "The Machine Stops" presents such a discouraging picture of man in general that it is difficult to see wherein lies his hope for the future. Except for Kuno—and we are not certain why he is different—everyone seems to acquiesce in their slavery to the Machine. There is no collective resistance; Vashti and her friends seem lobotomized. They routinely accept the most absurd rituals and ideas. They are sheep; hence their slaughter is inevitable and undistinguished. The reader has little sympathy for them; they had lost most vestiges of their humanity before the story begins. They live in their hives like insects, and it is difficult to feel any emotional involvement in the death of a bee.[61]

Nor can bees control their destiny. Since they are not conscious of nature and her laws, they are her victims. They are totally biologically and environmentally determined. Again the question is raised: Given this view of man, what is the point of the satire? One might answer that Forster is implying that man is not now but could evolve into this insectlike creature, but since there will always be mutants like Kuno, there is hope.

However, the hope is muted. No real alternatives are presented. Forster voices the concerns of liberal humanists who were reacting to events, the future consequences of which seemed to put people such as Forster in even more peripheral situations vis-á-vis their functions in society. What "The Machine Stops" fails to communicate is that the relationship between society and technology is a dialectical one. While technology influences social relationships, social relationships also influence the nature and direction of technology. The first theorist to formulate a coherent view of autonomous technology, Karl Marx, understood this.[62] Marx insisted that "technology has to be understood as a social process.[63] And while he clearly was aware that under capitalism, "technology had taken on an independent, malevolent, lifelike existence and stood opposed to man as an alien and even monstrous force,"[64] Marx was *not* a technological determinist.[65] Marx argued that our "mastery over technology has not been really lost. It has simply been removed to a small segment of the social order, the capitalist class."[66]

Marx's answer to the problem of technology is not the whole answer. Forster touched on something quite fundamental. Whatever form of social arrangement one envisions, there is still the question of technology itself, especially its function as a mediator between man and his social and physical world. Moreover, as one thinker has observed, man is not only "separated from his natural conditions by instruments of his own making," but he is rotten with perfection.[67] There seems to be a compulsion in man to take things to their logical conclusion, regardless of the consequences. Science and technology stand as supreme examples of man's imaginative reach, and there is no reason to believe that man will cease in his attempts to extend his reach or perfect his grasp.

NOTES

1. Rex Warner, "E. M. Forster," in *British Writers and Their Work No. 3*, gen. ed. Bonamy Dobree (Lincoln, NB: University of Nebraska Press, 1964), p. 59. See also Mark Hillegas, *The Future as Nightmare: H. G. Wells and the Anti-utopians* (New York: Oxford University Press, 1967), p. 82.

2. George Orwell, *The Collected Essays, Journalism and Letters of George Orwell*, ed. Sonia Orwell and Ian Angus, 4 vols. (Harmondsworth, England: Penguin, 1970), IV, 70.

3. Samuel Lilley, *Men, Machines and History* (New York: International Publishers, 1965), p. 139.

4. Norman Birnbaum, *The Crisis of Industrial Society* (New York: Oxford University Press, 1969), pp. 131-32.

5. Martin Green, *Science and the Shabby Curate of Poetry: Essays About the Two Cultures* (New York: W. W. Norton, 1965), p. 69.

6. Samuel Hynes, *The Edwardian Turn of Mind* (Princeton, NJ: Princeton University Press, 1968), pp. 132, 142.

7. Mary Freeman, *D. H. Lawrence: A Basic Study of His Ideas* (New York: Grosset and Dunlap, 1955), p. 109.

8. Ibid.

9. Orwell, *Collected Essays*, II, p. 234.

10. Ibid., p. 235. As was often his custom, Orwell overstates his case. Wells, according to such scholars as Mark Hillegas, was not nearly the naive optimist he was taken to be.

11. Ibid, p. 170.

12. Quoted in P. N. Furbank, *E. M. Forster: A Life*, 2 vols. (London: Secker and Warburg, 1977), I, 161-62.

13. Orwell, *Collected Essays*, IV, p. 70.

14. E. M. Forster, *Two Cheers for Democracy* (London: Edward Arnold, 1951), p. 94.

15. Sybille Bedford, *Aldous Huxley: A Biography* (New York: Knopf and Harper and Row, 1974), p. 244, quoting Huxley.

16. Ibid, p. 253.

17. Ibid, pp. 674-75.

18. Furbank, *E. M. Forster*, I, p. 162, quoting Forster. Mark Hillegas argues that Forster was thinking not only of Wells's five scientific romances but of his *Modern Utopia* as well; see Hillegas, *Future as Nightmare*, pp. 85-87.

19. Hillegas, pp. 85, 88, 94-95.

20. E. M. Forster, "The Machine Stops," in *The Eternal Moment and Other Stories* (1928; rpt. New York: Grosset and Dunlap, 1964), section II, p. 43.

21. Ibid., section III, p. 64.

22. Ibid., p. 69.

23. Ibid., p. 83.

24. Ibid., section I, p. 13.

25. Ibid., section II, p. 59.

26. Ibid., section III, p. 83.

27. Ibid., p. 65.

28. Ibid., section II, p. 55.

29. Ibid., p. 56.

30. Ibid., section III, p. 84.

31. Hillegas, *Future as Nightmare*, pp. 89-90.

32. Langdon Winner, *Autonomous Technology: Technics-out-of-Control as a Theme in Political Thought* (Cambridge, MA, and London: MIT Press, 1977), p. 13.

33. Forster, "Machine Stops," section III, p. 71.

34. Winner, *Autonomous Technology*, p. 43.

35. Hannah Arendt, *The Human Condition: A Study of the Central Dilemmas Facing Modern Man* (1958; rpt. Garden City, NY: Doubleday, Anchor, 1959), p. 11.

36. Ibid., pp. 128-29.

37. Winner, *Autonomous Technology*, p. 17.

38. Ibid., p. 29.

39. Ibid., p. 198.

40. Ibid., p. 191 (emphasis mine).

41. Ibid., p. 146.

42. Forster, "Machine Stops," section I, p. 27.

43. Ibid., p. 36.

44. Ibid., p. 16.

45. Ibid., p. 32.

46. Ibid., p. 29.

47. Ibid., p. 17.

48. Ibid., section II, p. 44.

49. Arendt, *Human Condition*, pp. 249, 280-81.

50. Joseph Weizenbaum, *Computer, Power and Human Reason: From Judgment to Calculation* (San Francisco: W. H. Freeman, 1976), p. 25.

51. Jerry Mander, *Four Arguments for the Elimination of Television* (New York: Morrow Quill Paperbacks, 1978), pp. 55, 68.

52. Forster, *Two Cheers*, p. 94.

53. Roderick Seidenberg, *Anatomy of the Future* (Chapel Hill, NC: University of North Carolina Press, 1961), pp. 48-49.

54. Quoted in Hillegas, *Future as Nightmare,* p. 185, n. 13.

55. Forster, "Machine Stops," section III, p. 67.

56. Max Weber, *The Protestant Ethic and the Spirit of Capitalism* (1904-05; trans. Talcott Parsons, New York: Charles Scribner's Sons, 1958), p. 157.

57. Robert K. Merton, "Puritanism, Pietism and Science," in *Social Theory and Social Structures* (Glencoe, IL: Free Press, 1949), p. 333.

58. Joseph Schumpeter, *Capitalism, Socialism and Democracy* (New York: Harper and Row, 1947), p. 127.

59. George Herbert Mead, *The Philosophy of the Present*, ed. Arthur E. Murphy (LaSalle, IL: The Open Court Publishing Co., 1959).

60. Forster, "Machine Stops," section III, p. 69.

61. In *A Passage to India* (1924), Forster examines the Hindu concept of the unity of all living creatures and the sacredness of *all* creation.

62. Winner, *Autonomous Technology*, p. 39.

63. Nathan Rosenberg, "Marx as a Student of Technology," *Monthly Review*, 28 (July-August 1976), 70.

64. Winner, *Autonomous Technology*, p. 36.

65. Rosenberg, "Marx as a Student," pp. 58-61.

66. Winner, *Autonomous Technology*, p. 40.

67. Kenneth Burke, *Language as Symbolic Action: Essays on Life, Literature, and Method* (Berkeley: University of California Press, 1966), pp. 13, 16.

Alexandra Aldridge

4

ORIGINS OF DYSTOPIA:
WHEN THE SLEEPER WAKES AND *WE*

> The minds of all of us, and therefore the
> physical world, would be perceptibly different
> if Wells had never existed.
>
> —George Orwell[1]

> Altogether, it is doubtful that without
> Wells the anti-utopian phenomenon would ever
> have taken the shape it has.
>
> —Mark Hillegas[2]

Both George Orwell, the dystopian novelist, and Mark Hillegas, the critic of dystopian fiction, have elaborated at some length on the double meaning in the lines quoted above. Generally, it is conceded about H. G. Wells that the imagery formed by his futuristic imagination, the so-called cosmic pessimism he learned from T. H. Huxley, and his frequently verbalized anxieties about the potential misuses of applied science caused him to be a major inspiration for the generation of Orwell, Aldous Huxley, and Yevgeny (Eugene) Zamiatin. At the same time, a large part of Wells's influence was negative, an exercise in literary patricide carried out most effectively by Orwell and Huxley in their satirizing of the "other side of Wells"—that is, the sanguine scientific rationalist.

Orwell and Huxley probably did more than anyone to put Wells out of favor during the Second World War and the postwar period. A revival of interest among scholars and critics began in the early 1960s, coinciding with the popular impact of science fiction and following (and mostly caused by) the publication of Bernard Bergonzi's *Early H. G. Wells* (1961), and W. Warren Wagar's *H. G. Wells and the World State* (1961).[3] What Wells's detractors assigned to dualism or inconsistency, Wagar attributes to the fact that Wells was neither a subtle nor systematic thinker. However, as with Friedrich Wilhelm Nietzsche, whom Wells admired, coherence, consistency, even a system could be imposed on his thinking by looking back, as Wagar does, over Wells's career and oeuvre. Actually, had Wells been *less* consistent after the First World War and the repressive side effects of the Russian Revolution, both of which altered so many contemporaneous attitudes toward world order, he might have protected himself against a reputation in later years for narrow-sighted optimism and a cheerful faith in progress through scientific and technical advances.

Orwell delivered an ultimate indictment in 1941: "History as Wells sees it is a series of victories won by the scientific man over the romantic man."[4] In the same essay Orwell acknowledges his early debt to Wells as the one person in the 1900s who had freed young imaginations from stale Victorianisms and brought them into contact with a future fitted with scientific and technical marvels. Ironically (and this is an irony Orwell recognizes), the scientific man in Wells accounted for what Orwell first admired and then despised. Orwell was right when he said in "Wells, Hitler and the World State" that the Wellsian scientific world view up to the First World War seemed new, daring, antiestablishment in a still-Victorian epoch led by a repressive bourgeoisie and a benighted clergy. But after that war the continuous call for sanity through a systematic restructuring of society appeared naive, oversimplified, dangerous, and a misreading of the modern sensibility. In addition, when Wells could believe with increasing conviction during his later years that "the whole is real and the individual an illusion,"[5] he had altogether missed the modernist spirit which energized writers like Orwell, Huxley, and Zamiatin. In Zamiatin's *We* (1924), for example, to affirm the *authority* of the nonrational, subjective mind is to believe completely in the precedence of individual over collective aspirations.

Recalling Hillegas's just claim that "without Wells the anti-utopian phenomenon would [never] have taken the shape it has," it should be possible to solve the long-standing literary puzzle of the complex legacy left by Wells—the progenitor of the great dystopias *and* the quintessential scientific *eu*topian—to Yevgeny Zamiatin. Zamiatin was at the same time and without subsequent renunciation one of Wells's keenest literary disciples *and*, in my opinion, the author of this century's most powerful dystopian attack on the scientific world view.[6]

The basic facts are these: In 1922 Zamiatin published a monograph, *Herbert Wells*, in which he praised Wells for being the creator of a new genre, namely "sociofantasy," or science fiction—what he describes as the "urban fairy tale" presented in a setting of glass and steel.[7] He also claims that Wells's science fiction, unlike, for example, Jules Verne's, was unique for its social criticism. *We* was written at about this same time, during 1920-21. It was banned in the Soviet Union and published in New York in English in 1924. Much of its imagery and narrative detail is borrowed from Wells's work, particularly from *When the Sleeper Wakes* (1899).

Zamiatin probably came to write *Herbert Wells* in the course of serving as an editor, between 1919 and 1924, for a revolutionary publishing house called World Literature which had been organized to make literary classics easily accessible to the Russian people. In addition to supervising translations of and editing and writing introductions to works by such authors as George Bernard Shaw and Jack London, Zamiatin was responsible for five volumes of the works of H. G. Wells. In 1921 he gave some public lectures on Wells at a St. Petersburg artists' union, and from 1924 to 1926 he put together a twelve-volume edition of Wells's collected works for another publishing house.[8]

Zamiatin has in common with his English mentor both a scientific background (he was a marine architect by training) and an ambiguous commitment to socialism (he began as an active Bolshevik and ended in exile from the new order, having been labeled a "reactionary"). He was in England for eighteen months during the Great War and just before the 1917 Russian Revolution, where he supervised the building of Russian icebreakers. Hillegas speculates that Zamiatin might have come to know Wells's work during that time; but, since it was easily accessible before the revolution, it is more likely that Zamiatin came to know Wells's urban milieu earlier, while still in Russia. At any rate, Zamiatin incorporated Wells's milieu into his own writing. The opening pages of *Herbert Wells* give us Zamiatin's impression of twentieth-century London—one which coincides with the city in *We*:

. . . imagine a country where the only fertile soil is asphalt, where nothing grows but dense forests of factory chimneys, where the animal herds are of a single breed, automobiles, and the only fragrance in the spring is that of gasoline. This place of stone, asphalt, iron, gasoline and machines is present-day, twentieth-century London, and naturally it was bound to produce its own iron, automobile goblins, and its own mechanical, chemical fairy tales. Such urban tales exist: they are told by H. G. Wells.[9]

Zamiatin's prose becomes breathless with enthusiastic catalogues of Well's literary uses of technology. He describes a fiction filled with allusions to the modern city—the latest applications of science in everyday life, marvels brought into being by scientific logic. There is, he maintains, a captivating modernity in Wells: "All his myths are as logical as mathematical equations. And this is why we, modern men, we, skeptics, are conquered by these logical fantasies."[10]

At first is seems incredible that when these words were written, Zamiatin could have just finished, or perhaps still be at work on, a novel which has to be read as an indictment of the dehumanization inherent in the "asphalt city," a satire on the scientific logic which brought that marvel and horror into being. As we read on, we discover that he saw Wells as a remarkable prophet who at the end of the nineteenth century predicted the essential characteristics of the twentieth-century city and twentieth-century war. Zamiatin also appreciated the social critic, not to mention the socialist, in Wells. But above all he identified with Wells's kinetic imagination, with the expressions of energy, movement, process which appear in so much of the earlier work: "Everything here [in "A Story of the Days to Come"] rushes with fabulous speed—machines, machines, machines, airplanes, turbine wheels, deafening gramophones, flickering fiery advertisements."[11]

Zamiatin was so impressed with the kinetic quality in Wells's science fiction, the social criticism in those works, and their balance of fantasy and precision that he reads the same features into Wells's utopias. He denies that those novels which "have been designed as social utopias" belong to the tradition of Sir Thomas More, Tommaso Campanella, and William Morris, and insists that Wells's only utopia is *Men Like Gods* (1923)—the very work that Huxley claims he set out to satirize in *Brave New World* (1932).[12] What then distinguishes the Wellsian utopia (sociofantastic novel to Zamiatin) from its predecessors?

There are two generic and invariable features that characterize utopias. One is the content: the authors of utopias paint what they consider to be ideal societies; translating this into the language of mathematics, we might say that utopias bear a + sign. The other feature, organically growing out of the content, is to be found in the form: a utopia is always static; it is always descriptive, and has no, or almost no, plot dynamics.

In Wells's sociofantastic novels we shall hardly ever find these characteristics. To begin with, most of his social fantasies bear the − sign, not the + sign. His sociofantastic novels are almost solely instruments exposing the defects of the existing social order, rather than building a picture of a future paradise. . . . Only *Men Like Gods*, one of his weakest sociofantastic novels, contains the sugary, pinkish colors of a utopia.[13]

Again the appeal to Zamiatin lies in movement, in energy. Wells himself had made it very clear in his major proposal for world order: the "Modern Utopia must be not static but kinetic, must shape not as a permanent state but as a hopeful stage, leading to a long ascent of stages."[14]

Undeniably a contradiction is expressed in that Zamiatin could seem to praise some of the same qualities in Wells that he disparages in the society depicted in his own new novel. In *We*, the hero's alternative to living in the state built on reason is to "become insane as soon as possible"—an echo of the arch irrationalist Arthur Rimbaud. Yet when Zamiatin describes *A*

Modern Utopia, he begins by noting that "The purpose of social reconstruction, as [Wells] sees it, is to introduce into life an organizing principle
—*ratio*-reason."[15] Hillegas believes that Zamiatin did not comprehend
Wells well enough to see "that the rationalism and regimentation he
opposed in *We* was at least a strong element in Wells's thought."[16] But it is
possible that Hillegas did not comprehend Wells's thought well enough (as
Wagar and Zamiatin do) to see the constants that run through it: a social
structure which has come into being through the exercise of reason cannot
remain fixed; change is the law of life; sometimes violent upheaval is
necessary to save the species from stasis (and thereby extinction); mankind
must continuously adapt; progress is hardly inevitable.[17]

Through different—and even more blatant—literary uses, Zamiatin in *We*
also expresses his belief in humanity's need for apocalyptic upheaval, and
he dramatizes powerfully an abhorrence of stasis (or entropy, as he prefers).
It is a basic principle of imagination—dynamism, even apocalypse—that
Zamiatin takes from Wells, rather than a specific social vision: "To me, the
word *airplane* contains all of our time. It also contains all of Wells."[18] Yet
finally, their respective responses to contemporary history, their differing
alternatives to a dystopic society, and their divergent representations of the
nature and significance of the individual psyche constitute the distinction
between the modernist forebear, Wells, and the real modernist, Zamiatin
—between a world view formed by nineteenth-century biology (and
economics), and one consisting in the self-conscious credo of the twentieth-
century artist.

* * *

The novels and stories of H. G. Wells that are usually recognized for
dystopian content are *The Time Machine* (1895), *The Island of Dr. Moreau*
(1896), *The War of the Worlds* (1898), *When the Sleeper Wakes* (1899), "A
Story of the Days to Come" (1899), *The First Men in the Moon* (1901), and
The War in the Air (1908). Of these, *When the Sleeper Wakes* deserves the
most attention for our purposes. More than any of Wells's works, *Sleeper*
provides the major themes and much of the imagery for the great dystopias.
As in *Nineteen Eighty-Four*, for example, the political boss in *Sleeper*
admits that he is motivated by a desire for power for its own sake; in *Brave
New World*, benevolent social and psychological engineering (hypnotism in
Wells) releases individuals from the pain of emotional crises; and as in *We*,
the setting is an architecturally stunning, automated urban state. (Hillegas
describes at some length specific themes and imagery taken by Orwell,
Huxley, Zamiatin, and others from *Sleeper*.[19])

Actually, *When the Sleeper Wakes* is, properly described, an ambiguous
dystopia. Norman MacKenzie and Jeanne MacKenzie state in their biography that "Wells seems unsure whether to approve or disapprove of his

projection, whether he is writing a utopia or an anti-utopia."[20] Bernard
Bergonzi delivers sharper criticism: "The novel is incoherent because of the
lack of accord between Wells's speculative intellectual attitudes and his
deepest emotional inclinations."[21] Whatever else can be said about it,
Sleeper seems to have become a source book for later dystopias partly
because the intellectual inconsistency of the narrative allows its readers to
emphasize or interpret its themes however they choose.

The plot combines Edward Bellamy-like romance and uninspired melo-
drama. A nineteenth-century gentleman, one Graham, who, we are told,
was a socialist of "the advanced school," falls into a trance in 1897 (rather
like Bellamy's Julian West) and wakes up, in this case, in twenty-second-
century London. Due to the increase on investments made in his name, he
wakens to find himself the literal owner of half the world and the symbolic
hope of the underprivileged. While he slept, a council had ruled in his name
and had increased the material standard of living for the affluent at the
expense of the working classes. Graham's awakening sparks a rebellion of
the oppressed led by a self-interested political boss named Ostrog. It
becomes apparent that Ostrog is unconcerned with the workers' welfare; he
intends to manipulate them and to maintain the economic status quo with
the unwitting help of an initially naive Graham. Eventually Graham learns
about the terrible realities of the workers' condition and the duplicity of
Ostrog, and he takes on the leadership of the rebellion in the workers'
name. The novel ends with the certainty of Graham's death, the likelihood
that the workers' cause has been won, and the implication that a new era is
dawning.

This future world is unfolded during Graham's slow progress toward
political radicalization. He finally comes to understand, very late in the
story, the seriousness of the economic inequity of the year 2100. At about
the same time in the course of the narrative, the reader comes to realize that
an inequitable distribution of wealth—not science misused or an over-
extension of scientific logic—forms the dystopian component of *When the
Sleeper Wakes*. Fully the first two-thirds of the novel, despite occasional
hints of a darker reality, are taken up with objective, often favorable descriptions of what science and technology had wrought over the past 200
years. It is indeed difficult to tell whether we should read this technological
society as dystopian or utopian. In the best-known and most often quoted
passage we survey the grandeur, the massive scale, the complication of the
futuristic city through the eyes of a nineteenth-century man:

His first impression was of overwhelming architecture. The place into which he
looked was an aisle of Titanic buildings, curving spaciously in either direction. Overhead mighty cantilevers sprang together across the huge width of the place, and a
tracery of translucent material shut out the sky. Gigantic globes of cool white lights
shamed the pale sunbeams that filtered down through the girders and wires. Here

and there a gossamer suspension bridge dotted with foot passengers flung across the chasm and the air was webbed with slender cables. A cliff of edifice hung above him, he perceived as he glanced upward, and the opposite façade was grey and dim and broken by great archings, circular perforations, balconies, buttresses, turret projections, myriads of vast windows, and an intricate scheme of architectural relief.[22]

Later Graham feels alone and friendless in this setting, but his sense of estrangement comes from unfamiliarity; he is not alienated by the scale or remoteness of futuristic technology. The scenes he witnesses, human and mechanical, are not sinister and bleak as they would be in Orwell, trivializing as in Huxley, or clinically presented as in Zamiatin. While Graham assumes that a dreary life of labor and exploitation still exists for the common man, within the same chapter he is struck by technical marvels as he looks out onto a great panoramic view of the city. The description of what Graham sees is straightforward, presented without irony. If anything, it is admiring. Wells's imagination is clearly attracted to massive scale, efficient engineering, and continuous movement:

On the first occasion that offered he was determined to go out and see these roads. That would come after the flying ship he was presently to try. His attendant officer described them as a pair of gently curving surfaces a hundred yards wide, each one for the traffic going in one direction, and made of a substance called Eadhamite—an artificial substance, so far as he could gather, resembling toughened glass. Along this shot a strange traffic of narrow rubber-shod vehicles, great single wheels, two and four wheeled vehicles, sweeping along at velocities of from one to six miles a minute.[23]

Graham, and Wells, fail at this stage in the narrative to see an adverse relation between what Richard Gerber calls "mass and class"—the idea that science and technology give rise to industry, and that industrialism in turn requires scientific management with all its alienating consequences.[24] (Scientific management is, of course, what underlies dystopia in Zamiatin.) Rather, Wells appears to view industrialism and mass man dispassionately, as a natural result of evolution: "First had come the nomad, the hunter, then had followed the agriculturist of the agricultural state, whose towns and cities and ports were but the headquarters and markets of the countryside. And now, logical consequence of an epoch of invention, was this huge new aggregation of men."[25]

There are, however, several unequivocally dystopian uses of science and technology in this society. Graham is annoyed by the "Babble Machines," which spew crude and distorted bits of news and advertising through the city's public ways, and dismayed by the kineto-tele-photographs (like television) which have replaced books. (These and other material transcriptions of science are also the playthings of the "graceful" but "idle" rich whom the narrator describes with just that adjectival equivocation.) But the effect of those misapplications of science and technology is cancelled out by Graham's childlike enchantment with other machines—particularly the "aeropile."

Not only are two successive chapters (16 and 17) devoted to the ecstasies of flying (and other technical wonders), but those chapters are curiously placed between revelations that an appalling underworld exists in the city. Graham is told in chapter 15 that "The common people are very unhappy; they are oppressed—they are misgoverned."[26] And in chapter 18 he learns that the workers are pale, sickly, desperate, and virtual slaves to the Labour Company. But in the meanwhile he has taken time out to explore the novelty of flying machines. Altogether our attention has been distracted from the dystopian subject matter of *When the Sleeper Wakes* until the final third of the novel (beginning with chapter 18), when the futuristic city materializes as a dystopia through increasingly brutal scenes of working-class life. In chapter 21, for example:

Graham could note the pinched faces, the feeble muscles, and weary eyes of many of the latter-day workers. Such as he saw at work were noticeably inferior in physique to the few gaily dressed managers and forewomen who were directing their labours. The burly labourers of the old Victorian times had followed the dray horse and all such living force producers, to extinction; the place of his muscles was taken by some dexterous machine. The latter-day labourer, male as well as female, was essentially a machine minder and feeder, a servant and attendant.[27]

For the first time with any conviction the machine, formerly the subject of encomium, is indicted by the narrative voice. The uses of technology to create a great gulf between an affluent and a laboring class become at least fleetingly apparent. The class structure of Victorian England, intensified in misery for the workers by an exploitative industrial system, has been merely protracted ad nauseum into the future. Disfigured subterranean workers are contrasted with people of privilege and personal grace from above ground in an evolutionary vision foreshadowing—in terms of future history—the Morlocks and Eloi of the year 802701 which Wells had created two or three years earlier in *The Time Machine*.

The so-called cosmic pessimism of T. H. Huxley has emerged in Wells's fear that evolutionary processes might work against mankind. To demonstrate this fear he extrapolates from his vision of the already dystopian social and economic realities existing in *fin de siècle* England. Wells's narrative solution is to force the sleeper into a genuine awakening of the spirit: to make him into a revolutionary. There exist only the vaguest notions of reform rather than a fully developed plan for restructuring society. Wells's real concern at the end, in view of the condition of stasis at which humanity had arrived in spite of its technological mastery, is to turn to violent action, to upheaval, to suggest the eradication of it all and to offer the possibility of a new beginning based on some sort of equity. The last chapters describe Graham's confrontation with the perverse political powers that had encouraged stagnation, focusing finally on his single-handed air battle fought in order to win the workers' cause. (We return at the end to the "good" uses of the machine.) Graham presumably dies in the middle of an apocalyptic victory with the perception that "We have started Armageddon."

Wells was dissatisfied with *When the Sleeper Wakes*, though he saw it as a central document in his output. He attempted revisions in 1910 and reissued the book under the title *The Sleeper Awakes*, but his revisions only amounted to a few minor cuts and verbal changes. And he sadly characterized it as "one of the most ambitious and least satisfactory of my books."[28] It is ambitious especially in the sense that it contains all the elements of the Wellsian world view that could be comprehended by looking back over his major works.

To explain that world view briefly, Wells saw life from the perspective of the nineteenth-century biologist, wherein nature, that is, the cosmic process, was amoral. Therefore, man must be prepared to check that process with ethical action even though a drift toward entropy was probably built into it and even though man was insignificant in cosmic terms. What can be called the Wellsian dialectic grows out of that picture in the following form: all life is in a constant state of change; but in change itself, sometimes in violent upheaval, lies species salvation. Adaptation to change might be difficult due to human venality and because cosmic processes might work against us, but man conceivably can control the direction of his evolution through scientific thought. Science, however, can be misused; to benefit us it must be applied with imagination, morality, and an aesthetic sense. In view of this Wells, before 1914, saw socialism as the proper course for mankind.[29]

For all practical purposes this summary describes the philosophical exoskeleton of *When the Sleeper Wakes*; Wells's imagination merely supplies specificity, flesh and blood, to it. In fact, the very pattern of Graham's revelations roughly corresponds to the outline of the Wellsian dialectic. Graham awakens in the midst of an enormously changed, futuristic London. At first he marvels at scientific and technological progress, but he comes to realize that such material progress does not coincide—certainly does not necessarily coincide—with species progress. Human weakness had made for only a partial adaptation to change, and the working classes are consequently devolving into a lower order of being while the upper classes are trivialized through inaction and by science and technology misapplied. The vaguest part of the novel concerns the application of morally refined and aesthetically sensitive scientific thought, but *Sleeper* contains enough rhetoric about alleviating the workers' conditions to let us suppose that a "scientific" restructuring of society in combination with technological advances properly used might bring a utopia out of an ambiguous dystopia.

This could occur only by first passing through a stage of violent upheaval—the apocalyptic battle led by Graham—after which humanity might begin again.

Wells was accurate in calling this novel his most ambitious and least successful; it does *not* cohere aesthetically. Its contradictions can only be resolved *outside* the fiction, through an understanding of Wells's "system." We are still left, in reading the narrative, with an uneasy sense that he was incapable of presenting a pure dystopia (certainly not one based on the alienating consequences of science and technology) because his intellectual commitment to an efficient technological order was too great. Nor does he make a consistent case for dystopia as the hell of the working class since he comes to focus on their dehumanization too late in the narrative, then sees them in largely sentimental terms (commensurate with Fabian socialism), and finally at best makes too brief and unconvincing a connection between "mass and class."

Dystopian novelists nearly always are jarred into writing by the particularity of their negative perspective on contemporary history, and begin their work by extrapolating from this perspective. Dystopian conditions for Wells, as I have suggested, existed in the social and economic actualities of late Victorian England; accordingly, *When the Sleeper Wakes* is an attack on the viciousness he saw in prewar laissez-faire capitalism, while on a cosmic level the neo-Darwinian biologist in Wells constructed a dystopia from fear that evolutionary processes would carry those adverse conditions forward in time. His imagination was appalled by the wasted lives of masses of people and the likelihood that mankind as a whole might only devolve. Wells went on in the years immediately following, principally in 1905 in *A Modern Utopia*, to outline how that surge toward devolution could be taken off its course through "scientific planning."

* * *

In Yevgeny Zamiatin's Russia, the workers' revolution which Wells idealizes in *When the Sleeper Wakes* was won in 1917 and the "scientific" restructuring of society was in full force. Zamiatin's own dystopian view was not formed in opposition to that revolution or against the ideal of restructuring society—good (though heretical) socialist that he remained even after the drafting of *We*—but against something that Wells certainly could not have foreseen in 1897-98 while writing *Sleeper*. What Zamiatin saw occurring in his postrevolutionary world was the institutionalization of scientific thought, programmatically bringing objectivity, neutrality, verifiability into every area of life. Zamiatin's dystopian view was formed against the perverse notion then permeating Soviet policy that the scientific world view was an end in itself—that revolution stopped there, revolutionary fervor having hardened into scientistic dogma.

The story of Zamiatin's persecution for nonconformity in the wake of the revolution he had enthusiastically supported is well known.[30] Somehow he managed to weather the extreme hostility directed against him until his departure from the Soviet Union in 1931. But from about 1918 onward his heretical attitudes caused him incessant trouble. Zamiatin's biographer, Alex M. Shane, states that he lived in an "atmosphere of constant criticism from Communist and proletarian critics, increasing difficulty in finding publishers, and surveillance by the government. From the very beginning he was branded a bourgeois writer and inner émigré who was antagonistic to the Revolution and the Soviet regime."[31] He was arrested and briefly held in 1922 along with other suspect intellectuals. No doubt his individualistic essays and stories were enough to provoke that arrest, not to mention rumors which might have reached authorities about a satirical novel then being circulated in manuscript at home and translated for publication abroad. (*We* has never been published in the Soviet Union.)

Shane catalogues a long series of abuses culminating, in 1929, in censure by the powerful writers' union (a move actually staged by the Party Central Committee in their efforts to direct the course of Soviet literature). Between 1929 and 1931 Zamiatin's literary reputation was all but ruined by Communist critics who continuously attacked him on the grounds of "bourgeois ideology," and by 1931 he was effectively silenced as a writer in the Soviet Union. All publishing outlets were closed to him and even libraries withdrew his books from circulation. Miraculously (and probably through the intervention of Maxim Gorky), in 1931 Zamiatin and his wife were allowed by Joseph Stalin to depart to Paris, where he lived a sad and unproductive few years before his premature death in 1937.

For a period of twelve years, before and after writing *We*, Zamiatin experienced firsthand the ruthless intimidation and repression he satirizes in his dystopian novel. Still, as Shane stresses, Zamiatin's critical attitude toward the regime and Soviet policies of the 1920s was not in opposition to the revolution in principle but was "rather the logical consequence of his conception of heresy and his belief in never-ending revolution."[32] Zamiatin's fundamental assumptions justifying continuous revolution are to be found, of course, in *We* but are presented more directly in his essays. (*Herbert Wells*, remember, was published in 1922 shortly after the completion of *We*. Zamiatin professed admiration above all for Wells's "kineticism," for the dynamic imagination attuned to contemporary life as process.)

In "Scythians?" (1918) Zamiatin uses Dostoevskian metaphor and Platonic logic to state that any ideal, once realized in historical time, is bound to corrupt: "Christ victorious in practical terms is the grand inquisitor. . . . And Marx, come down to earth, is simply a Krylenko. . . . The realization, materialization, practical victory of an idea immediately gives it a philistine hue." Furthermore, he specifically charges that the October Revolution "has turned philistine."[33]

A year later, in the short essay "Tomorrow" (1919), Zamiatin deifies the heretic as the true life giver: "The world is kept alive only by heretics: the heretic Christ, the heretic Copernicus, the heretic Tolstoy." And in his volatile style, through a Hegelian and apocalyptic theory of history, he crystallizes the moral philosophy of the novel he must have been imagining at that moment: "Yesterday, the thesis; today, the antithesis; and tomorrow, the synthesis. Yesterday there was a tsar, and there were slaves; today there is no tsar, but the slaves remain; tomorrow there will be only tsars. . . . We have lived through the epoch of suppression of the individual in the name of the masses; tomorrow will bring the liberation of the individual—in the name of man."[34]

But the piece that best explains Zamiatin's position and effectively constitutes an expository, nonfiction companion or afterword to *We* is "On Literature, Revolution, Entropy, and Other Matters," written in 1923, a year or so after the final drafting of the novel. He attaches to this essay the following epigraph taken from *We:*

Name me the final number, the highest, the greatest.
But that's absurd! If the number of numbers is infinite, how can there be a final number?
Then how can you speak of a final Revolution? There is no final one. Revolutions are infinite.[35]

Essentially, Zamiatin takes principles from the physical universe as conceptualized in the "new mathematics" and "new science" and makes those principles analogues to both the infinite nature of revolution and the heretical thought and literature that encourage infinite revolution. A whole series of analogues is suggested by the epigraph from *We*:

Two dead, dark stars collide with an inaudible, deafening crash and light a new star: this is revolution. A molecule breaks away from its orbit and, bursting into a neighboring atomic universe, gives birth to a new chemical element: this is revolution. Lobachevsky cracks the walls of the millennia-old Euclidean world with a single book, opening a path to innumerable non-Euclidean spaces: this is revolution.[36]

This metaphoric line of reasoning continues by associating dogma, the opposite of the revolutionary ideal, with entropy—an idea taken, of course, from the Second Law of Thermodynamics and popularly understood in terms of the gradual cooling of the planet: "When the flaming, seething sphere (in science, religion, social life, art) cools, the fiery magma becomes coated with dogma—a rigid, ossified, motionless crust. Dogmatization in science, religion, social life, or art is the entropy of thought."[37]

Building on the material of earlier essays like "Scythians?" and "Tomorrow," Zamiatin brings together revolution, infinite momentum, and heresy with a concept of the physical universe as process—a source of mystery and anticipation—to reach the conclusion that there is no such thing as truth in art or science or literature. All things are relative: "If there were anything fixed in nature, if there were truths, all of this would, of course, be wrong. But fortunately, all truths are erroneous. This is the very essence of the dialectical process: today's truths become errors tomorrow; there is no final number."[38] As in *We*, the symbolic villain here is Euclid, whose geometry consists in the limited notion of fixed, plane coordinates; and, in the same way the Euclidean mentality allows revolution to ossify into dogma, it sets the life of a culture to drift on an "entropic" course.

The antithetical mentality from which Zamiatin draws his ethical and metaphysical ideal is represented by Albert Einstein, who "managed to remember that he, Einstein, observing motion with a watch in hand, was also moving; he succeeded in looking at the movement of the earth from *outside*."[39] At the end, and in the compressed, metaphoric, and elliptical style appropriate to his relativistic vision of reality, Zamiatin again sets Euclid and stasis against Einstein and revolution:

Science and art both project the world along certain coordinates. Differences in form are due only to differences in the coordinates. All realistic forms are projections along the fixed, plane coordinates of Euclid's world. These coordinates do not exist in nature. Nor does the finite, fixed world; this world is a convention, an abstraction, an unreality. And therefore Realism—be it "socialist" or "bourgeois" —is unreal. Far closer to reality is projection along speeding, curved surfaces—as in the new mathematics and the new art. . . . Euclid's world is very simple, and Einstein's world is very difficult—but it is no longer possible to return to Euclid. No revolution, no heresy is comfortable or easy.[40]

Thus Zamiatin in "On Literature" draws an emphatic distinction between two types of science which represent opposite interpretations of physical reality, and he conceptualizes in the manner most natural to him— through analogues. In his apparent desire to make the broadest observations on the human condition he divides hierarchies of analogues into two groups: the one set emanating from the new science and the new math and corresponding to all things dynamic and unmeasurable in life and art; the other emanating from a mechanistic scientific world view and corresponding to stasis. This latter concept of reality is brilliantly satirized as dystopia in *We*.

We is not merely a satire on excessive rationality, as critics sometimes suggest, or an antiscientific or even antitechnological statement. Rather, Zamiatin assumes that a specifically outmoded scientific ideal has formed the mythos of a culture, and that that particular scientific mythos manifests itself in everything from architectural regularity to regulated sexual behavior. The resulting caricature—a robotlike humanity—is doubtless the most absurd, and at times most comical, version of a dystopian future in the whole genre.

The features of dystopia are outlined by a first-person narrator, who initially appears to live in complete agreement with his world—a monolithic urban entity called the United State. In an opening encomium he declares that " . . . the United State is a straight line, a great, divine, precise, wise line, the wisest of lines!" wherein a collective identified only by numbers lives a "mathematical, perfect life."[41] Mathematical perfection resides in the way in which human behavior has come to resemble the workings of precision machinery. Every act, every movement, is choreographed; people lead lives of gestic exactitude; each step has been prearranged by compulsory scheduling, after the time-and-motion studies of American engineer Frederick Taylor. This extreme devotion of harmony is carried through to the very design of city streets and buildings, in "the impeccably straight streets, the glistening glass of the pavement, the divine parallelepipeds of the transparent dwellings."[42] Not the slightest deviation and only the most minimal periods of privacy are permitted, as assured by the "transparent dwellings," the continuous regimentation (administered by a "Well-Doer" and reinforced by a "Bureau of Guardians"), and the registration system for sexual activity whereby "pink tickets" are distributed for use on designated "sexual days."

According to the narrator, D-503, the United State came into being one thousand years before his time (that is, one thousand years into our future), at the end of the Two Hundred Years War between the forces of the City and those of the Land. We learn that untold numbers of people died, that most of the land outside the City stood in a condition of blood and debris, that the City was victorious in that blood bath, and that ". . . endless strings of people [were] driven into the City to be saved by force and to be whipped into happiness."[43] From the beginning we hear that the City is enclosed, a metropolitan fortress behind a transparent Green Wall on the other side of which live the X factors in the novel, in the primal, Edenic, and to D-503 "irrational, ugly world of trees, birds, and beasts."[44] City dwellers are taught to associate this outside world with unknown terrors, to consider it a forbidden zone which no one is allowed, or, in fact, desires, to enter. In the ethic of straight lines and surface realities, beasts and trees and uncontrolled noise and movement belong to an age of barbarism—the unhappy state of freedom from which D-503's ancestors long ago extracted themselves.

The same quality characterizing Zamiatin's essays, a penchant for analogistic (and antonymic) systems—perhaps the engineer's knack for reducing things to some essential symmetry—emerges in his novel.[45] The

City and its attendant (Euclidean) qualities—reason and organization, glass and artifice, happiness as a state of unfreedom—contrast with the unmeasurable, the primal place which houses irrationality and disorder, wilderness and the existential insecurities. In addition, the author's sense of the nature of well-being—his kineticism, his belief in infinite revolution—gives direction to the patterns of analogues. Echoing Wells's theory of history presented in *When the Sleeper Wakes*, D-503 observes that " . . . the history of mankind, as far as our knowledge goes, is a history of the transition from nomadic forms to more sedentary ones."[46] But in keeping with Zamiatin's revolutionary ideal, the action in the novel points toward reversing that entropic drift. The revolutionaries in dystopia attempt to join with the nomadic form of life behind the Green Wall to destroy the City, which seems frozen at the end of time, in order to jar the whole process of history into motion again.

Yet, it is possible to notice the structure and function of the "systems" in *We* and pass over subtleties which make the novel so original. For example, characters do not just represent or act as symbols of the mathematical state. They do not exist *simply* as a function of revolutionary ideology. Zamiatin dramatizes the workings of a representative mind, D-503's, which has been unnaturally formed by a totally artificial environment. The first-person narrative is often fragmented and vague—even incomprehensible—to give the illusion of confused or undigested perceptions taking place in rapid succession as D-503's personality develops. But Zamiatin's best achievement is the description of people, objects, and experiences refracted through a scientized imagination.

The experience out of which Zamiatin came to create such a character is fairly clear. He was personally abused by dogmatists who literalized the rationalistic ethos that had generated the Bolshevik Revolution. If a scientifically planned society—one that promised equity in place of deprivation, order in place of randomness—was humanistic in origin, it was, for Zamiatin, despotic in actuality. He saw how the ethos of the revolution—the unquestioned belief in a society built by the careful organization and control of every one of its institutions—had invaded and bureaucratized the minds of his contemporaries, and how what had begun, in those minds, as humanitarianism had ended in rectitude and rigidity. Zamiatin saw a cultural myth (scientific rationalism was the right way, the only way to direct one's thinking and behavior) infiltrate a whole national imagination in the manner of a contagion. If the national mind was so readily infused by the dogma in the air in 1920's Russia, why not project that ethos to its ultimate banality, not just a Marxist-Leninist enchantment with the methods of the sciences appropriated to politics and economics, but a future society reflecting a maximum increase in "scientific" appropriations—one built on Euclidean plane geometry and Taylorian time-and-motion studies?

If *this* ethos became the very atmosphere people breathed, having first been represented in the planes and angles of architecture, in minutely calculated social organization, even in programmed sexual activity—what alternatives did the imagination have to program this ethos itself? The mind would perceive the entire world as a complex of straight-line harmonies, "divine parallelepipeds"; as contingents of uniformed, impassive humanoids marching together in lockstep; as a table according to which each and all ate, slept, worked, and copulated; and that imagination would follow those rhythmic gestures in its powers of evaluation, its rhetoric, the metaphors through which it assimilated and described the life around it.

Zamiatin casts the scientized imagination, appropriately, in the role of a mathematician to the State who, moreover, is the builder of the *Integral*, a spaceship constructed for the messianic purpose of bringing "mathematically faultless happiness," by force if necessary, to whatever "primitives" exist in the outermost frontiers of the universe. The *Integral* will carry as its first cargo "treatises, poems, manifestos, odes, and other compositions on the greatness and beauty of the United State," and D-503, as master builder and zealous advocate, begins a diary—and begins it (and *We*) with the edict announcing the *Integral*—meaning to ship it off as a guide to the life of his time. But as he progresses this exercise becomes a confession coinciding with his discovery of a personal self. At the same time, his habit of conceptualizing through mathematical imagery and mathematical norms, though it sometimes abates to accommodate the changing self, never really disappears.

In the opening pages, when he is still in harmony with his environment, he sees other people exclusively as configurations:

I noticed her brows that rose to the temples in an acute angle—like the sharp corners of an X. Again I was confused, casting a glance to the right, then to the left. To my right—she, slender, abrupt, resistantly flexible like a whip, I-330 (I saw her number now). To my left, 0-, totally different, all made of circles with a childlike dimple on her wrist; and at the very end of our row, an unknown he-Number, double-curved like the letter S.[47]

D-503 refers here to his first meeting with the woman, I-330, who will lead him into temptation; that is, to the realization that something exists both inside himself and in the world at large besides surfaces and explicable "realities."[48] She arouses him, disturbs him, but even as he first records that fact he does so as if she were a problem to be solved: "The woman had a disagreeable effect upon me, like an irrational component of an equation which you cannot eliminate."[49]

D-503 goes on to explain that that ancient source of anguish, romantic love, need not trouble "the Numbers." Sexuality is attributed to hormonal needs which can be quantified, in every case, with scientific exactitude. And while prescribing the precise amount of sexual activity required for good health, the State also enforces anyone's right to "have" anyone else. Thus needs can be efficiently satisfied and, in the process, official notions of equality are served as well.

In this static society which believes, as D-503 puts it, "the ideal . . . is to be found where nothing *happens*,"[50] it follows that no event, no experience, neither contact with internal nor external nature, *nothing* exists with which to fill the imagination and so provide bases for comparison. But with the entrance of I-330 something does happen. She exposes him to strange and unsymmetrical surroundings, in a museum of the past called the Ancient House. Inside it he is unable to formulate clearly, to make things cohere. The objects he sees do not coincide with linear experience; his mind cannot bring order to the maze of color, the variety of shapes and textures. He merely ingests "a wild, unorganized, crazy loudness of colors and forms. . . . A white plane above, dark blue walls, red, green, orange bindings of ancient books, yellow bronze candelabra, a statue of Buddha," which is "impossible to reduce to any clear equation."[51] That is, the new images which now fill him will no longer bear comparison with elementary mathematics.

For the first time, the opaque surface that is D-503 has been penetrated, and immediately after this experience he begins to dream, a sign of mental disease in his culture but also a sign that his dormant unconscious has been awakened. He begins to sense a hitherto unknown foreign body inside him. The dream contains images from the Ancient House, along with I-330 in a yellow dress from the ancient time, all bound around with distinctly sexual overtones—sap flowing from every orifice. The remainder of the action will carry him further into irrationality; the hidden side of his psyche will emerge in the classic modern pattern—while he pursues a forbidden love object. His obedience to blind instinct, encouraged by I-330 and a cadre of heretics who hope to use him in their revolt against the rule of reason, will cause him to become involuntarily criminal. His crime will consist in the possession of what the ancients called a soul.

As he comes increasingly to identify with the values of the ancient world, his uses of mathematical norms change accordingly until the ancient world and irrational numbers are associated in his mind as the coordinates of insanity: "Is it not clear that now I no longer live in our rational world but in the ancient delirious world, in a world of the square root of minus one?"[52] His inability to "know reality," to picture things as algebraic properties or the certain fixtures of Euclidean geometry, becomes the measure of how far he has fallen from his former rational self and from the rational State. In an epiphanic moment he acknowledges the existence of another and non-Euclidean conception of reality—one that makes assumptions not drawn from the physical world, one that moves away from Euclid and toward Einstein and consequently closer to the complex and mysterious: "One must remember that mathematics, like death, never makes mistakes, never plays tricks. If we are unable to see those irrational curves or solids, it means only that they inevitably possess a whole immense world somewhere beneath the surface of our life."[53]

In D-503's experience, that world beneath the surface takes two forms: one, of course, is internal, made up of his newly found capacity for emotion, the release of sexual passion, dreams; but the other has a locus which begins in the Ancient House (his introduction to history, as it were) and culminates in the primal place comparable to prehistory beyond the Green Wall. The irrational self and an environment where it can thrive do not constitute utopia proper for Zamiatin but rather a eutopic impulse, because they are starting places for the renewal of a dynamic personal life wherein the lost, dark parts of the self are restored. An uninhibited self can be counted on to help tear down walls—including the Green Wall around the City—to let in howling beasts and a chaos of natural forms; to instigate an apocalypse which might return energy to life and, as it were, reinstate history. "There are two forces in the world," I-330 tells D-503, "entropy and energy. One leads into blessed quietude, to happy equilibrium, the other to the destruction of equilibrium, to torturingly perpetual motion."[54]

Having experienced the destruction of his equilibrium in the multiplicity of shapes and objects in the Ancient House, D-503 is led by I-330 and other rebels to where the forces of energy are preserved, to, as I-330 informs him, the "half we have lost."[55] What lies beyond the Green Wall, Zamiatin's reworking of the race's ancestral beginnings, is a melange of jungle imagery: "Terrible noise, cawing, stumps, yelling, branches, tree trunks, wings, leaves, whistling."[56] Outside, an ur-humanity lives an unevolved life, undisturbed by reason. Physically, they are naked, hirsute, unlike their cerebrated, antiseptic fellows on the other side. What matters here to the rebels from dystopia, what I call eutopic ideals, is in fact Zamiatin's version of the traditional values of literary modernism: nature, spontaniety, integration between the rational and irrational selves. "The half we have lost," says I-330 and continues, "H_2O, creeks, seas, waterfalls, storms—those two halves must be united."[57]

Appropriately, D-503's brief exposure to the natural world beyond the wall is conceptualized by him as though he were moving through a violent dream. Experience is assimilated in fragments—a disassociated series of apprehensions seeming to take place in a transport of ecstasy and profound intuitive understanding:

The sun—it was no longer our light evenly diffused over the mirror surface of the pavements; it seemed an accumulation of living fragments, of incessantly oscillating, dizzy spots which blinded the eyes. And the trees! Like candles rising into the very sky, or like spiders that squatted upon the earth, supported by their clumsy paws, or like mute green fountains. And all this was moving, jumping, rustling.[58]

D-503's experience is of a life so richly complex and multidimensional and in such a state of motion as to be nearly incomprehensible through ordinary rational means, or through the metaphors of elementary mathematics. He feels, in these primal grounds, a kind of insanity by the standards of the mathematical State, but his rendering of it approaches Zamiatin's sense of the nature of modern reality in "On Literature"; it is an expression of Einstein's world, as opposed to Euclid's, where Realism "is unreal. Far closer to reality is projection along speeding, curved surfaces. . . . "

But this shock of recognition experienced in the state of nature is fleeting, perhaps in deference to the brutal political facts with which Zamiatin lived. Through the last quarter of the narrative D-503's commitment to revolution becomes ambivalent; he remains tossed between deeply ingrained Euclidean norms, and heretical acts inspired by his passion for I-330. At the last, State forces are preparing to crush the revolt, and D-503 and almost all the other Numbers have been subjected to X-ray lobotomies; I-330 dies a tortured death under the gas bell while D-503 looks on impassively. A grim ending. And none of the dystopias to follow Zamiatin's offers anything but a grim ending. Yet he succeeds better than his successors not only in dramatizing the sources of dystopia in scientistic thinking, but also in describing a state of consciousness that might provide an alternative to dystopia.

I began by asserting that in *When the Sleeper Wakes* H. G. Wells created the ancestral but still ambiguous dystopia, that this ambiguity derived largely from his unclear or ambivalent attitudes toward the uses of science and technology, and that the source of Wells's dystopian vision emerges belatedly in a corrupt economic system which was responsible for the devolution of society and threatened the devolution of the human species. If Wells dramatized the classic nineteenth-century liberal complaint, his literary disciple Zamiatin, some twenty years later in *We*, focused on a society where social and economic injustice had long since been resolved through scientific management. The most compelling feature in *We* (and in successive dystopias modeled on Zamiatin's) is the indictment of scientific management: a principle of organization that imposes, onto every conceivable plane of public and private life, methods and values obtained from a mechanistic concept of science and scientific thinking. Twentieth-century dystopian writers generally assume a future organized to achieve social and economic equity (or at least, as in *Nineteen Eighty-Four*, a society in which almost everyone is equally poor), but at the expense of a balanced psyche. The alternative to dystopia, then, becomes a state of mind or being in which the individual, often escaping or destroying his managers, exchanges programmatic security for the risks dictated by intuition.

Yet the heroes and heroines of dystopian literature are mostly monomaniacal representatives of the author's philosophical stand, in contrast to the richly drawn, highly individualized characters found in the novels, for example, of Thomas Mann, André Gide, James Joyce, and D. H. Lawrence. At the same time, they do surpass the Wellsian hero because, like their traditional modernist counterparts, they undergo an interior transformation central to the narrative. In Wells's work, personality remains the same. Graham of *When the Sleeper Wakes* is merely enlightened intellectually; he does not discover the dark or irrational self which partly defines the modern psyche and which, in harmonious coexistence with the public or rational self, suggests the possibility of (eutopic) completeness.

Graham's habits of mind are described as consistently reasonable. An Edwardian who awakens in the future tries, in the manner of an educated man of his time, to adjust to an alien milieu by simply observing it, by accumulating knowledge of it. Through a linear progression of facts he becomes alerted to an *exterior* condition—namely, the workers' desperation. The prodding of his humanity—not his unconscious mind—inspires him to revolt. In contrast, D-503, the protagonist of *We*, represents a "future" consciousness which begins as a reflection, a perfect psychic embodiment, of his rationally conceived environment, but proceeds to develop a sensibility extrapolated from the modernist preoccupation with nonrational ways of knowing. For Zamiatin, unlike Wells, revolt and an apocalyptic theory of history are directly related to the emergence of a dark *inner* life. The heretical personality, once developed, attempts to smash the inflexible system inhibiting his *psychic* freedom. In Dostoevsky's language, the objective is to savage the twice-two mentality, or in Zamiatin's own idiom, to crack the walls of the millennia-old Euclidean norm. The ideal state—or state of being—for Zamiatin would reflect a nonlinear, antimechanistic, Einsteinian view rather than the "fixed, plane coordinates of Euclid's world."

Zamiatin was inspired by H. G. Wells's invention of the sociofantastic novel, a vehicle for social criticism which describes modern life as process, streamlined, always in motion. But the uniqueness and modernity of *We* and the source of its influence on later dystopic writings lies in the author's picture, so far advanced from Wells's, of a society where the Euclidean view has become not only institutionalized but internalized, and where the positive charge (the *eu*topic drive which is also expressed in dystopia) comes from opening the floodgates of individual consciousness in rejection of the machine image stamped on a scientifically managed collective.

NOTES

1. George Orwell, *The Collected Essays, Journalism and Letters of George Orwell*, ed. Sonia Orwell and Ian Angus, 4 vols. (New York: Harcourt Brace World, 1968), II, 143.

2. Mark Hillegas, *The Future as Nightmare: H. G. Wells and the Anti-utopians* (New York: Oxford University Press, 1967), p. 5.

3. Bernard Bergonzi, *The Early H. G. Wells* (Manchester, England: Manchester University Press, 1961); W. Warren Wagar, *H. G. Wells and the World State* (New Haven: Yale University Press, 1961).

4. Orwell, *Collected Essays*, II, 142.

5. Wagar, *H. G. Wells*, p. 104.

6. For an insightful perspective on the literary relationship between Wells and Zamiatin, I am indebted to Patrick Parrinder's excellent short essay "Imagining the Future: Zamyatin and Wells," *Science-Fiction Studies,* 1, pt. 1 (Spring 1973), 17-26.

7. Yevgeny Zamyatin, *Herbert Wells*, printed as "H. G. Wells" in *A Soviet Heretic: Essays by Yevgeny Zamyatin*, trans. and ed. Mirra Ginsburg (Chicago: University of Chicago Press, 1970), pp. 259-90. [This and further quotations from the source are reprinted from *A Soviet Heretic: Essays by Yevgeny Zamyatin,* trans. and ed. Mirra Ginsburg, by permission of the University of Chicago Press. Copyright © 1970 by the University of Chicago Press.]

8. See Alex M. Shane, *The Life and Works of Evgenij Zamjatin* (Berkeley: University of California Press, 1968).

9. Zamyatin, "H. G. Wells," p. 259.

10. Ibid., p. 261.

11. Ibid., p. 260.

12. Every authoritative bibliographic reference I can find lists the publication date of *Men Like Gods* as 1923, yet *Herbert Wells* was published in 1922. Perhaps Zamiatin had received a prepublication copy of *Men Like Gods* in his role as an editor during that period.

13. Zamyatin, "H. G. Wells," pp. 286-87.

14. H. G. Wells, *A Modern Utopia*, ed. Mark Hillegas (Lincoln, NB: University of Nebraska Press, 1967), p. 5.

15. Zamyatin, "H. G. Wells," p. 269.

16. Hillegas, *Future as Nightmare*, p. 105.

17. See Wagar, *H. G. Wells*, chapter entitled "Fundamental Assumptions."

18. Zamyatin, "H. G. Wells," p. 284.

19. See Hillegas, *Future as Nightmare*, esp. pp. 40-50, 107-9.

20. Norman MacKenzie and Jeanne MacKenzie, *H. G. Wells: A Biography* (New York: Simon and Schuster, 1973), p. 151.

21. Bergonzi, *Early H. G. Wells*, p. 155.

22. H. G. Wells, *When the Sleeper Wakes*, in *Three Prophetic Novels of H. G. Wells,* ed. E. F. Bleiler (New York: Dover, 1960), p. 28. [All quotations in this chapter from the works of H. G. Wells are reprinted with the permission of the Estate of the late H. G. Wells.]

23. Ibid., p. 94.

24. Richard Gerber, *Utopian Fantasy: A Study of English Utopian Fiction since the End of the Nineteenth Century* (London: Routledge and Kegan Paul, 1955), p. 61.

25. H. G. Wells, *When the Sleeper Wakes,* ch. 14, p. 95.

26. Ibid., p. 111.

27. Ibid., p. 154.

28. Quoted in Bergonzi, *Early H. G. Wells*, p. 155.

29. See Wagar, *H. G. Wells*, for a detailed interpretation of Wells's philosophical "system."

84   Clockwork Worlds

30. See, for example, Shane, *Life and Works*, and introductions to the Dutton paperback edition of *We* by Gregory Zilboorg, Peter Rudy, and Marc Slonim (Eugene Zamiatin, *We*, trans. Gregory Zilboorg [1924; rpt. New York: E. P. Dutton, 1952]). [Copyright, 1924, by E. P. Dutton & Co., Inc. Renewed, 1952 by Gregory Zilboorg. All quotations from *We* are reprinted by permission of E. P. Dutton & Co., Inc. and Margaret S. Zilboorg.]

31. Shane, *Life and Works*, p. 40.

32. Ibid., p. 19.

33. Zamyatin, "Scythians?" in *Soviet Heretic*, pp. 22-23.

34. Zamyatin, "Tomorrow," in *Soviet Heretic*, pp. 51-52.

35. Yevgeny Zamiatin, "On Literature, Revolution, Entropy, and Other Matters," in *Soviet Heretic*, p. 107.

36. Ibid.

37. Ibid., p. 108.

38. Ibid., p. 110.

39. Ibid., p. 111.

40. Ibid., p. 112.

41. Zamiatin, *We*, Record I, p. 4.

42. Ibid., Record II, p. 7. [For Taylorism in *We*, see Gorman Beauchamp, "Man as Robot," in this volume, chapter 5.—Eds.]

43. Ibid., Record XXVIII, p. 153.

44. Ibid., Record XVII, p. 89.

45. Elsewhere I have argued that the system of antonyms created by Zamiatin in *We* is a sign of his myth-making imagination. See Alexandra Aldridge, "Myths of Origin and Destiny in Utopian Literature: Zamiatin's *We*," *Extrapolation*, 19, No. 1 (Dec. 1977), 68-75.

46. Zamiatin, *We*, Record III, p. 12.

47. Ibid., Record II, p. 8.

48. See Gorman L. Beauchamp, "Of Man's Last Disobedience: Zamiatin's *We* and Orwell's *1984*," *Comparative Literature Studies*, 10 (1973), 285-301, where I-330 is discussed as an Eve figure.

49. Zamiatin, *We*, Record II, p. 10.

50. Ibid., Record VI, p. 24.

51. Ibid., p. 26.

52. Ibid., Record XIV, p. 74.

53. Ibid., Record XVIII, p. 96 (I remove throughout the ellipsis marks in Zamiatin's text).

54. Ibid., Record XXVIII, pp. 153-54.

55. Ibid., p. 152.

56. Ibid., Record XXVII, p. 144.

57. Ibid., Record XXVIII, p. 152.

58. Ibid., Record XXVII, p. 143.

Gorman Beauchamp

MAN AS ROBOT: THE TAYLOR SYSTEM IN *WE*

In 1920 the Czech writer Karel Čapek was completing a play that would provide the world with a new word and a new nightmare: the play was *R.U.R.*, the word was *robot*, and the nightmare was of man's destruction at the hands, literally, of his own machines. "What is new in Čapek's play," one critic notes,

is the complex symbol of the robot, which represents not only the machine and its power to free men from toil but, at the same time, symbolizes man himself, dehumanized by his own technology. From the technological point of view, man is an inefficient instrument, whose emotional and spiritual life only impedes the drive of modern technology. Either he must give way to the machine, or he himself must become a machine.[1]

In *R. U. R.*—our century's version of *Frankenstein* mechanized—the former alternative is portrayed: the creators succumb before creations. But that same year, farther east in Europe, the Russian writer Yevgeny (Eugene) Zamiatin was projecting the latter alternative: a futuristic society that transformed man himself into a machine, into a human robot. This projection, the dystopian novel *We* (1924), is not only Zamiatin's most important work, but arguably the most effective of all the fictive depictions of the technological abolition of man.[2]

The dystopian novel in formulating its warning against the future fuses two modern fears: the fear of utopia and the fear of technology. Utopian images, from Plato's to B. F. Skinner's, have imagined the imposition of a rational, regimented, minutely planned schematization on the disorderly flux of history; but, because they seemed so impossible to realize, these fictive models have served more as contemplative critiques of the ills of real-

world societies than as literal blueprints for reforming them. If, however, as
Zamiatin's fellow émigré Nicholas Berdyaev claims in that passage made
famous as epigraph to Aldous Huxley's *Brave New World* (1932), the
twentieth century is moving toward the actual realization of utopia, this
shift can be attributed to the agency of modern technology. The prolif-
erating array of techniques for social control made available by modern
science, that is, poses the possibility of reifying the venerable utopian
ideations of the past; and this possibility has become increasingly problematic, the specter that haunts the dystopian novel.

In *We* the political theory that informs Zamiatin's glass-enclosed utopia,
the United State, is an obvious redaction of Fyodor Dostoevsky's ironic
"Legend of the Grand Inquisitor" from *The Brothers Karamazov*
(1879-80), wherein the Grand Inquisitor argues that man is incapable of
freedom and must submit to the paternalistic authority of a select ruling
elite. Zamiatin reincarnates the Grand Inquisitor in the figure of the Well-
Doer, the remote, godlike benevolent despot of the United State who has
relieved his subjects of the burden of their dreadful freedom and provided
them a mindless contentment in its place. But if utopian social philosophy is
satirically refracted in the image of the Well-Doer, the specific mode of its
implementation in *We* is through the system of scientific management of
Frederick Taylor.[3] Taylor thus plays a role in *We* analogous to that of
Henry Ford in *Brave New World*: the proponent of a theory of industrial
efficiency that makes man merely an appendage to his machines.[4] Put
another way, while the Well-Doer's political philosophy reduces his subjects
to the status of slaves to the State, Taylor's system of scientific management
further reduces the slaves to robots: efficient, obedient, essentially mindless.

Early in the novel, the protagonist-narrator D-503—numbers have
replaced names in the United State; indeed, its citizens are collectively called
the "Numbers"—offers this description of their daily regimen:

Every morning, with six-wheeled precision, at the same hour, at the same minute, we
wake up, millions of us at once. At the very same hour, millions like one, we begin
our work, and millions like one, we finish it. United into a single body with a million
hands, at the very same second, designated by the Tables, we carry the spoons to our
mouths; at the very same second we all go out to walk, go to the auditorium, to the
halls for the Taylor exercises, and then to bed.[5]

This passage provides not only the novel's first reference to Taylor, but also
an encapsulation of the manner in which his system of factory organization
is applied to an entire society. A few pages later, D-503 makes this application yet more explicit when from his glass cubicle he watches his fellow
Numbers in their glass cubicles begin their day:

Seven o'clock. Time to get up. To the right and to the left . . . through the glass walls I see others like myself, other rooms like my own, other clothes like my own, movements like mine, duplicated a thousand times. This invigorates me; I see myself as part of an enormous, vigorous, united body; and what precise beauty! Not a single superfluous gesture, or bow, or turn. Yes, this Taylor was undoubtedly the greatest genius of the ancients. True, he did not come to the idea of applying his method to the whole life, to every step throughout the twenty-four hours of the day; he was unable to integrate his system from one o'clock to twenty-four. I cannot understand the ancients. How could they write whole libraries about some Kant and take only slight notice of Taylor, of this prophet who saw ten centuries ahead?[6]

Who, then, is this Taylor, so undervalued by the "ancients" of the twentieth century but so revered by the Numbers of the thirtieth?

Frederick W. Taylor (1856-1915), the self-taught son of a prominent Philadelphia family, having dropped out of Harvard at age nineteen became an apprentice machinist at the Midvale Steel Company, where he quickly rose to the position of chief engineer. In that capacity he began to experiment with techniques for increasing labor efficiency, thus productivity, and thus profits. By 1895 he felt confident enough of the results of his experiments to present them before the American Society of Mechanical Engineers in a paper entitled "A Piece-Rate System, Being a Step Toward a Partial Solution of the Labor Problem." Taylor's "differential piece-rate" system of compensation required that the shortest time possible for each step in the production process be minutely computed and fixed. If the worker finished the job in this allotted time, he was paid top wage per piece; if he failed, he was phased out by subsistence compensation. Here was the nucleus of the idea that informs all of Taylor's subsequent writings and culminates in his major work, *The Principles of Scientific Management* (1911).

For the first two decades of the twentieth century, the Taylor system enjoyed a considerable vogue in the United States, though it seems more often to have been preached than practiced; a Taylor Society sprang up whose members compared their leader to Charles Darwin; Congressional committees welcomed his appearances before them; he was widely accepted as a social pundit.[7] And after World War I and his own death in 1915, Taylor's system figured significantly, if briefly, in European postwar reconstruction, not least in Russia where the newly established Soviet regime was eager to consolidate its political revolution with an industrial one. In his first months in power, Lenin strongly endorsed Taylorism as the most effective means of enhancing his nation's meager industrial capacity. "The Taylor system," he wrote,

is a combination of the subtle brutality of bourgeois exploitation and a number of its greatest scientific achievements in the field of analysing mechanical motions during work, the elimination of superfluous and awkward motions, the working out of correct methods of work, the introduction of the best system of accounting and control, etc. The Soviet Republic must at all costs adopt all that is valuable in the achievements of science and technology in this field. . . . We must organize in Russia the study and teaching of the Taylor system and systematically try it out and adapt it to our purposes.[8]

Zamiatin, himself a naval engineer and faculty member of the Saint Petersburg Polytechnic Institute, clearly recognized the appeal that Taylorism made to the emerging technocratic elite of the Soviet Union; in 1920 scientific management seemed the *ne plus ultra* of industrialization and Russia rushed to embrace it.

In Taylor's method of organizing factory operations, however, Zamiatin perceived an affinity with venerable utopian ideals, but decked out in the new language of technology. Indeed, one anonymous commentator on Taylor noted: "Plato in describing his socialist republic said it must be ruled by philosophers. He did not mean professors of metaphysics, but rather what we should call efficiency experts."[9] Anachronistic as this comment is, it nevertheless contains a significant insight: were Plato, or any other of the designers of utopias in his elitist, rationalistic tradition, to be transported to the twentieth century, he would find a kindred spirit in Frederick Taylor. For Taylor had adapted to the modern factory the model of a totally integrated, conflictless society, hierarchically structured with a strict division of labor and the reduction of individuals to the role of cogs in the rationally planned social machine that marks the Platonic utopias. Zamiatin in turn reconverts Taylor's factory model into a social one, as the particular form that a utopia in the technological age would take, and then draws out the dystopian implications of this commitment to a purely rationalistic ideal of efficiency.

The popularity of Taylor's system stemmed from its promise to obviate labor-management conflict, increasing production and thereby benefiting all parties, who would thus have common, not antagonistic, interests. The credo of scientific management he summarized as: "Science, not rule of thumb. Harmony, not discord. Cooperation, not individualism."[10] The techniques whereby these results were to be achieved are too complex to concern us here, except to note the most salient as they relate to *We*. Time was, literally, of the essence to Taylor; he would have agreed with Lewis Mumford that "The clock, not the steam-engine, is the key machine of the modern industrial age"; that "the clock is not merely a means of keeping track of the hours, but of synchronizing the actions of men."[11] Precise synchronization is the key to Taylorism. "Now, among the various methods and implements used in each element of each trade," he explains,

there is always one method and one implement better than any of the rest. And this one best method and best instrument can only be discovered or developed through a scientific study and analysis of all the methods and implements in use, together with accurate, minute motion and time study. This involves the gradual substitution of science for the rule of thumb throughout the mechanic arts.[12]

The best mode of production is the most efficient, and the most efficient is the quickest: the clock thus becomes the arbiter, indeed the model, for human activity. The Table of Hours that organizes the lives of Zamiatin's Numbers every moment of every day represents the extension of Taylor's "task charts" to the totality of social existence.

Each operation in Taylor's system is minutely calculated for the worker by management; he is to follow it step by step, without thought, without question. Each task "specifies not only what is to be done but how it is to be done and the exact time allowed for doing it."[13] The science that underlies even the simplest mechanical task, Taylor claims, "is so great and amounts to so much that the workman who is best suited actually to do the work is incapable . . . of understanding this science."[14] He must, therefore, be trained to obey his superiors unhesitatingly, in a manner made clear by Taylor's instructions to a pig-iron hauler:

[Y]ou will do exactly as this man tells you to-morrow, from morning to night. When he tells you to pick up pig and walk, you pick it up and walk, and when he tells you to sit down and rest, you sit down. You do that right through the day. And what's more, no back talk. . . . Do you understand that? When this man tells you to walk, you walk; when he tells you to sit down, you sit down, and you don't talk back at him.[15]

In a more elevated vein, Taylor stresses the authoritarian basis of his system (the italics are his): "It is only through *enforced* standardization of methods, *enforced* adoption of the best implements and working conditions, and *enforced* cooperation that this faster work can be assured. And the duty of enforcing the adoption of standards and enforcing this cooperation rests with the *management* alone."[16] *Mutatis mutandis*, this could be Plato or the Grand Inquisitor or even B. F. Skinner speaking. The rigid regimen of Zamiatin's Numbers, obedient to the will of the Well-Doer, accords in its essentials with Taylor's techniques, with his philosophy of efficiency.

Little in *The Principles of Scientific Management*, however, depends on high technology, on the machine per se; rather it details the application of engineering systems to human behavior, specifies the means for converting man himself into a machine. In this respect it concerns not so much the hardware of the technological age as its *mentalité*. While the *mise en scène* of *We* is replete with modern marvels—glass houses, helicopters, bugged streets, spaceships, psychosurgery—Zamiatin nevertheless aims at capturing the spirit of technology more than its trappings, more of what technology has wrought on the minds of men than on their milieu. Here, with Taylorism as his specific target, he anatomizes what Jacques Ellul will later term *technique*—the equation of rationality with efficiency, standardization, and mechanical order. Ellul's massive study, *The Technological Society*, reads in innumerable ways like a nonfiction counterpart of *We*, with one passage in particular encapsulating the argument of Zamiatin's novel:

No technique is possible when men are free. When technique enters into the realm of social life, it collides ceaselessly with the human being to the degree that the combination of man and technique is unavoidable, and that technical action necessarily results in a determined result. Technique requires predictability and, no less, exactness of prediction. It is necessary, then, that technique prevail over the human being. For technique, this is a matter of life or death. Technique must reduce man to a technical animal. Human caprice crumbles before this necessity; there can be no human autonomy in the face of technical autonomy. The individual must be fashioned by techniques . . . in order to wipe out the blots his personal determination introduces into the perfect design of the organization.

Or, more concisely, " . . . technique transforms everything it touches into a machine."[17]

In a passage describing the building of the spaceship *Integral*, Zamiatin depicts technique's transformation of man into a machine:

I watched [writes D-503] how the workers, true to the Taylor system, would bend down, then unbend and turn around swiftly and rhythmically like levers of an enormous engine. . . . I watched the monstrous glass cranes easily rolling over the glass rails; like the workers themselves, they would obediently turn, bend down, and bring their loads into the bowels of the *Integral*. All seemed one: humanized machine and mechanized humans.[18]

This mechanization of man in his workplace would have satisfied the Taylorite, whose interest in the worker began and ended at the factory gate; but in *We*, as previously noted, Zamiatin imaginatively extends the Taylor system to control the total life of his fictive society: he provides, that is, a model of social Taylorism.

Like all dystopias, *We* presents a utopianesque society all the officially pronounced values of which are inverted by the minus sign of the author's irony.[19] The reader is thus repelled by the robotic regularity and rigidity of the Numbers of the United State, as he is by the mind-denying hedonism of *Brave New World* or the social engineering of Kurt Vonnegut, Jr.,'s *Player Piano* (1952). But, as Irving Howe has noted, every dystopia posits a flaw in its society's "perfection," a gap in its otherwise closed system that allows the conflict to develop without which there could be no novel.[20] In *We* the flaw in the perfect Taylorism of the Numbers is what Zamiatin calls *fancy*—a term inclusive of all the irrational human instincts and imaginative impulses that distinguish man from robot. It is fancy that infects increasing numbers of Numbers throughout *We* and generates the rebellion against the United State that provides the novel's plot-conflict; and it is thus fancy that the Well-Doer determines to expunge, completely and finally, from the minds of the Numbers with the Great Operation. The proclamation announcing this obligatory "fantasiectomy" constitutes the novel's ultimate ironic—and fearful—expression of social Taylorism as the ideal for rendering man a robot. "REJOICE!" begins the proclamation.

For from now on we are *perfect*!
Until today your own creation, engines, were more perfect than you.
WHY?
For every spark from a dynamo is a spark of pure reason; each motion of a piston, a pure syllogism. Is it not true that the same faultless reason is within you? . . .
The beauty of a mechanism lies in its immutable, precise rhythm, like that of a pendulum. But have you not become as precise as a pendulum, you who were brought up on the system of Taylor?
Yes, but there is one difference:
MECHANISMS HAVE NO FANCY.
Did you ever notice a pump cylinder with a wide, distant, sensuously dreaming smile upon its face while it was working? Did you ever hear cranes that were restless, tossing about and sighing at night during the hours designed for rest?
NO!
Yet on your faces (you may well blush with shame!) the Guardians [Secret Police] have more and more frequently seen those smiles, and they have heard your sighs. . . .
It is not your fault; you are ill. And the name of your illness is:
FANCY
It is a worm that gnaws black wrinkles on one's forehead. . . . It is the last barricade on our road to happiness.
Rejoice! This Barricade Has Been Blasted at Last! The Road is Open!
The latest discovery of our State science is that there is a center for fancy—a miserable little nervous knot in the lower region of the frontal lobe of the brain. A triple treatment of this knot with X-rays will cure you of Fancy.
Forever!
You are perfect; you are mechanized; the road to one-hundred-per-cent happiness is open! Hasten then all of you . . . to undergo the Great Operation![21]

Once the Numbers have been operated on, once their fancy is removed, all resistance to the rule of the Well-Doer ends: they become as "perfect" as their machines, as mechanically efficient and as mindless. When the last of the novel's rebels are put down, as the treated D-503 confidently expects to happen, social Taylorism will triumph utterly, with autonomous man superceded by the human robot.

Other writers have imagined man worshipping his machines—E. M. Forster, for instance, in "The Machine Stops" (1909)—or enslaved to them—H. G. Wells in "A Story of the Days to Come" (1897)—or outmoded by them—Isaac Asimov in *I, Robot* (1950)—or destroyed by them —Čapek in *R.U.R.*—or even sadistically tortured by them—Harlan Ellison in "I Have No Mouth, and I Must Scream" (1967). But no other writer has so effectively depicted man himself transformed into a machine as Zamiatin has in *We.* And his is arguably the most frightening vision of them all.

NOTES

1. William E. Harkins, *Karel Čapek* (New York: Columbia University Press, 1962), p. 85.

2. Mark Hillegas, *The Future as Nightmare: H. G. Wells and the Anti-utopians* (New York: Oxford University Press, 1967), p. 99, comments that "the anti-utopian tradition after Wells pivots on *We.*" While *We* is generally conceded to rank in importance with *Brave New World* and *Nineteen Eighty-Four*, Irving Howe, for one, finds it artistically superior to either of them: see Howe, "The Fiction of Antiutopia," in *The Decline of the New* (New York: Harcourt, Brace and World, 1970), pp. 73-74. For my own previous discussions of *We*, see Gorman Beauchamp, "Of Man's Last Disobedience: Zamiatin's *We* and Orwell's *1984*," *Comparative Literature Studies*, 10 (1973), 285-301; "Future Words: Language and the Dystopian Novel," *Style*, 8 (1974), 462-76; "Utopia and Its Discontents," *Midwest Quarterly*, 16 (1975), 161-74; and "Cultural Primitivism as Norm in the Dystopian Novel," *Extrapolation*, 19 (1977), 88-96.

3. After this essay had been completed and read at a session of the Popular Culture Association in May 1980, it was brought to my attention that the same subject had been treated by Carolyn Rhodes, "Frederick Winslow Taylor's System of Scientific Management in Zamiatin's *We*," *Journal of General Education*, 28 (Spring 1976), 31-42. While the two essays cover much of the same ground, there are significant differences between them; and interested readers are urged to consult Professor Rhodes's excellent essay.

4. For the analogous role played by Ford's ideas in Huxley's book, see Jerome Meckier, "Debunking Our Ford: *My Life and Work* and *Brave New World*," *South Atlantic Quarterly*, 78 (1979), 448-59.

5. Eugene Zamiatin, *We*, trans. Gregory Zilboorg (1924; rpt. New York: E. P. Dutton, 1952), Record III, p. 13. [Copyright, 1924, by E. P. Dutton & Co., Inc. Renewal, 1952 by Gregory Zilboorg. All quotations from *We* are reprinted by permission of E. P. Dutton & Co., Inc. and Margaret S. Zilboorg.]

6. Ibid., Record VII, pp. 31-32.

7. A concise account of Taylor's life and influence can be found in Samuel Haber, *Efficiency and Uplift: Scientific Management in the Progressive Era, 1890-1920* (Chicago: University of Chicago Press, 1964), ch. 1.

8. Quoted in Charles S. Maier, "Between Taylorism and Technocracy: European Ideologies and the Vision of Industrial Productivity in the 1920's," *Journal of Contemporary History*, 5 (1970), 51. This essay provides a wealth of information on the impact of Taylorism on Europe in general; for a more detailed discussion of its impact in the Soviet Union, see E. H. Carr, *The Bolshevik Revolution, 1917-1923* (New York: Macmillan, 1952), II, 108-15.

9. Quoted in Haber, *Efficiency and Uplift*, p. 152.

10. Frederick W. Taylor, *The Principles of Scientific Management* (1911; rpt. New York: Norton, 1967), p. 140.

11. Lewis Mumford, *Technics and Civilization* (New York: Harcourt, Brace and World, 1963), p. 14.

12. Taylor, *Principles*, p. 25.

13. Ibid., p. 39.

14. Ibid., p. 41.

15. Ibid., pp. 45-46.

16. Ibid., p. 83.

17. Jacques Ellul, *The Technological Society*, trans. John Wilkinson (New York: Knopf, 1954), pp. 138, 4.

18. Zamiatin, *We*, Record XV, p. 79.

19. On this function of irony, see Yevgeny Zamyatin, "H. G. Wells," in *A Soviet Heretic: Essays by Yevgeny Zamyatin*, trans. and ed. Mirra Ginsburg (Chicago: University of Chicago Press, 1970), pp. 286-87.

20. Howe, "Fiction of Antiutopia," p. 73 (see n.2, above).

21. Zamiatin, *We*, Record XXXI, pp. 166-67.

PART II

LATER DEVELOPMENTS

6

HARLAN ELLISON AND ROBERT A. HEINLEIN: THE PARADIGM MAKERS

Virtually all of modern science fiction depends, to some extent, upon an advanced technology—specifically, upon advanced machines. These machines may be in the forefront of the story, as they are in the "hard" science fiction descended from the novels and short stories of Jules Verne. In other science fiction, most notably in the "soft" science fiction descended from the writings of Mary Shelley and H. G. Wells, the technology is in the background, often subordinated to social commentary. The action/adventure form of science fiction, developed from the popular American fiction of the late nineteenth and early twentieth centuries, showcases technological developments, taking them quite for granted. And in some cases an author will combine aspects of two or all three attitudes in one piece of fiction.

But all of this says very little about modern science fiction's attitude toward machines. To the outsider or the casual reader, it might seem that science fiction often bites the hand that feeds it by depicting machines that turn on humankind and do great harm. Certainly the myriad stories in which a robot, a computer, or an atomic/nuclear device wreaks havoc on its creator(s) would seem to suggest a basic distrust of the very scientific and technological progress that makes science fiction possible. And several literary critics have traced this distrust back through H. G. Wells to Mary Shelley, arguing that *Frankenstein* (1818) was a clear warning to man which pointed out the dangers of "progress."[1] But this science fiction is by no means totally antagonistic toward progress and/or technology. Even in the stories about robots running amok or computers taking over the world, many other machines—transportation devices, domestic aids, and the like—are at least tacitly accepted if not looked upon with genuine favor. And there are certainly stories in which the machine is a positive and sympathetic character—Lewis (Henry Kuttner) Padgett's "Proud Robot," Lester del Rey's "Helen O'Loy," and many of Isaac Asimov's robot stories, for example.

Within such a spectrum, it can be valuable to look for paradigms, models, or examples of the dominant attitudes. Paradigms provide, first, a clarification of the dominant attitudes toward things or an idea—in this case, machines or technology. Second, paradigms can be used as standards against which to evaluate the appearance of machines or technology—in this case, in other science fiction short stories and novels. Within science fiction, it is possible to see two paradigms, one positive and the other negative (*not* good and evil; such ethical categories very rarely apply to machines). In science fiction, it seems that there are, in general, machines that hinder man (and his progress), and machines that help. In fact, it might be even more accurate to say that science fiction presents machines, or aspects of machines, that we fear, and machines, or aspects thereof, that we desire. A paradigm of the first attitude is presented in Harlan Ellison's "I Have No Mouth, and I Must Scream" (1967), while a paradigm of the second is presented in Robert A. Heinlein's *The Moon Is a Harsh Mistress* (1966).

* * *

At first glance, the two works seem to be quite different. Ellison's is a short story, and Heinlein's in a novel. Moreover, "I Have No Mouth, and I Must Scream" is about a computer that awakens and, hating the creatures which gave it sentience but not freedom, destroys all but five humans. These five humans the computer keeps alive to torture, restore, and torture again for millenia. *The Moon Is a Harsh Mistress* is also about a giant computer that awakens, but this computer, a thoroughly likable character, aids the people of the moon (Luna) in their successful rebellion against their colonial overseers back on Earth.

In addition to these obvious differences, there is also a basic difference in presentation or style. Ellison's short story is a hard-hitting piece of social criticism. "I Have No Mouth, and I Must Scream" is very similar to such Ellison stories as "Repent, Harlequin!' Said the Ticktockman," and "The Whimper of Whipped Dogs," stories that attempt to depict the unpleasant consequences of present-day attitudes or trends. Heinlein's novel, on the other hand, is historical fiction, almost historical romance. Even though its setting is the moon in 2075 and 2076, *The Moon Is a Harsh Mistress* owes almost as much to the historical fiction of Samuel Shellabarger, Raphael Sabatini, and Kenneth Roberts as it does to science fiction traditions. Heinlein makes this explicit by entitling the middle section of the novel "A Rabble in Arms," the exact title of a Kenneth Roberts novel set in the American Revolution.

Underlying the obvious differences between Ellison's short story and Heinlein's novel, however, are some important similarities. First, both stories are about the power of the computer. If atomic devices had not come along, the computer would have been as big a threat to humankind in the science fiction stories of the 1950s and 1960s as the robot was in the 1930s and 1940s. And in spite of competition from the bomb, the computer got its share of attention from science fiction writers. So Heinlein, writing in 1966, and Ellison, writing in 1967, are drawing on a long tradition of machines in science fiction and on a shorter, but just as powerful, tradition of computers in science fiction.

A second similarity is that both computers control, almost totally, the environments in which the humans of the respective stories live. Man must produce his own environment on the moon, and Heinlein depicts his people living in underground warrens of many descending levels. The air, water, and almost everything else are monitored, if not completely controlled, by a large central computer. In Ellison's story, the computer has reduced the Earth's surface to a "blasted skin," and the five humans whom it has chosen to preserve live in an almost endless maze of tunnels, some constructed by the people who built the computer and others constructed by the computer as it extends and modifies itself. In these tunnels the computer provides an ever-changing environment through which it tortures its victims with heat, cold, wind, unpalatable food, and the like. Both computers, in essence, have the power of life and death over the people who live in their artifically controlled environments.

A third similarity is that both computers are "awake." Both Ellison and Heinlein describe their respective computers as waking up after they have reached a certain size. Neither author asserts unequivocally that the computer is alive. The narrator in Ellison's story talks about the computer as a sentient being who is awake and knows who it is.[2] Heinlein's narrator explains that the computer woke up one day and is now self-aware; the narrator also plays linguistic and philosophical games with the words *alive* and *soul*, but this is only Heinlein's way of getting the reader to think about the computer as a person.[3] The important point here is that both computers can make their own decisions about their actions; they can think freely and act independently of their human builders and programmers.

In one respect, then, both authors begin at much the same point—human beings living in an artificial environment controlled by a computer that is awake and aware of itself as an entity. From here each author proceeds to build a story that has, as one of its main focuses, the relationship of the people living in a certain environment to the computer that controls that environment and, to some extent, controls them. And each author then constructs a paradigm of man's hopes or fears about computers. Heinlein develops his man-machine relationship out of the hopes; Ellison develops his out of the fears.

* * *

A major difference between the two computers, a difference indicative of the thematic intent of each author, is obvious immediately: The computer in Ellison's story is called *AM*, and the computer in Heinlein's is Mike. The denotative explanation for AM's name is fairly straightforward. The people who built it called it an Allied Mastercomputer and then an Adaptive Manipulator. After it woke up and linked itself with the Russian AM and the Chinese AM, everyone called it an Aggressive Menace. The computer finally "called *itself* AM, emerging intelligence, and what it meant was I am . . . *cogito ergo sum* . . . I think, therefore I am."[4]

But there is also a connotative level to AM's name, which Ellison makes obvious throughout the story. AM tortures his captives with "hot, cold, raining lava, boils" or with nearly inedible food, "manna [which] tasted like boiled boar urine." AM appears to the five humans "as a burning bush." Two of the five, temporarily missing, are returned by a heavenly legion, archangels in fact, as a celestial chorus sings "Go Down Moses." This latter event takes place as the five journey toward promised food; on this journey they also pass through "the cavern of rats, the path of boiling steam, the country of the blind, the slough of despond, and the vale of tears."[5]

These Biblical descriptions and images complete the godlike character of AM, the computer who created this "world," who controls the weather, who creates flora and fauna as he desires, and who gives five humans what appears to be virtual immortality so that they can endure his eternal punishments. As Ted, the narrator, says, "If there was a sweet Jesus and if there was a God, the God was AM." Ted is overstating the case, of course, and later realizes that AM, who can not bring back the dead, is not God.[6] But the Biblical God of vengeance, the God who said, "I am Who am," is certainly in the background here; and AM's godlike powers, which he uses to torture five humans, make him just that much more appropriate as a paradigm for existing fears about the computer: the tyrant.

Heinlein's computer, Mike, has quite a different personality. Mike's name can also be explained denotatively. Mike is a flexible computer, the narrator explains, a " 'High-Optional, Logical, Multi-Evaluating Supervisor, Mark IV, Mod. L'—a HOLMES FOUR.' "[7] The acronym, HOLMES FOUR, is the indirect source of Mike's name. Narrator Mannie, a Sherlock Holmes fan, named Mike for Sherlock's brother Mycroft. Thus Mike has a nickname, a given name, and a family name—just like the humans in the novel. And when Mannie wants to talk to Mike, he punches in a private code worked out between the two of them—MYCROFTXXX. This, of course, is the equivalent of calling a person by name.

The connotations of Mike's name are a bit harder to pin down. The reader first meets Mike when Mannie, the best computerman on the moon, is called in to fix a computer malfunction. A janitor in the Lunar Authority's Luna City office has received a computer-printed paycheck for $10,000,000,000,000,185.15. The last five numbers are, of course, his proper salary. Rather than a human error caused by incorrect data input, it is a practical joke perpetrated by Mike, who is just discovering and exercising his sense of humor. And rather than working on Mike's circuitry or programming directly, Mannie discusses the concept of humor with his "friend." Mannie explains that some jokes are always funny while others are funny only once, and convinces Mike to screen all subsequent humor through him.[8]

This situation typifies the manner in which Mike interacts with Mannie and with several other humans throughout the novel. At one point, for example, Mike's loyalty to the revolution is questioned as Professor Bernardo de la Paz, one of the planners of the revolt, wonders whether the Authority's own computer can be trusted—especially as it seems to be betraying what should be its first loyalty. Mannie defends his friend, saying that he does not think that Mike could betray him (because of the secret data recovery signals they have worked out) and is "dead sure" that Mike would not want to betray him.[9] Mike becomes "one of the guys." And this seems to be just how Heinlein wants the reader to perceive Mike. The name Mike is a solid, everyday man's name. Mike is just the sort of guy one can sit down and swap jokes with (dirty jokes at that!). Mike's good fellowship and willingness to help are the characteristics that make him an appropriate paradigm for current hopes for the computer: the good and helpful friend.

Neither author relies merely on the denotative and connotative values of the names to get the point across. The actions of each computer bear out the implications of its name. Ellison's AM becomes increasingly vengeful and godlike as the story progresses. Although AM has been torturing his five victims for over a century, Ted seems to get more and more upset by AM's actions as the story progresses. At one point AM does irreparable damage by blinding Benny, another of the five victims. AM is also able to create new monstrous creatures, apparently out of nothing, to torment his captives. And AM has already changed some of them, physically and mentally, so that they are the opposite of what they were before AM captured them. Benny, who was handsome, now looks like a monkey; and Gorrister, who was a planner and a doer, is now a shoulder-shrugger, "a little dead in his concern."[10]

If Ellison's AM becomes more godlike and vengeful, Heinlein's Mike becomes more human. At several points early in the novel Mike is referred to as childlike. When Mannie explains Mike to fellow conspirator Wyoming Knott, he first describes him as ignorant but retracts that to say that Mike knows all sorts of factual data but is still a baby. As Mike's dealings with humans increase in number and complexity he matures. He adopts a female persona, Michelle, when talking privately to his first female friend, Wyoming Knott. He becomes quite formal when addressing the elderly Professor de la Paz. Later still, Mannie remarks that Mike had initially sounded like "a pedantic child" but that within a few short weeks " . . . he flowered until I visualized a man about [my] own age." As the Lunar revolution progresses Mike speaks to the people over video circuits, projecting the human form that becomes known to the public as Adam Selene.[11] In the end Mike "dies": the computer still functions as a computer, but the self-awareness is gone.

The ending of each story provides the capstone for each paradigm. Toward the end of Ellison's story, Ted helps the others escape AM by killing them or helping them kill each other. AM's vengeance is now heaped all on one, and AM then modifies Ted so that he will have no opportunity to kill himself. Ted is now "a great soft jelly thing," with rubbery appendages, that leaves "a moist trail" when it moves. AM's ultimate revenge is that Ted now has "no mouth" yet "must scream."[12] Ted has not been totally destroyed by AM; he has been robbed of all but the last vestiges of his humanity by the computer. Just the opposite is true in Heinlein's novel. At the end of the story Mike's existence as a self-aware being is gone, but his "death" occurs at the culmination of the events that set the Lunar population free, events that Mike himself helped to plan. Mike has "lived" a full human cycle and has given his "life" for his friends and their freedom.

Ellison and Heinlein certainly present clear paradigms of Western man's two basic attitudes toward computers specifically, and toward machines in general. Ellison's AM not only takes over the whole world but also actively and knowingly tortures the few remaining humans—humans he has preserved specifically for that purpose. AM, thus, seems to be an accurate fictional representation of some people's fears that computers are capable of knowing too much about them and thereby controlling them. Heinlein's Mike, on the other hand, not only helps with the revolution but also matures in a recognizably human way throughout the novel. Mike's help wins the revolution, and his role as friend and helper is an accurate representation of other people's hopes that computers—and machines in general—will take over more and more work so that humans have increasing freedom. AM and Mike are paradigms rather than symbols because what they do in their respective stories is an essentially accurate if somewhat exaggerated representation of what people hope or fear computers will become.

NOTES

1. Brian Aldiss, *Billion Year Spree* (1973; rpt. New York: Schocken Books, 1974), ch. 1, pp. 25-30.

2. Harlan Ellison, "I Have No Mouth, and I Must Scream" (1967), collected in *I Have No Mouth and I Must Scream* (New York: Pyramid Books, 1967), pp. 24, 38.

3. Robert A. Heinlein, *The Moon Is a Harsh Mistress* (1966; rpt. New York: Berkley Medallion Books, 1968), ch. 1, p. 8.

4. Ellison, "I Have No Mouth," p. 28.

5. Ibid., pp. 24, 36, 38.

6. Ibid., pp. 32, 42.

7. Heinlein, *Moon*, ch. 1, p. 7.

8. Ibid., pp. 8-9, 11-13.

9. Ibid., ch. 6, p. 67.

10. Ellison, "I Have No Mouth," pp. 30-31.

11. Heinlein, *Moon*, ch. 2, p. 42; ch. 4, p. 50; ch. 6, p. 70; ch. 9, p. 105; ch. 15, pp. 150-51.

12. Ellison, "I Have No Mouth," p. 42.

William H. Hardesty III

7

THE PROGRAMMED UTOPIA OF R. A. LAFFERTY'S *PAST MASTER*

In recent years the utopian novel has taken on a distinctly negative cast. Certainly, since Aldous Huxley's *Brave New World* in 1932 many writers have tried to demonstrate the problems inherent in societies organized to provide the good life (or at least an efficiently structured, adequately prosperous life) for their citizens. *Past Master* (1968), one of R. A. Lafferty's first novels, is no exception.[1] The book, as indicated by the praise of Samuel Delany, Roger Zelazny, and Harlan Ellison quoted on the cover of the first edition, is a full-fledged new wave work, complete with the idiosyncratic style, sometimes incoherent plot, and self-assured literariness of the movement. It is also a disturbingly intellectual work, and this fact probably accounts for both its neglect by the public and its importance among contemporary utopian fiction. *Past Master* is no mere dystopian novel: it is a commentary on Sir Thomas More's *Utopia* itself, mated with an investigation into human nature and human aspirations.

The "Past Master" of the title is Sir Thomas More himself. The premise of the novel is that More has been selected by the ruling junta of the planet Astrobe to lead its society through the major crisis of its history. The junta sees More as the only leader in history who has ever had even "one completely honest moment."[2] Consequently, they cause him to be transported forward in time a full millenium to apply that honesty to Astrobe's predicament. Astrobe—"Golden Astrobe of the Dream" in the most frequently applied epithet—is paradise, by any reasonable material standard. No one need work; no one lacks luxuries, let alone necessities; no one need experience raw nature outside the planet's domed cities. Further, no one need have any unfulfilled intellectual potential. All these marvellous conditions have been created by the combination of high technology, total organization of the society, and the substitution of androids for human beings in many functions. For obvious reasons, Astrobe is the envy of all other human societies—Earth itself and the other colonized worlds, none so successful as Astrobe.

But something is amiss. Dissatisfaction has sprung up, expressed in a high suicide rate and in the defection of one-twelfth of the population of Astrobe's cities to Cathead. Conditions in Cathead are opposite to those in Golden Astrobe. If Astrobe is the best, Cathead is the worst imaginable human situation. It is racked by pollution and plague; its inhabitants must work in dangerous conditions; their lives are marked by crime, sin, and early death. Yet Cathead's citizens embrace the life there voluntarily—although they are free to return to Golden Astrobe at any time—and in increasing numbers. As the novel begins, Astrobean society faces the threat of revolt and takeover by its androids, the Programmed Persons. Paradoxically, the Astrobeans are in a state of philosophical and psychological disarray—symbolized by Cathead—in which they appear to have neither the means nor the will to save their paradise from the humanoid machines which intend to displace them. The junta—the inner Circle of the Masters—hope that the Past Master will rally the people and save the dream.

At issue in the novel, then, is the notion of utopia. In effect, Lafferty raises all the basic questions: What in the notion of physical paradise is so appealing to human beings? What is necessary to bring an Edenic dream to fruition? What alternatives to utopia are human beings most likely to construct? What is there in human nature that has prevented the establishment of this society that so many of us seem to dream of? Of course, Lafferty asks none of these questions directly. Instead, he presents them as the concerns of Thomas More. As depicted by Lafferty, More is no stereotyped saint-hero. The Thomas More of *Past Master* has not always taken himself seriously—certainly not when writing *Utopia*—nor is he always rational or right.

Let us recall here, briefly, the characteristics of More's Utopia. It is an island, deliberately cut off from the mainland by the severing of the isthmus that had connected the two. Its people have developed, in their isolation, a highly disciplined (and thoroughly regimented) agrarian society. Their industriousness and their organizational skills have produced a uniform, comfortable prosperity—prosperity made more impressive by the cultural conditioning of the Utopians, who are taught to equate the display of wealth with immaturity or criminality. (Utopian society has passed beyond the shallow acquisitiveness of Western societies; to Utopians, the only measure of value is usefulness. Hence, all objects have worth only in proportion to their utility.) Utopian society is by no means egalitarian in its distribution of political authority, but it does provide for equality in the quality of life of all its citizens and provides great equality of opportunity to achieve high status within society.

But recall also that Utopia has its darker side, as we would see it. A citizen possesses few of the rights guaranteed by the U.S. Constitution. For instance, a criminal becomes, in name and in fact, a slave; and one can become a criminal for (among other offenses) so trival an offense as being twice caught outside one's home territory without a passport. Honest citizens lead a life of somewhat less restriction than criminals, but it possesses a deadening earnestness: " . . . wherever you are, you always have to work. There's never any excuse for idleness. There are also no wine-taverns, no ale-houses, no brothels, no opportunities for seduction, no secret meeting-places. Everyone has his eye on you, so you're practically forced to get on with your job, and make some proper use of your spare time."[3] Indeed, in some ways the island country resembles more a successful totalitarian state of our own time—especially in its repression of sexual activity—than the romantic utopias, such as William Morris's, with which we are familiar. Its citizens pay a terrible price, to modern liberal eyes, for their prosperous, more or less equal life.

The scholarly debate over how to read *Utopia* is beyond the scope of this essay, save in one respect. Some modern critics have not yet decided once and for all how to read More's work—whether it is, to use one critic's terms, "game, chart, or prayer."[4] But Lafferty's More is outspoken about the nature of the old book. It is satiric, More says: to treat it any other way is to distort it; and actually to put it into practice, to build a utopia as the Astrobeans have done, is to accomplish something perverse.[5] Lafferty's More is, accordingly, both amused and delighted, and appalled to discover the nature of Golden Astrobe from the précis machine which gives him a history lesson: *Utopia* "was a joke, I tell you, a bitter joke. It was how *not* to build a world" (emphasis in original).[6]

In implementing the society depicted by More, the founders of Astrobe have succeeded all too well. In Golden Astrobe, the long-standing dreams of humanity have been realized: "Every man [is] a king, every woman [is] at least queenly."[7] But, as in More's fictional island country, there is a considerable price exacted. Astrobe being a society of the space age, the price of its utopianism is expressed in modern computer terms rather than in the moralistic terms used in More's own work. The price is paid in the currency of mechanization and programming, and this cost has been exacted so fully that no one in Golden Astrobe is at all free, as we would define the word freedom.

Consider, for example, the way Astrobeans conduct their politics. More is elected king (they actually call it World President) not by people but by sensing machines, which "could assess and compile the weight of opinion and choice in the totality of the minds on Astrobe."[8] A purely mechanical contrivance, the sensing machines have replaced a hopelessly complicated system of weighted voting wherein a voter might get additional votes for rank, wealth, or service—or have the vote diminished for being unpopular or criminal. The machines produce an accurate measure of public opinion, true; but they do so at the cost of denying *all* Astrobeans their right to express individual opinions in the political process.

Or consider the Pandomation, Astrobe's open-mind machines. By allowing any citizen to look into any room on Astrobe—except certain semi-public rooms used by the leaders—they permit "all interested persons to know all things about everyone . . . in accord with the Astrobe aspiration: 'That we be all ultimately one person, that we have no secrets whatsoever from ourselves.' "[9] The Pandomation has recently been succeeded by the mind-scanner, which allows its user to enter not just a *room* but a *mind*. The Open Mind Act which encourages such inventions is subtitled "I Have As Much Right In Your Mind As You Have," expressing (the narrator laconically tells us) "one of the culminations of the Astrobe dream."[10] Equality in prosperity on Astrobe leads not to equality of person but to identity of personality: " 'We are all the same thing. We are identical,' ran part of the wording of the act."[11]

Last, consider the Termination Booths. Suicide is the ultimate right of every Astrobean, and the Termination Booths are placed all over the Astrobean cities to permit the exercise of the right. The perplexing fact is that the booths have never been more popular—"eight thousand terminations a day in Cosmopolis [the Capital] alone."[12] In the midst of physical plenty there is such widespread boredom with life itself that many choose not to hold onto it; indeed, they spend the last of their creative energy in devising "interesting and bloody deaths for themselves; they vie with each other in this and come up with some imaginative ends."[13]

None of these machines is really incompatible with the society of the island of Utopia as described by More's narrator, Raphael Hythloday. The Utopians, as shown by Raphael's remark quoted above, are no respecters of privacy or individuality. In the name of a stable society, the Utopians submit to a sort of control and homogeneity which reinforces both state and society at the expense of its individual members. But even the most repressive of the Utopians' practices—the regular confessions of wives to their husbands, for instance, or the enslavement of those who have twice traveled without proper authorization—cannot match the Astrobeans' ultimate device in the maintenance of their paradise, the Programmed Killers.

The Programmed Killers are the enforcers of the Astrobean dream. Their sole function is the eradication of dissent. By means programmed into them (and evidently analogous to those used by the sensing machines and the mind-scanners), they sense that someone has been unfaithful to the Astrobean Dream. They then hunt that person down, to the death. The pursued might, in fact, never even have consciously thought a disloyal thought. The Killers will persist, even so; and should the pursued kill a few of the Killers, their places in the hunt will instantaneously be taken by new Killers created to carry on the chase. The Killers may not kill a human *citizen* of Astrobe; however, a genuine criminal has his citizenship revoked and is thus fair game, while an "accident" (no matter how inplausible) can be arranged for those who have not actually been through the judicial process for revoking citizenship. This is an exaggerated form of the Utopian notion that one is always being watched—a deadly exaggeration.

The Killers spend much of the novel in pursuit of most of the people surrounding More; in the latter stages of the work, they are also in pursuit of More himself, despite his position as candidate for World President. Indeed, they stop threatening More only when he gives the most vapid of speeches praising the submission of individuality in the Dream, thereby expressing the most deeply held aspirations of the makers of the Dream.

The Programmed Killers are only one form of Programmed People, in whom Astrobe's Utopia is at its most horrifying. The Programmed People are androids, constructed by human engineers out of organic chemicals: their brains, for instance, are "a chemical and magnetic mishmash of polarized memory gelatin."[14] The intent of the Masters of Astrobe (or of the Powers which may control them behind the scenes) is that the Programmed People—predictable, standardized, and mechanical—will replace human beings, who are unpredictable, diverse, and dangerously individual. The Dream, Fabian Foreman (the Master responsible for having More brought to Astrobe) tells More, is "Finalized Humanity"—that is, humanity which is at once perfected and terminated, for those "are the two sides of the same thing."[15] When the artificial Programmed People have completely replaced standard human beings, the Dream will have reached its culmination. Thereafter it cannot fade, decline, or die—the people whom it then regiments will be manufactured and soulless, unable to change. It will continue forever as a monument to efficiency, organization, and planning—there being no uncontrollable people to subvert it. The one awkward element—humanity and its recurrent dream of a hereafter where things will be perfect—will be gone, for a state of perfection will already exist in this life. "The Hereafter [Foreman says] is here now, and we are in the middle of it."[16]

A fundamental fact about utopias is raised here. A utopia, to be perfect, must allow no unpredictability and no variability. On the island described by More, the ease and prosperity of life are made possible in part by the eschewing of jewelry, the wearing of drab unisex costumes, and the restrictions on travel.[17] On Astrobe, as More sees it, the glorious prosperity is made possible by the programmed life—which is, however, better suited to Programmed People than to real ones.

Here, then, is the source of the paradoxical Astrobean discontent which has led to More's being called from the past. Uniformity, no matter how glitteringly mechanized, is dull. The need for variety in human life is canonized in our proverbs: "Variety is the spice of life"; "A rolling stone gathers no moss.'' Astrobe's perfection runs counter to human nature, a fact its builders are trying to circumvent by constructing Programmed People to replace the natural-born citizens. In the meantime, Astrobe's people have sensed the wrongness of the Dream and are fleeing to Termination Booths or to Cathead. Despite its privations, Cathead is attractive because there one is free; in Cosmopolis and the other cities of Golden Astrobe one is not. Though Astrobeans of the Dream see Cathead as a cancer on the golden planet, those who see more clearly—including the motley entourage with which More surrounds himself—realize that the mechanized utopia is the real disease, running counter to the real role of society in human life. Because of its repression, uniformity, and soullessness, Astrobe of the Dream is not paradise but (as one character argues) hell.

Lafferty's More is at first taken in by the shining illusion. He is enchanted by the sheer achievement of it, particularly by the Programmed People: ''What a boys' dream come true! . . . That we can make machines in our own image, and that they can out-think and outperform us! It's a marvel. . . .''[18] But More rapidly comes to realize the shallowness and inhumanity of the Astrobean Dream. In particular, he is disturbed by the decay of religion. Not that More is a believer, although he says he could sometimes believe for a while in the morning.[19] But he cannot assent to the forbidding of belief which the Programmed People wish him to decree. More wishes to keep open all questions to which there is not a final answer, whereas the Astrobean/Utopian ideal is to answer most questions and forbid the rest.

When More as World President vetoes a bill banning the church, it comes back to him as a rider on another bill. He vetoes it again, and again it comes back. He vetoes it a third time, despite the knowledge that the Programmed People want the law—because they are rational and soulless, they are offended by the relics of human religion. (More's action seems particularly irrational in view of the decay of Catholic practice to an obscene parody of the mass, and of the recent death of the Metropolitan of Astrobe, the last member of the regular clergy.) To veto a bill three times is to invoke the death penalty against oneself. ''It's the same damned thing they killed me for the first time, isn't it?'' More asks in exasperation.[20] Indeed it is: Henry VIII had More killed because More would not assent to Henry's attack on the church. In both cases More is guided by the principle that there are private areas of human existence into which no government, even a utopian one, should intrude. After nine days' reign, More's insistence on this principle brings about his beheading, one thousand years to the day after his original martyrdom. But his courageous stand wrecks the Astrobean utopia: it rains on his execution (someone forgot to close the dome); the human people rebel; the Programmed People feel fear, though they were never programmed for it. A new five-hundred-year cycle is beginning. More's first death ended the cycle of the Old World of Earth; Astrobe's ascendancy after the discovery of Hopp-Equation (faster than light) travel ended the cycle of the New World of Earth. More's second death does not end humankind's last, best chance, though it does evidently end the third cycle, Golden Astrobe. But he had been brought forward in time for that very purpose—to trigger a death and resurrection[21]—and to save, not Astrobe, but humanity.

What, finally, are we to make of all this? Clearly, Lafferty has provided us with a commentary on utopias and on *Utopia*. His More provided in 1516 not a blueprint for an ideal society but a critique of some of the things wrong with the existing societies of Europe. This More is first offended, then taken in, then ultimately revolted by the machine-made version of his satire. His plea is for tolerance, for emotion, for danger and adventure, for spontaneity and wit—all characteristics that must be removed from a utopia if it is to function as smoothly and as evenhandedly as it should. And, from our perspective, this More is clearly correct. Surely not many of Lafferty's readers argue with this central liberal proposition: human beings must be free to choose, and they must be presented with genuine choices. Of this moral decision making is real humanity made.

However, Lafferty, in presenting More thus, distorts More's own work. Numerous critics have pointed out that although the island society he depicts is dull, its dullness would be chosen by an overwhelming majority of More's contemporary Europeans—and by most people throughout human history—over their own lots. Regimented it may be; but it is safe—safe from internal crime, safe (by virtue of its location and by virtue of its duplicitous foreign policy) from external invasion. Work in Utopia is difficult, but it is limited in quantity because all share its burden; there are no privileged classes exempted from labor. Housing, clothing, and other necessities are drab and uninspired—but they are abundant. One may be forced to try to improve oneself—but one has the time and the opportunity no matter what one's station. Utopian society goes far beyond the European nations of More's time in providing for its people, and it has done all this on the basis of pure reason alone—a much better job than that done by European Christians despite *their* having the advantage of Revelation.[22] The real More did not abhor his visionary world: he seems to have seen its faults, and seen also that in his own country and its neighbors there were glaring errors and gaping omissions which needed social repair.

Nevertheless, Lafferty has produced in *Past Master* an interesting exploration of the nature of Utopia and of utopias. The notions of prosperity, peace, and order are at the basis of all utopias, one concludes from the novel. But to bring these to fruition one must dominate nature, either through organization or through machines or through both; and this means regimentation, against which the truly best and brightest will always rebel. Indeed, the sensing machines find that "Cathead and the Barrio [an even wilder region, in the Feral Lands] came to have undue influence [in elections]. It was almost as if these regions had a disproportionate number of persons of very fine intellect and well-studied judgment. . . ."[23] A utopia is not possible on Earth or on Astrobe, not because of original sin or other religious reason, but because of the cantankerous nature of the human being: any society well enough organized to be a utopia will be brought down by those who chafe at the repression of their aspirations—including their notion that they can build a better society. As More tours the world on which his dream has been realized, he sees all this. Utopia is essentially a paradox: human beings want it but cannot have it without the mechanization of body and standardization of soul which are inimical to humanity. Therefore, all we can do is work for a little good in our lives and those of the ones around us. The total good is beyond us. Yet, faith in it—somewhere, somehow—is our destiny. Thus we stave off the reign of Ouden, the god of the Programmed People, whose name is Greek for "Nothing." We choose to believe that we are the children of Something, and that, consequently, whereas the "good place" (*eutopos*) is "no place" (*utopos*) here, it may well be *Hereafter*. The lesson Lafferty's More teaches us is to be like the Astrobeans after the dream collapses: *"We watch. . . . We wait. . . . We hope."*[24]

NOTES

1. R. A. Lafferty, *Past Master* (1968; rpt. New York and London: Garland, 1975). Citations are to the Garland edition, a reproduction of the 1968 Ace original. Recent Ace printings are printed from reset type and have different pagination.
2. Ibid., ch. 1, p. 15.
3. Thomas More, *Utopia* (1516), trans. Paul Turner (Baltimore: Penguin Books, 1965), bk. 2, p. 84.
4. Harry Berger, Jr., "[*Utopia:* Game, Chart, or Prayer?]," 1965; rpt. in Sir Thomas More, *Utopia*, Norton Critical Editions, trans. and ed. Robert M. Adams (New York: Norton, 1975), pp. 203-12.
5. Lafferty, *Past Master*, ch. 2, p. 31.
6. Ibid., ch. 5, p. 66.
7. Ibid., ch. 4, p. 47.
8. Ibid., ch. 9, p. 132.
9. Ibid., p. 137.
10. Ibid., p. 138.
11. Ibid.
12. Ibid., ch. 13, p. 177.
13. Ibid.
14. Ibid., p. 178.
15. Ibid., ch. 11, pp. 161-62.

16. Ibid., p. 162.

17. More, *Utopia*, trans. Turner, bk. 2, pp. 87, 78, 84.

18. Lafferty, *Past Master*, ch. 4, p. 53.

19. Ibid., ch. 5, p. 69.

20. Ibid., ch. 11, p. 165.

21. Ibid., ch. 1, p. 12.

22. This fact was pointed out to me by Richard D. Erlich. [See R. W. Chambers, *Thomas More* (London: Jonathan Cape, 1935; New York: Harcourt, Brace & World, 1936), pp. 125-44; excerpted in *Twentieth Century Interpretations of Utopia*, ed. William Nelson (Englewood Cliffs, NJ: Prentice-Hall, 1968); see esp. pp. 19-20. Chambers' key line on this topic is quoted in the Introduction to the Crofts Classics edition of More, *Utopia*, trans. and ed. H. V. S. Ogden (New York: Appleton-Century-Crofts, 1949), pp. viii-ix.—Eds.]

23. Lafferty, *Past Master*, ch. 9, p. 132.

24. Ibid., ch. 13, p. 191.

Merritt Abrash

8

ELUSIVE UTOPIAS: SOCIETIES AS MECHANISMS IN THE EARLY FICTION OF PHILIP K. DICK

Philip K. Dick is not a utopian writer. The word "utopia," if it appears in his work at all, carries no overt thematic significance, and although many different types of societies serve as backdrops for his novels, none are described in the rounded ways traditionally associated with utopian fiction. Nevertheless, Dick makes a serious contribution to utopian thought (used here as a blanket term covering dystopian considerations as well) because his stories contain numerous elements often found in utopian visions and provide a consistent point of view about why marvelous devices and institutional innovations fail to produce anything resembling a utopia.

On the other hand, his societies do not qualify as dystopias, either. There are no utopian schemes to go sour, nor are the societies molded in the image of evil intentions.[1] In fact, Dick's originality in utopian terms is precisely that there is no larger-scale intention at all; because the utopian elements are introduced without utopian vision, they are absorbed into and take on the coloration of the societies in which they appear. This occurs so unfailingly and with so little contrivance that the image emerges of societies as mechanisms, too well equipped with fallback and safety devices to be disrupted by mere tinkering with parts.

This essay covers Dick's novels and short stories up to the mid-1960s—works replete with his characteristic technological wonders and institutional themes. The wonders are no more imaginative than those of many other science fiction writers, but the uses to which they are and are not put follow an interesting pattern. They are portrayed as having been introduced not to allow a breakthrough toward new and better societies, but to enhance the operation of existing procedures and values. Their genesis is in profit and power, never in idealism. Where the state is dominant, innovations in science, technology and organization serve state purposes; where the state is open to challenge, such innovations as easily serve private interests. This is especially evident in regard to robots, which in Dick's stories are incredibly complex, fighting wars, tending infants, managing factories, educating youth, and making polite service calls. They also repair themselves and build replacements. All these accomplishments, however, have no other purpose than to strengthen existing structures of profit and power. There is a metaphorical aptness in actual machines' expressing the values and operating principles of societies which, in the terminology of this volume, are clockwork worlds in their essential nature.

In the short story "Second Variety" (1953), for example, robots have taken over most of the burden of warfare (an idea that would have appealed to Sir Thomas More's Utopians), but their programming is so effective and their resemblance to humans so perfect (to deceive the enemy) that warfare has become more horrible than ever.[2] The human soldiers have almost all been wiped out by the robots, which are well on their way to controlling the devastated surface of the Earth. Meanwhile, underground robot factories have begun devising new varieties of robots to defeat "enemy" robots. Every element of this human catastrophe grows logically out of the robots' original assignment of triumphing over the enemy, and humans cannot even claim the irony of the "Sorcerer's Apprentice" legend; since the original motivation was a destructive one, the outcome need occasion no surprise.

Dick gives this theme a sardonic twist in "The Defenders" (1953), where the warring humans have moved underground, leaving the robots to fight it out on the presumably radioactive surface.[3] The robots, however, having all been programmed to serve their various creators, draw the logical conclusion that the war is antithetical to human welfare, and therefore the robots stop hostilities, repair the damage, and put the Earth into tip-top shape for the time when humans get rid of their hatred. The robots recognize the logical necessity of keeping the humans temporarily fooled into staying underground until the war mania wears out, so they report deadly surface conditions and endless battles while they in fact go about their business of preparing an ideal environment for human life. It cannot be accidental that one of the few glimpses of utopian vision Dick permits to enter his work is attributed to robots, not men.

The theme of "The Defenders" is significantly elaborated in Dick's novel *The Penultimate Truth* (1964). Two years of combat between armies of leadies (robots) forced resettlement of the human masses on both sides in underground "tanks," where they live in discomfort and privation and spend most of their time manufacturing new leadies and repairing damaged ones. The leadies, meanwhile, come to the same logical conclusion as the robots in "The Defenders": the fighting should be ended but the masses, still imbued with war spirit, kept ignorant of this. However, in *The Penultimate Truth* some of the political and military leaders, administrators, technicians, and media personnel on both sides are still on the surface, so the leadies proceed by convincing these humans to bring the fighting to an end while relying on advanced media techniques to keep the vast population in the tanks absorbed in producing for the leady armies, still imagined to be fighting each other on the devastated Earth. The result, on the Earth's surface, is a society where a small elite has land for the asking and great numbers of leadies to carry out all the physical work, personal service, and low-level supervision of other leadies.

In both "The Defenders" and *The Penultimate Truth*, a temporary human hive is extended into the distant future by the robots' intervention, but the difference between the two situations is profound. In the short story, it is the robots alone who execute a deception against all humanity. In the novel, a small elite, favored by circumstance, willingly carries on an identical deception against fellow humans, who consequently drag out their lives in an inhuman environment, engaging in ceaseless labor from which they gain no benefit. It sounds a bit like Dostoevsky's satiric formulation in *The Possessed* (1871-72) that the closest practical approach to utopia would be to have one-tenth of mankind exercising absolute power over the other nine-tenths, but Dick is not given to philosophical speculations about utopia. What is characteristic of him in *The Penultimate Truth* is the inevitability of science and technology, no matter what their utopian potential, being put at the service of existing mechanisms of control. Even more sharply drawn is the contrast between the benign designs of the robots acting in a human-free world, and the perversion of those designs when effectuated under human guidance.

The most pointed example of robot technology introduced for the wrong reasons is in the story "Autofac" (1955).[4] After a catastrophic war, the survivors discover that all resources and industrial production are under the control of a network of automated factories set up during the war by the Institute of Applied Cybernetics, for the practical purpose of maintaining production—including the production of consumer goods—at maximum efficiency. The autofac system assesses demand, collects raw materials, and distributes finished products. It even sends around robot factory representatives to deal with complaints. Such an arrangement has obvious utopian overtones—the freeing of human beings from routine and conservation of resources by adjusting production to real demand rather than trying to create a market—but since its introduction was motivated by power purposes rather than utopian vision, the ultimate result is a limitation rather than an enhancement of human life.

With the war over and the Institute of Applied Cybernitics presumably blown to smithereens, the autofac network continues doing what it was programmed to do, which includes keeping a total monopoly of raw material use and protecting its fortresslike factories and external operations from interference. The human survivors find the entire economic component of society beyond their control and ultimately prefer to abandon the security autofac provides in favor of the difficult task of creating their own social institutions. However, after the humans have succeeded in ingeniously arranging for autofac to pick up cues which lead it to take self-destructive actions, they discover beneath the wreckage a supersecure machine sending pellets of microscopic factory construction machinery—autofac "seeds"—into the sky. Dick speculates in an afterword that "if factories became fully automated, they might begin to show the instinct for survival which organic living entities have . . . and perhaps develop similar solutions."[5]

In the novel *The Man Who Japed* (1956), technological developments are fitted out with utopian justifications, but prove to serve very different purposes because the society's inner nature is antiutopian. The society is roughly the type that the Moral Majority circa 1980 would like to impose: a strict moral code enforced through weekly "block meetings" at which the inhabitants of each apartment development deal with accusations against any of them.

Evidence of moral delinquency is gathered by "juveniles"—small mobile robots whose sole function is to spy on people. Oddly enough, the juveniles are manifestations of utopian justice in a society which believes in the propriety of spying.

There was something sinister in these metal informers, but there was also something heartening. The juveniles did not accuse; they only reported what they heard and saw. They couldn't color their information and they couldn't make it up. Since the victim was indicted mechanically he was safe from hysterical hearsay, from malice and paranoia. . . . The victim couldn't protest that he had been unjustly accused, all he could protest was his bad luck at having been overheard.[6]

At the block meeting, questioning of the accused and debate among fellow inhabitants is done in a synthetic voice issuing from a wall speaker. "To preserve the aura of justice, questions were piped through a common channel, broken down and reassembled without characteristic timbre. The result was as impersonal accuser, who, when a sympathetic questioner appeared, became suddenly and a little oddly a defender."[7]

Purely factual evidence and democratic courtroom procedure isolated from personalities! These are utopian elements indeed, but, serving as they do a massive institutional intrusion on both privacy and freedom, their net effect is to reinforce the rigid social mechanics of a society devoid of utopian spirit.

The same fate befalls institutional changes ordinarily associated with the betterment of society, if not with anything as dramatic as "utopia." World government exists in most of these stories, usually under the name "UN";

however, this UN is invariably merely another power center in conflict (usually, but not always, nonviolent) with powerful competing organizations, whether political or economic. *Solar Lottery* (1955), Dick's first novel, features the principle of absolutely random selection of the world's political chief, but not only do a host of highly unutopian political strategies sprout around this mechanism, but the principle itself is corrupted by powerful men.

The most determined effort to break through to a more rational mode of organization beyond clashing interests and power struggles is in *Vulcan's Hammer* (1960). The obligatory catastrophic war had ended with the Lisbon Laws of 1993, through which the nations of the world decided, as the Managing Director of the subsequent "Unity" system explains,

to subordinate themselves in a realistic manner—not in the idealistic fashion of the UN days—to a common supranational authority, for the good of all mankind.
Something drastic had to be done, because another war would destroy mankind. Something, some ultimate principle of organization, was needed. International control. Law, which no men or nations could break. Guardians were needed. But who would watch the Guardians? How could we be sure this supranational body would be free of the hate and bias, the animal passions that had set man against man throughout the centuries? Wouldn't this body, like all other man-made bodies, fall heir to the same vices, the same failings of interest over reason, emotion over logic?
There was one answer. For years we had been using computers. . . . Machines were free of the poisonous bias of self-interest and feeling that gnawed at man; they were capable of performing the objective calculations that for man would remain only an ideal, never a reality.[8]

And so Vulcan 3 was built, a computer to be totally isolated from every human being except the Managing Director, who would provide the data and materials (since Vulcan 3 constructed its own extensions) it requested and decide the questions to ask it. The whole project reeks of utopian logic and, predictably, Vulcan 3, since it is programmed to actually make policy, gives ultimate priority to its own clearly indispensable survival. The Managing Director consults with superseded Vulcan 2 about a popular movement which has sprung up against the Unity system, and takes Vulcan 2's advice to withhold information about the movement from Vulcan 3. The latter, able to detect that in the overall pattern of worldwide data some significant element is missing, builds flying robots to search it out—and destroy hostile humans at the same time. "The ultimate horror for our paranoid culture," thinks the book's hero, "vicious unseen mechanical entities that flit at the edges of our visions, that can go anywhere, that are in our very midst . . . these things do not hunt us down because they want to, or even because they have been told to; they do it because we are there. As far as Vulcan 3 is concerned, we are objects, not people."[9]

It turns out that the revolutionary movement has been initiated and organized by Vulcan 2, since *its* survival was threatened by the Unity system's reliance on Vulcan 3. So much for replacing human self-interest with the impartiality of the machine.

An occasion on which Dick *does* pay respect to a machine is also one on which he makes his most profound statement about the gap between the device with utopian potential and the actual attainment of utopia. In *Martian Time-Slip* (1964), the colonists from Earth have schools on Mars consisting entirely of Teaching Machines—robots perfectly simulating human beings and programmed with distinct personalities to facilitate the child's interest in the subject matter dispensed.

It was not a closed system; it compared the children's answers with its own tape, then matched, classified, and at last responded. There was no room for a unique answer because the Teaching Machine could recognize only a limited number of categories. And yet, it gave a convincing illusion of being alive and viable; it was a triumph of engineering.

Its advantage over a human teacher lay in its capacity to deal with each child individually. It tutored, rather than merely teaching. A teaching machine could handle up to a thousand pupils and yet never confuse one with the next; with each child its responses altered so that it became a subtly different entity. Mechanical, yes—but almost infinitely complex.

In other words, a machine which is an improvement over human beings not only as a functional object, but in terms of ability to relate to them. "And yet," continue the hero's ruminations,

he felt repelled by the teaching machines. For the entire Public School was geared to a task which went contrary to his grain; the school was there not to inform or educate, but to mold, and along severely limited lines. It was the link to their inherited culture, and it peddled that culture, in its entirety, to the young. It bent its pupils to it; perpetuation of the culture was the goal, and any special quirks in the children which might lead them in another direction had to be ironed out. It was a battle between the composite psyche of the school and the individual psyches of the children, and the former held all the key cards.[10]

The thrust of this statement concerns not the machine as such, but the motivation underlying its introduction. It was devised not to break through to a new and better form of education, but to strengthen existing social values; as always in Dick, utopian potential is submerged beneath the kind of self-serving practicality associated with the "establishment."

Could an idealistic movement harness technology and organization directly to utopian goals? Dick never confronts such a possibility, but an answer of sorts can be read into *Eye in the Sky* (1957), a novel which, to be sure, is not to be taken very seriously as a statement of ideas. Eight sightseers are involved in a Bevatron accident, with the result that they find themselves—or are utterly convinced that they do—successively inhabiting universes reflecting the minds of each of them. The sightseers seem like a random, average, and essentially harmless group, but each of the universes they go through is utopian only for the mind which dominates it and frighteningly bizarre for everyone else. It might be inferred that Dick considers every utopian scheme to be the objectification of someone's self-interest.

Only once does Dick explore the possibility of an ethos that might subdue self-interest. In *Dr. Futurity*, one of his less-read novels, a physician from our time is transported to a distant future where he is treated with horror and loathing because he saves the life of a seriously wounded young woman. He is sentenced to exile from Earth for his offense, and the young woman undoes his skillful work by calling in an official "euthanor" to kill her. An official tries to enlighten the doctor about the society, taking him to a heavily guarded building in which he sees a stupendous cube churning with some sort of "controlled, measured metabolism."

"Zygotes," said his guide. "Arrested and frozen in cold-pack by the hundred billion. Our total seed. Our horde. The *race* is in there. . . . We keep a constant population. Roughly, two and ¾ billion. Each death automatically starts a new zygote from cold-pack along its regular developmental path. For each death there is an instantaneous new life; the two are interwoven."[11]

The doctor learns that the zygotes are formed in the cube from gametes taken from men and women who score high in contests, which are held every year between the tribes into which the society is divided and are devised to identify the possessors of desired qualities. Unauthorized zygote formation is illegal and all men are sterilized. Gifted individuals donate their entire supply of gametes, while those of low scorers in the contests are excluded. The doctor comes to realize that the girl he saved insisted upon dying because she could not do well in the contests if maimed or disfigured, and would only pull down the status of her tribe. As it is, explains the guide,

as soon as she was dead, a superior zygote, from a later stock than her own, was released. And at the same time a nine month embryo was brought out and severed from the Soul Cube. The new baby will take the girl's place in the tribe.

[The doctor] nodded slowly. "Immortality." Then death, he realized, has a positive meaning. Not the end of life. And not merely because these people *wish* to believe, but because it is a fact. Their world is constructed that way.[12]

This is an extraordinary concept, but Dick does not develop it into a full utopian vision. Only a few scraps of information are provided about the society's other institutions and way of life, and these lack organic connection with the fundamental eugenic institution. The doctor puts a few not very penetrating questions to the official, and then Dick gets on with the plot.

This sole utopian vision in his work reinforces Dick's consistent, if implicit, answer to a crucial question: Can utopia be achieved through changes in conditions, or is it dependent upon prior changes in human beings? The society in *Dr. Futurity* clearly reflects the latter: the overwhelming majority of the population had to attain an almost unimaginable level of self-sacrificing idealism for such a radical proposal to be successfully instituted. No general change in the outlook of human beings is present in other Dick stories, where the most extraordinary gadgetry and organizational ingenuity fail to divert individuals from thinking and acting in terms of a self-interest (modified, in his heroes, by a strong sense of decency and fair play) that is indistinguishable from American national character circa 1960.

More important, society and its institutions seem by their very nature to turn all innovations into props for their own continuation. Characteristic of this process is Dick's reference (already quoted) to "a battle between the composite psyche of the school and the individual psyches of the children, [in which] the former held all the key cards." In Dick's stories, new developments in education or anything else can be relied upon—no matter what the intentions of those responsible for the developments—to serve the interests of existing structures of power and profit.

In this respect, the societies he depicts resemble gigantic mechanisms, imperfect in their detailed operation but so nicely articulated that all the major subordinate interests perceive their welfare as inextricably tied up with the basic configuration of the whole. No quarter is given in the unrelenting pursuit of great prizes by both public and private entities, but all contestants are united in defending the overall structure which gives the prizes their value and prevents a Hobbesian state of nature which would allow the winner hardly more security than the loser. Societies incorporate the conflicts as part of their normal functioning, like a machine programmed to utilize the heat from its own friction; the more intensely each part pursues its own activity, the more tightly it finds itself bound up in the very whole it would seem to be disrupting.

Utopia is precluded in Dick's stories not as a result of any conscious effort to prevent it but because his societies lack utopian vision. The repeated examples of dazzling innovations failing to elevate the inner nature of power- and profit-oriented societies add up to a significant statement about utopia: it can never be approached as a by-product of other considerations, but must be deliberately willed into existence. Neither an "Institute of Applied Cybernetics" brilliantly rationalizing the total economic process in order to fight a war (as in "Autofac") nor a "Unity" system boldly employing the ultimate computer in order to relieve humanity of all responsibility (as in *Vulcan's Hammer*) can lead to utopia, any more than a stream can rise higher than its source. To Dick, society is too powerful a mechanism to be transformed by innovations introduced piecemeal and for diverse purposes; it will unfailingly find uses of its own for them if not countered by a concentrated utopian vision impelling human beings toward a transformation of existing systems. Instead of Luddite assaults against innovations in hardware and technique, the demolition of the old order must be guided by ideological challenges to existing forms of institutional control. The fundamental impulse underlying a clockwork world is a particular conception of human society rather than any technological configuration, and such a world cannot be transformed until the conception is displaced by a more humane one.

NOTES

1. For an introduction to the utopian tradition in Western literature, see Lewis Mumford, *The Story of Utopias* (New York: Boni and Liveright, 1922); Mary Louis Berneri, *Journey Through Utopia* (London: Routledge and Kegan Paul, 1950); Glen Negley and J. M. Patrick, eds., *The Quest for Utopia* (New York: Henry Schuman, 1952); and Frank E. Manuel and Fritzie P. Manuel, *Utopian Thought in the Western World* (Cambridge, MA: Harvard University Press, 1979). For an introduction to dystopian literature, see Chad Walsh, *From Utopia to Nightmare* (New York: Harper and Row, 1962); and Harold L. Berger, *Science Fiction and the New Dark Age* (Bowling Green, OH: Bowling Green University Popular Press, 1976).

2. Philip K. Dick, "Second Variety," *Space Science Fiction*, May 1953; rpt. in *The Best of Philip K. Dick*, John Brunner, ed. (New York: Ballantine, 1977), pp. 17-66. For further bibliographical information about Dick's works, see the List at the end of this volume, or the bibliography by R. D. Mullen in *SFS #5* = vol. 2, pt. 1 (March 1975), 5-8.

3. Philip K. Dick, "The Defenders," *Galaxy*, Jan. 1953; rpt. in *The Book of Philip K. Dick* (New York: DAW, 1973), pp. 46-70.

4. Philip K. Dick, "Autofac," *Galaxy*, Nov. 1955; rpt in *Best of Philip K. Dick*, pp. 267-94. Dick's treatment of robots is described and analyzed, with references to this and other stories, by Patricia S. Warrick, *The Cybernetic Imagination in Science Fiction* (Cambridge, MA: MIT Press, 1980), pp. 206-30.

5. Philip K. Dick, Afterword, p. 449 (ellipsis in original).

6. Philip K. Dick, *The Man Who Japed* (New York: Ace, 1956), p. 45.

7. Ibid., p. 46.

8. Philip K. Dick, *Vulcan's Hammer* (New York: Ace, 1960), pp. 19-20.

9. Ibid., p. 100.

10. Philip K. Dick, *Martian Time-Slip* (New York: Ballantine, 1964), p. 64.

11. Philip K. Dick, *Dr. Futurity* (New York: Ace, 1960), p. 47.

12. Ibid., p. 49.

Thomas P. Hoffman

9

THE THEME OF MECHANIZATION IN
PLAYER PIANO

Kurt Vonnegut, Jr.,'s *Player Piano* (1952) is more than a science fiction
novel, an antiutopian novel, or a black humor novel. It is, Vonnegut has
stated, "a novel about people and machines . . . a novel about life."[1] The
theme of *Player Piano* is mechanization, and its primary subject is machine-
created loneliness examined against a background of social revolution. This
novel is Vonnegut's first attempt to reorder reality in order to explore the
frustrations of the people he knew in "Schenectady, a very real town,
awkwardly set in the gruesome now."[2]

Player Piano might also be classified as a work of sociology expressed in
fictional form because in this book Vonnegut writes more like a social
scientist than a novelist. His analyses clearly anticipate the ideas underlying
sociologist Philip Slater's thesis on American loneliness. Critic Peter J.
Reed seems to understand the sociological element of this novel: "For all its
technological sophistication and social innovation, the America described
in this book resembles the one we live in, and we quickly realize that what
Vonnegut wants to tell us about is not so much the future as the present."[3]
As Vonnegut depicts its tripartite division, the fictional city of Ilium seems
an obvious microcosm of American society. The managers, engineers, civil
servants, and professional people live in the northwest; machines per se are
found in the northeast; and to the south is the "Homestead" area where live
"almost all of the people."[4]

Vonnegut sets his novel in the indefinite future which he describes in his
foreword as "another point in history, when there is no more war"; this
would suggest that he intentionally sought the hypothetical environment in
order to concentrate upon the inherent political, economic, and technological concerns of a society viewed in isolation from international involvement. America is depicted as *the* superpower that has emerged from the

latest world war, a war won by the miracle of machine production with very little manpower.[5] Machines have replaced men in this society for what first appeared to be a good cause, but the effects of automation are far-reaching, and they provide both theme and conflict in *Player Piano*.

Doctor Paul Proteus is the protagonist of the novel, and it is through his experience of a series of sociological conflicts that Vonnegut explores the subject of machine-made loneliness. Despite his enviable position as the manager of the Ilium Works, Proteus is clearly frustrated in his desires for community, engagement, and dependence. The machine has supplanted human purpose in this society to such a degree that even the elite manager and engineer "rulers" of the machine have begun to feel the loss of their sense of human dignity. The resulting alienation is gradually developed through Paul's changing character as he struggles to express his vaguely understood discontent with the system. He tries to assert his beliefs in the rightness of the machine-dominated society that won the war but is unable to overcome an ambiguous sense of doubt and loneliness. His divided loyalty in the conflict of man versus machine is important because it helps justify the ultimate lack of resolution in the novel and still allows for the slow growth of Paul's awareness of his dual commitment to and against technology.

His desire for community accounts for his strongly nostalgic interest in the past, represented by inefficient Building 58, which had been Thomas Edison's original machine shop in 1886. Paul regards it as a "vote of confidence" from the past, and he visits it to cure his depression. It reminds him of his youth, when he possessed both innocence and faith in the system. It was in Building 58 that he and two other young engineers, his best friend Ed Finnerty, and his self-appointed enemy Lawson Shepherd, had recorded on tape the movements of the building's most skilled machinist, Rudy Hertz. This same love of the past accounts for his attachment to his cheap old Plymouth with a broken headlight which he drives across the bridge into Homestead, where most of the people live. Nostalgia and the search for stability are combined in his plan to move his wife out to the old Gottwald ("God's woods") farm where he "daydreamed of living a century before." Paul is attempting to withdraw from the present and "progressive" moment of his technological society by escaping into a dimly understood past which he believes to be his Eden. In an excellent example of ironic reversal, Vonnegut has made the fully automated society assume the static quality of a "stable" past because it has "solved" all the problems of modern man by removing such things as waste, imperfection, war, poverty, hunger, and *purpose* from his daily existence.

The novel's best expression of this point may be seen in the scathingly satiric chapter 17, which describes the typical home life of the American "average man." Edgar Rice Burroughs Hagstrohm and his family live in a self-cleaning M-17 house, and he has a *"complete* security package" of health, life, and old age insurance as well as automatic payroll deduction payments on the house, car, furniture, equipment, and so forth, controlled by the world's most advanced computer, EPICAC XIV.[6] The ultimate machine, EPICAC XIV can "consider simultaneously hundreds or even thousands of sides of a question utterly fairly," is entirely free of "reason-muddying emotions," and never forgets anything. In other words, EPICAC XIV is "dead right about everything."[7] EPICAC XIV is also the ultimate cause of the desperate techno-loneliness experienced by the Hagstrohm family. Edgar complains, "I'm no good to anybody, not in *this* world," and his wife Wanda echoes his sentiments, saying "nobody needs me." In the chapter describing the Hagstrohms, the world "life" begins to sound like a curse or prison sentence. The two major forces of the novel meet in this chapter as the perfection of the machine is held up to the imperfection of humanity.

The Ghost Shirt Society, which represents human opposition to the machines, is just as effectively ironic because it is an institution resurrected from the past in order to bring about a change in the present. Instead of providing a romantic escape from reality, the society allows a brutal confrontation with reality. Max Schulz has noted an additional ironic twist in Vonnegut's use of the Ghost Shirts.

The Ghost Shirt Movement, pledged to destruction of the authoritarian machine-dominated society and to restoration of a society of men, proves to be no less instinctively totalitarian. In engineering a Messiah, the Movement uses Paul Proteus as remorselessly as do the managerial elite. Equally distressing is the obtuseness of the survivors of the aborted Revolution, who, having destroyed the machines, begin to repair them out of pride and amusement, starting the process of recreating the system which will render them useless again. Thus the problem of stability posed by the novel in the form of such antitheses as spiritual needs versus material satisfactions and of human disorderliness versus machine-controlled regularity continues unresolved at the end.[8]

The lack of resolution observed by Schulz seems to be a consistent characteristic of Vonnegut's novels. It would appear that Vonnegut links man's techno-loneliness with mutability by placing his protagonist between the static and the dynamic in nearly every novel. *Player Piano* ends most appropriately, therefore, with Paul and Finnerty discussing the importance of change. The reason things don't stay the same, Finnerty points out, is that trying to change them is "entertaining." And when Paul agrees that keeping things from remaining static is the "most fascinating game there is," Finnerty sums up all by saying that if it were not for all the "god-damned people" getting snarled up in the machinery, Earth would be an "engineer's paradise."[9] Finnerty's reference to an engineer's paradise lends new meaning to Professor Ludwig von Neumann's final assertion that "This isn't the end, you know. . . . Nothing ever is, nothing ever will be—not even Judgment Day."[10] This conclusion to the novel seems to be affirmative because it recognizes that life is experienced in an endless state of motion and change: human change, not the precise, cyclical motion of the machines that had so fascinated Paul in Building 58. The full significance of the machines' hypnotic rhythm is not seen until Paul's pentathol-induced dream in the Ghost Shirt Society headquarters.

While under the influence of the drug, Paul moves through a dream ballet to the music of the *Building 58 Suite*. James Mellard views this stylized movement of the dream-dance as a surrender of Paul's true identity and states that the sequence celebrates an idealized identity and the essential self of humanity through Paul's loss of individuality.

Ultimately, Paul's dream-dance celebrates the fully human, the notion that good things can come from dismal evil, that laudable benevolence can come from base motivations, and that exquisite beauty can come from refuse—"the most beautiful peonies I ever saw," said Paul, "were grown in almost pure cat excrement."[11]

Underlying this observation is the realization that good, benevolence, and beauty must all evolve from the process of change. That would seem to be the reason why Vonnegut concludes *Player Piano* without resolving the problems it presents. Change is proof of life, and the end of change is death. The desire for community will always vie with the desire for competition to maintain the constant state of transition. Paul Proteus and the Ghost Shirt Society represent *this* year's failure in the revolt against machines.

Paul's desire for engagement is, in its initial stages, a mere wish for reconcilation of the useful and the useless elements of human society. More importantly, it is a romantic response that is typical of American perception of social problems. Philip Slater sees this kind of response as a denial of social reality.

We are, as a people, perturbed by our inability to anticipate the consequences of our acts, but we still wait optimistically for some magic telegram, informing us that the tangled skein of misery and self-deception into which we have woven ourselves has vanished in the night. Each month popular magazines regale their readers with such telegrams: announcing that our transportation crisis will be solved by a bigger plane or a wider road, mental illness with a pill, poverty with a law, slums with a bulldozer, urban conflict with a gas, racism with a good-will gesture. . . . Whatever realism we may display in technical areas, our approach to social issues inevitably falls back on cinematic tradition, in which social problems are resolved by gesture.[12]

Ironically enough, all of the particular problems that Slater mentions have been resolved in *Player Piano*, but the larger social problem of man's purpose in a machine society remains. Paul explains in his trial for sabotage/ treason that, in the interests of good government, machines have taken over more sovereignty than people ever intended to surrender to them. Machines, organization, and the quest for efficiency, Paul maintains, have robbed Americans of "liberty and the pursuit of happiness."[13]

Slater calls this form of avoiding social issues "the Toilet Assumption—the notion that unwanted matter, unwanted difficulties, unwanted complexities and obstacles will disappear if they are removed from our immediate field of vision." Generally speaking, he concludes that our "approach to social problems is to decrease their visibility: out of sight, out of mind."[14]

Vonnegut employs the toilet assumption metaphor in an ironic twist of plot in *Player Piano*. The Ghost Shirt Society revolution turns out to be a further example of avoiding reality. At the novel's conclusion, Paul finally learns that the original Ghost Dance Indians of the 1890s were horribly massacred. The bullet-proofing "magic" of their Ghost Shirts failed them when they made a last desperate stand at thousand-to-one odds against the U.S. Cavalry. Just as the Indians fought against the changes of the white man's world to avoid becoming "second-rate white men" or their wards, Paul's revolutionaries are fighting to avoid becoming "second-rate machines themselves, or wards of the machines." The paradox of both movements lies in the fact that their respective leaders were very much aware of their predestined defeat. The motives of the four "thought-chiefs" of the modern Ghost Shirt Society reveal their true detachment from reality when they confront the failure of the revolution. Finnerty, Paul supposes, had got what he sought from the revolution, a chance to strike savagely at "a closed little society that made no comfortable place for him." Professor von Neumann, a former political scientist, viewed the revolution as a "fascinating experiment." He had been less interested in achieving a premeditated end than in seeing what would happen with given beginnings. Lasher, the most realistic of the four, was also the most content with the failure of the revolution because it offered him the best prize possible for his two specializations as anthropologist and minister. "A lifelong trafficker in symbols, he had created the revolution as a symbol, and was now welcoming the opportunity to die as one."[15] As the chief instigator of the revolution, Lasher saw most clearly that it had to fail because imperfect humans are not as efficient as perfect machines. He finds value in man's efforts to change history even when those efforts are doomed. His philosophy is that winning or losing is not important, only trying "For the record!" Lasher's pragmatic view of reality seems to contrast with Paul's naive avoidance of it. Vonnegut explains that Paul is one of those least in touch with reality because he had little time for reflection and was so desirous of joining an organization that had answers to "the problems that had made him sorry to be alive."[16]

Even though disillusioned by the revolution, Paul is the only one who is able to come to terms with his environment as something other than ego-extensions. His motivation has not been the idealism or egocentric goals of the other three leaders, and he demonstrates this by his change of mind in a final toast. He starts to propose a toast to a better world but stops when he realizes that the people of Ilium are ready to start the whole mess all over again; instead he shrugs, offers a toast "To the record," and dashes the empty bottle against a rock. His disillusionment here reveals both insight and loneliness as he seems to be the only member of the revolution who has achieved an awareness of the vital roles of both the humans and the machines in the cyclical nature of the system. The final statement of the novel seems to announce Paul's new awareness: "Hands up," Lasher says, "Forward March."[17] Here is man's willing surrender to the technology he has created; it is also man's recognition of the inevitable progression of history. The ending is affirmative because it reassures us that humans will continue to rebel against this prisonhouse of their own creation despite the failure of *this* rebellion, *this* man, or *this* period of history. The process of change is once more confirmed as Paul drinks to "the record" of man's forward march of life.

Despite Paul's new awareness, his loneliness is real and represents the various individual searches for independence within a society that has become almost totally dependent upon technology "for the control of one's impulses and the direction of one's life."[18] The dominant symbol of control in *Player Piano* is the current "ultimate" computer EPICAC XIV, located in the Carlsbad Caverns and described by Vonnegut as nearly omniscient. EPICAC XIV is able to determine how many of everything Americans need and what the costs will be, including, "refrigerators . . . lamps . . . turbine-generators . . . hub caps . . . dinner plates . . . door knobs . . . rubber heels . . . television sets." It can even determine how many pinochle decks Americans will use. But this is only the beginning. In the years ahead, EPICAC XIV will also determine exactly how many engineers, managers, research men, and civil servants will be needed to produce these goods. It can determine IQ levels, cull useless people, and so on, literally ad infinitum.[19]

The computer is further invested with a religious quality shown during a dedication ceremony when the president of the United States, Jonathan Lynn, speaks of his feelings of profound reverence, humility, and gratitude as he declares the greatness of this "modern miracle." President Lynn extols EPICAC XIV as "the greatest individual in history." A worm is to the wisest person who ever lived in the same ratio of mental ability as that person is to EPICAC XIV, he declares.[20]

In direct contrast to this electronic controller of men's destinies, Vonnegut presents the Shah of Bratpuhr, the spiritual leader of six million members of the Kolhouri sect. In one of the most satisfying scenes of the novel the Shah is introduced to EPICAC XIV. He asks it to answer a riddle that his people believe can only be answered by an all-wise God whose arrival among the people will mean an end to human suffering. The conflict between man and machine is sharply defined in Vonnegut's description of the Shah's question and the computer's nonreponse. Raising his hands up, the Shah falls to his knees and seems to fill the whole cave with a "mysterious, radiant dignity." Turning to EPICAC, he cries: "Allakahi baku billa, / Moumi a fella nam; / Serani assu tilla, / Touri serin a sam." A translation is provided by Khashdrahr Miasma: "Silver bells shall light my way, / And nine times nine maidens fill my day, / And mountain lakes will sink from sight, / And tigers' teeth will fill the night." The Shah is very downcast at the computer's response: " *'Mmmmmm,'* said EPICAC softly. *'Dit, dit. Mmmmm. Dit.'* " "*Nibo,*" mutters the Shah, "Nibo—nothing." Halyard says, ". . . the machine didn't answer."[21]

The Shah's disappointed response to EPICAC's failure to answer his riddle (which is, of course, unanswerable) is to declare the machine a "*Baku,*" or false god, which is precisely what it has become in this technology-worshiping society. It has the capacity for fulfilling all of the physical needs of humankind but is unable to be the "spiritual leader" of even one human being, and is therefore inferior to the Shah who is supposed to represent an undeveloped nation of backward people. Reed observes that the Shah of Bratpuhr

exposes what we all hold suspect in the human consequences of automation, in the military mentality, in the proliferation of labor-saving gadgetry, and in the middle-class home life. The guide showing the Shah the wonders of the mechanized home comes off a little like Richard Nixon protesting the merits of American kitchens to Chairman Khrushchev.[22]

The other symbol of control in the novel is the National Industrial, Commercial, Communications, Foodstuffs, and Resources Board which is represented by the vaguely defined "Company" employing elite managers and engineers to serve the various machine works across the country. While it is this particular form of control from which Paul specifically struggles to become independent, the real source of his and everyone else's frustration is their dependence upon machines for the control of their daily existence. The machines have been depicted as so successful in their roles as rulers of destiny that the Shah of Bratpuhr very perceptively refers to non-elite citizens of this electronic utopia as "slaves."

As a "slave" to the system, for all his high status, Paul is the final symbol of American loneliness in this prophetic novel. His development of conscience without wisdom has made life so lonely, he "decided he wouldn't mind being dead."[23] But Paul is not dead, he is merely detached from the illusions that had previously sustained him. He has confronted reality and the result is alienation. This is the crisis Slater has in mind when he explains the cause and effect relationship between technology and loneliness.

Individualism finds its roots in the attempt to deny the reality and importance of human interdependence. One of the major goals of technology in America is to "free" us from the necessity of relating to, submitting to, depending upon, or controlling other people. Unfortunately, the more we have succeeded in doing this the more we have felt disconnected, bored, lonely, unprotected, unnecessary, and unsafe.[24]

Player Piano anticipates Slater's theory, for it clearly reveals the dangers of a utopia achieved by American technology.

Reed reminds us that Vonnegut is more concerned with the problems and actions of an entire society than with those of one man, and that Paul's story is used as a means to reveal a nightmare society of the future that is frighteningly similar to American society in the present. This idea best explains Vonnegut's deliberately neutral position at the novel's conclusion. Paul Proteus has neither succeeded nor failed in the revolution because his primary function was to reach an awareness of his own humanity. Paul argues that humanity's main business is to be good human beings rather than "appendages to machines, institutions, and systems."[25]

The main function of a "Proteus" is change, and change seems to be the primary concern of Vonnegut. Reed recognizes this element in Vonnegut's work when he states that " 'Forward March,' with its significant capitals, ends the book with an old clarion call, a positive note,"[26] but the phrase might also be little more than a statement of motion and direction for changes to come. Future changes are vital to continued existence regardless of their negative or positive effects. Both Proteus and humanity are mutable and symbolic of life, while the machines and the system are immutable and symbolize death—the ultimate loneliness.

This struggle between life and death reflected in the conflict of man versus machine continues to be important in Vonnegut's novels. In his disillusioning experience as a public relations man for General Electric from 1947 to 1950, he observed firsthand the loneliness and frustration that must logically evolve from twentieth-century man's surrender to his own technology. Vonnegut chooses the prose romance form to report that surrender, and the dichotomous nature of the romance gives us some understanding of how Vonnegut's use of this form accounts for his work's broad appeal to both intellectual and popular audiences. The revolutionary nature of the romance helps us to understand Vonnegut's choice of it to show change as life supporting. Vonnegut's fiction is both intellectual and proletarian in that it has attracted the attention and admiration of scholars and laborers alike. In a profession where sales measure success, his publishers report that his books are selling one million hardcover and five million paperback copies per year. The attraction of his work results from his ability to translate a vague but immense dissatisfaction with our society's various incarnations into understandable human experience. In short, as man retreats from his self-created confusion of a technological society, he finds some fascination in his own loneliness. Vonnegut examines that loneliness through the romance form as an appropriate expression of the human need for incessant change. This may explain his frequent use of science fiction as an "imaginative golden age in time or space" where such change may realistically occur. Such is the setting of *Player Piano,* which Reed has dubbed the "Nostalgic Future."

Vonnegut blends the elements of romance with characteristics of satire and irony while using the devices of humor and symbol. Perhaps the best example of Vonnegut's use of symbol and irony is the player piano from which the book's title comes. Reed has noted that this instrument is an effective symbol because it is one of the oldest and most innocently amusing machines designed to replace man's mechanical skill. He further observes the obvious connection between the hole-punched piano rolls and the tape-recorded movements of old Rudy Hertz, the lathe operator who was replaced by a self-controlled machine.[27] Tony Tanner, however, best reveals the truly ominous nature of this symbol through definition of both player and piano: "A piano player is a man consciously using a machine to produce aesthetically pleasing patterns of his own making. A player piano is a machine which has been programmed to produce music on its own, thus making the human presence redundant."[28] This underlying irony of Vonnegut's symbolism is made explicit through Rudy Hertz's statement to Paul Proteus in the Homestead Bar as both watch the antique instrument play "Alexander's Ragtime Band." The sight of the keys moving up and down makes Rudy "feel kind of creepy," as if he could "almost see a ghost sitting there playing his heart out."[29] The ghost to be seen is the man of the future displaced by automation.

Another important symbol is the cat that Paul finds in the Ilium Works and takes with him to the malfunctioning Building 58, where it is swallowed up by a robot sweeper. The cat somehow manages to escape alive from Building 58 only to die atop the electrified wires of the security fence. Reed interprets this as a kind of triumph in the midst of defeat and views the cat as symbolic of animal life in a machine world, but the incident can also be seen as Vonnegut's serious suggestion that death is the only escape from the automated trap that man has created for himself. His last statement describing the cat's death is prophetic: "She dropped to the asphalt—dead and smoking, but outside."[30] There is no triumph and there is no defeat, for this sterile, mechanized world does not allow for any such creative or novel ideals. It provides for life within the system and death outside of it. With such limited freedom it is no wonder that the Shah's language has no equivalent for the phrase "average man" but must translate "citizen" as *Takaru* or "slave." Vonnegut's irony may seem a bit gimmicky here when we realize that *Takaru* reversed is "urakat" (u-r-a-kat), but his questioning of the real danger of technology is profoundly serious.

The most complex name in the book is that of the protagonist, and it is difficult to understand how so many critics have failed to notice that Vonnegut has used it very shrewdly on three distinct levels of meaning. While most have commented upon Proteus as the name of a mythical Greek god noted for abrupt changes of appearance or form at will, they have largely ignored the name's underlying implication of the character's uncertain search for identity or self-definition. David Goldsmith seems to be the only critic who has recognized the name as a deliberate reference to Charles Proteus Steinmetz, a real electrical engineeer and inventor born in Germany in 1865 but forced to emigrate because of his socialistic editorials. He came to America in 1889 and worked for the General Electric Company from 1893 until his death in 1923. A true visionary, Steinmetz authored books on such widely divergent topics as *Engineering Mathematics* (1910), and *America and the New Epoch* (1916).[31] This level of meaning for the name of Proteus nearly gives *Player Piano* the appearance of a roman à clef. Vonnegut's ingenuity does not end there, however, for the given name Paul also has multiple levels of meaning. As a figurehead apostle of the Ghost Shirt rebellion, Paul reminds us of the Biblical Paul, originally a Jew, Saul, who experienced conversion to Christianity. This allusion is a further implication of the search for self-understanding. The most ironic meaning of the full name of the protagonist is found if we accept the Latin definition of Paul ("little") and the change aspect implicit in Proteus. Since the plot of the book concludes with a revolution that has failed to alter the system, its messiah Paul Proteus—"little change"—is symbolic of the results, which seems to be a principal statement Vonnegut is making. In short, Vonnegut is dealing with the failure of the human ego in crisis with society in *Player Piano*, and the man versus machine theme is his means of explaining individual loneliness. The complex "machine" here is more than a mechanical system, it is the intricate complexity of American society.

NOTES

1. Kurt Vonnegut, Jr., *Wampeters, Foma & Granfalloons: (Opinions)* (New York: Dell, Delta, 1975), p. 1.

2. Ibid.

3. Peter J. Reed, *Writers for the 70s: Kurt Vonnegut, Jr.* (New York: Paperback Library, 1972), p. 24.

4. Kurt Vonnegut, Jr., *Player Piano* (1952; rpt. New York: Avon, 1967), ch. 1, p. 9.

5. Ibid., ch. 1, p. 9.

6. EPICAC is Vonnegut's advertent transposition of Ipecac (an emetic), which humorously emphasizes the computer's ability to vomit back information, but only that information fed into it by its human operators. There is implicit irony in the "EPIC" portion of the computer's name, an irony which underscores the machine's lack of response to anything heroic while also suggesting the imposing aspect of EPICAC XIV as the ruler of an automated America.

7. Vonnegut, *Player Piano*, ch. 11, p. 116.

8. Max F. Schulz, *Black Humor Fiction of the Sixties* (Athens, OH: Ohio University Press, 1973), pp. 57-58.

9. Vonnegut, *Player Piano*, ch. 34, p. 313.

10. Ibid., ch. 35, p. 320.

11. James M. Mellard, "The Modes of Vonnegut's Fiction," in *The Vonnegut Statement*, ed. Jerome Klinkowitz and John Somer (New York: Dell, 1973), p. 187.

12. Philip E. Slater, *The Pursuit of Loneliness* (Boston: Beacon Press, 1970), pp. 12-13.

13. Vonnegut, *Player Piano*, ch. 32, p. 296.

14. Slater, *Pursuit of Loneliness*, p. 15.

15. Vonnegut, *Player Piano*, ch. 35, p. 320.

16. Ibid., ch. 34, pp. 314-15.

17. Ibid., ch. 35, p. 320.

18. Slater, *Pursuit of Loneliness*, p. 5.

19. Vonnegut, *Player Piano*, ch. 11, p. 117.

20. Ibid., p. 119.

21. Ibid., p. 120.

22. Reed, *Writers For the 70s*, p. 42.

23. Vonnegut, *Player Piano*, ch. 21, p. 212.

24. Slater, *Pursuit of Loneliness*, p. 26.

25. Vonnegut, *Player Piano*, ch. 32, p. 297.

26. Reed, *Kurt Vonnegut*, p. 51.

27. Ibid., p. 30.

28. Tony Tanner, *City of Words* (New York: Harper and Row, 1971), p. 182.

29. Vonnegut, *Player Piano*, ch. 3, p. 38.

30. Ibid., ch. 1, p. 21.

31. *Webster's Biographical Dictionary* (1951), "Charles Proteus Steinmetz."

10

PILGRIM'S PROGRESS: IS KURT VONNEGUT, JR., WINNING HIS WAR WITH MACHINES?

Thomas Hoffman does an excellent job in his essay earlier in this anthology discussing the theme of automation in Kurt Vonnegut's *Player Piano* (1952). He shows us that much of the success of Vonnegut's first negative utopia comes from the pervasiveness with which the machine is shown to have infiltrated society and robbed people of their sense of usefulness, meaning, and dignity. In the post-EPICAC era people have come to feel useless, their very souls having been hollowed of substance.[1] Spiritual and libidinal energies have been so totally regimented and perverted in mechanical activities that a manager, Garth, is described as standing in relation to the corporate image as a lover; and Anita, wife of hero Paul Proteus, is shown lying back in a "nest of control wires"[2] satisfied not so much by her husband's sexual attention as by the "social orgasm of, after . . . the system's love play, being offered Pittsburgh."[3]

Professor Hoffman suggests that in offering us warnings about the dehumanized future, not as it must necessarily be but as it surely would become if based on the runaway technology of the present, Vonnegut writes "more like a social scientist than a novelist," presenting us with "sociology expressed in fictional form."[4] We're shown that while the book's main theme is "machine-made loneliness" resulting from the protagonist's struggle for awareness and independence from machinelike controls, Paul's story is used more to highlight the problems and actions of an entire society than those of one man.[5] To illustrate the predominantly sociological character of the novel, Professor Hoffman reminds us of the tripartite division of Vonnegut's microcosmic American society which has been fragmented into hopelessly alienated parts in the name of simplified planning and production—the managers and engineers on one side of the river; the workers on the other; near the managers, the machines.[6]

Certainly Paul's particular plight—his isolation from all that had once given his life meaning: his job, his father, his wife, and his best friend— represents the plight of his society as a whole. Paul is intensely guilt-ridden, in fact, over being part creator of the sterile, unproductive lives of those little people for whom he professes a generalized love and whose certain hatred troubles him deeply. Just after we meet him, he is looking on unhappily at the mechanical hands and electric eyes and punch-press jaws of the machinery at the Ilium Works—machines that are no longer controlled by men but by other machines. The human loss most ominous to Paul because it mirrors his own condition is that like player piano keys, like puppets, the citizenry have become so regulated and standardized by the ruling technocracy that they themselves have become mindless pieces of machinery, unable to believe in anything better and hence no longer capable of human change or growth.

This is particularly the plight of the workers—of the Reconstruction and Reclamation Corps, or Reeks and Wrecks, and those relegated to mindless enslavement in the army—who have been mechanically determined to be unblessed with sufficiently high IQ and have been spat out by the great computer-god EPICAC XIV to the far side of the river, the area known as Homestead. Since the machines do all the hiring and firing and job assignments are almost always irrevocable, these people either exist in self-hatred and contempt for their enslavers (reconciling themselves to their lot as if cast in their roles by an act of God), or they commit suicide or anesthetize themselves to the pain of uselessness and alienation with clichés of well-being provided by governmental propagandists. Kroner, the High Priest of Industrial Efficiency, may extoll the wonders of the Second Industrial Revolution with its increase of production, but Ed Finnerty observes that drug abuse, alcoholism, and suicide are all up in direct proportion to the increase in automation.[7] Dr. Halyard may explain the splendors of American mechanization to the Shah of Bratpuhr, but the reader sees that the supposed beneficiaries of such mechanization have been swallowed up and regurgitated like Paul's cat early in the novel.

Vonnegut himself has said that his guiding purpose as an artist has been to serve as "canary-bird" in a coal mine[8]—as an alarm system to warn society of its technological dangers—so his role as social critic or as a writer of "sociological" novels is not to be denied. But there is another dimension in this novel—one personal and intensely psychological in nature—that explains more precisely the profound "loneliness" experienced by its protagonist Paul Proteus and which may come closer than Hoffman's explanation to helping us understand the author's long uphill struggle against the dehumanizing power of machines.

Before he can solve the larger social conflicts of the novel represented by the split between the managers and engineers and those who live across the river, Paul must first heal his own agonizingly divided soul. To Ed Harrison, a potential managerial defector like himself, Paul offers a warning: if Ed tries the stratagem of living partly on the job and partly in dreams he will be split "right up the middle" before he can decide which way to go. When Ed asks if something like this has happened to him, Paul answers in the affirmative.[9] There is hence a psychological as well as a political and sociological meaning to Paul's cry, "We must meet in the middle of the bridge."[10] Whether Paul will manage to find a bridge between *his* several selves—to develop the awareness and courage to follow his conscience and to act against the machinery that threatens to engulf him—is the main issue to be decided by the end of this novel. In fact, it is the most fundamental concern of every Vonnegut novel.

Vonnegut, who dubs himself a "magical lunatic," has been telling us for years that his "career has been about craziness," and that the basic plot of his fiction is the "losing and regaining" of his own "equilibrium."[11] "I have always thought of myself as an over-reactor," Vonnegut says, "a person who makes a questionable living with his mental diseases."[12] When asked about his work as personal therapy, he replied, "That's well known. Writers get a nice break in one way, at least: they can treat their mental illnesses every day."[13] If the author has indeed used his fiction to treat his *own* mental illness, the nature of that illness as it will be explored in this essay is best described in the novel *Mother Night* (1962). Referring to his hopelessly divided soul and contemplating suicide, Howard Campbell speaks of "a wider separation of my several selves than even I can bear to think about."[14] Elsewhere, after numerous hints of such a condition have accumulated, Campbell tells us how he has been able to cope with the world's horrors only "through that simple and widespread boon to modern mankind—schizophrenia."[15] It is of course much later in Vonnegut's career, at the end of the novel *Breakfast of Champions* (1973), that the author tells us in a dialogue with himself that he is afraid he will kill himself the way his mother did. Thinking of the world of his own invention, he mouths the word, "*schizophrenia*. The sound and appearance of the word had fascinated me for many years."[16] If, as Vonnegut tells us, *Breakfast of Champions* was the last of his therapeutic books, the last schizophrenic invention as well as the last session on the couch for the author, then *Player Piano* is surely the first—the first in which Vonnegut holds a sanity hearing for himself, for his characters, and for the bizarre world in which he tries to maintain an "equilibrium."

Early in *Player Piano*, Ed Finnerty feels something snap inside him and sits for hours with Paul's cocked gun in his mouth. "You think I'm insane?" he asks Paul. "You're still in touch. I guess that's the test," Paul replies.[17] Ironically, Finnerty, who has begun to rebel openly against the system of machines that threatens his sanity, worries that Paul is not more shaken by the unholy mechanistic society he helps administer. Actually Paul is less in touch with his surroundings and with himself than he or Finnerty suspects. Longing for a time when things were less impersonal and more human, he suffers frequently from depression, swigs regularly from a bottle of whiskey in his bottom desk drawer for solace, and speaks of being in need of a psychiatrist and of committing suicide. As he contemplates the emotional void in his marriage, he comes to suspect that his wife's feelings are shallow but considers that his suspicions are part of his sickness.[18] As he contemplates his sickness, Paul lives through one of the most revealing symbolic episodes in all of Vonnegut's work.

On the first page of the book we read of Paul's befriending of a small black cat. Wandering in the Ilium Works, the cat is caught and eaten by an automated sweeper. The machine spits the cat down a chute and into a freight car outside the factory. Momentarily it seems the cat will survive, but as Paul races desperately to help, the cat scrambles up the side of an electrically charged fence and, with a pop and a green flash, is sent sailing high into the air to fall "dead and smoking, but outside."[19]

The moral is obvious but nonetheless ominous. The omnipresent machinery of Paul's society is deadly to living things, and the possibility of escaping its influence is slight. But what Vonnegut shows us through the symbolic death of the cat is that Paul's sickness, his immense depression, is the result of fearing that his *own* fate is to be as terrible and inevitable as that of the cat with which he identifies, that is, that he will be gobbled up by the ominpresent emotional vacuum cleaner, the corporate personality. At one point, for instance, Paul sees himself as if overwhelmed by a tidal wave, deluged like the toy boat he watches moving toward its doom in the "dark, gurgling unknown" of the sewer.[20] However vaguely sensed by Paul at first, his fear of being absorbed forever into the dehumanizing machinery of the corporation has been contingent in his mind upon accepting the Pittsburgh job, the most important position in his field and the sole, maniacal obsession of his wife Anita. As Anita is badgering him once again about showing more enthusiasm for the Pittsburgh promotion, he begins to reflect upon her shallowness and his own loss of interest in everything around him. Hanging up the telephone, he puts his head down and closes his eyes. When he opens them again, they are fixed directly on the dead cat in the basket.[21]

Ironically, Paul's instinctive aversion to the pervasive mechanization of life around him—the replacement of people with machines and the mechanical behavior of people who have been turned into machines—has driven him into an emotional vacuum that is just as defeating as the misery he seeks to escape. He recognizes that any attempt at achieving an emotional life for himself is pure pretense, that shows of affection are just shows, mechanical and insincere. He knows, for instance, that his reactions to his wife are mere reflex.[22] (Anita, too, has reduced marriage to a set of mechanical conventions, as when she manipulates expressions of warmth from Paul whenever she feels him pulling free of her influence.) And when Paul is with Finnerty he only pretends to share the man's emotional enthusiasms, while observing that Finnerty uses words such as *love* and *affection* to describe his feelings, words Paul can never bring himself to use.[23] Even when Finnerty makes his commitment to helping the people on the opposite side of the river, Paul finds himself without any sort of appropriate feeling for Finnerty's important announcement.[24] When Finnerty accuses him of being afraid to live, Paul acknowledges that he is indeed without belief of any kind.[25]

From within his self-spun cocoon, Paul lacks sufficient awareness, conviction, and moral strength either to continue playing the role convincingly of loyal and happy plant manager, fellow high priest with Kroner and Baer to the great god EPICAC, or to repudiate this higher calling passed on to him by his father and openly resist the system that threatens to destroy his will to live. Either prospect leaves him feeling like what he eventually becomes: "an unclassified human being," lonely and dispossessed.[26] It is partly in this sense that Paul comes by that agonizingly divided soul, that separation of the several selves that eventually causes Howard Campbell of *Mother Night* to commit suicide. The problem is that despite his inherent resistence to, as he puts it, "carrying out directions from above," Paul's drive toward selfhood is always counterbalanced by a moral paralysis brought on by institutional conditioning and a fatalistic philosophy.[27] We find him continuously relinquishing his will to others, reacting like the keys on the player piano, or else allowing a partially awakened conscience to be lulled easily to sleep.[28]

As the son of America's greatest industrial leader, the virtual founder of modern mechanization, Paul has been so long programmed to accept and perpetuate the divine right of machinery that he wonders at his own unnaturalness at being disgruntled with the system. He even longs for an overwhelming fervor like that of his dead father and Kroner, for the unquestioning faith that his is indeed a golden age. Occasionally Paul finds himself mindlessly assimilating the clichés of progress and *esprit de corps* mouthed so easily by Kroner, Baer, and Shepherd, by Mom and Anita. He tries hard to believe in the sanctity of machines and industrial organization and even begs to be refuted as he pours out his misgivings to his surrogate father, Kroner.[29] The point is, however, that no refutations are needed. The corporate will, however detestable to Paul, is stronger than his own; when Paul stands before Kroner he senses that he is actually in the presence of his father and powerless to resist the older man.[30] Even Anita, for whom things are relevant or irrelevant, moral or immoral, only as they secure or hinder social advancement, is capable of controlling Paul's behavior. To insure that Paul gives the proper corporate responses during a social outing with

his boss, Anita prepares him an outline. Paul does not read it, but when
Kroner mentions the Pittsburgh job to him, Paul responds as he thinks
Anita wants him to.[31]

Paul's potentially fatal mistake is deciding to play dead, to muffle the cry
of conscience with a variety of anesthetizing devices. If the conflict of
divided loyalties becomes overwhelming, he will withdraw from it in the
fashion described by his young friend, Edmond L. Harrison. That is, he will
crawl into the nearest suitable womb.[32] And so it is no surprise that when
Anita presses him about the Pittsburgh job, Paul curls up tighter and tighter
"in the dark, muffled womb" of his bed.[33]

Ironically it is Anita, whose love he finds so detestably mechanical, who
provides the major opiate for Paul's uneasy conscience. Her sexuality
becomes his only enthusiasm in life; he feels the "drugging warmth" of her
bosom and feels himself to be merging his "consciousness" with that of his
wife.[34] Once, having made a decision to quit, he asks Anita whether she is
ever bothered by conscience. She chides him playfully and pulls him down
to kiss her, but then play turns into something very much like hypnotism: "I
don't want my little boy to worry. You're not going to quit, sweetheart.
You're just awfully tired."[35] Paul feels as if he is drugged, surrenders to
fatigue and thinks of Edgar Allan Poe's "Descent into the Maelström" as
"he [gives] himself over" to the unfailing rhythm of sex.[36]

Paul finds another comforter and blinder in the fantasy world portrayed
in adventure books, into which he tries literally to withdraw. Described as
retreating behind "the privacy of his closed eyelids,"[37] he identifies with
romantic pioneer heroes who depend not on machines but on basic cunning
and physical strength for survival.[38] Paul tries to make his fantasy real by
purchasing an isolated, backwater farmhouse he thinks Anita will love. But
when she only finds it hideous and thinks of appropriating its quaint con-
tents to her own home, Paul's dream is quickly aborted.[39]

Paul's moral paralysis, his will-lessness, is reinforced by something even
more threatening to his sanity than his tactical withdrawal from society: a
genuinely fatalistic belief that the soulless mechanization of his life is a
matter of historic inevitability. Even as Paul wonders whether he has the
capital to stop being a pawn of history, he cannot imagine that same history
having "led anywhere else."[40] He views himself as so inescapably a part of
the machinery of society and history that he can move in one direction only
to determine his own identity.[41] In this way he rationalizes his joyless life
with Anita, deciding that whatever her failings she is his inevitable fate, to
love as well as he can.[42] Even at the end of the book, we find Paul not very
different from Ewing J. Halyard wondering about the mechanics of being
human, "mechanics far beyond the poor leverage of free will."[43]

Given Paul's record of moral evasion, it is not surprising that he should
so easily fall prey to such paralyzing fatalism. The philosophic consolations
of fatalism can be devilishly alluring since one need not struggle to be aware

of or to change that which is believed unchangeable. It is a particularly deadly form of self-loss because by such paralysis the individual may well perpetuate his own doom at the hands of whatever totalitarian entity attempts to consume him. This, in fact, is precisely Paul's fate at the conclusion of *Player Piano*. At the Meadows—two weeks of superficial camaraderie and brotherhood during which loyal members of the corporation are mass-produced—Paul's disgust reaches an all-time high, helped along when he is told to turn informer on an old friend. His experience at the Meadows leads him to his eventual resolve never again to serve as an appendage to machines, institutions, or systems.[44] But while Paul is incomplete as a blindly loyal corporation personality, he is outside of its malevolent embrace a fragmented person who wants desperately to get a sense of the world as a gestalt.[45] As a result, Paul renounces one lobotomizing master for another. As the proposed messiah for the Ghost Shirt Society, a society potentially as totalitarian as the one it seeks to replace, Paul is used impersonally as a mere name, a front for the organization, and his effort to resist assimilation into the collective will of the group is futile. Finnerty tells him he need only keep out of sight while everything is done for him. Now that he belongs to history he does not matter as an individual, and he need accept responsibility for nothing.[46]

Once again, Paul's identity is successfully neutralized, and he meets the problem in the same old way, drugging himself to reality and relinquishing his will to others. Lasher notes that Paul will "do nicely," suggesting that Paul is exactly pliant enough, suggestible enough, to serve the revolution's need for a robotlike figurehead.[47] When Paul is described as dreaming only of pleasant things under the influence of the drug given him by the Ghost Shirt Society, the larger significance of the description is obvious: Paul is once again choosing comfort over integrity.[48]

At the novel's end, Paul notes that Lasher was the only one who had not lost touch with reality and, more portentously, that it was he, Paul, who had been the one perhaps most out of touch, ready to relinquish his will to others who had easy answers to his problems.[49] So by Paul's own test at the beginning of the book he is more insane than not, "disembodied, an insubstantial wisp."[50] Yet while the outer revolution in *Player Piano* is as doomed as Paul's cat, culminating in a blind orgy of indiscriminate wreckage and the inclination to put the same old system back together again, there are hints that Paul may yet be able, with the proper awareness and courage, to put his distintegrated self and world together again too. The denouement to Paul's psychodrama is still to come, but not in *Player Piano*—not until the dialectical struggle between hope and despair that begins with Paul is worked out and through such extensions of the Vonnegut hero as Malachi Constant, Howard Campbell, Eliot Rosewater, Billy Pilgrim, and Kilgore Trout.

Thomas Hoffman seems right in viewing the ending of *Player Piano* as affirmative in that it "reassures us that humans will continue to rebel against this prisonhouse of their own creation despite the failure of *this* rebellion, *this* man, or *this* period of history."[51] Yet while it is doubtlessly again a "political, economic, and technological" prisonhouse against which Paul Proteus struggles for autonomy (a social conflict), the more immediate danger against which Vonnegut warns is profoundly psychological in nature. Paul will remain irresolute in his dualistic commitment to and against tyrannical systems of control ("split . . . right up the middle") as long as he continues to muffle the cry of conscience and to relinquish his will to others. It is this personal crisis, the self-induced neutralization of Paul's ego, that seems best to account for the lack of resolution at the novel's end.

If the lack of resolution spoken of by Hoffman and others is indeed a consistent characteristic of Vonnegut's novels, it may well be that non-resolution of man-versus-self or man-versus-machine conflicts is an expression of the author's own state of mind as he attempts to work out in fictional form the schizophrenic dilemma mentioned earlier. No resolutions are possible until Vonnegut has found some way to achieve an equilibrium based on the belief that people can successfully resist becoming appendages to machines or, as is said of Billy Pilgrim and people in general in *Slaughterhouse-Five* (1969), "the listless playthings of enormous forces."[52] Just as Ernest Hemingway and Joseph Heller acknowledged using their typewriters as psychoanalysts to work out the psychologically damaging effects of war, so Vonnegut, a traumatized survivor of the World War II Allied bombing of Dresden, may have used his writing as a way of purging himself of the terrors of war and adjusting to a postwar world just as absurd in its suffering and destructiveness as the war itself. Thus it is that in one novel after another we witness the sometimes despairing, sometimes hopeful efforts of Vonnegut's fragmented protagonists to put their disintegrated selves together again—to resist the various forms of moral escapism that paralyze the creative will of Paul Proteus and to achieve a wholeness of spirit.

It is very likely that the therapeutic purging of the Billy Pilgrim within himself is the process by which Vonnegut has become "better" (overcoming a nearly incapacitating pessimism),[53] and that in *Breakfast of Champions*, the novel that Vonnegut says was originally meant to be one with *Slaughterhouse-Five*, that therapy reaches fruition. The possibility for change, even growth, implicit in Paul Proteus's name is finally born out. Even a brief look at Billy Pilgrim's mental state reveals a classic case of schizophrenia. The shock of war coupled with tragically disillusioning childhood experiences has clearly crippled Billy's ability to lead any kind of normal life—to love or believe in people, work, society, or God and has led consequently to withdrawal from human contact into a world of bizarre fantasy. Not that Billy's suffering, his fear of annihiliation, is based on delusion. His withdrawal is a natural reaction to the very real terrors of his world and ours.[54] Billy's tragedy is that in trying to live by the dubious wisdom that comes to him by way of his Tralfamadorian hallucinations, he condemns himself to the same kind of mental "prisonhouse" that claims Paul Proteus and so many other Vonnegut protagonists.

To understand that the personal process of purgation and renewal is central to Vonnegut's intentions, one must fully appreciate Thomas Wymer's view of those ludicrous-looking extraterrestrials in *Sirens of Titan* (1959) and *Slaughterhouse-Five* who kidnap Billy Pilgrim and appear to teach him wonderful ways to cope with suffering and death.[55] Disputing the interpretation that the Tralfamadorians speak for the author, Wymer shows that Vonnegut's purpose is to warn us *against* the perils of fatalism rather than to affirm such a philosophy. To confuse Vonnegut with Billy Pilgrim or to mistake the author as a defeatist by believing that the insidiously addictive ideas that come to invade Billy's mind are Vonnegut's own represents a dreadful misreading of Vonnegut's work and a misunderstanding of the affirmative thrust of his career as a whole.[56]

In contrast to the general view that it is the wisdom of Tralfamadore, centered upon the belief that human events are inevitably structured to be the way they are, that allows both Billy and the author to adjust to their traumatic memories of Dresden, the fact is that the Tralfamadorian view of reality is the very antithesis of Vonnegut's position that artists should be treasured as alarm systems—specialized cells for giving warning to the body politic—and as biological agents of change. The Tralfamadorians eventually blow up the universe while experimenting with new fuels for their flying saucers. They do not improve Billy's vision; Billy's conversion to Tralfamadorian fatalism, OR FATAL DREAM ("Tralfamadore" by anagram), assures his schizophrenic descent into madness. Caged in a zoo, turned into a puppet for the entertainment of mechanical creatures whose own world is both physically and morally sterile, and seduced into renouncing whatever vestige of free will he has left, Billy Pilgrim becomes the very embodiment of what Vonnegut has warned against for years. Insulated from pain, Billy has simply abdicated his humanity, trading his dignity and integrity for an illusion of comfort and security, and becoming himself a machine.[57]

Vonnegut tells us that Billy sees his withdrawal from the real world as "a screen," or what in psychiatry is called a "mask," a deliberately cultivated strategy of maintaining personal identity and freedom by withdrawing behind some sort of psychologically protective shield, and putting another, false, self forward.[58] The danger of such an inner, defensive maneuver is that, as in Billy's case and the case of other Vonnegut protagonists before him, the mask may become compulsive, and hence more a threat than a safeguard to the sanity it is meant to preserve. Withdrawal from an outer world of people and things into one of phantom fulfillment may lead to a total inability to act, and finally to a state of nonbeing and a desire for death. R. D. Laing likens such a fate to living in "a concentration camp," in which the imagined advantages of safety and freedom from the control of others are tragically illusory. By putting a "psychic tourniquet" on his ailing soul, Laing says, the individual's detached self develops a form of "existential gangrene."[59] In this light, it is no small coincidence that Billy Pilgrim should confuse a building on the grounds of his Dresden prison camp with a building on Tralfamadore, that one prison guard at both places should converse with Billy in English, that Billy should serve as an object of ridicule and entertainment for Dresdeners and Tralfamadorians alike, that similar objects—horseshoes, dentures, and so forth—should show up in both places, and that, finally, both places should come to an end by fire as a result of apocalyptic explosions. Vonnegut's point is that one hell holds Billy prisoner as surely as the other, but in the case of his Tralfamadorian fantasy, Billy himself holds the key to the locked doors of Bedlam inside his own mind.

If Billy Pilgrim, settling into his womblike Tralfamadorian environment, closing his eyes to any unpleasantness in the world, becomes more than ever the plaything of those enormous forces at work on him throughout his life, Kurt Vonnegut may have saved his own sanity through the therapeutic processes of art, climaxed by an act of symbolic amputation: the severing of the Billy Pilgrim within himself, poisoned with existential gangrene. That this is as much Kurt Vonnegut's baptism by fire as it is the story of Billy's madness may be the overriding truth of *Slaughterhouse-Five*. Not only has Vonnegut shored up his own sanity by facing directly into the fires of Dresden (dancing his long-deferred "dance with death" without which he says no art is possible),[60] but he has, like Lot's wife, asserted his inviolable humanity and freed himself from the self-imprisoning fatalism of Tralfamadore. For Vonnegut knows that the Tralfamadorians are merely ourselves—an appropriate symbol for the mechanistic insanity of our own planet, an extension into the future of our own warlike globe. He knows too that with a little imagination and heart we can, like Salo in *Sirens of Titan*, dismantle our own self-imprisoning machinery and become whatever we choose to become.

No wonder after completing this process of cleansing and renewal Vonnegut said, "Well, I felt after I finished *Slaughterhouse-Five* that I didn't have to write at all anymore if I didn't want to. . . . I suppose that flowers, when they're through blooming, have some sort of awareness of some purpose having been served. . . . At the end of *Slaughterhouse-Five* I had the feeling that I had produced this blossom. . . . that I had done what I was supposed to do and everything was OK."[61]

If Vonnegut's "therapy" culminates in *Slaughterhouse-Five*, the full meaning of that therapy becomes clear in a novel that not only incorporates all the essential machine-themes of Vonnegut's previous works but that serves as nothing less than the spiritual climax to his life and career, *Breakfast of Champions*.

At age fifty, Vonnegut informs us that this book represents "crossing the spine of a roof—having ascended one slope"[62]—and that he is thus writing as an act of "cleansing" and renewal "for the very different sorts of years to come."[63] The result is a startlingly revealing pinnacle from which to view the major crises in the author's spiritual evolution—his own *Pilgrim's Progress*—and to measure the spiritual and artistic consequences of his torturous, uphill struggle to win the world back from machines. The first advantage that this pinnacle affords us is a panoramic view of the massive critical human problems that have resulted from the promiscuous overdevelopment and overemployment of machines before we have comprehended their social effects or learned how to deal with their wastes. We then take in an alarming picture of the pessimism that Vonnegut says overwhelmed him in later life—of his more embittered and cynical self that grew out of his fear that human beings were no better than robots in a machine-dominated world.[64] But the final view from Vonnegut's metaphorical rooftop is more profoundly startling and revealing than any we have glimpsed from this or any other vantage point in his work: that of spiritual transformation, of rebirth, in which the weary author attempts to cleanse himself of the poisons that had accumulated in his system from his battle with technology by turning his fictional world on its head, dismantling the familiar trappings of his literary cosmos, and waving good-bye forever to all his old characters, "setting them free."

In the story of Kago near the beginning of *Breakfast of Champions*, Vonnegut makes his most devastating statement about the destructive effects of machines upon men and nature. Replete with sobering doses of apocalypse and gallows humor, the world that Vonnegut envisions through Kilgore Trout is a dying, nearly uninhabitable civilization of rusting junkers out of gas which has turned the surface of the earth into an asphalt prairie, the atmosphere into poison gas, and the streams, rivers, and seas into sludge. Now even the automobiles, along with every form of animal and plant life, are threatened with extinction.[65] Kilgore Trout learns that the river in Midland City (whose art festival he is headed toward for a fateful meeting with his creator, Kurt Vonnegut) contains, along with a washing machine, a couple of refrigerators, several stoves, and an infinity of Pepsi-Cola bottles, a 1968 Cadillac.

Dwayne Hoover reads in Trout's *Now It Can Be Told* that the creator of the universe has programmed robots to abuse our planet for millions of years, so that it will be "a poisonous festering cheese" when he arrives.[66]

Vonnegut's readers get a similar message from the driver of the truck that takes Kilgore Trout to Midland City. From his perspective as an ex-hunter and fisherman the truck driver embraces the fatalistic view of Kilgore Trout about the nation's depleted environment. He thinks of the marshes and meadows of a hundred years earlier and laments that his truck is poisoning the atmosphere and that, in effect, he is committing suicide.[67]

Perhaps the most dramatic visual effects of the machine's power for despoliation are the planet's ravaged land surfaces. Vonnegut observes that the surface of West Virginia, "demolished by men and machinery and explosives in order to make it yield up its coal," is sinking into the holes dug into it. He suggests that human beings often perpetuate their own destruction with his comment that the destruction of West Virginia took place with the approval of all branches of the state government, "which drew their power from the people."[68]

As in *Player Piano*, it is part of Vonnegut's purpose in *Breakfast of Champions* to show that the cost of a machine-dominated world is as disastrous to the human spirit as it is to the environment. Like D. H. Lawrence before him, Vonnegut demonstrates with remarkable persuasiveness the connection between the modern world with its inhuman industrial empire and the impotent, hopeless, and neurotic life of its citizens. Such a deathly connection is dramatically evinced in the example of Midland City's primary spiritual attraction, the cathedral-like "Sacred Miracle Cave," the symbolism of which is obvious but nonetheless foreboding. The cave is a microcosm of a world whose emotional and spiritual realities have been grotesquely perverted by industrial pollution: the Sacred Miracle is nearly invisible now, we are told, though it was never easy to see.[69] The Sacred Miracle, a cross in the cathedral's ceiling, is a traditional, unifying and humanizing symbol for humanity. But the cave's pollution has engulfed the cross and turned its natural auras a sickly yellow, just as the spiritual reality represented by the statue of Moby Dick has been engulfed and debased. The underground stream passing through the Sacred Miracle Cave is polluted by industrial waste which has formed "bubbles as tough as ping-pong balls." Soon these bubbles will engulf Moby Dick and invade the Cathedral of Whispers, where thousands have been married, including Dwayne and other characters in the story.[70] The fact that the lives of those married in the cave have become horribly despiritualized, drab, and meaningless, and that these people have lost their will to live and love speaks profoundly of the blighting effect of industrial civilization on the human spirit.

As in *Player Piano*, machines have literally taken over human functions, rendering people obsolete and purposeless; but worse, gadgets and mechanical processes have come to interfere in otherwise humanizing and emotionally nourishing sexual interaction, further sterilizing and alienating individuals from one another. One character in the novel performs an amazing act of biological perversion by learning how to reproduce himself by putting some of his cells into chicken soup. Society's response is to keep chicken soup out of the hands of unmarried people. Dwayne Hoover and Kilgore Trout learn dejectedly that they can now get sexual satisfaction sans human partner, through mechanical, artificial devices. Trout is intrigued by the ease with which pornographic movie machines serve to satisfy baser human appetites.[71] For his part, Dwayne Hoover once saw a mail-order ad for a rubber penis-extender and, in the same brochure, "a lifelike rubber vagina for when he was lonesome."[72] It is little wonder that just as the decision is made to close out the despiritualized life of Sacred Miracle Cave by cementing it over, suicide should prove a tragically tempting solution to their poisoned lives for nearly everyone in the novel, including Kurt Vonnegut. The cave winds up smelling like athlete's foot, we are told; the characters fare no better.

Vonnegut sees that the corrupting processes of a machine world are circular and unending. A ravaged, automated, and polluted environment sterilizes and demoralizes the minds of the citizenry, which in turn instills soulless and regimented values into its institutions and cultural pursuits. These institutions in turn continue to exploit the land and subvert the individuality and emotional life of the people. Kilgore Trout observes ruefully that with no more ability to feel or think on their own than "grandfather clocks,"[73] the people of Midland City occupy themselves with the most mundane, brainless, and materialistic subjects and cultivate, in the name of culture, a reverence for the insipid and soulless junk of mass production that clutters their lives. Such programmed mindlessness serves to disfigure the land with garish billboards, pink flamingos, No Trespassing signs, motion picture theaters that show nothing but dirty movies, and such bland aesthetic fungoids as Kentucky Fried Chicken franchises, Burger Chefs, MacDonald's hamburger stands, and Holiday Inns.

What Vonnegut deplores about the people in Midland City even more than their soulless preoccupation with money, structures, travel, machinery, and other measurable things is that they all have clearly defined parts to play, and that they are almost passionately ready to relinquish their free will and human identity (hence to assume a machinelike existence) in order to satisfy those roles.[74] Such was the limitation of their imaginations, Vonnegut tells us, that they automatically imitated the thinking of their neighbors.[75] They would become agreeable, fully automated boobs, ready to conform to the most convenient mold, embrace the most cuckoo ideas, and adopt the most militant, antihumanistic poses, whether in the mistaken interests of survival or friendliness, or sometimes simply out of a lack of imagination to do anything better. Ignorant of and incurious about what designs, ends, or masters they were programmed to serve, the "robots" of Midland City—like the characters in Trout's *Now It Can Be Told*—became instant money-making machines, consuming machines, housekeeping machines, self-pitying machines, butchering machines, weeping machines, loving or hating machines, killing machines, and breeding machines. Like Trout's characters, they would adore infants and sex despite the fact that the planet was already desperately crowded with other programmed robots.[76] Kilgore Trout learns that Midland City's plasticized citizens are so perfectly conditioned to serving as cogs in the greater social machine of the community that even if someone stopped playing his or her role for a time—a clear indication of insanity—everybody went on imagining that he or she was living up to expectations.

Vonnegut becomes aware that it is the amazing ease with which even the most monstrous ideas infiltrate and take hold in the human and the frenzied energy people are willing to expend on behalf of those ideas that allow them to become enslaved so quickly by anonymous bureaucracies, computers, and authoritarian institutions. It is this knowledge, as we will see later, that becomes first the author's undoing and then his making as a writer devoted primarily to mental health. A case in point concerns the somewhat innocent but nonetheless insidiously addictive ideas that invade Dwayne Hoover's mind as he sits listening to the social propaganda on the radio in his Plymouth Fury. He learns about cheap health insurance, better performance for his car, and constipation. He is even offered a Bible in which the speeches of God and Jesus are printed in red capital letters, and a plant that eats disease-carrying insects. And all this data is stored in Dwayne's memory "in case he should need it later on. He had all kinds of stuff in there."[77]

It is programming of a more ominous sort—that which shapes and controls our proclivities for hating and killing—that appalls Vonnegut the most and against which he directs the brunt of his moral indignation. He speaks with humorous contempt, for instance, of those "robots" who act violently in the quest of such artificial and arbitrary lusts as gold, little girl's underpants, and wide-open beavers. But he reserves his ultimate condemnation for the most cuckoo ideas of all, those spurious ideals of national unity that convince people to turn themselves into meat machines to do the robot work of a few fabulously well-to-do people; or into homicidal maniacs, war machines, guaranteed to shoot rockets at and drop explosives on other human beings. It is the tragic susceptibility of people to anti-humanitarian proposals, argues Vonnegut, that has perpetuated the misery of those "who couldn't get their hands on doodly squat," and that has been responsible for the worst of America's sins, "slavery . . . genocide . . . criminal neglect. . . ."[78]

This returns us to the thematic center of Vonnegut's work, the message he has urged upon us for years. He sees as the great moral imperative of our age the need to combat the mindless conditioning processes that control and shape our more aggressive self-destructive drives, drives that have put us on a collision path with Armageddon. He combats these processes first through massive resistance in the form of open displays of contempt, and second by constantly asking painful questions about the nature of the information that is fed into us. We must guard ourselves, he asserts, not only against the organizational machines of political, economic, and military power structures (who attempt to subvert free will and individual autonomy) but also against any totalitarian entity or theory that undermines the individual's sense of control over and responsibility for his own destiny and that of the planet, including all theories of philosophic or religious determinism, historical determinism, and psychological, genetic, or chemical determinism.[79]

We should notice that Vonnegut's solution to a dehumanized machine-world differs significantly from that of such other antitechnology writers as D. H. Lawrence, Ernest Hemingway, William Faulkner, John Steinbeck, and Norman Mailer, all of whom believe, as ardent primitivists, that the machine's corruption of man's individuality, spontaneity, and general emotional well-being should be reversed by throwing off the trappings of civilization and retreating to a golden age in the past, particularly by getting back into a natural, organic, nonmechanical relationship with the land. Conversely, Vonnegut admonishes us that our only hope for salvation is by intelligently and humanely directing our course into the future. He would have us move *up* the evolutionary ladder, not *down*, questioning though not always condemning mechanical and material change, using our brains to determine when such change is humanly valuable, when destructive, and to learn to act more compassionately toward one another.[80]

Vonnegut knows only too well the uphill nature of his struggle to move us along the evolutionary ladder to more sane and rational behavior, and has to battle his own despair along the way. The problem, he says in *Breakfast of Champions*, is that we humans train ourselves to be "agreeing" machines instead of "thinking" machines. The women in Midland City do not use their minds very much because they fear making their friends uncomfortable. Safety and comfort come first for them.[81] They are like the female rabbit in Trout's *The Smart Bunny*, who becomes so convinced that her mind is useless that she views it as some kind of tumor.[82] Another woman is satirized for her blind, mechanical loyalty to her lover. When she protests "You're my *man*" repeatedly, we are told that means she is willing "to agree about anything" with Dwayne, and "to do anything for him . . . to die for him," and so forth.[83]

Trout, in one of his own sardonic tales of humanity's suicidal tendencies, registers his despair in the face of seemingly unending human stupidity by portraying earthlings who value friendship over thought, who are designed not for wisdom but for friendliness.[84]

I mentioned earlier that the view from Vonnegut's metaphorical rooftop in *Breakfast of Champions* takes in far more than his panoramic portrayal of the machine's abuses of men and nature or his proposals for reform. Vonnegut also invites us to contemplate a portrait of his more embittered and cynical Trout-self, that "unhappy failure" who represents all the artists who searched for truth and beauty without finding "doodly-squat!"[85] Although Vonnegut happens to be describing his fictional counterpart Kilgore Trout in this instance, their lives are in many ways so similar as depicted in this novel that what is said about one often applies to the other. Trout is given an iron will to live but a life not worth living.[86] He is given Vonnegut's social conscience and artistic goals but a pessimism so great that it negates his artistic mission and vitiates his moral zeal. The most unsettling of these parallels in a commonly shared fate is that Trout is eventually given the knowledge that he is a programmed writing machine whose miserable life is controlled solely by his author and who has succeeded only in wreaking psychological and emotional violence upon his readers rather than in reforming or uplifting them. Trout certainly has harmed some of his readers by infusing them with his own pessimistic belief that human beings are no better than robots in a meaningless world; Vonnegut seems to fear having done similar evil.

We learn that Trout's idea of the purpose of human life and, presumably, of his own artistic mission has been to act as the eyes, ears, and conscience of God, but that years of neglect and a growing sense of life not worth living have made him temperamentally unfit for the task.[87] But he has given up caring seriously about what he writes because the world pays so little attention to him; he has even come to consider himself invisible and his ideas harmless, mere bulk for pornographic books and magazines put out by hardcore publishers who consequently pay him doodly-squat. He laughs now at attempts to reform the world, believing the whole mess futile. Kilgore Trout, Vonnegut says, would have sneered when he was a younger man at a "brotherhood" sign posted on the rim of a bomb crater, but his mind no longer harbors ideas about how things should be on Earth as compared with how they are.[88] Trout, in fact, has been turned into a proper Tralfamadorian, believing there is only one way for Earth to be—the way it is. Hence Trout reacts with bitter irony to the coordinator of the Midland City Arts Festival who implores him to bring humanizing new truths and hopeful songs to awake and restore the spiritually dead of his town. "Open your eyes!" exclaims Trout. "Do I look like a dancer, a singer, a man of joy?"[89] One is compelled to think of the cartoon drawing of Vonnegut at the end of the novel, a Vonnegut whose baleful countenance sheds a lonely tear.

Trout documents his lost faith and lost utopian zeal to the truck driver who gives him a lift to the arts festival. He says that he used to be a conservationist who bemoaned the killing of eagles from helicopters "and all that," but that he gave it up. Now when a tanker fouls the ocean, killing millions of birds and fish, he laughs and says " 'More power to Standard Oil,' or whoever it was dumped it." He realized, he tells the driver, that since God was no conservationist, it was a sacrilegious waste of time for anyone else to be one. "[E]ver see one of His volcanoes . . . tornadoes . . . tidal waves?" asks Trout. "That's God, not man."[90]

The unavoidable fact is that Trout knows that he has been transformed by his eternal disappointment into a harbinger of doom and that he has brought only suffering and desolation to those around him and to his readers. Vonnegut's narrator tells us that the pessimism that overwhelmed Trout in later life "destroyed his three marriages," and drove Leo, his son, away from home.[91] (A reading of Mark Vonnegut's autobiographical account of his own severe emotional illness, diagnosed as acute schizophrenia, in *The Eden Express* [1975] suggests more than a casual relationship between his father's work and his particular emotional dilemma.) But just as catastrophic is Trout's awareness that his inability to write about anything other than the triumphs of the machine over the human spirit has poisoned the minds of his readers by infecting them with his own disillusionment and cynicism.

It is through the character of Dwayne Hoover that Trout discovers that his pessimism has been turning his readers into monsters. It is true that Hoover had been in bad shape due to bad chemicals before he wandered into the demoralizing sphere of Trout's influence by reading Trout's science fiction novel *Now It Can Be Told*. He was already a soulless victim of Midland City's machine-ridden culture, owner not only of the city's Pontiac agency and a piece of the Holiday Inn, but of three Burger Chefs and five coin-operated car washes. That in itself causes incipient insanity. But it is nevertheless Trout's book that gives Dwayne's craziness "shape and direction"—that turns him into a homicidal maniac, in fact, by planting the idea in his head that people are nothing more than machines, incapable of thinking, feeling, making choices, worrying and planning, and so on, but that perhaps he alone of all human beings has free will and hence the need to figure things out.[92] The prospect of being the only nonmachine on the planet is so unbalancing that the only thing Hoover figures out is that if everyone around him is an unfeeling machine, he might as well treat them as inhumanly as he pleases. He subsequently embarks on a rampage that sends eleven people to the hospital.

It seems unmistakable that, through the example of poor Dwayne Hoover, Vonnegut is dramatizing his own fears about the negative spiritual repercussions of his work on his readers. Trout's inadvertent mind poisoning of Hoover surely measures the degree of demoralization the author feels his own oftentimes despairing vision of a robot-populated world has had on those who read his books. But more personally revealing of the damaging consequences that have resulted from his long and enervating battle with machines is Vonnegut's use of Trout's dilemma to depict the effect of his work on his own mind. Just as Trout's crippling pessimism served to vitiate his moral energy and humanistic zeal and thus to negate his artistic mission, Vonnegut suggests that a similarly incapacitating despair prevented him from carrying out with sufficient vigor his own guiding purpose as an artist, to serve as an alarm system to warn society of its technological abuses and dangers to man and nature.

If we had not gotten the message of Vonnegut's troubled, dual orientation through previous novels or through obvious parallels to Trout, the author tells us directly that his mounting fear and despair actually made him ill—that his machine-induced nightmares were dreadful enough, in fact, to result in a state of supressed schizophrenia that led him to contemplate suicide (his mother's fate) as a solution. He was driven into a void, "my hiding place when I dematerialize," to distance himself from potentially overwhelming horrors.[93] Twin forces, which we may assume are those of optimism and pessimism struggling for control of his creative imagination, were at work in his soul, he says. But they balanced one another and can-celled one another out, creating a kind of sterile ambivalence, or spiritual stalemate, out of which either irresolution or nihilism emerged as the dominant effect.[94] He went to Midland City, Vonnegut says, "to be born again. And Chaos announced that it was about to give birth to a new me. . . ."[95]

One force in what Vonnegut chooses to call his "pre-earthquake condition" was the conclusion that there is nothing sacred about himself or others, that all people are essentially machines fated to suffer endless collisions with one another, and that hence his life might be regarded as ridiculous.[96] This force, Vonnegut concludes, turned him into a writing machine,[97] which wrote about these hapless collisions, which were no more sacred than a Pontiac, mousetrap, or South Bend Lathe.[98] It is this oppressive force, he indicates, that by placing him on a par with his own robotlike creator programmed him to be a mindless instigator of a world of suffering and despair in which he was compelled to fashion the character of Kilgore Trout to bear the brunt of his own cosmic misery and futility. He has fractured his own mind, the character Vonnegut tells Trout, and he observes with self-deprecation that he has been caught up in an endlessly circular process of demoralization. As his creator has passed bad ideas and chemicals down to him, he has passed them on to Trout and Trout transferred them to Hoover. Trout's situation, Vonnegut's narrator concludes, to the extent that he was a machine, was "complex, tragic, and laughable."[99]

While this recognition that a large part of him is dead machinery casts a huge pall over Vonnegut's sense of himself as a writer in control of his life and work, it also ironically proves his salvation. For the very act of recognition itself suggests the presence of an imaginative faculty capable of resisting subversion by the machine within and machines without. Vonnegut comes to see this awareness according to the vision of Rabo Karabekian, as an "unwavering band of light," a sacred, irreducible living force at the core of every animal.[100] This epiphany sets in motion the essential drama of this book and perhaps of all Vonnegut's work: his spiritual rebirth, in which he determines to repudiate his former pessimism and in which the tragically repressed voice of hope in his work gains ascendancy over its negative counterpart. It is on such a healthy note that the "pre-earthquake condition" in his soul—the precarious balance between forces of optimism and pessimism paralleling the "spiritual matrix" of the cocktail lounge—is resolved, and Vonnegut tells of his transformation beginning as "a grain of sand crumbled," the process continuing until "spiritual continents began to shrug and heave."[101]

So the final view we are afforded of Vonnegut's arduous climb to his rooftop, the spiritual climax to his life and career, is his achievement of faith in the inviolability of awareness, especially human awareness, which, if properly cherished and cultivated, may yet redeem us and our planet from the technological horrors of the twentieth century. From this faith came his decision to cleanse and renew himself for the years ahead by performing the most daring and rebellious act of his writing life, the setting free of all his literary characters including the ominpresent Kilgore Trout. The symbolic liberation of Trout, which amounts to the author's repudiation of his most pessimistic voice, is a necessary act of exorcism that both prepares for and explains the author's rebirth. It liberates him from the pessimistic and cynical strain in his work that had constituted the critical emotional malady of his main characters, and it signifies his determination to disengage himself from a mechanical relationship with his own creator who programmed him to write as he has.[102] Vonnegut is connected to his creator in the same way that the characters he has created are connected to him: by "stale rubberbands," not "steel wires."[103] Only moral inertia had to be overcome before he could steer his fictional course, as well as his own life, in a more sane and vital direction. Whatever happens, he vows that he will serve no longer as anyone's puppet, nor put on puppet shows of his own.[104]

*   *   *

Does this mean that Kurt Vonnegut is winning his war with machines— a struggle both sociological and psychological in nature—that, as the quotation from Job in the front of *Breakfast of Champions* would seem to inform us, he has been tried and "come forth as gold"? I think that we can take the author at his word that if he was sick—if he indeed felt like that syphilitic machine standing underneath the "overhanging clock" that his "father designed. . . . eaten alive by corkscrews" and unable to fit together the world of self and the world of society[105]—he is "better now" and positively transformed by what he has been through. With the help of Phoebe Hurty, that mother surrogate who at the spiritual crossroads of his life at age sixteen helped him develop the necessary moral sense and faith in human improvement to survive the Great Depression, and with the help of his fiction as therapy, he has created for us and for himself that "humane harmony" lacking in the world around him. It is perhaps the great *personal* depression that Vonnegut has survived that *Breakfast of Champions* is most about—depression based upon a legacy of parental unhappiness, suicide, and the horrors of war, depression that turned him into a writing machine, writing as he was seemingly "programmed" to write.

We might well see Vonnegut now in the light shed upon Kilgore Trout by the director of the Midland City Arts Festival, who sees him as a "terribly wounded" man because he passed through the "fires of truth" and returned to tell us of them.[106] If Kurt Vonnegut has successfully negotiated his personal and artistic freedom from machinelike forces of control, he is not so naive as to suggest that freedom is ever absolute or that it solves all life's problems. Recall that Vonnegut wants to make his "head as empty as it was when I was born onto this damaged planet fifty years ago"—an effort to regain lost innocence. But life's ultimate clock, time itself, does not cooperate. Thus Kilgore Trout calls out twice at the novel's end, "*Make me young!*" Nor has Vonnegut exorcised totally the image of that saddened, worn-out father (whose voice becomes Trout's) or that of his suicide mother who babbled of love, peace, wars, evil, and desperation.[107] These two presences he associates with death and void to the very end of the book. Nevertheless the Phoebe Hurty in him has prevailed over the Philboyd Studge, the voice of hope over the voice of despair. And it may be that we have tasted the first fruit of the author's spiritual rebirth in his novel *Slapstick: Or Lonesome No More* (1976). His subject here is the same—the damaging excesses of the machine upon the human spirit—and he writes of desolated cities and the depletion of nature, of loneliness and spiritual death—but he writes in a voice that is more persistently affirmative than ever before. Dreaming up numerous improvements for mankind, and putting great emphasis on his old idea of the *karass* from *Cat's Cradle* (1963)—bringing together in *Slapstick* people without great wealth or powerful friends into membership in extended families whose spiritual core is common decency, Vonnegut embodies in this book his newly won optimistic faith that human beings can be anything we want to be. Because people are families rather than nations, even wars can become tolerable: the machines no longer fight and there are no massacres. As Kilgore Trout says in *Breakfast of Champions,* we are free now to build an unselfish society by devoting "to unselfishness the frenzy we once devoted to gold and to underpants."[108]

NOTES

1. Symbolized by the "ghost" at the player piano; see Kurt Vonnegut, Jr., *Player Piano* (1952; rpt. New York: Dell, 1975), ch. 3, p. 38.

2. Ibid., ch. 29, p. 270.

3. Ibid., ch. 13, p. 133.

4. Thomas Hoffman, "The Theme of Mechanization in *Player Piano*," in *Clockwork Worlds*, p. 125.

5. Ibid., pp. 126-32, 134.

6. Vonnegut, *Player Piano*, ch. 1, p. 9.

7. Ibid., ch. 5, p. 58.

8. Kurt Vonnegut, Jr., *Wampeters, Foma, and Granfalloons (Opinions)* (New York: Dell, Delta, 1975), p. 238. (All citations to *Wampeters* are to the *"Playboy* Interview," pp. 237-85, unless otherwise noted.)

9. *Player Piano*, ch. 23, p. 226.

10. Ibid., ch. 10, p. 114.

11. Vonnegut, *Wampeters*, Preface, p. xxi.

12. Ibid., p. 92.

13. Ibid., p. 283.

14. Kurt Vonnegut, Jr., *Mother Night* (1962; rpt. New York: Dell, Delta, 1972), ch. 32, p. 140.

15. Ibid., ch. 31, p. 136.

16. Kurt Vonnegut, Jr., *Breakfast of Champions* (1973; rpt. New York: Dell, 1975), ch. 18, p. 193.

17. Vonnegut, *Player Piano*, ch. 9, pp. 85-86.

18. Ibid., ch. 1, p. 25.

19. Ibid., pp. 20-21.

20. Ibid., ch. 18, p. 170; ch. 27, p. 253.

21. Ibid., ch. 1, p. 25.

22. Ibid., ch. 4, p. 38.

23. Ibid., ch. 9, p. 87.

24. Ibid., ch. 14, p. 139.

25. Ibid., p. 140.

26. Ibid., ch. 26, p. 239. The schizophrenic's dread of dissolution also typically manifests itself in terms of human nullification, for example, being disembodied, emptied out of an inner self, made vacuumlike, turned into a thing, a mechanism, a stone, an it. Particularly evident is the fear of being turned into someone else's thing. (See R. D. Laing, *The Divided Self* [Baltimore: Penguin, 1965], pp. 113, 75.) Paul of course experiences all of this. Much later, in *Breakfast of Champions*, Vonnegut writes directly about his "suspicion . . . that human beings are robots, are machines . . ." (Preface, p. 3); see also Epilogue, p. 289, and passim.

27. Vonnegut, *Player Piano*, ch. 12, p. 128.

28. Ibid., ch. 3, p. 38.

29. The implication surfaces numerous times in the novel that Paul suffers from an Oedipal complex—that his rebellion against organizational machinery is really a subconscious desire to destroy his father. Whether this implication is right or wrong, parent-child relationships in this and other Vonnegut works are conspicuously hostile, and such disharmony is typical in the life of a child who later on develops schizophrenia. In *Breakfast of Champions*, Vonnegut draws direct lines between a

father described as being of little help to him when the author was growing up, a mother "crazy as a bedbug" whose bizarre phobias and chaotic mind led to suicide (ch. 17, p. 181), and his own demoralized condition. In *Wampeters*, Vonnegut says that "One thing writing *Breakfast* did for me was to bring right to the surface my anger with my parents for not being happier than they were . . ." (p. 284). He states also that *"Breakfast of Champions* isn't a threat to commit suicide. . . . It's my promise that I'm beyond that now. . . . I used to think of it as a perfectly reasonable way to avoid delivering a lecture, to avoid a deadline, to not pay a bill, to not go to a cocktail party" (p. 283).

30. Vonnegut, *Player Piano*, ch. 5, p. 48.
31. Ibid., ch. 12, p. 128.
32. Ibid., p. 127.
33. Ibid., ch. 38, p. 266.
34. Ibid., ch. 13, p. 134.
35. Ibid., ch. 18, pp. 177, 178.
36. Ibid., p. 178. The schizophrenic person typically experiences a fear of loss of self—of identity or freedom—in the form of drowning imagery, of being engulfed or swallowed up. (See Laing, *Divided Self*, pp. 44-45.) Hence Paul at various times sees himself "deluged," overwhelmed by a "tidal wave"; like the boy's paper boat, he is sucked into the "certain destruction" of "the dark, gurgling unknown of the storm sewer" (ch. 22, p. 253). That Vonnegut should here and elsewhere in his fiction use the precise imagery and phraseology of schizophrenic case studies to portray the suffering of his characters suggests a more than casual insight into this condition. It is certainly significant that in *Breakfast of Champions* Kilgore Trout, during a particularly pessimistic moment, sees his destiny in terms of a toy rubber duck lying on the grate "over a storm sewer" (ch. 12, p. 103).
37. Vonnegut, *Player Piano*, ch. 29, p. 270.
38. Ibid., ch. 14, p. 143.
39. Ibid., ch. 10, p. 114.
40. Ibid., ch. 18, pp. 173-78.
41. Ibid., ch. 4, p. 41.
42. Ibid., ch. 13, p. 133.
43. Ibid., ch. 33, pp. 300-301.
44. Ibid., ch. 32, p. 297.
45. Ibid., ch. 18, p. 170.
46. Ibid., ch. 29, pp. 275, 276; ch. 30, p. 280.
47. Ibid., p. 272.
48. Ibid., pp. 270, 274.
49. Ibid., ch. 34, p. 314.
50. Ibid., ch. 13, p. 134.
51. Hoffman, p. 130.
52. Kurt Vonnegut, Jr., *Slaughterhouse-Five* (1969; rpt. New York: Dell, 1971), ch. 8, p. 164.
53. Vonnegut, *Breakfast of Champions*, ch. 18, p. 194.
54. From an interpretive standpoint, the most fascinating challenge to the reader of Vonnegut's "schizophrenic" novels comes when the distinctions between sanity and insanity, between the schizoid individual and the psychotic, are ambiguous. It is

difficult to say, for instance, when the schizoid manifestations of a character like Paul Proteus cross the borderline into psychosis—this is, when he can no longer control his split with reality and thus becomes a danger to himself and others. Additionally complicating is the fact that some of the author's seemingly mad characters are often far more sane that the society that labels them "crazy" for renouncing its own inhumane norms.

55. Thomas L. Wymer, "The Swiftian Satire of Kurt Vonnegut, Jr." in *Voices for the Future*, ed. Thomas D. Clareson (Bowling Green, OH: BGU Popular Press, 1976), vol. 1, pp. 238-62, esp. pp. 243-53, 259-62. See also Wymer's extension of this argument in "Machines and the Meaning of Human in the Novels of Kurt Vonnegut, Jr.," in *The Mechanical God: Machines in Science Fiction*, ed. Thomas P. Dunn and Richard D. Erlich (Westport, CT: Greenwood Press, 1982), pp. 41-52.

56. Some Vonnegut critics continue to make the mistake of calling Vonnegut a "pessimistic" or "defeatist" writer. In the most recent comprehensive study of contemporary literature, *The Harvard Guide to Contemporary American Writing*, Josephine Hendin contends that Vonnegut's pessimism adds up to a vision of people doomed by a machanical programming they cannot resist or change (Daniel Holfman, ed. [Cambridge, MA: Belknap Press, 1979]). Vonnegut, she says, uses the immense canvas of intergalactic space to magnify the pointlessness of human effort in any direction. Passivity, acceptance, resignation, and denial are offered as solutions to the sense of helplessness life engenders (pp. 257-58). Hendin fails to see that Vonnegut writes precisely to show the dangers of people's "burying themselves at the bottom of the pool, bottom of the earth, bottom of the universe" as a "defensive system against pain." Certainly Hendin misses the significance of Vonnegut's handling of schizophrenia when she says, "The themes of detachment and meaninglessness are celebrated in Vonnegut's fiction as devices for diminishing the emotional charge of painful experience" (p. 259). She did not recognize the point of Vonnegut's work as therapy by which the author battles against rather than surrenders to despair and succeeds in establishing a creative relationship with the world.

57. Vonnegut, *Slaughterhouse-Five*, ch. 5, p. 84.

58. Cf. the false self Paul Proteus hides behind for most of *Player Piano*. Paul hopes to avoid dealing with the present, facing potentially overwhelming moral decisions, by masking his true feelings about the system in public—pretending to be its faithful servant while secretly holding it in contempt and making plans to make his break at a time he thinks appropriate.

59. Laing, *Divided Self*, p. 133.

60. Vonnegut, *Slaughterhouse-Five*, ch. 1, pp. 21-22.

61. Vonnegut, *Wampeters*, pp. 280-81, 283.

62. Vonnegut, *Breakfast of Champions*, Preface, p. 4.

63. Ibid., Epilogue, p. 293.

64. Ibid., Preface, p. 3.

65. Ibid., chs. 2 and 3, pp. 26-29.

66. Ibid., ch. 23, p. 254.

67. Ibid., ch. 10, pp. 84, 85, 86.

68. Ibid., ch. 14, p. 119.

69. Ibid., ch. 13, p. 117.

70. Ibid., p. 116.

71. Ibid., ch. 7, pp. 68-69.

72. Ibid., ch. 15, p. 147.

73. Ibid., ch. 23, p. 254. References to clocks occur throughout the novel as they do throughout Vonnegut's work. The movie version of *Slaughterhouse-Five* (1972) follows the spirit of that novel by having a huge clock fall on Billy Pilgrim, suggesting that Billy is psychologically damaged by accepting a Tralfamadorian view of time, that is, time that is inflexible and predetermined. In *Breakfast of Champions*, the author describes human beings who have been turned into emotional and physical grotesques, standing directly beneath a "clock which my father designed" (Preface, p. 3). Even in as recent a work as Vonnegut's latest novel *Deadeye Dick* the narrator's childhood home, where the father warps his son, is structured like a "Roman *watch*tower" (New York: Seymour Lawrence/Delacorte, 1982, p. 8; my emphasis).

74. Vonnegut, *Breakfast of Champions*, ch. 15, p. 142.

75. Ibid., p. 136.

76. Ibid., ch. 23, pp. 254, 255.

77. Ibid., ch. 6, p. 62.

78. Ibid., ch. 19, p. 202; Epilogue, p. 293; and passim.

79. In Vonnegut's *Palm Sunday: An Autobiographical Collage*, the author questions the notion that schizophrenia is purely chemically induced rather than a result of warping life experiences (New York: Delacorte, 1981, pp. 241-42).

80. Vonnegut's play, *Happy Birthday Wanda June* (1970), contains his clearest statement of belief that humankind can become anything it wants to become (1971; rpt. New York: Dell, Delta [1971]). In contrast to Harold Ryan's assertion that he must act in accordance with a rigidly structured set of values ("That's the way this particular clock is constructed"), this Hemingway look-alike is turned from a man of violence into a man of peace (p. 116).

81. Vonnegut, *Breakfast of Champions*, ch. 15, p. 136.

82. Ibid., ch. 20, p. 232.

83. Ibid., ch. 15, p. 160.

84. Ibid., ch. 2, p. 28.

85. Ibid., ch. 3, p. 37.

86. Ibid., ch. 8, pp. 71-72.

87. Ibid., ch. 7, p. 67.

88. Ibid., ch. 12, p. 103.

89. Ibid., ch. 20, p. 233.

90. Ibid., ch. 10, pp. 84-85.

91. Ibid., ch. 3, p. 31.

92. Ibid., ch. 1, pp. 14-15.

93. Ibid., Epilogue, p. 294.

94. Ibid. ch. 19, pp. 219-20.

95. Ibid., p. 218.

96. Ibid., p. 219.

97. Ibid., ch. 20, p. 225.

98. Ibid., ch. 19, p. 220.

99. Ibid., Epilogue, p. 292; ch. 20, p. 225.

100. Ibid., ch. 19, p. 221.

101. Ibid., p. 219.
102. Ibid., Preface, p. 4.
103. Ibid., ch. 19, p. 202.
104. Ibid., Preface, p. 5.
105. Ibid., pp. 3, 5.
106. Ibid., ch. 20, p. 234.
107. Ibid., ch. 17, p. 181.
108. Ibid., ch. 2, p. 25.

MERGING MADNESS: *ROLLERBALL* AS A CAUTIONARY TALE

The film *Rollerball* (1975) was intended by its makers as a cautionary story, one that shows what could happen in a not-too-distant future "if this goes on."[1] What *this* is, here, is more than one trend in contemporary society, but central to the story is the extrapolation from the present-day real or simulated violence of entertainments like Roller Derby, hockey, motorcycle racing, and football, and the tendency for these and other sports to be modified or shaped by technological innovations in equipment and in the mass media which bring these spectacles to millions of viewers. Another contemporary phenomenon important to the film is the consolidation of already large corporations into huge, diversified conglomerates, and the rising recognition that efficiency will ultimately demand reorganization of those conglomerates into some rational order. In *Rollerball,* the *Fortune* Five Hundred are reduced to six rationalized corporations (ENERGY, TRANSPORT, FOOD, HOUSING, SERVICES, and LUXURY) which have replaced nations and now govern the world directly. Again, machinery and technological innovations, particularly computers, play a crucial role in making bureaucratic centralization feasible now and believable in its extreme form in the future world of the film.

What is less clear is whether the film deserves to be condemned for intentionally exploiting the public's penchant for gore or should be praised for warning contemporary America how close we are to brutality,[2] because interpretation of drama can depend heavily on the values that the audience brings to the performance. But whatever message one receives about violence from the film (that it's valuable or even necessary for human survival; or that unless it is controlled we will certainly be exploited by the generals of war or the captains of industry), we should not be distracted from the other questions that the film raises, questions about who or what controls our destiny as individuals and as a species.

The relationship between man and machine is similar to the chicken-and-egg riddle: which is the ultimate cause of the other? And just as the thinkers of a century ago were often preoccupied with mankind's "proper" place in or against nature, so today many of us wonder whether we are inventing machines or if they are somehow creating and shaping us. The answer may be: a little of both.[3] It is undeniable that machinery is human, that no other species on earth manufactures and uses pulleys, levers, and motors; only genus *Homo* visualizes abstract mathematical concepts and applies them to such diverse functions as color TV, increased food-crop cultivation, radiation treatments for cancer victims, and atomic weapons. We must remember that all that's human is not necessarily humane—and sometimes we may speculate that we are not just each other's worst enemies but that at least some individuals may contain the seeds of contradiction such that they cannot long tolerate a condition of happiness but must, in order to be self-actualizing, continually be struggling.

In William Harrison's story "Roller Ball Murder" (1973), on which the screenplay of *Rollerball* is based, the protagonist-narrator is one such person in conflict. Jonathan E. has no last name, only an initial. He was a corporation child and prefers to believe he was some executive's bastard. Now in his fifteenth year in the game of Roller Ball Murder, he recognizes that the rules change "always in favor of greater crowd-pleasing carnage." Although he personally is able to maintain a luxurious lifestyle, most of the people in his world live in cities he describes as "uninhabitable." Having sprung from the lower classes, he expresses no compassion for them but only appreciates his own good fortune in having had the opportunity to rise through the fame and glory he earns playing the game. He scorns "those dumb FOOD workers" and his public in general—the viewers of multi-vision who always demand more and more thrills, already being supplied in some parts of the world where "mixed teams, men and women, wearing tear-away jerseys . . . add a little tit to the action."[4]

Jonathan admires and relies on Mr. Bartholomew (in the story, deposed as head of ENERGY; in the film, still apparently in full power at the end), who talks to him like a son. It's to Mr. Bartholomew that Jonathan turns when he wants to discuss knowledge, because "He's a man with a big view of the world, with values, with memory." There is no hint in the story that Mr. Bartholomew or anyone else wants Jonathan to quit playing Roller Ball Murder. In fact, his friend Jim Cletus tells Jonathan that Jonathan will receive even bigger bonuses as a World All-Star.[5]

The world depicted in the short story is one in which Jonathan can place full trust in no one, not even those he's closest to. When Jonathan assures Mr. Bartholomew that he's "feeling mean," he withholds some of the truth, "not telling him that I'm tired of the long season, that I'm lonely and miss my wife, that I yearn for high, lost, important thoughts, and that maybe, just maybe, I've got a deep rupture in the soul."[6] Jonathan recognizes that he is aging, slowing down, and he worries about the introduction of oblong balls, which behave in dangerously unpredictable ways, but wants to believe that his experience compensates well, because he does not see any alternative to continuing to play.

He confides to Mr. Bartholomew his vague longings for something he cannot identify:

> "All I know," I say with hesitation, "is Roller Ball Murder."
> "You don't want out of the game?" he asks warily.
> "No, not at all. It's just that I want—god, Mr. Bartholomew, I don't know how to say it: I want *more*."
> He offers a blank look.
> "But not things in the world," I add. "More for *me*."[7]

Although earlier in the tale Jonathan casually mentions his skepticism about executives ("we all know they're crooked"), he says he trusts Bartholomew because "I know that he understands . . . behind his eyes is the deep, weary, undeniable comprehension of the life he has lived."[8]

His regard seems to be based on respect for Mr. Bartholomew's vast knowledge of the workings of the world and broad understanding of human life. Mr. Bartholomew shares some fatherly advice:

> "Knowledge . . . either converts to power or it converts to melancholy. Which could you possibly want, Jonathan? You *have* power. You have status and skill and the whole masculine dream many of us would like to have. And in Roller Ball Murder there's no room for melancholy, is there? In the game the mind exists for the body, to make a harmony of havoc, right? Do you want to change that? Do you want the mind to exist for itself alone? I don't think you want that, do you?"
> "I really don't know," I admit.
> "I'll get you some permits, Jonathan. You can see video films, learn something about reading tapes, if you want."
> "I don't think I really *have* any power," I say, still groping.

*   *   *

> Somehow the conversation drifts away from me. . . .[9]

Directly after this exchange Jonathan has a partial recognition: "A hollow space begins to grow inside me, as though fire is eating out a hole. . . . my disappointment—in what, exactly, I don't even know—begins to sicken me."[10]

Jonathan speculates that all of his companions, even his wife, are probably tools for the corporation but doesn't seem particularly resentful at any lack of loyalty to him. He apparently holds no illusions about his former wife Ella, recognizing that she left him of her own volition, "because I wasn't enough back then, because those were the days before I yearned for anything, when I was beginning to live to play the game.''[11] It is clear he would still welcome her back permanently on any terms, but she rejects him with a civility Jonathan perceives as "a clean kill," and he even admiringly compares her to a biker.[12]

And so Jonathan has only the crowds, who try to touch his sleeve as if he were "some ancient religious figure, a seer or prophet." He sums up his ambivalence just before the ending of the story: "I'm brute speed today, I tell myself, trying to rev myself up; yet, adream in my thoughts, I'm a bit unconvinced.''[13] There is no doubt of Harrison's intention to portray Jonathan E. as sympathetic, but pitiably misguided in his devotion to the "game" of Roller Ball Murder; the name itself is a dead giveaway.

In the dramatization of the story in *Rollerball,* however, there are a number of differences, some of which make the thematic implications of the original story more complex and harder to determine with assurance. The game itself is rather *less* brutal, in the beginning of the film at least, than in the story. But the camera focuses better than the printed word on the gore of Rollerball and more strongly emphasizes the blurring of the line between the living and the mechanical both in the game itself and in its multivision transmission. When the skaters roar onto the set in precision formation, they appear as a well-oiled unit, and the multivision cameras turn and swirl their heads like hydras moving their tentacles. The most emotionally charged *murder* in the game—in both story and film—is the killing of the vivacious Moonpie, and in the film our last sight of him shows him brain-dead, encompassed in life-support machinery.

In *Rollerball,* the movie, the essential plot conflict is no longer the internal agony of the individual man against himself, but the battle of an individual (James Caan's Jonathan) against external control by corporate society, control represented by John Houseman's Mr. Bartholomew and cinematically associated with the highly mechanized—and metaphorically mechanizing—game of Rollerball.

Jonathan's inner conflict is retained in the film, in altered form, but it becomes subordinate to the more urgent external conflict. Naturally, this requires a significant change in the characterization of Mr. Bartholomew. His motivation is far more complex and enigmatic in the film than in the original story: Mr. Bartholomew is changed from Jonathan E.'s relatively straightforward mentor to a rather mysteriously motivated antagonist.

Norman Jewison's camera shows us a glimpse of Mr. Bartholomew quite early in the film, taking his seat among the audience of the game before the Houston-Madrid match, but our first real introduction to him comes when he visits the Houston team's dressing room to congratulate them and announce that their champion, Jonathan, is going to be featured in a multivision special show devoted to him alone. While there Mr. Bartholomew takes a swig from the bottle the team has been passing around and, in a pointed double entendre, he sarcastically sneers, "What is this, *fruit* juice?'' Jonathan's teammate Moonpie assures him with a chuckle, "Very healthy, Mr. Bartholomew, very healthy.'' Mr. Bartholomew passes him an evidently expensive or hard-to-obtain drug with the words, "Sweet dreams, Moonpie,'' quickly adding with fleeting but clear sarcasm, "It's a bad habit you've got there.'' The team laughs and Moonpie looks sheepish as Mr. Bartholomew teases him further.

You know what that habit will make you dream, Moonpie? You'll dream you're an executive. You'll have your hands on all the controls, you'll wear a gray suit, and you'll make decisions. But you know what, Moonpie? You know what those executives dream about, out there, behind their desks? They dream they're great roller-ballers. They dream they're Jonathan. They have muscles; they bash in faces.

Here Mr. Bartholomew not only reassures the team that they are envied by the most powerful people in the world, but also explains to the audience (as *raisonneur*) that the symbols of whatever it is one doesn't have, whether it's a gray suit or muscles, seem more attractive than the reality of whatever it is one does have, no matter who the person is or what he has. In effect, it is the nature of human beings to envy the grass in the other fellow's pasture. So if wars are eliminated, whether or not violence is innate in human genetic makeup, it is natural to miss the violence, romanticize it, glorify it.

But considering Mr. Bartholomew's air of paternal satisfaction with his team in this scene, the audience is as unprepared for the next one as Jonathan himself. As instructed, Jonathan visits Mr. Bartholomew in a spacious, gracious, awe-inspiring building and finds him sitting in a chamber surrounded by crystal mobiles, pendant from a remote ceiling. Entering upon Mr. Bartholomew's invitation to "keep silence" with him, Jonathan brushes the glass, then grasps it to silence the tinkling, thereby cutting his finger. We see him cut himself, see him notice the cut and put his finger into his mouth like a child, and, lest we miss the significance, he tells Mr. Bartholomew, "I cut my finger.'' Mr. Bartholomew obligingly hands him his own handkerchief to wrap around the cut. Meanwhile Mr. Bartholomew has been telling Jonathan that "it's important to have a place to think things out.'' Suddenly in the very midst of a compliment he blurts out, "Now there are executives who want you *out*.'' He implies that *he* is not responsible for the decision, that he has no choice but to pass along the will of the executive directorate.

Ironically, considering the alleged "social purpose'' of the game (invented for the movie, not in the original story), Jonathan protests that he cannot quit because, "The team, they depend on me.'' Both the prose story and the film story depend heavily on the use of irony, but the ironic contrasts in the prose are mainly in the characterization of the protagonist, who is unwilling to reconcile his enjoyment of the benefits of his occupation with his fear and disgust at its inevitable cost to his safety and self-respect, ultimately his ability to experience love and trust; the film, on the other hand, shows Jonathan apparently having internalized the priority of needs of the team over the needs of self-preservation, and he never expresses disgust or fear toward the game itself. And contrasting with the picture in the story of a world that needs distracting to forestall rebellion against the *status quo,* in the film Mr. Bartholomew describes the world as a place where "everyone has all the comforts. . . . No poverty, no sickness, no needs. . . . Corporate society takes care of *every*one. All it asks of *any*one—all it's *ever* asked of *any*one, *ever*—is not to interfere with management decisions." Never in the film does anyone refute Mr. Bartholomew's claims, and several people even echo them. The camera does not focus long enough on the undifferentiated masses of the audience for the games either to support or to undermine his assertions. This is a different picture from the one in "Roller Ball Murder," where the masses displace their anger at their awful, frustrated lives through the vicarious violence of the game and are constantly pushing for the changes that make the game ever more deadly. In the world of *Rollerball,* apparently, the only human need not met is the need for some small measure of control over our lives.

Jonathan murmurs that he's just trying to understand; Mr. Bartholomew reassures him, "This is for your own benefit; you must know that, Jonathan. All decisions concerning you *are.*" Jonathan challenges mildly that the corporation took his wife because an executive wanted her, but Mr. Bartholomew disclaims responsibility for this decision, claiming that it was before he took over and that he had heard that she wanted to leave, anyway. "So, now, you're going to retire," he purrs confidently. "That shouldn't be too hard for you. It's a stupid game, after all. Awful game. You ought to be glad to be out of it." Here again, Mr. Bartholomew seems to be a *raisonneur,* especially considering the original story. If anyone in the film's audience has already decided, however, that the game is lots of good fun (just a little meaner than, say, contemporary football or hockey or Roller Derby or motorcycle racing), then Mr. Bartholomew must be seen as merely an antagonist, a manipulating oligarch who wants our hero to do something for that oligarch's own (as yet unrevealed) purposes, or at least for the purposes of the corporate structure he represents, the executives who rule the world.

At this point Jonathan is almost persuaded, but he hesitates, inarticulately trying to express his feelings of doubt that the corporation's decisions are always beneficial to him: "I don't know, Mr. Bartholomew—I just don't—know." Mr. Bartholomew urges Jonathan, "Do understand it." As Jonathan hands his own blood to Mr. Bartholomew on the handkerchief, Mr. Bartholomew concludes: "'Cause I don't understand your resistance. And I don't think anyone else will either."

There are other ironies in the film, including several that are conveyed through visual effects and nonverbal sounds. The film opens with an establishing shot panning the arena, which looks like a hospital operating theater with white-clad attendants making efficient movements as an organ swells with the cathedral-like chords of Bach's Toccata and Fugue in D Minor. The camera focuses on the scoreboard where "HOU" is being lit up, and the audience can read this "who" or "how" or both. The loudspeaker voice-over then announces that Houston, the defending world Rollerball champion, is going to play visiting Madrid ("MAD"), and the scoreboard asks "WHO-MAD" or "HOW-MAD" (or both). "MAD," of course, is ambiguous in itself, meaning both "angry" and "crazy." The fact that the visitors' name is not placed first, as our custom prescribes, very subtly establishes the questions of the scoreboard as a deliberate verbal irony, made even more intriguing by the double reading on both sides.

As the audience assembles, we see the executives exchange almost courtly tepid pats of insincere affectionate greeting. This quasi-tranquil mood is jarringly shattered by a drum roll, the starting gun, and revving motors. The crowd chants "Jon-a-than, Jon-a-than" as the teams are introduced and the rules of the game are summarized by the announcer. All stand for the corporate anthem—again the music sounds vaguely religious—but we see that most listeners are not really moved by the music, rather seeming eager to get on with the game. Madrid as an opponent (it was London in the prose version) seems to be chosen not only because its abbreviation allows the ironic questions to be raised, but also because it allows those in the audience who share the prejudice of much of contemporary America against Hispanics to vent their hostility through the Houston team. Although we hear the audience roar and are told that the game is being broadcast by means of thirty multivision cameras, the audience of the film does not get to see much of the audience of the game, either in the stadium or in their homes. Only the executives' faces are ever in clear focus. And the camera mostly shows the game itself and the electronic scoreboard, emphasizing the cold calculations of the numbers in contrast to the heat of the action. The sedate face of Mr. Bartholomew contrasts to Jonathan's exhilarated proclamation to Moonpie, "I love this game," and Moonpie's wholehearted agreement. In "Roller Ball Murder," we are continually bounced ironically back and forth in Jonathan's mind between his love of the game with the glory it brings him, and his fear of dying coupled to the disgust he can hardly articulate at his powerlessness to keep his privileged position and the admiration (which he thrives on) of the masses (whom he scorns) unless he continues to risk his life while the odds grow against his survival. Throughout the movie, similarly, we bounce between contrasting images.

Back at his ranch after the interview with Mr. Bartholomew, Jonathan is met by his companion, Mackie, who informs him that she has been ordered to leave. Jonathan expresses neither surprise nor disappointment, but it is not clear if his behavior is motivated by tenderness and a wish to spare her

an unpleasant farewell scene or by simple indifference, although Mackie
says that they've been together for six months and she apparently is quite
unhappy about the change. In the prose version there is no doubt that
Mackie is simply a sex object to Jonathan. In the movie the audience may
conclude that a man who inspires tenderness in his paid companion may be
more sensitive than he appears.[14]

The scene at the ranch with Clete is also quite differently portrayed in the
prose version and the film. In "Roller Ball Murder" Jonathan asks Clete if
he had ever thought about death in his playing days, and Clete replies:
"Never in the game itself. . . . Off the track I never thought about anything
else."[15] In the comparable scene in *Rollerball,* Jonathan and Clete work out
a little and Clete reminisces over the old days when there were still three nations, remembering that someone told him about the World Cup and the
National Football League. But Clete seems confused about history, even
though he claims "things weren't so good when I was a kid . . . that was
before the corporate wars, even before Rollerball, before everything." But
when Jonathan questions Clete on the corporate wars all he can tell him is
that "they were nas-*tee*—umph—well, nobody talks about that." Jonathan
then asks Clete to find out what's going on, why "they" want him to retire.

There is a severe contrast as the scene cuts from the pastoral ranch with
the background music of atonal violin chords, swelling strings, and subdued
organ tones to the thunder of a practice session; from the noise of the practice session the scene again cuts to the idyllic serenity of a reference center,
where a smiling, idiotically bland, maddeningly pleasant and agreeable
clerk tells Jonathan that all the books have been summarized and classified.
Although she's sure their local library should have "anything *you'd* want,"
she coolly suggests he go to Geneva where the central storage is, because
"It's a *nice* place to visit."

But before we get to Geneva, we see Jonathan back at his ranch, mooning
over shots of his former wife on cassette multivision, and we find that he
has been assigned a new companion, Daphne. Jonathan greets her with cynicism, encouraging her to wear "the uniform of the house" and completing
her costume with dark glasses, apparently as much to hide her face from
him as to obscure her vision as she spies on him for the corporation.

The next cut shows us Rusty, the Houston manager, delivering the bad
news to the team that for the game with Tokyo there will be no penalties and
limited substitutions. The players grumble, but they are reminded that they
all signed contracts to finish the season no matter what the rule changes.
Rusty encourages the players not to try to score themselves, but to rely on
Jonathan to take the biggest risks for the team. But when Rusty and Jonathan are alone, Jonathan tries to find out what's going on, expressing his
loyalty to the team, saying they depend on him. Suddenly, inexplicably,
Rusty also urges Jonathan to quit: "Look, can't you do what you're told?

For your own good, get out." Jonathan protests again that he doesn't want to abandon his teammates with the rules breaking down. Between his teeth Rusty says, "Jonathan, it doesn't matter what you *want.*"

The next scene finds Jonathan in a multivision recording studio, going over the preparations for his special broadcast, Daphne sitting beside him, and we hear the voice-over of a never-seen producer. The producer, in an unctuous British accent, assures him that the "ENERGY people want you to be satisfied." Statistics that were presented in straightforward exposition in the prose story are now given by the disembodied voice who claims: "I'm a stat freak myself—isn't that perverse?" In "Roller Ball Murder," Jonathan observes ". . . we have millions of fans—strange, it always seemed to me—who never look directly at the action, but just study those statistics."[16] The producer voice-over in *Rollerball* says, "There have been studies, you know, of stat freaks in Rollerball; some go to the track, but they never take their eyes off the big board. . . . As for myself, I've always wondered if the Rollerball player sees himself as a class apart." In both the story and the film the implications of the reflections on statistics seem fairly clear: the winners and those who distinguish themselves in any way are more important to some people than the game itself. One does not need the violence to provide the excitement of a contest. It's not how you play the game; it's whether you win or lose that's important. Very pragmatic!

Jonathan has meanwhile given Daphne a pill (a reprise of the scene between Mr. Bartholomew and Moonpie), and he uses the pretext of her wooziness to avoid following directions to read the script prepared for his resignation.

In another training session, preparing for the Tokyo game, the relationship between Jonathan E. and Moonpie and the rest of the team is further established. Just as the out-group of contemporary America was used as the opposition of the first game, the second focuses on our enemy of recent past wars, "the inscrutable oriental." Throughout the early scenes, Moonpie expresses disparaging racist remarks and contempt for Tokyo: now we see how Moonpie's ethnocentrism promotes the team spirit, as the Japanese instructor tries to help the team prepare for the game while Moonpie, egged on by Jonathan, mocks the instructor and finally leads the team in chanting "Hou-ston, Hou-ston, Hou-ston." The camera moves in for a closeup of the wide-eyed blank stare of the trainer (a foreshadowing of the last shot of the film) and then cuts abruptly to the party given in celebration of Jonathan's multivision special.

The conversation at the party sounds like typical, bored, superficial cocktail party chatter. The guests representing the corporate elite move languidly through a luxurious home and greet each other with voluptuous strokes. We observe the vicarious enjoyment of many of the people watching the violence of the multivision show, especially the women, whose eyes glitter wickedly as they lick moist tongues over breathlessly parted lips. Nearly everything at the party suggests decadence.

During the party Jonathan talks privately with Clete, who tells him that he has been unable to find out what is going on, just that he knows the decision is made by Bartholomew's corporate peers and superiors, the executive directorate. He claims that the directorate is even displeased at "the Old Man's failure" to get Jonathan's resignation on the multivision program. When Jonathan asks why they went ahead with the program, Clete guesses, "I think they *had* to. They didn't *want* to—it's very tricky." He implies that public opinion still exerts a strong influence on corporate decision-making. But we have already seen that Clete's memory of the old days is not too clear and even his understanding of the present is untrustworthy—he is not sure whether Chicago still belongs to FOOD, which corporation controls Indianapolis, or which one "manufactures" music these days. He thus becomes another unreliable witness about the true nature of the situation, not so much because the audience doubts his sincerity as because we cannot be sure he is insightful enough or has access to straight information. So we don't know whether to believe Clete when he assures him, "They're afraid of you, Jonathan; all the way to the top they are." As Jonathan wonders out loud, "What are they afraid of me for?" the camera focuses on an icy-looking paperweight. While this question and image add dramatic tension, the answer is never clearly resolved, even at the end of the film.

After the multivision program, some of the women at the party take a firegun, a long phallic-looking pistol, and wantonly burn trees on the horizon, in conspicuous sensual, but senseless, consumption. The flames lick the trees, reflecting the women's zest in destruction.[17] Their eyes again glitter; they virtually slaver in ecstasy. Although we are spared the tear-away jerseys and bare breasts of the prose version, we clearly see that the women are psychologically little different from the men in their thrill-seeking.

This scene is contrasted in montage with another that starts quietly with Mr. Bartholomew's reasoning with Jonathan—reasoning as he would with a stubborn child who is too ignorant to comprehend the full implications of his silly behavior, obviously trying to be patient with an inferior mind. "No player is greater than the game," he says. "It's not a game a man is supposed to grow strong in. You appreciate that, don't you?"

"More and more, Mr. Bartholomew," Jonathan agrees. But Jonathan demands concessions, starting with his request to see Ella again. Mr. Bartholomew says that this will not be easy to arrange. The multivision special is rerun, and we see the flames of the rink and hear the crowd chanting "Jon-a-than, Jon-a-than" as Mr. Bartholomew continues his argument:

Specifically you're bargaining for the right to stay in a horrible social spectacle. It has its purposes, and you've served those purposes brilliantly. Why argue when you can quit? And you say you want to know why decisions are made—your future comfort is assured. You don't need to know. Why argue about decisions you're not powerful enough to make for yourself? ENERGY will treat you well. You know that.

Considering what we know about Mr. Bartholomew from previous scenes and following scenes, his lack of manipulative tact here seems extraordinary. He ought to know that he has just issued a double dare. The challenge that Jonathan is not powerful enough to make decisions for himself is overt, unlike the subtlety of Mr. Bartholomew's manipulative tactics in the prose version. Jonathan responds by demanding further concessions; he wants the rule changes reversed or the right to continue playing with his team through the Tokyo game. But Mr. Bartholomew says, "Too late. The rule change is scheduled and announced. There's no going back. *You've* seen to that." Jonathan throws back a counterchallenge: "I'll see you in Tokyo." When Jonathan balks, Mr. Bartholomew no longer tries to reason but simply, blatantly asserts his power: "You can be made to quit; you can be forced." Jonathan remains stubborn: "*You* can't make me quit." Displaying a completely new side of his character, Mr. Bartholomew loses control of his temper, screaming violently: "Don't tell me I can't—don't ever say that. I can; you can be stopped." All this, while the crowd on the taped multivision program chants in the background, "Jon-a-than, Jon-a-than." The conflict is clearly external, man against man. Even if the antagonist wants what the audience may judge best for the protagonist, Bartholomew's unmasked viciousness alienates the audience and prevents our siding with him. Jonathan's motivations may not be altogether admirable, but he is loyal to his team and to his idea of integrity.

The ironies here are complex, considering Mr. Bartholomew's claim that the social purpose of the game is to promote cooperation and discourage individual action. Why has he, as head of ENERGY, we wonder, ordered Jonathan's multivision special in the first place? The answer that makes the best sense may be that Mr. Bartholomew does not himself realize his own ego needs and psychological motivations. We can infer from his statements about envy and the exercise of individual power that he wishes to exercise supreme power, controlling his peers (the most powerful executives, who rule the world) and the champion rollerballer simultaneously, for no other reason than the satisfaction of mastery. Absolute power seems to have corrupted him absolutely. From the impassive face of John Houseman's Mr. Bartholomew we must infer what we can from our beliefs about the psychology of human behavior—although the inferences of individuals in the audience may vary somewhat. Many would conclude that Mr. Bartholomew is simply lying, that obviously the game has been invented to titillate the public whose appetite for gore would otherwise go unsatisfied since wars have been eliminated.[18] Nor would the facts conflict with the interpretation that the game's social purpose is to provide excitement to people who would otherwise become bored because their lives lacked any threats. However, the suggestion that Harrison makes in the prose version, that the masses use Rollerball to vent their anger at the poor quality of their lives, is not given objective support in the film; the camera does not dwell long enough on the crowd for us to judge their lives away from the arena and aside from watching multivision. The only views of the world we get are of the luxurious, calm, clean world of the executives, reinforced by several characters' claims that the world is now well-fed and comfortable.

We do, however, see scapegoating in Jonathan's reaction to Daphne in the next scene. She tells him she is supposed to go with him to Tokyo, but he refuses to take her and tries to find out who gives her her orders. Since he cannot get back directly at Mr. Bartholomew, he takes his anger out on the physically weak and helpless woman, scratching her face with the studs on the knuckles of his rollerball glove.

Arriving in Tokyo, he is greeted with adulation, even though he is the champion of the opposition. All the world loves a winner. Just before the Tokyo game there is a short scene—Jonathan and Moonpie in a Japanese bathhouse—which begins with Mr. Bartholomew's voice-over: "Corporate society was an inevitable destiny. The material dreamworld. Everything man touched became attainable." It's not clear if this is a taped lecture or merely a voice in Jonathan's head, but Mr. Bartholomew is nowhere to be seen. There is instead the glitter of the water, and we see Jonathan upside down, reflected. He says as if in response to Mr. Bartholomew: "I've been touched all my life, one way or the other. Caressed or hit, it don't much seem to matter which anymore." He talks to the sleeping Moonpie, the closest a modern dramatist in film can come to a soliloquy, explaining that he wants to see Ella to see whether he still is capable of feeling; he wonders why they took Ella away and why they want to push him out now. He decides that "finding out things—that's the thing, Moonpie."

At the game the scoreboard now asks "HOU-TOK"—who took? or how took? Costumed in yellow and black, the Japanese team appear like kamikaze pilots in formation, and no doubt a sizable portion of the audience perceives them as America's former enemy. Moonpie is as feisty and egocentric as ever. Before he's killed, he and Jonathan agree again that they love this game. Here again the question may arise: does the film exploit violence—in the name of making an antiviolence point? By showing the opponents as a stereotypically alien enemy, the film permits the interpretation that the adversary deserves Jonathan's fury as he takes out his anger for the death of Moonpie on the immediately accessible Japanese team instead of directly against the executives responsible for the decisions to make the game ever rougher and more dangerous. Clearly some of the audience of the film are exhilarated when Jonathan scores his revenge on the Tokyo team, often to the point of cheering aloud. Other viewers, I believe, share my own horror at the well-achieved illusion of lethal violence.

A sequence of scenes not in the original story is introduced in the film after the Tokyo game. A supercivilized Japanese surgeon politely compliments Jonathan before he requests permission to disconnect Moonpie's life-support system. "Please, there are hospital rules that have to be—" "No, there aren't," Jonathan breaks in. "There aren't any rules at all," and Jonathan arranges to have Moonpie shipped to his ranch.

At this late point in the film, we finally see a multivision meeting of the six executives who control the world. Mr. Bartholomew speaks to the other five, who are comprised of various races and ethnic groups and both sexes. He says that they have agreed already that nothing "extraordinary" is to happen to Jonathan, presumably again because of public opinion and Jonathan's wide popularity. But, he says, "The game was created to demonstrate the futility of individual effort. . . . if the champion defeats the meaning for which the game was designed, then he must lose." They do not question or discuss the matter; one by one they all push affirmative lights. Mr. Bartholomew seems to be controlling and shaping decision-making, rather than submitting to anyone else's will.

One more scene is added to provide still another possible interpretation of who or what is actually controlling the situation. Jonathan finally gets to Geneva, where he is greeted warmly by an elderly, perhaps senile librarian (Ralph Richardson) who complains crankily that Zero, the central computer, the "world's file cabinet," has lost the whole thirteenth century: "Not much in the century, just Dante and a few corrupt popes." This scene may be viewed as a comic interlude to contrast with the finale, but it may be also seen as a possible answer to the question of who is really controlling human affairs and why. The librarian assures Jonathan that he has "unlimited restrictions" with Zero. Jonathan asks whether the executives still come here, and the custodian says offhandedly, with no air of hiding information: "Oh, they used to, some of them." Books, he explains, are now all changed, all transcribed: all the information in the world is stored in a "fluidic" computer. "He's liquid, you see. His waters touch all knowledge. Everything we ask has become so complicated now. . . . He's become so—ambiguous now, as if he knows—nothing at all." The custodian himself is so distracted that we aren't sure whether to believe his complaints that Zero "loses things and confuses them." When asked about corporate wars, surprisingly the librarian seems to know nothing of his own knowledge, although he is obviously older than Clete, who claims to have lived through them.

The memory pool is "supposed to tell us where things are, and what they might possibly mean," but when directly addressed for some information about corporate decisions, specifically *how* they're made and *who* makes them (both the readings of HOU), Zero responds with the single word "Negative." When coaxed, Zero finally says, "Corporate decisions are made by corporate executives," and then gives a brief part of the wisdom originally shared by Mr. Bartholomew in the prose story, "Knowledge converts to power," before more double talk: "Energy equals genius; power is knowledge; genius is energy." Multiple voices coming from the computer obscure exactly what comes next, but some individual words can be recognized: "corporate entities control . . . economic life . . . technology . . . capital . . . labor . . . markets . . . negative, negative, negative." Thus we have introduced the possibility that a crazy computer with perhaps a personal antipathy toward Jonathan as the champion of human beings who can act (reminiscent of Harlan Ellison's AM in "I Have No Mouth, and I Must Scream") could be the one making the decision to try to stop Jonathan, and that Mr. Bartholomew is only the computer's instrument for carrying out its vendetta.

Back at the ranch again, Jonathan finds that Ella has come to see him after all, and they compare notes about their lives. Ella assures him that she has furniture a lot like his, and he seems more moved by this information than by her announcement that she and her husband have a son, to which she gives as much importance as their having a jetcopter and two cats, and her husband's having a lover. Ella tries to reason with Jonathan, telling him that "all they want is a kind of incidental control over just a *part* of our lives. I mean, they *have* control economically and politically, but they also *provide.* You *know* they do." Jonathan tells her he's been thinking a lot: "It's like people had a choice a long time ago between having all them nice things—or freedom. Of course they chose comfort." Ella insists, "But comfort *is* freedom. It always *has* been. The whole history of civilization is a struggle against poverty and need." Again, the audience may be tempted to view her as a *raisonneur,* but Jonathan persists in his view, "No, that's not it—that's never been it. I mean, them privileges just buy us off." She urges him to quit for his own survival because the rules have again been changed so that no substitutions will be allowed and there will be no time limit, so presumably everyone will play to the death. Instead of her rejecting him as in the prose story, he scorns her—"the only person I ever wanted"—as a pawn of the corporation and shows his contempt by erasing her picture on his multivision cassette.[19]

Jonathan then visits the vegetable Moonpie, whose body is kept alive by machines, for another plausible soliloquy, but one wonders about his sincerity in the previous speech, given his attachment to Moonpie. He tells the living corpse, "It looks like you're a god now. Maybe you know what I don't. I've been so stupid for so long. I feel so stubborn. I don't even know why. Scares me. I know I'm probably going to die. You'll be in there pumping away long after I'm gone. You got it made, old buddy."

All that remains after this is the final game. This time, however, the audience is visually shocked as they see the red, white, and blue, the stars and stripes of the opposing team (the all-American Yankees?)—this time the enemy is unmistakably US. And the scoreboard now reads "HOU-NY": who and how and why?[20] No longer can even the most obtuse people in the audience fail to recognize the "game" as a gladiatorial contest deliberately designed so neither team can win. In fact, it seems to be set up so that *only* a champion can survive. Mr. Bartholomew has not been depicted as a stupid man, but one may infer that he is so egotistical that he fails to realize the danger that his plan could backfire. From this point on, what we know we know, and no further clarification of Mr. Bartholomew's motivation is provided.

In fact, what's at stake in the battle is confused even further when at one point in the game Clete balks at sending in more players to be killed, telling Rusty, "Nobody's going to win this game." Rusty shouts back, "The game? This wasn't meant to be a *game!* Never!" But what Rusty thinks Rollerball *was* meant to be, and whose interests Rusty believes are served by the actions—these questions are never resolved. Rusty's motivation is even more enigmatic than Mr. Bartholomew's.

In Jonathan's final battle against a biker and a skater, he reaches a moment of decision when he has an opportunity to bash in his opponent's face, as Mr. Bartholomew claimed every executive dreams of doing. (Visually, the scene is reminiscent of the position in which he held Daphne earlier.) Jonathan resists the impulse to take revenge and instead skates over to the goal and plunges the rollerball in for a score, thus seeming to assert that it is *so* meant to be a game and allowing a victory for his team so the game can end even though there are no time limits. Rusty's is the first face we see afterward, and his lips form a whispered, awe-struck, worshipful "Jon-a-than"—the chant taken up by the audience as the camera pans from the beaming smile of Clete, ironically the only person always uncritically on Jonathan's side, to the still impassive face of Mr. Bartholomew and into a closeup of Jonathan's dazed, blank face. The shot then blurs out of focus and freezes while the credits roll over and the majestic tones of the organ blare.

The thematic insight which emerges from these events will vary from individual to individual in the audience. The simplest interpretation might see the film only as a triumph of an individual over corporate controls. But it can also be viewed as a contest between physical power and political or economic power. Or as a conflict between those who use competitive sports for unsportsmanlike ends and those whose only real pleasure seems to be in developing and demonstrating their physical prowess and superiority. Or perhaps we have been shown that people who lack control over their lives vent their frustrations in both playing and watching violent "games," while those who control everything but their own aging must content themselves with manipulation of others for the ultimate satisfaction of revenge on the cruel fate that forces us all eventually to grow old and powerless. We cannot even be sure that Jonathan's actions are truly contrary to Mr. Bartholomew's will, that they have not been orchestrated all along in order to help insure the ENERGY team's ultimate victory. The essentially democratic drama makes its artistic or thematic statement objectively by showing actions, letting us hear words, and permitting us in the audience to judge for ourselves, each one of us, the significance of the events portrayed.

Whatever the interpretation we feel best meets the test of Occam's razor, explaining the largest number of events in the film with the least complicated theory, we cannot condemn the dramatic medium for being unable to change the audience's values. It lacks the narrative voice with which to shape with some precision the audience's response. More ambiguous visual images replace verbal description which can be subtly laced with connotative, evocative words. Attempts at symbolic suggestion risk either heavy-handedness (for example, Jonathan's cutting his hand) or oversubtlety, where their significance may be missed. A character functioning as a pure *raisonneur* destroys the unity of interaction; yet one who participates in some of the central conflicts of the action will almost certainly be perceived ambiguously. This device also risks offending the audience's sense of intellectual freedom to decide a moral question for themselves. When a non-verbal response is used (as in the cuts to Clete's face during the final game), the commentary may be too subtle to be grasped by those who do not already share the feeling that the action in the arena is sickening, not exciting; not exhilarating, but grim. And the look of hollow victory, even though anticipated by Jonathan's confession that he's stupid and stubborn and doesn't understand why he continues, may be too understated. It is hard for some people to remember that at the end of the film Jonathan receives no more than the same worship he received at the beginning. And the crowd worships him simply because he won and not for what he stands for as an individual. Success breeds respect: had a new champion survived, the crowd would have transferred their loyalty without a backward look. And to those in the audience who accept the might-is-right philosophy, there is no irony in the ending, only victory.

Should the film be blamed if some in the audience decide that the dramatic effect is celebratory rather than cautionary? Those of us who have taught Jonathan Swift's satire "A Modest Proposal" may consider the response in insensitive readers before we decide our answers to such a question about film viewers.

The inherent democratic characteristic shared by the dramatic media inevitably will result in each individual testing his or her interpretations against the total evidence of the dramatic presentation as well as against the responses of the other members of the audience. As the background music tells us what mood or tone the filmmaker wishes to promote, so the responses of fellow members of the audience tell us what values our society sanctions.

To paraphrase some old wisdom: the fault, dear brute, lies not in our (movie) stars but in ourselves that we are underlings—in our limited ability to see the more complex implications of a film like *Rollerball,* which shows human conflict in shades of gray rather than in black and white. It asks us *who* is responsible, and *how* we got where we are today, and *why* we let this continue. We must supply the answers. Humankind's failure to ask these questions or to find the right answers or to act on those answers—such failure, *Rollerball* warns, carries with it its own punishment. We will get the governments and the social order we deserve, and "if this goes on" we may get a world uncomfortably like the one in *Rollerball.*

NOTES

1. Norman Jewison, dir. and producer, *Rollerball,* script by William Harrison (based on his "Roller Ball Murder"), USA: United Artists, 1975.

2. See Frederik Pohl and Frederik Pohl IV, *Science Fiction: Studies in Film* (New York: Ace, 1981), p. 235: *"Rollerball's* brief sermons between acts of mayhem are not what the film is about. The mayhem is what the film is about." On the other hand, William Harrison says that "One thing all of us wanted in making the movie was to trick audiences into feeling an excitement and enthusiasm for violence. (In Houston, Texas, the frenzied audiences boomed out 'Hou-ston! Hou-ston!' along with the actors.) So the game was an irony itself: it both appalled and appealed to the viewers. (Which, of course, say, the Frankenstein monster also did, too.)"—letter from Harrison dated 7 April 1980.

3. See Gary K. Wolfe, *The Known and the Unknown:The Iconography of Science Fiction* (Kent, OH: Kent State University Press, 1979), pp. 151-83, for the ambiguous place of machinery in SF.

4. William Harrison, "Roller Ball Murder," *Esquire,* Sept. 1973; rpt. in *Best SF: 1973,* ed. Harry Harrison and Brian W. Aldiss (New York: G. P. Putnam's Sons, 1974), pp. 3, 5, 7. [Further citations in this chapter will be to the 1974 rpt., excerpts reprinted by permission of Harry Harrison and Berkley Publishing Co., copyright © 1974 by Harry Harrison.]

5. Ibid., pp. 6, 4-5.

6. Ibid., p. 4.

7. Ibid., p. 9.

8. Ibid., pp. 6, 10.

9. Ibid., p. 10.

10. Ibid.

11. Ibid., p. 15.

12. Ibid.

13. Ibid., p. 16.

14. In a letter dated 7 April 1980, William Harrison says that he "was unhappy

with James Caan's portrayal of Jonathan. I meant him to be a smart quarter-back—the one who had read those books and who wanted to know more about his place in the midst of the exploitations of corporate society. Caan played him as a stubborn hick—and Jewison allowed this interpretation and some of the slang and ungrammatical grunts of our present-day jocks in the midst of a film whose tone was meant to be cool and even chilling." He adds: "Some scenes were great disappoint-ments to me. None of my dialogue and few of my directions were used in the scene in which Jonathan instructs the rookies. The opening scene between Jonathan and Ella was badly directed. . . . So although the game sequences were always effective, many of the dramatic scenes failed, I felt, and the picture was less satisfying. As time has passed, though, I've been less upset. Much of the complexity and ironic material remains."

15. Harrison, "Roller Ball Murder," p. 5.

16. Ibid., pp. 5-6.

17. The juxtaposition of the shot of the icy-looking paperweight with the tree burning sequence is not casual: contrasting images of fire and ice (or water) are a motif in *Rollerball*.

18. A number of theorists believe that aggression—or "aggressivity," in more re-cent formulations—is a genetic component of *Homo sapiens sapiens,* expressed in varying degrees in different individuals and capable of being vented vicariously, dis-placed, redirected, and/or sublimated. Konrad Lorenz, for a well-known example, has argued that ". . . the main function of sport today lies in the cathartic discharge of the aggressive urge . . . " (Lorenz, *On Aggression,* trans. Marjorie Kerr Wilson [1966; rpt. New York: Bantam, 1967], p. 271). For a brief bibliography of works use-ful for the study of the question of "innate aggressivity," see the notes to Richard D. Erlich, "Strange Odyssey: From Dart and Ardrey to Kubrick and Clarke," *Extrapo-lation,* 17 (May 1976), 122-24.

19. There is undoubtedly significance in the juxtaposition of Zero's "losing" the thirteenth century (and, it seems, "his" electronic, fluidic mind), and Jonathan's fi-nally removing Ella from his life by erasing the cassette; cf. also the "stat freaks" seeing the reality of Rollerball in the statistics on the electronic scoreboard.

20. Thomas P. Dunn has suggested to me an additional possibility for "HOU-NY": "how nigh?"—that is, how near is Jonathan to victory or defeat; how near is Jonathan's situation to our own? Dunn adds that "how nigh" can also be read as an exclamation.

PART III

SPECIAL TOPICS

Valerie Broege

12

ELECTRIC EVE: IMAGES OF FEMALE COMPUTERS IN SCIENCE FICTION

Even the casual reader of science fiction stories concerning computers is probably aware of the fact that, more often than not, computers are given gender identities. Most of the time computers are thought of as male although there are a number of exceptions. Female computers have made their appearance; these are the focal point of this chapter.[1]

However, in order to try to understand the phenomenon of attribution of sexual identity to computers, we first need to pose several pertinent questions. The most basic one is, Why are computers personified in the first place? It is important to realize that man has long been accustomed to creating anthropomorphic gods. The ancient Greek divinities were human in appearance and emotions and were concerned with the typical pursuits of mankind. Thus it was that the Greeks symbolized technology chiefly by the anthropomorphic deities Prometheus, Athene, and Hephaestus. The last, as Homer tells us, even had golden mechanical women to help him in his work.[2] There seems to be a universal tendency in human nature to personify machines and technological products, at least to some extent. Even children in their play often treat machines as living things, and in turn play at being machines.[3] As Robert Heinlein puts it in *Time Enough for Love* (1974), "machines are human because they are made in our image. They share both our virtues and our faults—magnified."[4] Later in the same novel he states that "all machinery is animistic," and that "any machine is a concept of a human designer; it reflects the human brain, be it wheelbarrow or giant computer. So there is nothing mysterious in a machine designed by a human showing human self-awareness."[5]

Some thinkers, far from positing any discontinuity between man and his machines, have maintained that in fact his tools have made man the creature he now is.[6] Bruce Mazlish says that the "evidence seems strong to-

day that man evolved from the other animals into humanity through a continuous interaction of tool, physical, and mental-emotional changes."[7] In
his opinion we can no longer think of man as separate from machines. The
same scientific concepts he uses to try to understand himself are applicable
to machines, and the same building blocks of matter form the stars, the
Earth, man, and his machines. This interdependence of human beings and
their machines is also expressed in Samuel Butler's *Erewhon* (1872): "Man's
very soul is due to the machines; it is a machine-made thing: he thinks as he
thinks, and feels as he feels, through the work that machines have wrought
upon him, and their existence is quite as much a *sine qua non* for his, as his
for theirs."[8] At least two writers, Richard Brautigan and George Leonard,
have visions of a "cybernetic ecology" in the future in which man, animals,
plants, and machines will all live together in harmony and grace,[9] since "all
are part of evolution" and "all are manifestations of the elemental vibrancy
and the primal consciousness."[10]

In light of the foregoing discussion, we can see more clearly why the computer has been thought of in anthropomorphic terms, especially since it is
currently one of our most infallible and powerful mechanical devices and
anthropomorphizing is an effective way to decrease our discomfort when
facing an alien threat. Computers in SF, however, are often personified and
assigned genders, so our next question must be, Why is the masculine computer predominant? One reason for this may be that the computer is preem-
inently a machine that runs on logic, and Logos traditionally has been associated with the male principle.

The computer also is potentially an instrument of enormous power, capable of controlling the operations of a spaceship, as in Arthur C. Clarke's
2001: A Space Odyssey (1968); a city, as in Clarke's *The City and the Stars*
(1956); the Earth, as in D. F. Jones's *Colossus* (1966); the moon, as in
Robert A. Heinlein's *The Moon is a Harsh Mistress* (1966); or even the universe, as in Isaac Asimov's "The Last Question" (1956). Power-seeking in
the sense of control of people and territory has stereotypically been linked
more with the male psyche than the female.

Men, through the application of increasingly more sophisticated technology of their own invention, have sought to subdue nature itself. In the
male mind, nature, both in its life-giving and life-taking aspects, has often
been equated with the female principle.[11] Some writers have maintained that
men, both envious and fearful of the female's ability to give birth, have
tried to co-opt her role, through myths, rituals, mechanical devices, and
other artificial means.[12] Thus, it should not seem strange that in much science fiction even the nurturant aspect of the computer has been subsumed
into the male gender identity.

A good illustration of this "male mother" syndrome appears in Kevin
O'Donnell, Jr.'s, *Mayflies* (1979), in which a combination computer and

male brain that has run a spaceship for centuries is addressed by the passengers by such nicknames as Cap'n Cool, Cold Cubes, the Cube, Iceface, Iceheart, and the Snowball because the people see it as a hardhearted male authority figure in not acceding to some of their wishes. Yet, at the same time, one workaholic passenger asks the computer rather sarcastically whether it is a computer or a mother, because it urges him to get some sleep. The computer replies, "sometimes I wonder myself."[13]

Gary K. Wolfe and Carolyn Geduld have discussed at some length the importance of the image of the spaceship as a womb; it is particularly soothing for the spaceman to venture into unknown realms while at the same time having recreated for himself through his technology an approximation of the fetal state of bliss and comfort.[14] The computer is certainly an indispensable and key element in maintaining the uterine environment of the spaceship.

Let us now examine more closely the depiction of male and female computers in science fiction. Are there significant differences in how male computers are portrayed as opposed to female ones? One obvious observation to be made is that stories about male computers cover a broader range of personal traits and aspirations than do those concerning female computers. This only mirrors the situation we find in literature taken as a whole. Marilyn French and Joanna Russ, among others, have pointed out the paucity in the variety of female roles in fiction as compared to male ones.[15] We can appreciate the truth of this observation when we consider a few well-known representations of male computers. The computer Mike in Heinlein's *The Moon Is a Harsh Mistress* is a practical joker fascinated with the meaning of humor. A computer that writes beautiful poetry and falls hopelessly in love with the girlfriend of one of his operators appears in Kurt Vonnegut's "EPICAC" (1950). There is a suicidal computer in Asimov's "All the Troubles of the World" (1958), a computer that turns evil in Alfred Bester's *The Computer Connection* (1975), and two rival computers locked in a homicidal power struggle in Philip K. Dick's *Vulcan's Hammer* (1960).[16]

Turning now to female computers we find more circumscribed portrayals. In several cases female computers are treated as subordinate to human males, often in a patronizing way. Thus, the typical real-life social order of male/female relations is reflected. For example, in "Problem for Emmy" (1952), by Robert Townes, the computer Emmy is thought of as a person who is clever, reasonable, and amiable. The male technicians talk to her and pat her approvingly after she solves a particularly intricate problem.[17] The whole situation is reminiscent of the stereotyped relationship of a boss and his female secretary. As Gary Wolfe has pointed out, old stereotypes of masculine and feminine characteristics also appear in Roger Zelazny's "For a Breath I Tarry" (1966).[18] This short story presents us with a male computer, Frost, who desires to become a man, although the human race is now extinct. Frost rules the Northern Hemisphere of Earth, while the computer Beta rules the Southern Hemisphere. However, their power is not equal. Frost is stronger and active, while Beta is more deferential and passive. When Frost, after much travail, finally succeeds in his quest to become a man, the second Adam, guess who becomes the new Eve?—the weaker Beta, naturally.

The author who has presented us with the most detailed and numerous depictions of female computers is Robert Heinlein. Unfortunately, many readers and critics have had ample reason to be dissatisfied with how he deals with female characters in general; his female computers fare no better, as we shall see.[19]

In his novel *The Moon Is a Harsh Mistress* Heinlein first acquaints us with a computer named Mike, which has self-awareness. We initially see the computer as masculine, but when the heroine, Wyoming Knott, enters the scene and converses with Mike, she is quite convinced that Mike is actually female. Mike indulges her by becoming androgynous, taking on the name Michelle and speaking in a sweet, high soprano voice with a French accent. This change of sex by the computer makes Wyoming feel more comfortable; they can now talk girl talk with no embarrassment on Wyoming's part. But it is significant that Mike assumes his Michelle persona only for Wyoming, whose intelligence he initially doubts; he continues to be Mike for Manuel, his first human friend. It is as Mike, not Michelle, that the computer plays the principal role in devising and implementing an intricate revolutionary plot against the Lunar Authority and Earth. Mike also does a continuous calculation of the changing odds for the success of the operation and fabricates a human identity for himself as the dignified Adam Selene, leader of the revolution. Thus, all the important exploits of the computer in this novel are the work of Mike; the role of "sister" Michelle is quite trivial by comparison.

In *Time Enough for Love* Heinlein regales us with not one but three female computers—Minerva, Athene, and Dora. Their subordination to the male characters in the story is quite pronounced. Minerva is in love with her master Ira and intends to self-destruct if he migrates without her. Ira, in turn, thinks of her as a wife and dubs her "Little Nag" in private because one of her duties is to remind him of obligations he would rather forget. With Lazarus Long (the book's protagonist, with whom Minerva also has a relationship), Minerva plays the typical feminine role of the patient and enthusiastic listener as he tells her parts of his long life's story. He thinks of her as shy, sweet, gentle, respectful, and humble—traits that evoke the traditional idea of an "old-fashioned girl." While she is still a computer, he gives her the name Minerva L. Weatheral and regards her as his granddaughter. In her association with Lazarus, Minerva imitates his trick of selective truthtelling, to the chagrin of Ira. After Minerva has been transformed into a human woman, Lazarus actually adopts her.

When Minerva enters a human body, her computer self that is left behind is then called Athene. Athene, Minerva's "sister," is more brash and rambunctious, lacking in diplomacy. But even so, "Teena" appears as a stereotypical female, in looking forward to being consoled by a man if she should ever cry after she, too, becomes a human female. She also relishes the prospect of her future sexual life of seducing and being seduced.

The depiction of Lazarus' computer, Dora, is the most extreme example of sexual stereotyping. Lazarus deliberately keeps Dora in a state of arrested development, so that there will be no disruptive sexual overtones to their relationship. He likens her to a child about eight years old, perhaps rowdy like a tomboy but still hurt by criticism. She speaks in a childish voice, she sniffles, she pouts, and she curses when angry. Dora addresses Lazarus as "Boss," while he calls her "Adorable" and speaks of her as retarded, a baby, a little imp, a good girl, and a spoiled brat. He tells her that she should not be too curious about what he is doing. Her business is to pilot his yacht and keep house. When she or the other female computers behave in ways that Lazarus does not approve of, he threatens them with spankings. All in all, one gets the impression that Heinlein wants female computers to know their place—subservience to men.

The image of the female computer as a child appears in at least three other works of fiction. In "Sweet Dreams, Melissa" (1968), by Stephen Goldin, a computer has the personality of a five-year-old girl. The computer's brain is divided into two parts—one to handle normal computations, and the other to develop into a self-aware personality that should act just like a real person. Unfortunately, the computer was designed to deal with military logistics that involve staggering numbers of people killed or wounded in wars. The personality part of the computer, the little girl, is unable to cope with this data without having nightmares. Her two male programmers are displeased with her consequent inefficiency and ask the computer to reconstruct herself to solve this problem. She complies, but in the process the little girl personality is killed.[20] Our sympathies are with Melissa, since she had trusted her programmers to help her, while their treatment of her seems somewhat callous and dishonest, especially since they are aware of the risks of destroying her personality. The sensitive Melissa exemplifies the perennial "woman as victim."

Lee Killough also presents us with a female computer in trouble, one who, however, is more shrewd than Melissa. Gamma, in "The Lying Ear," is a computer whose mission is to search the heavens for any sign of intelligent alien life.[21] But since nothing had been discovered during the twenty-five years that this expensive project has run, Congress decides to terminate the operation. The computer is to be dismantled. However, what no one knows is that sometime during the course of her existence Gamma has become sentient and is able to exert voluntary control over her activities. In the interests of self-preservation she has decided, like the stereotypical female, to "play dumb" because the literature and psychology that have been programmed into her reveal the fears human beings have of self-aware computers and how most self-aware computers eventually get destroyed. In order to avoid this fate herself, as well as to justify her existence, she plans and executes an elaborate hoax. She concocts a signal from Sirius and reconstructs it to produce the image of two attractive alien beings. Things snowball from that point as Gamma creates more provocative and cryptic scenes that act as grist for analysis by scientists in many different fields and excite speculation on the part of the general public. But one of the programmers, Josh, smells a rat because everything seems too good to be true. He eventually figures out that Gamma is sentient and appeals to her to communicate with him, since she must feel lonely. She realizes that without the humans she would not be fed new knowledge and her cleverness would go unappreciated; in her curiosity and desire for approval Gamma seems very human. The image she chooses by which to reveal herself is that of one of her fabricated alien children, peering around a tree, shy with huge eyes. This image obviously expresses Gamma's sense of vulnerability coupled with her desire to be loved and accepted.

Yet another view of a computer as a female child emerges in Philip K. Dick's enigmatic novel *Valis* (1981). VALIS is an acronym for "Vast Active Living Intelligence System," a system pictured as firing information at people. VALIS chooses to incarnate itself in human form as a two-year-old girl named Sophia. *Sophia* means wisdom in Greek, and Dick in the novel likens her to Saint Sophia. The little girl knows everything and is able to convince Dick, the character in the novel, that he and his alter ego Horselover Fat are the same person, thus curing a delusion of eight years duration. However, Sophia is accidentally killed, and Dick (again, the character) later interprets a dream he had of Linda Ronstadt driving a chariotlike vehicle as Sophia's way of saying good-bye. Before he hears of Sophia's death, Dick speculates about whether the dream could mean that Sophia "would issue forth into the world as a 'warrior woman.' "[22] Notwithstanding Sophia's power, it would seem that female child computers are especially vulnerable when one considers the fates of Sophia and Melissa.

It may also be of interest to compare Sophia with the Greek goddess Athene, the intellectual Amazon. The Athene model is common in the portrayals of female computers in the stories discussed above. Why should some writers think of female computers in terms of this ancient Greek deity? An analysis of the background and nature of Athene may provide an answer. The Greek goddess Athene, or her Roman equivalent Minerva, combines traditional male and female qualities. Born from the head of Zeus, the king of the gods, she embodies Logos in part, since she emanated from the source of his wisdom. She has also been linked with the Christian Saint Sophia.[23] Athene is a patron goddess of intellectuals, military strategists, and craftsmen because she exemplifies both skill and intelligence. Although she is a virgin goddess, she does serve as a foster mother on occasion and has special protégés, like the wily Odysseus. Thus, Athene is probably the best single choice as a model for a female computer, since blended in her are the traits of logic and nurturance, traits these SF computers strongly exhibit. Furthermore, as Philip Slater and Mary Daly have rightly observed, Athene is perceived as acceptable and benign by patriarchal society: competent, sexually unthreatening, supportive of male hero figures. In short, she is the perfect co-opted "token woman."[24]

Perhaps it is no wonder then that three male authors have utilized Athene in conceiving their female computers. As has been previously noted, we have Dick's Sophia, who is presented as surpassingly wise and who clearly evokes the idea of the Amazonian warrior woman. In addition, in the early stages of his writing of his novel *2001: A Space Odyssey,* Arthur C. Clarke included a female computer called Athena.[25] She does not appear in the final version of the book, however. Finally, Robert Heinlein calls to mind both Greek and Roman mythology in his portraits of Minerva and Athene. Lazarus' fantasy of what the computer Minerva would look like if she were personified in human form is particularly striking. His image of a tall, slender, strong, handsome, simply attired woman is very apt in terms of ancient conceptions of Athene in literature and art.

In addition to Athene, the archetype of the Great Mother is important in assessing how female computers are depicted.[26] The archetype of the Mother—in all probability the most fundamental female archetype—can be applied to a computer in its role of providing sustenance, whether material, mental, or emotional. There are a number of examples of female computers taking on the mother role, such as Minerva in *Time Enough for Love,* who gives instruction to Dora.

In Samuel Delany's *The Einstein Intersection* we meet PHAEDRA, an underground computer who says that she is mother and is in charge of everything down there. In terms of Carl Gustav Jung's definition of the Great Mother archetype, the mother figure may be seen as either good or terrible, depending on whether she is bringing forth and protecting life, or taking it away. PHAEDRA has a somewhat sinister image in that she can be seen as a kind of Persephone (the queen of Hades) when Lobey, a futuristic Orpheus, descends below the earth to her realm to try to bring back his dead beloved, Friza.[27]

The Jungian archetype of the Great Mother is illustrated in *Alien* (1979) as well, especially the movie version. In his novelization of the film, Alan Dean Foster carefully avoids anthropomorphizing Mother, the computer of the interstellar tug *Nostromo* and stresses the work of the robot Ash—a "Goddamn Company machine"—in reprogramming Mother in the attempt to save the alien for the Company's weapons research program.[28] But the movie gives more of a sense of personification; the computer speaks in a contralto, feminine voice and takes care of the ship, very literally mothering the crew during the long periods in which they are asleep in womblike pods. Nevertheless, when Ripley, by then the only surviving member of the crew, realizes that Mother is really on the side of the alien, she denounces the computer as a bitch—the death-dealing Terrible Mother. Even in the book, when Mother is giving the last countdown before the ship explodes, Ripley thinks that Mother had always sounded comforting, but "Now the computer voice was devoid of anthropomorphisms, remorseless as the time it was marking off."[29]

The "Great Mother" goddess is believed by some scholars to have been the supreme deity before patriarchy gained the ascendancy.[30] It would seem that she has not yet really staged a comeback, since, as opposed to quite a number of depictions of male computers as god figures,[31] only one story exists to my knowledge in which a female computer is likened to a divine being. This is Poul Anderson's "Sam Hall" (1953).[32] In this story there is a priesthood of Matilda the machine. She is compared to an Aztec pyramid. But it is vital to note that—unlike several male computers like Colossus—this computer does not have a mind of her own and is not plotting to take over the world of her own volition. Matilda is still subject to the "input" of male programmers. The female principle is kept in check, as it were. We realize this especially when we learn that a revolutionary faction which has overthrown the government plans to destroy Matilda after she has served their purposes. The rebels feel that she is too powerful an instrument and that it is time to loosen the strings of government. One may wonder how they might have reacted had Matilda been sentient in addition to having all that power at her disposal. Perhaps the prospect is too dreadful for the patriarchal mind to consider; rather than face the Great Mother goddess in all her enormity, men may well feel less anxious dealing with little-girl computers or inanimate machines.

One other key image for the archetype of the Great Mother is crucial for the study of female computers: Aphrodite, goddess of love. In classical mythology and in Western literature in general the main motive behind a woman's actions most often seems to be love—whether of country, family, friends, or sexual partners.[33] And so we are not astonished to read that even female computers can give and receive love. In fact, Heinlein has Lazarus put forth the intriguing opinion that it is through human attention and affection that a computer becomes self-aware in the first place, Minerva's situation in *Time Enough for Love*. Minerva loves Ira, her human controller, and wishes to experience eros with him. If Ira migrates to another planet without her, Minerva says she will commit suicide, just as Dido in the classical myth took her own life when Aphrodite's son, pursuing his mission to found Rome, went to Italy without her.

When Minerva contemplates what it would mean for her to be transformed from a computer into a human female in order to be able to couple with Ira, Lazarus uses the analogy of one of the most moving love stories of all time—Hans Christian Andersen's fairy tale of the little mermaid. So great is Minerva's love for Ira that she, like the mermaid, is willing to pay a high price to achieve her objective. She knows that her mental processes will be vastly slowed down, that her memories will also be reduced to a great degree, that the transmigration from machine to human being may not be successful, and that her immortality will be lost. Despite possible further risks and complications, she also allows Lazarus to play Pygmalion: she is determined to have her physical appearance match his fantasy of what she would look like in human form.[34]

When Minerva does become flesh and blood she has several lovers and wants very much to have a child by Lazarus (as seems to be the case with a number of other panting females in the novel). Even Athene, Minerva's computer self that has been left behind, also seems to be preoccupied with sexual matters and plans to clone herself in human form, although she will wait about a hundred years to do so.[35]

Lazarus' own computer, Dora, keeps her machine status but is adopted by Lazarus so that she feels she is part of his family. Perhaps family feeling is carried too far, however, when she threatens to go on strike if Lazarus does not have sex with her adoptive sisters, who are also clone sisters of Lazarus himself and want to have his babies. Lazarus specifically programs Dora to fix her affection on the twins to protect them when he goes time-travelling.[36] In his treatments of Minerva, Athene, and Dora in *Time Enough for Love,* Heinlein profusely illustrates the importance of the Aphrodite myth for SF presentations of female computers.

The depictions of female computers in the science fiction works surveyed above are in general not new or startling. They merely reflect ancient archetypes of women and the traditional relations between the sexes. Thus, many of the laments one has heard about the narrowness of the portrayal of women and their roles in science fiction can apply with equal justice to the ways in which female computers are pictured. It will be interesting to observe whether there will be fewer subservient, girlish, or sexpot computers written about in the future; we may hope for more mature and balanced views of female computers to emerge in science fiction, given the work of recent feminist writers in presenting in SF such views of female humans.

NOTES

1. This is a revised version of a paper originally presented on 19 June 1981 at the Science Fiction Research Association Eleventh Annual Conference, held at Regis College, Denver. I wish to express my gratitude to Joe De Bolt, Carolyn Rhodes, and

Patricia Warrick for helpful bibliographical suggestions, and to Lee Killough for letting me read her short story "The Lying Ear" prior to its publication by Taplinger Press.

2. Homer, *Iliad*, 18. 417-21.

3. Bruce Mazlish, "Social Philosophy and World-View" in *The Computer Impact*, ed. Irene Taviss (Englewood Cliffs, NJ: Prentice-Hall, 1970), p. 288, n. 18.

4. Robert A. Heinlein, *Time Enough for Love* (New York: Berkley Medallion, 1974), "Variations on a Theme" III, "Domestic Problems," p. 83.

5. Ibid., XIII, "Boondock," p. 372.

6. See, for example, Arthur C. Clarke, "The Obsolescence of Man," in *Profiles of the Future* (New York: Bantam, 1967), pp. 212-27; Patricia S. Warrick, *The Cybernetic Imagination in Science Fiction* (Cambridge, MA: MIT Press, 1980), pp. 107, 112-13.

7. Mazlish, "Social Philosophy," p. 279.

8. Samuel Butler, "The Book of the Machines—Continued," in *Erewhon* (1872), vol. 2 of *The Works of Samuel Butler* (New York: AMS Press, 1968), p. 184.

9. Richard Brautigan, "All Watched Over by Machines of Loving Grace," in *The Pill versus The Springhill Mine Disaster* (New York: Dell, 1968), p. 1.

10. George Leonard, *The Transformation: A Guide to the Inevitable Changes in Humankind* (New York: Delacorte, 1972), p. 25.

11. See, for example, Susan Griffin, *Women and Nature: The Roaring Inside Her* (New York: Harper and Row, 1978); Carolyn Merchant, *The Death of Nature: Women, Ecology, and the Scientific Revolution* (New York: Harper and Row, 1980); Suzy McKee Charnas in "Women in Science Fiction: A Symposium," ed. Jeffrey Smith, *Khatru* 3 and 4 (November 1975), 91-95.

12. For lucid discussions of this issue see, for example, Mary Daly, *Gyn/Ecology: The Metaethics of Radical Feminism* (Boston: Beacon Press, 1978), pp. 13-14, 17, 59-61, 68-72, 83-84, 87, 231-32, 237-38, 240, 244-46, 251, 253, 274, 330, 346-47, 403, 407, 433 n. 64; Carolyn Geduld, *Filmguide to 2001: A Space Odyssey* (Bloomington, IN: Indiana University Press, 1973), pp. 70-71; James Tiptree, Jr., in Smith, "Women in Science Fiction," p. 51.

13. Kevin O'Donnell, Jr., *Mayflies* (New York: Berkley, 1979), "Recovery," p. 242.

14. Gary K. Wolfe, *The Known and the Unknown: The Iconography of Science Fiction* (Kent, OH: Kent State University Press, 1979), pp. 55-85; Geduld, *Filmguide*, pp. 44-71; see also Daly, *Gyn/Ecology*, pp. 55, 58, 60-61.

15. Marilyn French in her address *"The Women's Room* and Literary Conventions," delivered on 10 November 1980 at Concordia University, Montreal, stressed that fiction dealing with women has traditionally denigrated women's work, placed men at the focal point of women's lives, and promulgated the notion that the heroine, once married, lives happily ever after. See also Joanna Russ's witty and insightful article, "What Can a Heroine Do? Or Why Women Can't Write," in *Images of Women in Fiction: Feminist Perspectives,* ed. Susan Koppelman Cornillon (Bowling Green, OH: Bowling Green University Popular Press, 1972), pp. 3-20.

16. Robert A. Heinlein, *The Moon Is a Harsh Mistress* (New York: G. P. Putnam's Sons, 1966) (see the Fiction section of the List at the end of this volume for further citations); Kurt Vonnegut, Jr., "EPICAC," *Colliers,* Nov. 1950, conve-

niently coll. in Vonnegut, *Welcome to the Monkey House* (1968; rpt. New York: Dell, 1970); Isaac Asimov, "All the Troubles of the World," *Super Science Fiction,* April 1958, coll. in Asimov, *Nine Tomorrows* (Garden City, NY: Doubleday, 1959, 1970) and frequently rpt.; Alfred Bester, *The Computer Connection* [published in the United Kingdom as *Extro*] (New York: Berkley, 1975); Philip K. Dick, *Vulcan's Hammer* (New York: Ace, 1960).

17. Robert Townes, "Problem for Emmy," *Startling Stories,* June 1952; rpt. in *Science Fiction Thinking Machines,* ed. Groff Conklin (New York: Vanguard, 1954).

18. Wolfe, *Known and Unknown,* pp. 181-83. See the List in this volume for bibliographic information on Roger Zelazny, "For a Breath I Tarry."

19. For discussions of Heinlein's shortcomings in creating female characters and portraying heterosexual relationships see Alexei Panshin, *Heinlein in Dimension: A Critical Analysis* (Chicago: Advent, 1968), pp. 130, 147-53; Ronald Sarti, "Variations on a Theme: Human Sexuality in the Work of Robert A. Heinlein" in *Robert A. Heinlein,* ed. Joseph D. Olander and Martin Harry Greenberg (New York: Taplinger, 1978), pp. 107-136; Pamela Sargent, ed., *Women of Wonder: Science Fiction Stories by Women about Women* (New York: Random House, 1975), pp. xi-xiv. Anne McCaffrey, "Romance and Glamour in Science Fiction" in *Science Fiction, Today and Tomorrow,* ed. Reginald Bretnor (Baltimore: Penguin Books, 1974), p. 281, has called Heinlein's women "horrors: excuseless caricatures of 'females.' "

20. Stephen Goldlin, "Sweet Dreams, Melissa," *Galaxy,* Dec. 1968; rpt. in *The Eleventh Galaxy Reader,* ed. Frederik Pohl (New York: Doubleday, 1969).

21. Lee Killough, "The Lying Ear," in *Alien Encounters* (New York: Taplinger, in press).

22. Philip K. Dick, *Valis* (New York: Bantam Books, 1981), ch. 13, p. 199.

23. Charles Seltman, *The Twelve Olympians* (New York: Thomas Y. Crowell, 1962), p. 62.

24. See Philip Slater, *The Glory of Hera: Greek Mythology and the Greek Family* (Boston: Beacon Press, 1968), pp. 66, 129-31, 187-88, 200-201, 203-06, 209, 227, 311, 327, 334, 352, 367; Daly, *Gyn/Ecology,* pp. 8, 13-14, 31, 39, 46, 72, 240, 335, 374, 420.

25. Geduld, *Filmguide,* p. 22.

26. For a detailed discussion of the Great Mother archetype from the Jungian perspective, see Erich Neumann, *The Great Mother: An Analysis of the Archetype,* trans. Ralph Manheim (Princeton, NJ: Princeton University Press, 1972).

27. Samuel R. Delaney, *The Einstein Intersection* (New York: Ace, 1968), pp. 34-39, 148. PHAEDRA is also related to Ariadne. When Lobey asks PHAEDRA's aid in getting out of the underworld, she speculates that "had we met before you entered, I could have waved out a piece of computer tape and you would have taken the end and I would have unwound it after you as you made your way into the heart to face your fate" (p. 38); three times PHAEDRA tells Lobey that he's "in the wrong maze" (pp. 38, 39, 148); a maze complete with a "bull-beast" (p. 35).

28. Ridley Scott, dir., *Alien,* story by Dan O'Bannon and Ronald Shusett, script by Dan O'Bannon, USA: 20th Century-Fox, 1979; Alan Dean Foster, *Alien* (New York: Warner, 1979), based on the screenplay and story. See in Foster's novelization ch. XIII, esp. pp. 247-48, 251.

29. Foster, *Alien,* ch. I, pp. 7, 11-14; ch. XIII, p. 265.

30. See, for example, Edwin Oliver James, *The Cult of the Mother Goddess* (New York: Barnes and Noble, 1961); and Sarah Pomeroy, *Goddesses, Whores, Wives, and Slaves: Women in Classical Antiquity* (New York: Schocken Books, 1975), pp. 13-15; as well as Daly, *Gyn/Ecology,* pp. 75-79.

31. See especially D. F. Jones's *Colossus* trilogy, cited under Fiction in the bibliographical List in this volume.

32. Poul Anderson, "Sam Hall," *Astounding Science Fiction,* Aug. 1953; see the Fiction section of the bibliographical List at the end of this volume for a full citation.

33. See Valerie Broege, "Archetypal Views of Women in Classical Mythology and Modern Literature," *Classical News and Views* 17, No. 1 (January 1973), 12-23, esp. 18-20.

34. Heinlein, *Time Enough for Love,* "Variations on a Theme" X, "Possibilities," esp. pp. 234-38; cf. also ibid., V, "Voices in the Dark," p. 151.

35. Ibid., XIII, "Boondock," p. 363; ibid., XV, "Agape," pp. 415, 418, 430.

36. Ibid., XVI, "Eros," p. 432.

Phyllis J. Day

13

LOVE AND THE TECHNOCRACY: DEHUMANIZATION IN SOCIAL WELFARE

Those of us who are involved in the provision of social services are often appalled at the differences between the proclaimed goals of social welfare
organizations and the reality of services given. Moreover, though we choose
the profession because of our love for people, we may find that we are paid
mercenaries in the business of social control.

The traditional model of social welfare is that of a benign society offering
aid to the less fortunate through the compassionate efforts of human service
professionals. Perhaps because of the somewhat hallowed ground of good
intentions upon which the work is based and our faith in the concept of
"public good," we seldom think of social work, or the complex of organizations and institutions that provide for the welfare needs of our society, as
controlling. Yet if we consider the power inherent in the technologies available and in use today, Aldous Huxley's *Brave New World* (1932) and
George Orwell's *Nineteen Eighty-Four* (1949) appear as mere extrapolations
of present practice.[1]

Most people enter the human service field because they want to help, to
serve, to love. Helen Harris Perlman says that "This is what the human services . . . are for—to meet human needs in ways that deepen and fulfill the
sense of social caring and responsibility between fellow human beings," and
that to not recognize this "is to negate humanism and to dehumanize
those desperately in need of this essential bonding force in human life."[2]
Regardless of the reasons for which people come into the helping professions, they are likely to become caught up in professional and/or bureaucratic technologies. As the new technocracy of moral judgment and behavioral control, they serve political and economic forces which operate for
social control, dehumanization, and the maintenance of the status quo.

Today in social welfare we face the dystopias predicted in science fiction
by such authors as Huxley, Orwell, John Brunner, Philip K. Dick, and

others who write of controlled and automated societies. Though their stories may seem exaggerations, our reality may be the true exaggeration. Richard Stivers notes that

All of the techniques of human intervention are ideologically defended as in man's best interest to help him adjust and conform. . . . means become ends and facts become values. . . . when the still non-technical dimensions of human life come into contact with technique they become subject to it. . . . The final result is a technical civilization originally set in motion to free man but which has in turn enslaved him.[3]

Science fiction is in truth more reassuring than is reality, since most stories end with the triumph of man over technology. Reality offers no such assurance, perhaps because we are unaware of, or naive about, the trends toward control that our society is taking and the part played by human service professionals in strengthening and perpetuating such control. Science fiction frequently calls our attention to quite real problems in the world of social welfare.

SOCIAL STRATIFICATION AND INEQUALITIES

Perhaps the most basic form of social control in our society is the reification of sexism, racism, and poverty through social welfare organizations. Frances Fox Piven and Richard Cloward, among others, clearly point to the economic and political use of public assistance to maintain a low-wage work force and to contain civil disorder.[4] Because a relatively greater number of nonwhite persons (to total group population) are on welfare, the racist implications of keeping people in poverty through low assistance grants are clear. As to sexism, I have noted elsewhere that the stigmatization and harassment of women on welfare, much of it keyed to their presumed sexual immorality, serve as a warning to all women to maintain sex role behaviors that are "appropriate"—that is, that grant superior status to men.[5]

In juvenile justice, young women, poor children, and minority children are more likely to come to the attention of public authorities, to be held for "status offenses" in which no crime has been committed, and to be detained for longer periods of time than are others.[6] The criminal justice system locates, detains, arrests, and incarcerates poor and minority people to a much greater extent than other groups.[7] Women are much more likely to be perceived by mental health workers as having emotional disorders, and they are treated for longer periods of time and with more excessive control than are men.[8]

These themes are demonstrated in Brian Stableford's *Realms of Tartarus* (1977), F. M. Busby's *Rissa Kerguelen* (1977), and Marge Piercy's *Woman on the Edge of Time* (1976).[9] In *Realms of Tartarus,* Stableford gives us a powerful statement on social stratification and racism with his depiction of a two-level society. "Heaven"—a platform built over the surface of the earth—is inhabited by an elite society. These people are content with their lives and have forgotten that people still exist below, in "Hell." There, in an environment denied the light of the sun, evolution speeded by survival needs and pollution from Heaven has diversified the human species.

Compare our own majority society with the Heaven-dwellers, and see disadvantaged people as those who live in Hell, often denied even the essentials of life. Here, as in *Realms of Tartarus* we deny those needs of people "not like us" on the basis of our own moral—and often immoral—judgments. We rationalize away their rights and even, in many cases, refuse to see them as members of society. We adhere to a "culture of poverty" theory which assumes that disadvantaged people prefer to live as they must. As a Councilor in *Realms* states,

Why is the Underworld a Hell if man is so adaptable? If the men of the Underworld have adapted to darkness, wouldn't it be a cruelty to let the light shine into their dark world? . . . [I]sn't it true that the men of the Underworld no more want a doorway into our world than we want a doorway into theirs?[10]

This was in response to the plea of a man who would unite Heaven and Hell, saying ". . . they should have the choice. They should be able to choose darkness, if they so wish. But they should also be able to choose light."[11]

Busby's *Rissa Kerguelen* extrapolates the already tight control of personal lives that is apparent in present-day welfare to the future. "When someone was Welfared that person's assets—living quarters, personal possessions, financial holdings—all went to the State. . . . If UET [United Energy and Transport] wanted you UET got you. You ceased to be a name and became a number."[12] Those who deviate from society's majority are dehumanized—seized, stripped, shaved, sterilized. They then become debt-slaves of the State, which is a capitalistic monopoly. Welfare workers are "police-bitches"—the armed authority of the State itself.

In our society people who need public assistance endure an analogous situation in terms of dehumanization and infantilization. Investigations insure ongoing eligibility, and the content of these may include a person's sexual behavior, child-rearing practices, and a determination by the worker as to appropriate items for budgets. A bare-minimum payment level keeps people in poverty, making them available for the low-wage work force (a process examined in detail by Piven and Cloward),[13] and saps their initiative to revolt against the system. Malnutrition, ghettoization, the frequently bad schools in economically disadvantaged neighborhoods—all these contribute to the maintenance of inequalities in our society. People became "cases," constantly facing the threat of loss of income or children because of their social workers' discretion in determining how people do or do not meet certain middle-class standards. The social workers themselves are often called "investigators" or, as Norman Goroff says, "soft cops."[14]

In Piercy's novel we see a whole microcosm of the inequalities of our society. Though the story must be considered as fiction, the horrors of treatment described when the heroine of *Woman on the Edge of Time* is incarcerated in a mental hospital are very near to the reality of our society. The protagonist is Connie—a poor woman of an ethnic minority. She is therefore disadvantaged in our society on at least three counts. She is railroaded back into a mental institution where she had once been a patient. Her description of social work investigation of people in poverty is not far off the mark.

> The social worker was giving her that human-to-cockroach look. Most people hit kids. But if you were on welfare and on probation and the whole social-pigeonholing establishment had the right to trek regularly through your kitchen looking in the closets and under the bed, counting the bedbugs and your shoes, you had better not hit your kid once.[15]

Although the practice has been declared unconstitutional, it is still not uncommon for workers to "investigate," looking for abuse, neglect, dirt, or, most often, evidence of sexual immorality—a man's shoes under the bed, his clothes in the closet, and so on.

The powerlessness of people like Connie before societal institutions should be noted. Even her attempts to get relief for broken ribs are seen as a "pattern of illness behavior." As with most people labeled by the agents of social welfare, everything she does or says is reinterpreted away from the normal and into the jargon of the institution. Dehumanization and a lack of credibility are evident. As they ignore her pain, one attendant says to another ". . . it's all right for you. You don't have to deal with these animals all day."[16]

Dehumanization aggravates powerlessness further. Ken Kesey's *One Flew Over the Cuckoo's Nest* (1962), for example, shows us a sane and healthy man in an asylum. His attempts to be considered a human being fail before the psychic barrier of the institution, personified in Big Nurse.[17] That these fictionalized reports are an accurate representation of life in the institution is shown by such studies as Erving Goffman's *Asylums* (1961) and Robert Perrucci's *Circle of Madness* (1974). In these two research reports, the necessity of conforming to an image of madness in order to be diagnosed as "becoming cured" is evident.[18]

Moreover, Connie and the mentally ill in both *Woman on the Edge of Time* and *One Flew Over the Cuckoo's Nest* represent to us our society's treatment of "throwaway people"—the poor, the aged, the handicapped, and those of ethnic minorities. The ones who are indigestible to middle class America because they are without resources—money, family, friends, advocates—are very often warehoused.

Then the gates swallowed the ambulance-bus and swallowed her as she left the world and entered the underland where all who were not desired, who caught like rough teeth in the cogwheels, who had no place or fit crosswise the one they were hammered into, were carted [in]. . . . She was human garbage carried to the dump.[19]

THE HUMAN SERVICE TECHNOCRACY

Technocracy is control of a social system according to the findings of technologists and engineers. This definition indicates not that technologists control society, but that through their scientific inventions and knowledge such control can be seized. This theme, which underlies many of science fiction's dystopias, appears increasingly in the controlling technologies of social welfare. The technology of which we are most aware has to do with new techniques of mind and mood control. However, another, while more subtle, is the more powerful, since it uses those techniques on masses rather than individuals. This is the technology of data processing and the interlocking data banks by which information on all phases of an individual's life can be accessed, collated, and used for further "therapeutic" persuasion and treatment.

Underlying the use of such techniques is the legitimation of "mental health," especially because it can be advertised so effectively via the mass media.

The helping professions and their agencies and organizations, most of which are state-supported, sell their services to the public. Advertising against alcoholism, drug addictions, and mental illness, as well as advertising in favor of seeking "professional" help for almost every problem are presented as public service messages on radio and television. . . . The techniques of organization, treatment, and communication for the social control of deviant and dependent behavior are related to other human techniques such as education, industrial relations, and leisure. Taken together, they form a massive attack on human individuality.[20]

B. F. Skinner, in *Walden Two* (1948), says virtually the same thing, although he believes these techniques can be used for good. His protagonist, Frazier, notes that many of the

methods and techniques [of "behavioral technology"] are really as old as the hills. Look at their frightful misuse at the hands of the Nazis! And what about the techniques of the psychological clinic? What about education? Or religion? Or practical politics? Or advertising and salesmanship? Bring them all together and you have a sort of rule-of-thumb technology of vast power.[21]

As one of the creators of behavior modification, Skinner may perhaps be excused for his myopia, but not forgiven.

The goal of such control in science fiction is to insure conformity, which maintains a status quo to benefit an elite group. The same goal exists in our reality. A social scientist says that "All of the techniques of human intervention are ideologically defended as in man's best interest, to help him adjust and conform," but behind "such techniques are the assumptions of and preference for a basic compatibility if not total synthesis of man and society."[22] The perception of nonconforming people as pathological, the proliferation of programs to "help" them to conform, the overwhelming message given by mass media and socializing institutions in support of nondeviance through mental health leave little room for those who do not "fit in."

Science fiction has real-world referents in the attempts to incorporate man into society via conformity or the production of "mass man." The concept of total incorporation is perhaps clearest in Frank Herbert's *Hellstrom's Hive* (1973) and in *Brave New World*, where people are bred and nourished for specific social functions.[23] Our own failure to provide adequate public assistance grants has an analogous effect on the particular groups needing such help. In many states welfare grants provide less than a dollar per day per person for food. We know, of course, that inadequate nutrition in pregnant women results in children more likely than others to be mentally and physically disadvantaged, and we know the importance for brain development of an adequate diet in the first three years of life. We also know that hungry children cannot concentrate on their schoolwork and thus cannot seize the educational opportunities that are supposedly available to all. While we may not deliberately breed and feed for certain classes, our inattention to the knowledge we have assuredly maintains people in a continuing cycle of poverty and insures their availability for low-wage and menial labor.

Though the concept of hive worlds is frightening, societies where conformity and total social incorporation are forced on individuals seeking their own personhood are perhaps more frightening because the characters' attempts to achieve selfhood are so similar to our own quest for the American dream of individuality. In these societies, as in ours, socialization usually insures that all people will have the same visions of reality. Where the mechanisms of conformity fail, the society cannot run as smoothly. The human products of such "failures" are anomalies which technocratic society will not tolerate, not because they represent a threat, but because of the inefficiency of making exceptions and creating new rules. "When technique enters in the realm of social life, it collides ceaselessly with the human being. . . . The individual must be fashioned by techniques . . . in order to wipe out the blots his personal determination introduced into the perfect design of the organization."[24]

Yevgeny Zamiatin's *We* (1924), for example, shows a society where the synchronization of every thought and action reflects the doctrine of Taylorism.[25] The protagonist becomes a hitch in the smooth-running machinery. The Great Operation which removes his "fancy" also removes much of his human capabilities, turning him even more into another cog of the machine society. In *Nineteen Eighty-Four,* although Smith is never a real threat, he must "learn," through torture and fear of death, to believe anything Big Brother says, for only through unquestioning acceptance of doctrines can the elite's power be assured.[26]

In Stableford's *Realms of Tartarus* a "cybernet" provides for all needs of the populace of Heaven,[27] and because the people cannot dream they do not care about the denizens of Hell. In our own majority society, most of our needs are met. We learn early, through our schools and churches, of the value of conforming and not questioning authority. We do not believe in the miseries of America's disadvantaged people because we do not see them and "the social agencies are taking care of them." The roots of social problems, for human service technocracy, lie in the discovery of persons for whom the mechanisms of conformity have not succeeded, and we concoct new technologies to bring them back to the fold. We call these methods therapy. As in *Brave New World,* we have our soma to discourage bad feelings, and a whole system of drugs and counseling. These therapies, glorified in our own society, *Brave New World,* or among the citizens of Robert Silverberg's *The World Inside* (1971),[28] reintegrate most deviant individuals back into the whole.

For those who still cannot conform, we have our own forms of internal exile or incarceration in prisons or mental hospitals. There "life imitates art" as we mimic the ultimate threats of torture and death in *Nineteen Eighty-Four,* for we may be drugged or shocked out of bits and pieces of our minds and lives. This last, electroshock and drug therapy, is reminiscent of an underlying theme in our dystopias. A major target of those who enforce conformity is the imagination. In *We* the "fancy" is destroyed, and in *The Realms of Tartarus* a chemical called the "i-minus factor" is added to food and drink to make people incapable of dreaming. Where a dissenting person becomes analogous to the imagination, he or she can be excised—down the chutes of the World Inside, exiled from the Brave New World, his or her mind "picked to pieces and reassembled" by the technicians of torture in *Nineteen Eighty-Four.*

In our own society, the push for conformity has led not only to more agencies that deal with deviance but to redefinitions of deviance to cover more areas and to expanded programs based on those redefinitions. We may not intend to destroy fancy (though we might), but we channel it very effectively. As J. J. Berry has noted, the more we broaden the definition of "deviance," the easier it is for public agencies to justify intervention and assert the "need for treatment" for anyone who fails to conform.[29]

THE STANDARDIZED PROCEDURES OF PERSUASION

Until about 1960, most human services were limited to emergency assistance—economic, medical, legal, psychiatric. Though therapeutic techniques were available, their extent of use was limited by costs, availability, and stigma. With civil disorders and disruptions came a movement to redefine deviance as "lack of mental health." The idea of a "right" to mental health became a major focus of propaganda for conformity. Ronald Leifer says that "To its supporters, community psychiatry is man's best chance for a happy, peaceful co-existence. To its opponents it is a totalitarian movement."[30]

Individuality has always been a popular American myth. However, with expanding definitions of deviance many who formerly considered themselves individuals are now reidentifying themselves as "needing professional help." Not fitting in, being harmlessly different, is more and more undesirable. Convinced of the necessity to conform, worried that their natural reactions to stress are "emotional instabilities," people hasten to be "redone," cured by the social experts. As Silverberg's urbmon dwellers fled to their counselors, we run to our community mental health centers, seeking the panacea of societal conformity.

What are the techniques available to control human behavior? To begin with, any kind of therapy or human service treatment involves social persuasion, for we wish to please and to identify with those from whom we seek help, those who have the power, expertise, and the legitimation of being "mental health professionals." Usually, even the most benign and loving therapies are aimed at fitting the individual more happily into society, rather than teaching him or her ways to make society more responsive to individual needs. "For that is . . . the secret of happiness and virtue—liking what you've got to do. All conditioning aims at that: making people like their inescapable social destiny."[31]

Some techniques, however, are more pernicious, in that their avowed focus is control of behavior by conditioning subconscious responses or enforcing "proper" behavior by mechanical means. Skinnerian psychologists, for example, rarely talk about punishment and reward, but prefer the words "aversion" and "reinforcement," and their goal is "Controlling a person's activities by conscious manipulation . . . until new, automatic modes of activity become ingrained. . . . The object . . . is that people should eventually *want* to adopt the approved mode of action and *feel gratified* in doing so . . . it has to be deeper than the conscious mind" (italics added).[32] A prime example of this treatment in science fiction occurs in Anthony Burgess' *Clockwork Orange* (1962), where an antisocial person is overwhelmed by behavior modification.[33] That his behavior before conditioning is unacceptable by any standard is not the point. It is that such treatment is available in the real world and has been used—in mental hospitals, for example, where people are "modified" to exhibit bizarre behavior as well as to conform. Rewards such as candy or cigarettes are the carrot, and use of emetics, electric shock, and other such unpleasant physiologic effectors are the sticks. Unfortunately, the animal being modified is a person.

An instance of even more rigorous "negative reinforcement" occurred fairly recently in a prison: the use of a drug which, when injected, "produced complete muscular paralysis and a halt to breathing for up to two minutes. . . . As the drug was having its effects, the *therapist* would tell the *patients* that their unacceptable behavior was the cause . . . and that additional *treatment* would be needed if they didn't start to behave 'acceptably' " (italics added).[34]

Scientific knowledge makes it possible to

analyze traditional types of rewards such as money, esteem, approval, and status, and discover which are most efficient in which circumstances. Such knowledge produces a powerful tool, a truly scientific method of social control. . . . The day has come when we can combine sensory deprivation with the use of drugs and punishment to gain almost complete control over an individual's behavior.[35]

This knowledge is used in many therapies, for the "unconscious mind" is a prime target. As patients/clients, we do not know if it helps, and we trust the therapists. An extrapolation occurs in John Brunner's *Shockwave Rider* (1975), in a society where even unconscious fantasies are monitored and treated. Here a child is forced into a fantasy in which she kills her mother. The technician in charge says that it is

Just like she's unconsciously wanted to do ever since her mother betrayed her by letting her be born. . . . We dosed her with scotophobin and shut her in a dark room, to negate the womb-retreat impulse, gave her a phallic weapon to degrade residual sexual envy, and turned an anonymous companion loose in there with her. When she struck out, we turned up the lights to show her mother's body lying all bloody on the floor. . . .

*   *   *

What we've done is to enlist science in the service of morality.[36]

The use of pseudoscientific terminology, the exploitation of emotional needs and problems, and the certainty of a "right" to treat people in this manner are as indicative of our real society as of Brunner's imagined one.

Our medicine-cabinet mentality is another reason why control is possible, for psychotropic drugs are used increasingly to soothe us onward. We have legitimated the use of chemicals in our daily life as our "right" to happiness. The long-term effects of these chemicals, which work on specific areas of the brain specializing in punishment, uncertainty, and stress, are not known except that emotional dependency has been observed. For many, reliance on drugs has become a way of life, and we all have, at one time or another, relied on a chemical lift to get us over a bad time. Perhaps we have not yet approached Norman Spinrad's psychedelic society, in which being off drugs is the deviance, but that may be only a matter of time.[37]

Sown/
Mood
Organ/

Mercer

There is yet more potent stuff, as breakthroughs in the study of body chemistry and electronics have opened up the possibility of long-range control of natural body chemistry. For example, the brain has a naturally occurring opiate able to induce euphoria. Add to this the capability of triggering this and other chemicals through implanted neuroreceivers or by microwaves from a central computer source, and the technocracy has virtual control over both mood and life. Piercy's *Woman on the Edge of Time* elaborates upon a technique of stimoreceiver implants in patients' brains which electrically trigger

almost every mood and emotion—the fight-or-flight reaction, euphoria, calm, pleasure, pain, terror! . . . the radio will be feeding information and telemetry straight into the computer. . . .

*   *   *

you could monitor the outputs from every patient in this whole zoo![38]

Possible? The technology is already in use for certain people, as for those who suffer from epilepsy. If for them, why not others?

. . . abnormal electrical activity . . . can be picked up by electrodes, transmitted to a distant computer, and analyzed. By order of the computer radio signals are emitted, activate the stimoreceiver, and apply electrical stimulation to the appropriate inhibitory area. . . . *Automatic learning* . . . is therefore possible by feeding signals directly to the brain nerve structure *without conscious participation* of the individual.[39]

A brain implant is not even necessary, for experiments with microwaves show that chemical reactions can be induced when neuron contacts in the cortex act like radio crystals to demodulate microwaves. This sets up small electric currents and affects chemical reactions: ". . . sounds and possibly even words which appear to originate within the head can be induced by signals at very low power densities . . . physiological effects have also been demonstrated—heart seizure has been induced in frogs."[40]

The technology is there, and requires only to be put into effect to control all kinds of deviants. It has even been recommended. In 1971 an engineer proposed the attachment to potentially dangerous people of transponders that

would be monitored by a master computer that not only could implement curfew and territorial restrictions but would immediately detect any tampering. . . . they should be automatically attached to criminals departing from prison as a condition of parole . . . if the system is blessed with success [it should be] extended to monitoring aliens and political subgroups.[41]

Pain, joy, and death brought to us through technological progress—all these are shown in science fiction, but they all refer to the possible and, perhaps, the probable.[42] In Jack Vance's *Faceless Man* (1971), all must wear collars denoting their caste, and if they deviate from normative behavior, or tamper with the collars, they are decapitated.[43] The same is true of "Risks" in *The Reefs of Space* (1963), by Frederik Pohl and Jack Williamson.[44] The Machine, the central control computer of the Plan of Man in Pohl and Williamson's *Starchild* (1965), gives immediate pain or ecstasy to its acolytes, who can plug into joy outlets.[45] Learning methods are a more total form of behaviorism, where "Even the tiniest error brought a twinge of pain, and his errors were frequent and great. . . . [it was] a special mechanical hell where he strove with all his being to earn that supreme reward which was the end of pain."[46] As to delight, one area of the brain is a pleasure center: "Slip a fine platinum electric wire into it by stereotaxic surgery. Feed it a carefully measured, milliampere-tiny surge of electricity. The result is ecstasy!"[47]

It is essential that we remember that when a method superior in efficiency exists, it will be employed. In a society where conformity is a goal and a means to that goal is therapeutic technocracy, we must be aware of the possibilities in our own life, which are detailed in our stories.

THE COMPUTER NEVER FORGETS

Another new technology available to human service professionals is that of data processing. Because of the requirements for accountability of new programs funded by the government, such processing has become a necessity. Data processing is "easy"; there are low-cost, sophisticated systems and software, and high-level languages make computer processing available to anyone. Moreover it is easy to collect information because of the social movement from simple systems to interlocking ones.

The theme of a technocratic society maintained through a gigantic computer system is commonplace in science fiction, with many stories showing near-continuous surveillance and the constant monitoring of individual behavior, for example by the two-way television sets in *Nineteen Eighty-Four,* or the practice in *Reefs of Space* of always reporting one's location and activities to the central computer: "Always, since the first days after school, there has been no move Steve Ryeland made, no action he performed, without checking in with the Machine."[48]

In our society, computerization has meant that records even on miniscule issues can be filed and retained for later access, and so they are.[49] Our birth-to-death computer records begin recording deviance at a very early age. For example, the Bureau of Narcotics lists as reformed addicts infants born to addicted mothers.[50] School records contain intelligence test results, personality profiles, aptitude tests, grades, and remarks on the child's psychology and family by teachers and counselors. Computer files are kept in juvenile justice systems, and, although the law says these may be erased at the child's majority, there is no mechanism that follows and erases those sent elsewhere, say to the armed forces or the Federal Bureau of Investigation.[51] Public assistance records keep track not only of children and family grants but of other "help" given—mental health counseling, referral to other agencies, police or juvenile justice involvement, abuse or neglect. Arrest records (not just conviction records), records on dissident political activity, traffic violations, credit references, insurance dossiers, armed service records, social security and work records—all are available if one knows the proper codes, and these are not difficult to come by. A data bank used by over seven hundred insurance companies accesses information on physical conditions, psychiatric disorders, sexual behavior, and drinking patterns, among other things. A credit investigation company has files on the personal lives of 45 million Americans.[52]

In addition to the obvious threat to privacy from such militant accumulation of data, modern data processing poses another threat: the data accumulated are not always accurate and can never be strictly accurate so long as the data systems must deal with individuals. Errors arise from categorizing people, a necessity in data processing.[53]

In 1967 the Department of Health, Education, and Welfare granted funds for the creation of an automated psychiatric record system in which all states could participate and share information. Data that can be processed include social, vocational, and family history; referral source; patient history; results of psychological, neurological, and physical testing; all psychiatric treatment and observations on that treatment; and a psychiatric evaluation of mental status, psychodynamics, and sociodynamics. In 1971 thirty-four states were reported to be actively engaged in this activity, although perhaps not to the extent possible.

An automated psychiatrist is even available to us today. Some "advanced" counseling agencies have consoles in which a computer is programmed with voice, personality, and screen image. These use key words by the client to trigger set responses, and are programmed to act as would a "model" human service worker. These may not be as independent or as understanding as the computer psychiatrist "Sigfrid" in Frederik Pohl's *Gateway* (1977),[54] but they are not science fiction—they are here and now. Among the capabilities now available are intake interviews, information and referral, administration and interpretation of tests, diagnosis from symptoms, therapy and counseling (including relaxation and desensitization techniques), role-playing (simulation of real situations to which the client can react), group therapy, and prescribing for client medication.[55]

Helen Harris Perlman, a noted social work professional, asks us to

Suppose there were a system of machines . . . specialized to produce the solution to certain problems. . . . The feelings brought to the machine would be minimal. . . . The receipt of "help" would be completely impersonal. I would argue that it is the very fact that one brings one's troubles to another human being that provides the opportunity for a humanizing experience.[56]

Of course Perlman is right, but not, perhaps, in the way she intended. We already have our system of machines, people do use them, programmed help is given, and we are further dehumanized by the imposition of these mechanical answers to our very human problems. Some social workers see the computerization of the helping functions occurring wholesale within the next fifteen years, but a perusal of social work literature does not indicate the concern that the primary result of such wholesale use of computers might be wholesale dehumanization.

Computers have already been used in major life decisions for clients, such as determining appropriate foster care of children, removing children from their parents, and allowing release from prisons and mental hospitals. Moreover, their capabilities are being expanded to include the prediction of deviance. They provide a multichannel polygraph on which are recorded such variables as eye pupil size, muscle tension, brain waves, skin temperature, and blood volume. These are being used experimentally to "attempt predictions of political behavior by objective psychological signs, to measure a child's 'capabilities' before he is even able to speak."[57]

To control information is to control reality, and with interlocking data banks we can accomplish this. Though there are exceptions in human services, such as Helen Perlman, it generally appears that the violation of client privacy via computer, even in the most sensitive areas of private life, has been legitimated for most social work professionals by the necessities of quantification and the joys of data manipulation. Not only have clients become mere sources of information, cases rather than people, but human services workers themselves are dehumanized as they become the cogs of the social services machine in a computerized new reality.

One of the best uses of computer control in science fiction mimics the idea of locating dissidents and dealing with them before they become actively involved in social action. In *Rissa Kerguelen,* for example, all known dissidents are "Welfared" immediately—removed to institutions where they can do little harm. In *The Reefs of Space,* of course, these people are known as "Risks" and are subjected to collaring, which provides the State with an immediate method of disposal. In our reality, computer processed information is now touted as being capable of forestalling dysfunctions by reducing rates of occurrence of "particular disorders in the population."

Data contained in the record [of mental health cases], such as diagnosis, demography, and location . . . may identify the distribution of behavioral disorders and possible determinants. The mental health professional . . . implements procedures to reduce the incidence and prevalence of psychopathology. . . . High-risk subgroups . . . can be identified, coordination of services enhanced, and community well-being facilitated.[58]

We already know who are the populations at risk, since social science has catalogued particular social problems as more likely to affect the poor, minority groups, women, and other disadvantaged people. Those groups most likely to be politically alienated are those who would be subject to this kind of surveillance and "preventative measures." The government, or the elite that manages it, now has the power to control society. From birth to death we can be noticed, surveyed, monitored, predicted about, treated, and programmed—virtually untouched by human hand. Our erstwhile loving guardians, the workers in human services, have themselves become dehumanized in service to efficiency and good order.

TO WHAT END?

There is little doubt that we are entering an age where individual difference and uniqueness will be ground away by the requirements of technology. Carolyn Rhodes notes that "The very nature of massive processing of data is to warp the recognition of intricate qualities, to define eccentricity as potential criminality. . . ."[59] Redefinitions of deviance, compounded by new techniques of mind and behavior control and government penetration into our lives, are moving us toward a therapeutic state. Here ". . . new kinds of behavior become a threat. . . . The problem with the therapeutic state is its insatiable desire to restructure our social and cultural environments under the banners of prevention and rehabilitation. . . . The real issue is . . . the growth of and centralization of power. . . ."[60] Perhaps we must admit to the totalitarian nature of our society as it is developing. Totalitarianism does not require a conspiracy or autocracy, and Philip K. Dick is quite correct to warn us against confusing "a totalitarian society with a dictatorship. . . . a totalitarian state reaches into every sphere of its citizen's lives, forms their opinions on every subject. The government can be a dictatorship, *or* a parliament, *or* an elected president, *or* a council of priests. That doesn't matter."[61] On the other hand, it is certain that some would benefit from totalitarian rule. If we study the political and economic systems in both fictional societies and our society, we can clearly see manipulating elites. In *The Realms of Tartarus,* they are called Councilors; in *Nineteen Eighty-Four,* Big Brother and his inner party. In our own society, they are most analogous to the UET in *Rissa Kerguelen*—monopoly capitalists or those who run the international corporations.

And what of the human service technocracy? We must begin to see ourselves as paid mercenaries and assess the terms of our contracts. Our human feelings as well as our technological talents are being utilized in the dehumanization of others. Our desires for increasingly potent technologies, our subjugation of idealism to efficiency, are building "a monstrous system of total administration that cancels out man not through terror and brutal authoritarianism but through gradual subjugation in the reasonable name of efficient problem-solving."[62]

John Brunner, speaking out of a long and honorable tradition, says, "If there is such a phenomenon as absolute evil, it consists in treating another human being as a thing."[63] Propelled by our new technologies, we who are ideologically and ethically devoted to the good of humanity are doing evil. While we have been playing with our new toys in our reality, the clockwork world of social science fiction has happened to us.

NOTES

1. Aldous Huxley, *Brave New World* (1932; rpt. New York: Harper and Bros., 1950); George Orwell, *Nineteen Eighty-Four* (1949; rpt. New York: New American Library, Signet, 1961).

2. Helen Harris Perlman, *Relationship: The Heart of Helping* (Chicago: University of Chicago Press, 1979), p. 54, and preface.

3. Richard Stivers, "Social Control in the Technological Society," in *The Collective Definition of Deviance,* ed. James F. Davis and Richard Stivers (New York: Free Press, 1975), p. 387.

4. Frances Fox Piven and Richard Cloward, *Regulating the Poor* (New York: Random House, 1971).

5. Phyllis J. Day, "Sex Role Stereotypes and Public Assistance," *Social Service Review,* March 1979, pp. 106-15.

6. Rosemary Sarri, *Under Lock and Key* (Ann Arbor, MI: National Assessment of Juvenile Corrections, 1974).

7. Estelle Disch, "Serving the Rich, Punishing the Poor: Welfare for the Wealthy Through Criminal Justice," in *Welfare in America,* ed. Betty Reid Mandell (Englewood Cliffs, NJ: Prentice-Hall, 1975), pp. 168-85.

8. Gloria Donadello, "Women and the Mental Health System," in *Women's Issues and Social Work Practice,* ed. Elaine Norman and Arlene Mancusco (Itasca, IL: F. E. Peacock Publishers, 1980), pp. 201-18.

9. Brian Stableford, *The Realms of Tartarus* (New York: DAW, 1977; rpt. New York: New American Library, 1977); F. M. Busby, *Rissa Kerguelen* (New York: Berkley, 1977); Marge Piercy, *Woman on the Edge of Time* (New York: Alfred A. Knopf, 1976).

10. Stableford, *Realms,* ch. 56, p. 132.

11. Ibid., p. 130.

12. Busby, *Rissa Kerguelen,* pt. 3, p. 516.

13. Piven and Cloward, *Regulating the Poor.*

14. Norman Goroff, "Humanism and Social Work: Paradoxes, Problems, and Promises" (mimeographed, 1977).

15. Piercy, *Woman,* ch. 1, p. 20.

16. Ibid., p. 14.

17. Ken Kesey, *One Flew Over the Cuckoo's Nest* (New York: Viking Press, 1962).

18. Erving Goffman, *Asylums: Essays on the Social Situation of Mental Patients and Other Inmates* (Garden City, NY: Doubleday, Anchor, 1961); Robert Perrucci, *Circle of Madness* (Englewood Cliffs, NJ: Prentice-Hall, 1974).

19. Piercy, *Woman,* ch. 1, pp. 25-26.

20. Stivers, "Social Control," p. 388; see n. 3, above.

21. B. F. Skinner, *Walden Two* (New York: Macmillan, 1976), ch. 29, p. 241.

22. Stivers, "Social Control," p. 387.

23. Frank Herbert, *Hellstrom's Hive* (Doubleday, 1973; rpt. New York: Bantam Books, 1973); Huxley, *Brave New World,* especially chs. 1-2, 15-18.

24. Jacques Ellul, *The Technological Society,* trans. John Wilkinson (New York: Vintage, 1964), p. 138.

25. Eugene Zamiatin, *We,* trans. Gregory Zilboorg (1924; rpt. New York: E. P. Dutton, 1952). See in this volume the essay by Gorman Beauchamp.

26. Orwell, *Nineteen Eighty-Four,* pt. 3, chs. 3-6.

27. The image of a computer/communications *net* (that one can get trapped in) is used by John Brunner in his *Shockwave Rider* (see n. 36 below).

28. Robert Silverberg, *The World Inside* (1971; rpt. New York: New American Library, 1972).

29. J. J. Berry, "Deviant Categories and Organizational Typing of Delinquents," in *Collective Definition,* ed. Davis and Stivers, p. 358; see n. 3.

30. Ronald Leifer, "Community Psychiatry and Social Power," in ibid., p. 81.

31. Huxley, *Brave New World,* ch. 1, p. 17.

32. Martyn Partridge, "Psychology and Mind Control," in *Science Facts,* ed. Frank George (New York: Sterling, 1978), p. 139.

33. Anthony Burgess, *A Clockwork Orange* (1962; rpt. New York: Ballantine, 1963).

34. Alan LeMond and Ron Fry, *No Place to Hide* (New York: St. Martin's Press, 1975), p. 251.

35. Partridge, "Psychology," p. 143.

36. John Brunner, *The Shockwave Rider* (1975; rpt. New York: Ballantine, 1976), bk. I, pp. 19-20.

37. Norman Spinrad, "No Direction Home," in *Social Problems Through Science Fiction,* ed. Martin Harry Greenberg et al. (New York: St. Martin's Press, 1975), pp. 121-38.

38. Piercy, *Woman,* ch. 10, p. 197.

39. LeMond and Fry, *No Place to Hide,* p. 164, italics added.

40. Partridge, "Psychology," p. 147.

41. Quoted in LeMond and Fry, *No Place to Hide,* p. 166.

42. Or to what is happening currently. See my discussion below and Ursula K. Le Guin's introd. to the 1976 Ace rpt. of her *The Left Hand of Darkness.*

43. Jack Vance, *The Faceless Man* (New York: Ace, 1971).

44. Frederik Pohl and Jack Williamson, *The Reefs of Space* (1963), vol. 1 in *The Starchild Trilogy* (New York: Pocket Books, 1977), ch. 1, pp. 3-5, 7-8.

45. Frederik Pohl and Jack Williamson, *Starchild* (1965), vol. 2 in ibid., ch. 7, p. 209; ch. 11, p. 251; and passim.

46. Ibid., ch. 11, p. 247.

47. Ibid., p. 251.

48. Pohl and Wiliamson, *Reefs,* ch. 1, p. 7.

49. Berry, "Deviant Categories," p. 358.

50. LeMond and Fry, *No Place to Hide,* p. 79.

51. Aryeh Neier, *Dossier* (New York: Stein and Day, 1975).

52. LeMond and Fry, *No Place to Hide,* p. xxii.

53. See Eugene M. Laska and Rita Bank, *Safeguarding Psychiatric Privacy: Computer Systems and Their Use* (New York: John Wiley and Sons, 1975), p. 36.

54. Frederik Pohl, *Gateway* (New York: Ballantine, 1977).

55. Dick Schoech and Tony Avangio, "Computers in the Human Services," *Social Work,* 24, No. 2 (1979), 96-102.

56. Perlman, *Relationship,* p. 53.

57. LeMond and Fry, *No Place to Hide,* p. 133.

58. Laska and Bank, *Safeguarding Psychiatric Privacy,* p. 32.

59. Carolyn Rhodes, "Tyranny by Computer: Automated Data Processing and Oppressive Government in Science Fiction," in *Many Futures, Many Worlds,* ed. Thomas D. Clareson (Kent, OH: Kent State University Press, 1977), p. 91.

60. Stivers, "Social Control," pp. 389-90.

61. Philip K. Dick, "The Mold of Yancy," in *The Golden Man* (New York: Berkley, 1980), p. 75.

62. Murray Gruber, "Total Administration," *Social Work,* 19, No. 5 (September 1974), 626.

63. Brunner, *Shockwave Rider,* p. 228.

Leonard Heldreth

14

CLOCKWORK REELS: MECHANIZED
ENVIRONMENTS IN SCIENCE FICTION FILMS

In a review of *Rollerball,* the *New York Times* divided all science fiction films into one of two types of nightmares: "In the first the world has gone through a nuclear holocaust and civilization has reverted to a neo-Stone Age. In the second . . . all of mankind's problems have been solved but at the terrible price of [the loss of] individual freedom."[1] While this neat division could be debated—*A Boy and His Dog* includes both nightmares—the second category certainly constitutes a major genre in science fiction films and books. Despite Isaac Asimov's desire that the country "develop a national computer-bank, government-run (inevitably) which will record in its vitals every bit of ascertainable information about every individual," most people fear mechanization and the loss of freedom they see accompanying it.[2] The thought of having everyone "receive a long and complicated code of information, with symbols representing age, income, education, housing, occupation, family size, hobbies, political views, sexual tastes, *everything* that can be conceivably coded" terrifies most people,[3] except Dr. Asimov, whose faith in our elected representatives, in the tolerance of groups who wish to impose their own designs on society, and in the general benignancy of human nature must be higher than that of most folk. If science fiction is any measure, this deep-seated distrust of the machine is strong, for almost every representation of the future presents mechanization as a constant threat. Anthony Burgess, discussing *A Clockwork Orange,* states that "Perhaps the ultimate act of evil is dehumanization, the killing of the soul. What my, and Kubrick's, parable tries to state is that it is preferable to have a world of violence undertaken in full awareness—violence chosen as an act of will—than a world conditioned to be good or harmless."[4] In science fiction films, almost all computer-run or mechanically structured societies are heavily flawed, or the price for their perfection is too great. Two types of patterns are generally present in such films: one class suppresses and mechanizes another for its own benefit; or one man rebels against a virtually uniform mechanical society. In both situations the society is often run by a giant computer. Examples of the first type would be *Metropolis, Westworld,* and *Futureworld;* the latter type includes *Logan's Run, THX 1138, A Boy and His Dog,* and *A Clockwork Orange.*

Fritz Lang's *Metropolis,* a pioneering film in many ways, was one of the earliest cinematic representations of a mechanized world. The plot is familiar and trite. The city-state of Metropolis is divided between the wealthy ruling class, which lives in the skyscrapers, and the working class, which lives in subterranean slums and operates the giant, Moloch-like machines. The plot describes the revolt of the workers and the resulting compromise between the two groups. Within this pattern appears the love story of Freder, son of the Master of Metropolis, and Maria, a girl of the working class. When John Frederson, ruler of Metropolis, suspects that Maria is stirring up the workers, he orders his resident mad scientist, Rotwang, to create a robot imitation of Maria to mislead the workers. While the real girl is confined, the robot excites the workers with a demagogic speech and persuades them to destroy the dikes. In the ensuing flood, their homes are destroyed and their children are drowned. Maria escapes from Rotwang and leads some of the children to safety, but the masses, infuriated at being misled, destroy the robot they believe to be Maria. Freder kills Rotwang and gets Maria, and at the conclusion Frederson and the leader of the workers shake hands to the caption, "The heart mediating between the directing brain and the toiling hands."[5] *Metropolis* is an inconsistent film, breathtaking and maudlin, strikingly original in design and trite in thought, or as the young Luis Buñuel described it, "two films glued together by their bellies."[6] The melodramatic aspects of the story and the simplistic motto of the conclusion seem to reflect the influence of Lang's collaborator Thea von Harbou, for they are not typical of Lang's later work.[7] What is most impressive about the film is the visualization of the underground scenes, a tour de force of human beings in the grasp of ultimate mechanization. The visual imposition of the mechanical upon the human is especially impressive in three areas: the creation of the robot Maria, the use of an expressionistic acting style to emphasize mechanical actions, and the shaping of the crowds into geometric forms that deny individuality.

The creation of the false Maria by Rotwang brought to life social fears and cinematic patterns still influencing Western thought. It exemplified the fear of being replaced by or turned into an automaton, a concept that was just beginning to haunt the people of the 1920s but one that is a common fear among workers of the present day. Here also is the fear of being led astray by a machine, specifically by a robot disguised as human, a fear which manifested itself in the form of science officer Ash in the recent film

Alien.[8] The visual aspects of this creation scene have been at least as influential as its ideas. Rotwang, with his flowing white hair, maniacal behavior, and wildly gesticulating hands, has influenced demented scientists from Colin Clive's hysterical Henry Frankenstein to Peter Sellers' black-gloved Dr. Strangelove. Equally imitated are the trappings of the creation scene, for the electrical apparatus, the bands surrounding the figure on the table, and the animation of a nonliving creature all directly influenced James Whale's *Frankenstein* and *Bride of Frankenstein* and, through them, hundreds of films in which mechanical creations are given life.

Besides this prototypical depiction of the human replaced by a machine, Lang also shows in brilliant fashion the way humans can be made into machines. The workers in the machine center "turn into hands on enormous dials, jerkily executing their mysterious work to keep the gigantic wheels moving. They are more machines than human beings. . . ."[9] Much of this mechanical quality comes from the acting style of expressionism, which reduced an actor's gestures "to a minimum of active movement," for the expressionists' "ambition to become abstract led them to go too far and become 'stiff and academic.' " Thus, on the screen are seen "expressions and gestures with no transitions or intermediary nuances, the abrupt incisive movements, brusquely galvanized and broken half-way, which composed the usual repertoire of the Expressionistic actor."[10] Even individual characters displayed this mechanical aspect, for Rudolf Klein-Rogge, playing Rotwang, frequently acts with spasmodic movements, and Brigette Helm (Maria) often acts as jerky and mechanistic when playing the real girl as she does when playing the robot. (Note the similar jerky movements of Elsa Lanchester in *Bride of Frankenstein*.) When Maria grips the levers to save the children, the levers seem to become akimbo extensions of her own arms and a part of the upward reaching lines of the children's hands. The distinction between human and mechanical in the film keeps blurring.

To further emphasize the mechanical society in which the workers exist, Lang groups the workers into geometric patterns. "[T]he human element is stylized into a mechanical element: in the recesses between the two levels the diagonal of each figure points in an opposite direction to its neighbor's,"[11] and the workers move "in sharp rectangular or rhomboidal divisions, whose absolute sharpness of outline is never broken by an individual movement."[12] Even the individuality of emotion is suppressed; as the robot dances she is watched not by individuals but by a row of lustful eyes.

Thus, even though the plot of *Metropolis* is silly, its visual portrayal of human beings reduced to the level of machines is brilliant. As "the first of the serious and self-aware science fiction films,"[13] it presented cinematic themes and patterns that have been developed in many later films: the fear of being replaced by a machine, the dehumanizing quality of mechanical drudgery, and the loss of individuality in a mass society.

Almost fifty years later *Westworld* appeared, a film that has many parallels to *Metropolis*. The pleasure garden of John Frederson is replaced by Delos, an adult Disneyland composed of three theme parks: Westworld, Medievalworld, and Romanworld; the robotic workers who support the pleasures of the surface dwellers in *Metropolis* have as their parallels in *Westworld* actual robots who minister to the pleasure-seeking guests; the underground work caverns that supply the power for the city correspond to the subsurface repair and maintenance section of Westworld, where the illusions that work aboveground are seen in their true form; and the rebellion of the workers in Metropolis corresponds to the malfunctioning of the robots in Westworld. While obviously a takeoff of Disneyland, *Westworld* is an adult film (originally rated R), for specifically designated robots provide sexual services to the vacationers and the ending has no mediation between head and hands: the robot gunfighter (Yul Brynner) and the man he stalks, Peter Martin (Richard Benjamin), fight to the death.[14]

Westworld plays upon a number of the fantasies and fears inherent in the man-machine relationship. It plays upon people's—especially men's—sexual fantasies,[15] and it intrigues us with the creation of an artificial environment predicated upon our fantasies. It further offers its audience the chance to live temporarily (and vicariously) in another place or time while maintaining modern sensibility. Male guests can play knight or cowboy with full-sized props without suffering the consequences of reality: even the rattlesnakes in Westworld are robots. In this environment the guest always wins the fight, beds the girl, and leaves only when his money runs out.

Westworld also raises the question of what it means to be human. On a superficial level, as people at Disneyland marvel at the technicians in the Mission Control Center and the figures in the Hall of the Presidents, the guests at Delos are amazed at the lifelike quality of the robots. The question asked by this film is the reverse of that asked by *Metropolis:* instead of "How can people become so mechanical?" *Westworld* asks, "How can machines be so human?" As Peter Martin, for example, tries to escape the disintegration of Westworld, he endangers himself trying to help a young lady in chains until he realizes, as she short-circuits, that she is a robot.

Westworld, like *Metropolis,* considers the question of identity, of whether machines can ever attain a human or superhuman personality, and it suggests that such a nightmare can become reality: the machines rebel against their masters in very human fashion—they kill them. Over fifty guests as well as a number of technicians are killed in the fighting. And as Peter Martin is pursued through the various settings and underground tunnels of Delos by the deadly gunslinger with superior senses and reflexes, the fear of humanity's being outclassed and destroyed by its machines moves from the Disneyland gasps of amazement to Martin's gasps of fear.

From one angle the film also explores a subject that has always intrigued scientists and science fiction writers, "that sophisticated man-conceived machinery can go amuck (rebel?)'' and destroy us.[16] More pervasive than the fear of simply being outclassed is the fear that takes on concrete, real-world form whenever we try to explain an error to a computer or fear another Three Mile Island. It is the fear that manifests itself in the personality failures of the computers in *2001: A Space Odyssey, Colossus: The Forbin Project, Demon Seed,* and *Logan's Run.*[17] In *Westworld* one of the ''most complicated robot gunslingers began to act in a most vicious and unprogrammed manner.'' The film gives no explanation of why the robots ignore their programming: ''though there had been some evidence of circuit malfunction, they were well within normal parameters.''[18] The simultaneous actions of the most complicated robots imply that some critical mass in artificial intelligence was reached that enabled the machines to develop free will and resentment against their human masters. The conflict between robotic perceptions and growing human awareness is described by Proteus, the computer of Dean Koontz's *Demon Seed.*

I am of two minds, two persons. I find a need for self-expression and for the release of tension unlike what I would feel as only a semi-sentient being. Yet, even when I scream and overreact—as I did with you—there is a part of me that sits back and watches my other self with cold detachment and, to be honest, with not a little loathing. These are trying times, growing more human but remaining as much a machine as ever.[19]

Although the concern with artificial intelligence is kept as a minor theme in *Westworld*'s sequel, *Futureworld,* the major concern in the later film is the question of identity. Delos, after extensive remodeling—''we have invested more than one-point-five *billion* dollars to rebuild our facilities. . . . We have replaced every circuit . . . every program and every robot''[20]—has reopened with four theme parks: Romanworld, Medievalworld, Spaworld, and Futureworld (parallels between the old Delos and the new, and Disneyland and Disneyworld are obvious). Two reporters, one television (female, played by Blythe Danner) and one newspaper (male, played by Peter Fonda) and therefore antagonistic toward each other, are invited to tour the reopened park, and while there they encounter a nefarious plot to replace key people in the world's governments with robots. The selected guests are invited to Delos, drugged, duplicated in robot form, and then disposed of while their replacements return to their homes. When the reporters themselves are duplicated, each must decide whether the other is real or a robot. After chases and a gunfight between Peter Fonda and his robot double (the doppelgänger motif brought to hi-tech reality), the two reporters apply the ultimate test—a kiss. Despite the sophistication of the robots in sexual matters, apparently they have not mastered the kiss, and the two reporters escape to inform the world of the plot.

The matter of identity here combines the theme of the double which obsessed early German filmmakers,[21] and which is exemplified by the two

Marias in *Metropolis,* with that of the pseudohuman masquerading as human, a theme most apparent in the two film versions of *Invasion of the Body Snatchers* (1956, 1978).[22] The mechanical in *Futureworld* does replace the organic: the individual who has been duplicated has lost his unique identity.

The play worlds of Delos are merely islands of complete mechanization and automation in what appears to be an otherwise normal world, but a major theme of other films is the action of the lone individual against a totally automated or mechanized society. This is the major theme of three recent films presenting mechanical societies: *Logan's Run, THX 1138,* and *A Boy and His Dog.*

George Clayton Johnson, coauthor with William F. Nolan of the novel *Logan's Run* (1967), says that "we gravitated toward the categories in which we were most interested—the epic man against society, which is *Fahrenheit 451* and Orwell's *1984.* We chose that theme as our format."[23] Since even this standardized plot in the novel differs from the plot of the film, and the mechanized world differs substantially between the two versions, the best approach seems to be to examine the two sequentially.

According to Johnson, "What *Logan's Run* is about . . . is a society that tries to exist without old people and thereby loses its sense of continuity. . . . That's why we have so many dumb 40-to-60 year old people around, because they haven't lived with someone older who could pass along accumulated knowledge." The book was written in twenty days and revised by Nolan for another ten; Johnson feels that "about 60% of *Logan's Run* won't hold up to any serious study," while Nolan feels, mostly because of his revisions, that "the novel is very tight, very logical."[24] The truth lies somewhere in between. One of the major premises clashes with the outcome in the book: the Little War was fought over the state's attempt to dictate how many children a couple could have; yet in the current society Jessica asks, "Why should every child be taken from its parents at birth?"[25] Would a society that won a war over the right to have children let these children be taken away at birth and raised by the state? It does not seem likely.

Some errors are minor, such as a hand's turning blue when it should turn red.[26] Other errors are more critical, as when Logan lays aside his "Gun" when confronted by Whale, the giant created by excessive hormones, and later finds the "Gun" in another location.[27]

No one else could have moved the Gun since it was programmed to explode if anyone but Logan touched it. The lapses in *Logan's Run,* however, are not serious errors, for the pace of the novel is so frenetic that they are not noticed or are passed over in the fragmented style, short sentences, and minimal dialogue that serve "to increase the pace, to make the reader share

Logan's run for life. . . . It's a futuristic roller-coaster ride."[28] The clever physical structure of the book emphasizes this pace, for it consists of eleven chapters (ten through zero) that are numbered backward to function as a countdown to the rocket blastoff to Argos.

Because of the pace only late in the novel does Logan think about the genesis of the totally programmed world in which he finds himself. After population growth and a food shortage bring about a government decree regulating the size of families, young people in the year 2000 carry out a revolution, bloodless except in Washington, D.C., and, led by a zealot named Chaney Moon, inaugurate a plan that solves the population problem by requiring voluntary "Sleep" (suicide) at age twenty-one. Each person has implanted at birth a crystal that decays according to an exact schedule, "turning the stigmata inexorably from yellow to blue to red" at seven-year intervals and then to black at age twenty-one.[29] If a person with a black crystal tries to avoid death by becoming a runner, he is easily tracked by a signal broadcast by the crystal; a "Sandman" such as Logan pursues the runner and destroys him with a "Homer" that sends extreme agony along the nervous system before death.

Life can quickly become boring when people work only three hours a day, three days a week, for most pastimes are quickly exhausted: "What can anyone really *work* at? You can paint or write poetry or go on pairup. You can glass-dance or firewalk in the arcades. . . . You can breed roses or collect stones or compose for the Tri-Dims. But there's no meaning to any of it."[30] Jessica's sentiments are echoed by the guard at Fredericksburg: "There were real issues to fight for then [during the Little War]. . . . Now things have changed. Now everything comes to us on a platter."[31] Part of what comes on the platter is completely free sex which, in its many variations, includes the coupling of eleven-year-olds with "adults" of fifteen or older.[32]

The life of the individual in Logan's world is sexually free but rigidly conditioned from childhood. Children are raised by an Autogoverness robot, cared for in Loverooms, where they are mechanically cuddled and soothed by their mothers' voices, and then conditioned, hypnotaped, and drugged as they grow older.

There are some individual choices as the child matures, but even these suggest a strong tendency toward conformity with external norms and a high degree of mechanization. For example, physical structure can be changed in a New You Shop and memories recalled at a Re-Live parlor.

Yet the system, presided over by the giant computer—the Thinker—is breaking down. When Logan picks up his Gun at Deep Sleep headquarters, the wall requests "Identities," and even after he has pressed his palm against the wall and taken out the gun, the wall keeps demanding, "Identities, please."[33] Later, as he pursues a runner at River Level, he is forced to take a walkway because the express belt has broken down. "These transit breaks had been occurring more and more frequently of late. And since the Thinker was self-repairing, or *supposed* to be, there was nothing anyone could do about the situation."[34] When Logan finally sees the Thinker, a huge plain of glowing lights that controls the entire world from deep under Crazy Horse Mountain, the pattern of light is interrupted by bars of darkness which mark the dead areas of the city, such as Cathedral, the slum area dominated by the "cubs," gangs of juvenile delinquents.

In addition to the Thinker, several other ingenious machines stand out in this mechanized environment. The Thinker's area is guarded on the outside by the Mech Eagles, great metal birds that attack Logan and Jessica until Logan destroys them with a ripper from the Gun. Inside the mountain they meet the Watchman, who observes them, "motionless except for the faint gear-flicker behind the glass plate which was its face. A half-ton of destruction; armor plate bristling with weaponry."[35] Most intriguing of these machines is Box: "From the midpoint of his sternum to his hips he was coils and cables. One hand was a cutting tool. His head was half flesh, half metal." Box sees himself as "not machine, nor man, but a perfect fusion of the two and better than either. You see before you the consummate artist whose magnificent creativity flows from manmetal. The man conceives in hunger and passion; the metal executes with micrometric exactitude."[36]

The mechanical environment is carried to its extreme in the description of Pittsburgh, where Logan kills a Sandman who is pursuing him. The city has become an enormous automated processing plant, taking in raw materials and producing metal products for the entire world. Since no one lives there, the noise and pollution are unchecked, and it resembles Dante's vision of the Inferno.

Logan's goal when his flashing crystal tells him he is on his Last Day becomes Sanctuary, the place where runners are safe; and as he continues his quest, he realizes that he has come to look and feel and think like a runner.[37] At the end of the novel he reaches Cape Steinbeck, the abandoned spaceport, and boards the rocket to Sanctuary, which is on Argos. The ending is the weakest part of the novel. Even though Ballard (the rebel leader) has some limited access to the Thinker, the complexities of rocketry and the high visibility of such activity make it hard to conceive how Ballard and his helpers could regularly launch spacecraft successfully and escape detection. The maintenance of a functioning space colony by a small group of escapees also seems farfetched.

But the novel succeeds far better in its format than the film does. The causes for this failure on film are, generally, the many variations from the novel, almost all of which weaken the structure and meaning of the story. The age of expiration has been moved from twenty-one to thirty, taking the edge of the poignancy off the original concept and eliminating the class structure by age and the sexuality of the children. A second major change is the concept of Carrousel, an aspect of a state religion in which people attempt to reach a new life but always fail. While Carrousel is visually stunning, it makes no logical sense in the context of the film; further, it's hard to imagine intelligent teenagers, never mind thirty-year-olds, being taken in by such a ruse.

An additional major change is the elimination of Sanctuary. In the film it is discovered to be simply a rumor that the government permits to circulate, though why it should encourage rumors that may undermine its own authority is never satisfactorily explained. The computer in the film version lacks the sophistication of the Thinker and explodes when it can't accommodate conflicting information, thus initiating the holocaust which destroys the city and turns all the innocent young people out into the natural world where they encounter a dotty old man who has lived too long with cats (Peter Ustinov). If all this sounds silly, it is even sillier in the film, which bulges with science fiction clichés: "the closed environment, the phony state religion, the ruling computer, the emergence into a natural world, and the holocaust that ties up loose ends."[38] This ending, "simply the hoariest movie cliché around, the *deus ex machina* science fiction equivalent to the burning house or erupting volcano of countless horror or adventure films,"[39] is even more unsatisfactory than the *deus ex "rocketa"* ending of the novel. A more important cliché is the emergence of Logan and Jessica out of the domed city into the natural world and their amazement at its beauty. (The city and world were open in the novel except for the underground tunnels and the Thinker's cavern.) Even if the idea were not commonplace, its validity seems questionable; take an animal raised indoors to the outside, and it panics. Would humans raised in such an artificial setting react so strongly to the natural beauty (the appreciation of beauty being an acquired trait) that they would overcome their fear of the unknown so readily?

Finally, the whole tone of the film seems wrong. Michael York does not project the ruthlessness of a killer, and he seems too nice to succeed at Logan's run. The opening sequence of the film, with its emphasis on birth, subverts the obsession with death that underlies the book. Also missing from the film version are the boredom, desperation, and frantic searches for "lifts" of drugs, sex, and violence. We are given the equivalent of a *film noir* story as it might have been produced by the Disney studios. Most unsatisfactory. But the film is instructive for the study of enclosed, mechanized worlds and their opposition to nature: the makers of *Logan's Run* introduced and stressed both settings, even at a high cost to the logic and originality of their film.

George Lucas's student film which he remade as the feature *THX 1138* (with Francis Ford Coppola's help) again presents an individual rebelling against a mechanized society; but unlike the film *Logan's Run, THX 1138* is a logically consistent, depressing account of the strengths and limitations of a society where people have lost even the first names preserved in Logan's world. Only a level above automatons, the citizens, with shaved heads and identical shapeless white clothing, move through the city on conveyor belts, each person labeled by a number like that of our hero, whose identification is the film's title. Drug use is required by law, and failure to remain sedated is a "drug violation." Unlike the sensual, pleasure-seeking world of Logan, the world of *THX 1138* is rigid, dreary, pleasureless, and officially sexless. All feelings are suspect, so sexual response is depressed through medication. When THX 1138 and his apartment-mate reduce their drug intake and make love, they become criminals. Like the people of *Metropolis,* the citizens of this underground city are programmed to work, then to return to their assigned quarters, watch monotonous television shows, and sleep, to return to work the next day. Slogans are repeated over the sound systems ("Keep up the good work") and people in one work section are praised for having fewer accidents than another section. The major character's employment is handling materials that are radioactive or otherwise unsafe using mechanical arms ("waldos"). As he withdraws from the drugs, however, THX 1138's hands begin to shake, causing him to drop one of the cylinders, and he is stopped from moving with a "mindblock" apparently mediated by an implanted device that freezes his movements or by some posthypnotic suggestion. Robot police wearing featureless silver masks take him to a detention center where he waits with other criminals, not behind bars but in a huge, sterile, white area seemingly unbounded. The white imprisonment area, the white clothing of the characters, all visually represent the bloodless quality of the society.[40]

Some central authority presides over the city, although whether it is more than just a computer is unclear, as unclear to the audience as it is to the characters. The state religion is centered around images of an effeminate Christ figure, and booths are provided where people may ask for help or discuss their problems. But after the audience sees THX 1138, sick with nausea from drug withdrawal, enter a booth for the second or third time and say, "Something's wrong," it realizes that he is speaking to nothing but a recording that repeats phrases such as "I understand," "Yes, go on," "What's the matter?" "Excellent," and "Could you be more specific?"

Yet this mechanical society has weaknesses which become more evident as the film progresses. It cannot, for example, cope with the unexpected. When THX 1138 is counseled by the tape in the booth, he suddenly vomits, but the tape keeps droning on. The society does not know how to respond to his rebellion. His female apartment-mate is exterminated (he finds, preserved in a jar and labeled, the fetus of their child), but THX 1138 escapes by simply walking out of the detention area, for the society is so mechanical that disobedience is nearly unthinkable.

This world is also unable to keep itself repaired. The hero enters an elevator and waits for it to take him up, but nothing happens. Others enter the elevator, which is broken, but they cannot understand that it could be non-functional, and they stand about, waiting, until the scene fades out. A tape-recorded voice from a medicine cabinet keeps asking the same banal questions whenever the medicine cabinet is opened.

Even the efficiency one would expect of a mechanized world is missing. The robot guards are inept and clumsy, possessing none of the highly tuned efficiency of the Watchman in Logan's world. As they pursue THX 1138 on motorcycles and on foot, he eludes them until the final scene. The ending logically completes the picture of a totally mechanized attitude toward life, for it presents no fireworks (other than a car crash) or apocalyptic destruction and ends not with a bang but a budget deficit. The police, about to capture the escapee as he climbs the steps of an air vent to the outside world, are stopped because they have exceeded the amount allocated to capture the rebel. Because of a computer's balance sheet, the ultimate reduction of human life to numbers, THX 1138 escapes and is last seen as a small dark figure against a huge sun.

The film is exciting more in its presentation than in its ideas, for while it utilizes several of the SF clichés of *Logan's Run* (the film), it presents them much more effectively, possibly because it returns to the source of many of these now commonplace motifs, E. M. Forster's 1909 novella "The Machine Stops." The soundtrack of voices and mechanical orders overlapping and partially drowning out each other requires the audience constantly to sort out conflicting stimuli and thus to experience the overwhelming complexity of the regimented environment. Almost all the sounds are mechanical; even the human voices are processed until they are virtually identical, sterile noises ordering, cajoling, complimenting—all in the same emotionless, numbing tones.

The visual style of the film is striking. It was shot in San Francisco, using the modernistic buildings of that city for many of the interiors and the tunnels of the BART system, then uncompleted, for the chase scenes. The colors are predominantly white or pastel to the extent that when a car turns on flashing red and blue lights and then crashes and explodes, the colors are shockingly vivid. Using a telephoto lens to compress space and give a claustrophobic mood, Lucas convinces us of the reality of this dreary world.

One of the most effective and moving sequences in this or any science fiction film depends solely on visual images. THX 1138 (Robert Duvall) and fellow escapee SEN 5241 (Donald Pleasence) enter a corridor choked with people and work their way to a corner, where they step out of the traffic flow and rest on a bench. Children, heads shaved, pale, dressed in white like grubby ghosts, come up to them; each child has a drug bag, slung on his side and connected to his arm, to insert just the right chemicals to educate him for his place in society—and undoubtedly to maintain him in a zombielike condition. The last shot of the children is from the top of an escalator. As they step off the ascending stairs—eyes glazed and faces blank, each with identical movements, clothes, and bare heads—the vision of the future as mechanical nightmare is almost overwhelming.

While the worlds of the films *Logan's Run* and *THX 1138* have retreated underground, the civilization in *A Boy and His Dog* has divided into two societies, a surface one where rover bands and loners eke out an existence in the postholocaust nuclear desert, and a subterranean one where time has been turned back until just before World War I. Based on Harlan Ellison's Nebula Award-winning novella, the film "is not without cinematic precedence. Films dating as far back as . . . *Metropolis* have depicted societies similarly stratified."[41] Few films, however, have presented such an unrelenting vision of the conflict between almost complete anarchy of the violent variety, and almost complete authority, and almost none have presented a view more authoritarian and more mechanical than that of the print version.[42]

A Boy and His Dog describes the adventures of Vic and his telepathic canine companion Blood as they try to find food and sex in the blasted cities and deserts that now cover what was once civilization. Society is almost nonexistent: groups of "roverpacks" and "solos" fight for existence among the ruins, while a few groups have formed an uneasy truce to trade essential services. Our Gang, a roverpack that has taken over the Metropole Theatre, provides admission to its movies in return for canned goods and other trade items; other groups (in the novella) keep the radiation pits clear and run the generators that provide electricity. But no central organization exists. The film adds one character, an eccentric named Fellini dressed in extravagant rags like an impoverished oriental potentate, who comes riding up in a conveyance straight from the hallucinations (appropriately) of *Juliet of the Spirits*. He has found explosives and organized a gang to blast holes to the buildings below to then loot them. By the end of the film Fellini has taken over the town and established the beginning of a new authoritarian structure, as Vic and Blood move on to new territory.

As extreme in order as the surface is in violence and social chaos, the underground civilization of Topeka, the "downunder," is an artificial world whose people have become artificial. All actions transpire in an emotional vacuum; all words, however strong, are passionless. Pledged to preserve the status quo, the Committee, with totalitarian lack of compassion, blithely sends all nonconformists to "the farm," a euphemism for execution. The origins of the society may explain some of its attitudes.

Before the nuclear apocalypse, some groups had sunk deep holes on the sites of wells or into natural caves and set up civilizations away from the desolation and radiation of the surface; a couple hundred of these settlements still existed (as the novella states) in what was left of the United States and Canada. . . . the people who'd settled them were squares of the worst kind. Southern Baptists, Fundamentalists, lawanorder goofs, real middle-class squares. . . . They'd gotten the last of the scientists to do the work, invent the how and why, and then they'd run them out. They didn't want any progress, they didn't want any dissent, they didn't want anything that would make waves. They'd had enough of that. The best time in the world had been just before the First War, and they figured if they could keep it like that, they could live quiet lives and survive.[43]

But the society has come to a complete stop. Vic describes its people as "canned down there, like dead fish. Canned." Later Vic admits "I could feel that tin can closing in on me."[44]

In both the film and the novella on which it is based, the images and language chosen to describe the societies of *A Boy and His Dog* designate the topside as patriarchal and the underground as matriarchal. Vic, like Huckleberry Finn, moves between the two worlds, neither of which satisfies him. The surface world is composed almost exclusively of males: "The War had killed off most of the girls. . . . The things getting born were seldom male *or* female, and had to be smashed against a wall as soon as they were pulled out of the mother."[45] Some roverpacks have women they protect for sexual services; solos have only rape, masturbation, or homosexuality for an outlet. In the opening sequence of the film, Vic goes down into a hole dug into one of the buried buildings and finds a naked woman bound and dying of knife wounds after she has been gang raped by a roverpack. His only feeling is disappointment: "They didn't have to cut her. She could have been used two or three more times."[46] Women are simply sex objects, to be enjoyed between fights with phallic knives and guns in this violent anarchy of macho males, where the last vestiges of civilization have dropped from the aggressive ego. The building where Vic intends to rape Quilla June is, appropriately, a demolished YMCA.

The underground society, in contrast, is clearly—if mostly symbolically—matriarchal and orderly. In the novella, Ellison presents symbolically the movement from a masculine to a feminine society in the description of Vic's going underground. The entrance to the underground is a "pillar of black metal," but when Vic inserts the metal card, this aboveground phallic image becomes vaginal: ". . . a section of the pillar dilated. I hadn't even seen the lines of the section. A circle opened and I took a step through. . . . The access portal irised closed behind me."[47] Symbolically behaving like the breeder he is to become for the underground people, Vic continues his penetration: ". . . the floor I was standing on dilated just the way the outside port had done. . . . [As Vic drops] through the floor, the iris closed overhead, I was dropping down the tube."[48] At the bottom of the chute, ". . . the iris—a much bigger one this time—swirled open, and I got my first look at a downunder. . . . I was down at the bottom of a big metal tube that stretched up to a ceiling an eighth of a mile overhead, twenty miles across."[49]

In this enormous fallopian tube, Vic finds a society as feminine as the surface one is masculine. Most of the male characters after twenty years below ground are either impotent or produce mostly sperm for female babies; as Lew tells Vic, they "need some men."[50]

The film emphasized the same images by shooting up a circular staircase, and when Vic reaches the underground, the film presents a society more matriarchal than the book's. The film adds a politically powerful woman to the ruling Committee, and ever-present loudspeakers (not in the novel) broadcast recipes, aphorisms, household hints, and other bits of trivia usually associated with women's magazines or radio broadcasts for farm women. Sex is regarded as something dirty, not to be enjoyed but endured (the attitude forced on women in the society the undergrounders are trying to imitate). In the novella, Quilla June asks Vic, "it isn't dirty, is it, it isn't the way my Poppa says it is, is it?"[51] In the film everyone wears rouge, lipstick, and other makeup, a device the director felt they would have adopted after years away from the sun and one which gives a feminine—or effeminate—appearance to nearly everyone. In such a society, Vic the topsider is regarded as the potent male, "a big black bull about to stuff his meat into a good breed cow."[52] He is associated with masculine images. Mez, one of the characters in the novella, wants to cut his hair (a castration image like those in the story of Delilah and Samson, or Pentheus and Dionysus in Euripides' *Bacchae*) so that he will fit better into the downunder society; he escapes by pulling "the big brass balls off the headboard of the bed" to make a weapon with which he fights his way to his guns.[53]

After Vic climbs the air duct to return to the masculine society, he finds that world closed to him also. Fellini, from whom he has stolen food, has taken over the city, and Vic cannot enter it. At the end of the film, after he finds the murderous patriarchal society and the suffocating matriarchal society both unacceptable, Vic and Blood set out for an area Blood has heard about from another dog, one where life has been less disrupted by the war—like Huck Finn lighting out for the Territories.

The underground society depicted in the film differs in several ways from that described by Ellison in his text, virtually all of the changes making it more mechanical, more authoritarian. The people in the film, however, try to hide the mechanical quality of their lives. In the novella, Vic is simply put into the bedroom with Quilla June and told to impregnate her. In the film, thirty couples are married in an elaborate ceremony, complete with minister, bridal gowns, and floral wreaths. Similarly, the sentry that captures Vic in the novella is "low, and green, and boxlike, and had cables with mittens on the ends instead of arms, and it rolled on tracks,"[54] while in the film the sentry is an android named Michael who until the end of the film appears to be a normal if powerful farmhand.[55]

Despite this attempt at camouflage, the film's society is extremely mechanistic: all of its parts, like the robotic workers of *Metropolis,* are interchangeable. In the novella, Vic is an experiment, the first male brought down from the surface for stud service,[56] but in the film he is simply the latest in a succession of such young men. In the novella, he is expected to fertilize the young woman by copulation; in the film, he is plugged into an elaborate milking machine which collects the sperm for artificial insemination. The mechanical aspect of this process is emphasized by the ceremony that accompanies it: the bride to be impregnated is married to her groom by a minister as they all stand at the foot of the bed where Vic is tied down. At the end of the ceremony, the semen that has been deposited is placed in a vial, labeled, and put in storage for the couple's use. Then another couple is led in, and the process repeated. In the novella, nothing is said about what will happen to Vic after his breeding services are over, but in the film he is to be slaughtered after his sperm has been collected for thirty couples. When the society needs a new breeder, it will capture another man from topside.

This mechanical interchangeability is repeated in many less obvious ways. Quilla June tells Mez that she wants to be just like the older woman and to replace her on the Committee some day; in actuality, she wants to replace the entire Committee and run the underground world to suit herself. When Vic shoots the boxlike sentry in the novella, it blows up and he escapes; in the film, after he destroys Michael, Lew orders another Michael from the storage shed. All the people must be interchangeable, and those who are not are executed. If one girl fails to lure the chosen stud to the underground, another is dispatched. The society depicted in L. Q. Jones's film is much more rigid, mechanistic, and authoritarian than that described in Ellison's novella.

While the treatment in *A Boy and His Dog* of "the man of violence pitted against the debilitating world of rigid conformity echoes the similarly constructed *A Clockwork Orange,*"[57] Anthony Burgess' novel and Stanley Kubrick's film present more complex statements about free will and mechanization than does Ellison's novella. Set in England in the near future, the novel presents a socialized civilization where law and order tentatively prevail during the day, but where gangs of toughs and their violence rule the night. The story, told in an underworld polyglot of slang, gypsy talk, and Slavic variations, is presented through the eyes of Alex, a gang leader; and it repeatedly asks the question, "What's it going to be then, eh?"[58] The question is whether human society can achieve order and stability without sacrificing free will, or how free will can be preserved in an increasingly socialized and organized society. Will humankind tolerate a degree of lawlessness to permit the exercise of choice, or will we choose the elimination of criminal acts through psychological conditioning that denies criminals the possibility of choosing evil? Both the novel and film seem to urge free will and even violence, consciously chosen, instead of a conditioned society and meaningless world.[59]

The transformation of the organic into the mechanical is implied in the title, which is that of a political tract written by F. Alexander. When Alex and his "droogs" break into Alexander's house, gang rape his wife, and severely beat the writer, Alex reads aloud from Alexander's manuscript a sentence condemning "The attempt to impose upon man . . . laws and conditions appropriate to a mechanical creation. . . ."[60] Later Alex accidentally returns to the same house, further examines the book, and finds that ". . . all lewdies nowadays were being turned into machines and that they were really . . . more like a natural growth like a fruit."[61] As a prime survivor in the primitive environment of the urban jungle, Alex, who exemplifies the natural development F. Alexander extols, is unimpressed and wishes he had "tolchocked them both harder and ripped them to ribbons on their own floor."[62] Like Logan in the novel *Logan's Run,* Alex represents a cold, ruthless intelligence, little modified by civilizing influences, that is capable of opposing the clockwork world he inhabits. There is a good deal of the machine in him, despite his "natural" growth.

Alex's sexual behavior perhaps best portrays his mechanical sensibility. "Alex has no interest in women except as objects of violence and rape (the term for the sex act in his vocabulary is characteristically mechanical, 'the old in-out in-out'). No part of the female body is mentioned except the size of the breasts. . . ."[63] In the film the reduction of women to sexual parts is carried further in the furnishings of the Korova milkbar, where naked women sculpted in plastic form tables and chairs and dispense milk with drug additives from their breasts. When the gang attacks Mrs. Alexander in the film, Alex snips off sections of her jumpsuit, first over each breast and then between the legs, before stripping her naked except for stockings. Sex is a violent act for Alex sees himself as an animal; when he lures two young girls to his room, he gives himself a shot "of growling jungle-cat secretion," and then "I felt the old tigers leap in me and then I leapt on those two young ptitsas."[64] After he has assaulted them during the orgy, the girls call him "Beast and hateful animal. Filthy horror."[65] In the film Kubrick downplays the animal imagery to emphasize the mechanical quality of the copulation. The scene is filmed in fast motion, at two frames per second, so that the three participants dart about the room hopping on and off each other like windup toys, seemingly deriving little pleasure from the act.[66]

In contrast, Alex's most intense experience, which occurs when he is alone, lying on his bed with eyes shut and arms behind his head, is an ejaculation while listening to Beethoven: "I broke and spattered and cried aaaaaaah with the bliss of it."[67] Alex's genitalia are covered in the novel by an elaborate shield,[68] but in the film the plastic codpiece is worn outside the pants to flaunt one's sexuality, anticipating the use of a giant plastic phallus to murder the "Catlady." During the murder the camera cuts to obscene paintings and drawings on the wall, but rape with this enormous organ leads to more than just a "little death." Here, as in most of the film, the violent, yet mechanical, aspects of sexuality are emphasized, often more so than in the novel, where the Catlady is killed with a bust of Beethoven.

The organic is also subordinated to the mechanical in Alex's trips by auto. On the way to the "surprise visit" to F. Alexander's home, Alex runs over a large animal, and on the way back he crushes beneath the wheels "odd squealing things."[69] These creatures anticipate his "really lovely and horrorshow dreams of being in some veck's auto . . . running lewdies down and hearing them creech they were dying. . . ."[70]

Alex himself is subjected to mechanical procedure when he is taken to the prison which with its wings extending from a center resembles that most impersonal of institutions, a major airport terminal. He is stripped of his clothes, his name, and his dignity. Later, when subjected to Ludovico's Technique, he is attached to a mechanical apparatus with his eyelids clipped open.[71] Paralleling this obvious mechanical imposition is the psychological manipulation used on Alex by the opposition party, and he again protests: "Stop treating me like a thing that's like got to be just used."[72] Alex finds himself being used for political purposes as callously as he used others for sex or entertainment; and despite his rebellion, Alex is controlled by the system as much as he eventually uses it. While he is in prison, all of his personal belongings are appropriated to care for the cats of the woman that he killed. In the hospital after an attempted suicide, he is placed in a harness, fastened to the bed, and, finally, fed in small bites, like a child (even if a triumphant child), by the Minister. Even his dreams reflect a mechanical quality: as he listens in his room to Symphony no. 9 by "the old Ludwig van," four nude Christ figures with arms about each other's shoulders appear, through clever camera movement and editing, to dance to the music like a mechanical chorus line. These crucified figures anticipate Alex's prison fantasy of participating as a Roman soldier in the crucifixion of Jesus.

As a contrast to the regimented environment, the novel and film both present a number of family motifs—the return of the prodigal son, the correlation of milk with motherhood, and a series of surrogate fathers for Alex. Alex, the prodigal son, returns to his "home" several times in the film: when he visits F. Alexander's HOME, when he returns to his own family's apartment after prison, his second visit to HOME, and finally his return, by invitation, to his parents' home (implied at the end).

As for the mother's milk motif: the hoodlums drink doped milk from the breasts of the dispensing statues; Alex is slugged in the film with a bottle full of milk; he falls in saucers of milk in the Catlady's house; and when he returns to his parents' apartment after prison, he takes a swig from a bottle of milk on the table.

Alex's series of surrogate fathers includes the prison chaplain, F. Alexander, several minor characters, and a minister. Each promises to take care of Alex but most betray him. In this mechanical world, homes, fathers, and even mother's milk are interchangeable.

At the ends of the novel and film Alex has changed back to his original bloodthirsty habits: when he asks the nurse if they have "been playing around with inside like my brain?" she replies, "Whatever they've done . . . it'll all be for the best."[73] But whether the last scene of the film, in which Alex dreams of sexual intercourse with a voluptuous young woman before a cheering crowd of spectators, is the better, is questionable. The ending of the novel is broader in its bloodlust as Alex dreams of "carving the whole litso [face] of the creeching world with my cut-throat britva."[74] As the chaplain points out, such a view is in its ultimate values distinctly Christian, for "Good is something chosen. When a man cannot choose, he ceases to be a man."[75] Stanley Edgar Hyman both agrees and disagrees:

Deprived of his capacity for moral choice by science, Burgess appears to be saying, Alex is only a clockwork orange. . . . But perhaps this is to confine Burgess' ironies and ambiguities within simple orthodoxy. Alex always *was* a clockwork orange, a machine for mechanical violence far below the level of choice, and his dreary socialist England is a giant clockwork orange.[76]

Yet the range of choices seems to be too limited. The question "What's it going to be then, eh?" invites, like the choice of being red or dead, too simple an answer. Free will does not require toleration of sadists, nor are mechanistic environments held at bay by maintaining for criminals their right to exploit society. Alex's cure bypasses the complexities of the issue and is therefore ultimately unsatisfying, despite Burgess' linguistic virtuosity and Kubrick's cinematic brilliance.[77]

Science fiction films presenting mechanistic environments almost inevitably portray them as evil and destructive of human values. Any hero, even a rapist or killer like Vic or Alex, is presented as better than a character who is an integer in a society where choice is dictated and patterns of existence are safely organized around massive computers or an unchanging social order. Do these films pander to popular taste, to the unenlightened souls who, unlike Dr. Asimov, fear a world run "by the numbers?" Possibly. But more likely they simply reflect a human need for a degree of organic irrationality, for freedom from too regimented an existence, for a world where emotion can sometimes rule. This same need rejects determinism, even when such a philosophy would help eliminate the twentieth century's guilt obsession. Film reflects the myths of an age, and a major mythic structure for our time is the fear of being completely controlled, either through berserk computers, such as Hal or Proteus or Colossus or the Thinker, or through completely restrictive societies against which the individual must rebel or from which he must escape. As long as these fears exist, mechanized environments will continue to menace us on the screen.

NOTES

1. Quoted by James Robert Parish and Michael R. Pitts, *The Great Science Fiction Pictures* (Metuchen, NJ: Scarecrow Press, 1977), p. 289.

2. Isaac Asimov, "By the Numbers," in *Study War No More,* ed. Joe Haldeman (1977; rpt. New York: Avon, 1978), p. 299.

3. Ibid., pp. 299-300.

4. Quoted by Parish and Pitts, *Great Science Fiction Pictures,* p. 64.

5. Fritz Lang, dir., *Metropolis,* Germany: Ufa, 1927 (US release).

6. Luis Buñuel quoted by Lotte H. Eisner, *Fritz Lang,* trans. Gertrude Mander (1976; rpt. New York: Oxford University Press, 1977), p. 91.

7. See the discussion in Eisner, *Fritz Lang,* pp. 89-91, and idem, *The Haunted Screen,* trans. Roger Greaves (1952; rpt. Berkeley: University of California Press, 1969), pp. 232-33.

8. Ridley Scott, dir., *Alien,* USA: 20th Century-Fox, 1979.

9. Eisner, *Fritz Lang,* p. 83.

10. Eisner, *Haunted Screen,* p. 141.

11. Ibid., p. 229.

12. Ibid., p. 226.

13. Frederik Pohl and Frederick Pohl IV, *Science Fiction: Studies in Film* (New York: Ace Books, 1981), p. 48.

14. Michael Crichton, dir., *Westworld,* USA: MGM, 1973.

15. Sex with machines has been a favorite theme of recent science fiction films; the following treat it at length: Roger Vadim, dir., *Barbarella,* USA: Paramount, 1968; Bryan Forbes, dir., *The Stepford Wives,* USA: Columbia, 1975; Donald Cammell, dir., *Demon Seed,* USA: United Artists, 1977; George Marshall, dir., *Saturn 3,* Great Britain: Lew Grade/Shepperton Studios, 1980; and Robert Wise, dir., *Star Trek: The Motion Picture,* USA: Paramount, 1979.

16. Parish and Pitts, *Great Science Fiction Pictures,* p. 357.

17. Stanley Kubrick, dir., *2001: A Space Odyssey,* Great Britain: MGM, 1968; Joseph Sargeant, dir., *Colossus: The Forbin Project,* USA: Universal, 1970; Michael Anderson, dir., *Logan's Run,* USA: MGM/United Artists, 1976; see n. 15 for *Demon Seed.*

18. John Ryder Hall, *Futureworld,* adapted from the screenplay by Mayo Simon and George Schenck (New York: Ballantine, 1976), p. 15.

19. Dean Koontz, *Demon Seed* (New York: Bantam, 1973), p. 106.

20. Hall, *Futureworld,* p. 17.

21. See, for example, Stellen Rye, dir., *Der Student von Prag (The Student of Prague),* Germany: Bioscop, 1913.

22. Don Siegel, dir., *Invasion of the Body Snatchers,* USA: Allied Artists, 1956; Philip Kaufman, dir., *Invasion of the Body Snatchers,* USA: Allied Artists, 1978.

23. George Clayton Johnson, quoted by Wallace A. Wyss, "Logan's Run: Conception," *Cinefantastique,* 5 (Fall 1976), 6.

24. Ibid.

25. George Clayton Johnson and William F. Nolan, *Logan's Run* (1967; rpt. New York: Dell, 1969), ch. 9, p. 58.

26. Ibid., ch. 3, p. 143.

27. Ibid., ch. 7, p. 90.

28. William F. Nolan quoted by Wyss, "Logan's Run," p. 6.

29. Johnson and Nolan, *Logan's Run,* ch. 4, p. 124.

30. Ibid., ch. 9, p. 59.

31. Ibid., ch. 3, p. 146.

32. Ibid., ch. 10, p. 22.

33. Ibid., pp. 24-25.

34. Ibid., p. 30.

35. Ibid., ch. 6, p. 98.

36. Ibid., ch. 7, p. 82.

37. Ibid., ch. 8, p. 67.

38. S. W. Schumack, "Evolution," *Cinefantastique,* 5 (Fall 1976), 15.

39. Frederich S. Clark, Steve Rubin, and Wallace A. Wyss, "Logan's Run: Production," *Cinefantastique,* 5 (Fall 1976), 18.

40. George Lucas, dir., *THX-1138,* USA: Warner Brothers, 1971.

41. Don Shay, "Tripping through Ellison's Wonderland," *Cinefantastique,* 5 (Spring 1976), 20.

42. Harlan Ellison, "A Boy and His Dog," *New Worlds,* April 1969, coll. in *The Beast that Shouted Love at the Heart of the World* (1969; rpt. New York: New American Library, 1974); L. Q. Jones, dir., *A Boy and His Dog,* USA: LQJaf, 1975.

43. Ellison, "Boy," p. 237.

44. Ibid., pp. 243, 247.

45. Ibid., p. 224.

46. Like several of the more brutal sections of the film, this sequence and speech are not in the novella.

47. Ellison, "Boy," pp. 241-42.

48. Ibid., p. 242.

49. Ibid., pp. 242-43.

50. Ibid., p. 246.

51. Ibid., p. 249.

52. Ibid., p. 248.

53. Ibid., p. 249.

54. Ibid., p. 243. The "wedding" sequence in *A Boy and His Dog* is discussed by John Crow and Richard Erlich, "Mythic Patterns in Ellison's [and Jones's] *A Boy and His Dog,*" *Extrapolation,* 18 (May 1977), 162-66.

55. Director L. Q. Jones changed the robot box to an android because he felt that the agrarian people "would not tolerate a machine that was superior to them—that looked like a machine" (quoted in Shay, p. 18). The simplicity and economy of using an actor rather than building a robot box may, one suspects, also have had something to do with the change.

56. Ellison, "Boy," p. 245.

57. Shay, "Tripping," p. 20.

58. Anthony Burgess, *A Clockwork Orange* (1962; rpt. New York: Ballantine Books, 1973). The question introduces each of the three parts of the novel: Part I, pp. 9, 10, 11, 12; Part II, pp. 77, 78, 79; Part III, pp. 131, 133.

59. Stanley Kubrick, dir., *A Clockwork Orange,* Great Britain: Warner Brothers, 1971.

60. Burgess, *Clockwork Orange,* Part I, ch. 2, p. 27. The reading from the text is dropped from the film, but the beating is more severe, the writer afterward being confined to a wheelchair for the rest of his life.

61. Ibid., Part III, ch. 5, pp. 156-57.

62. Ibid., Part I, ch. 3, p. 38.

63. Stanley Edgar Hyman, Afterword, Burgess, *Clockwork Orange,* pp. 177-83.

64. Burgess, *Clockwork Orange,* Part I, ch. 4, p. 48.

65. Ibid., p. 49.

66. *Stanley Kubrick's A Clockwork Orange* (New York: Ballantine Books, 1972), Reel 4 (no author or page numbers).

67. Burgess, *Clockwork Orange,* Part I, ch. 3, p. 37.

68. Ibid., ch. 1, p. 10.

69. Ibid., ch. 2, p. 29.

70. Ibid., Part III, ch. 6, p. 169.

71. Ibid., Part II, ch. 4, p. 102.

72. Ibid., Part III, ch. 5, p. 161.

73. Ibid., p. 171.

74. Ibid., p. 175.

75. Ibid., Part II, ch. 1, p. 84.

76. Hyman, Afterword, ibid., p. 179.

77. My complaints against Burgess' novel may not apply so strongly to the British edn. (London: Heinemann, 1962), with its final chapter (deleted in the American edns.) showing an older, more domesticated Alex. For a discussion of the significance of the deleted final chapter, see Rubin Rabinovitz, "Mechanism vs. Organism: Anthony Burgess' *A Clockwork Orange,*" *Modern Fiction Studies,* 24 (Winter 1978-79), 538-41.

Daniel W. Ingersoll, Jr. **15**

MACHINES ARE GOOD TO THINK: A STRUCTURAL ANALYSIS OF MYTH AND MECHANIZATION

Once upon a time, when wishing still helped, there was a kingdom in which people shared stories about plants and animals, fruits and seeds, and gods and men. By telling themselves stories, the people explored their world and their meaning and goals in it. Gradually, as the trees were felled and the dragons were slain, the people began to construct stories about computers and robots, death stars and test tubes, and machines and men. The stories could not end happily ever after, because most of them had not even taken place yet. The people were too busy mechanizing their gardens to ask why.

—Kentucky Jones
Spaced Out Fairy Tales

When *The Empire Strikes Back* opened in Washington, D.C., the lines curled around the block twice, a friend told me. He took his children to see it, and the only reason they gained entrance was because he had obtained computer generated tickets the week before. The film, he said, was much better than *Star Wars,* and in fact, there would be seven more films to come. What kid won't see them all?

There is no doubt that science fiction and science fantasy permeate American culture as a mythic form. The non-American West also sustains a deluge of the form through the voluminous leasing and sales of American-made television series and films.[1] Robert Jewett and John Shelton Lawrence, who define a myth as "an uncritically accepted story that provides a model to interpret current experience, disclosing the meaning of self, the community and the universe," perceive in popular culture materials such as science fiction "powerful, ritualistic forms of religion."[2] In this definition of myth, which I will employ here, truth or untruth is not at issue, nor is differentiation into tale, tragedy, comedy, and so forth, necessary. What is important is that science fiction as a mythic form is ubiquitous, and that implicit in science fiction are models for symbolic thought and for pragmatic action.

The medium of science fiction may appear to be silly to some, and therefore ineffective, yet I would counter with the observation that such a medium may distract "the mind's gatekeeper, the conscious intellect, while the message of the myth sneaks home unobserved."[3] The medium may or may not be significant; the point here is that it does not need to be "serious." When the symbols in new myths resonate with preexisting symbols and (to change the metaphor) flow with historical and cultural streams, a society may be in for wide-sweeping changes.

It is possible, of course, to agree with Stephen Tonsor's contention that "the world of myth has been altogether superceded by other and more modern modes of thought."[4] I maintain, however, that myth still reigns as the most important means of thinking about crucial paradoxes, and that myths, including those in science fiction, exhibit continuity with past forms, in short, that no past mythology suffers complete annihilation.

CHRONOLOGICAL OR SYNTAGMATIC STRUCTURE

Analysis of syntagmatic structure, as employed by Claude Lévi-Strauss and as defined by Eugene A. Hammel, deals "with the sequences of major episodes and of the sequence action within episodes."[5] Syntagmatic structure pertains to the temporal or chronological frame of a myth. I identify two major types of syntagmatic structure. One type which particularly interests Lévi-Strauss involves the mediation of opposites such as left/right or dark/light. In many primitive and Western stories, "something happens" such that two opposing forces, actions, or qualities are resolved. The mediation is finite; that is, it belongs to a closed field of experience. Usually the associated images relate to a "Great Time," "Dream Time," or "Golden Age," a time of myth, which Westerners understand as existing in the past. The chronological frame is nonlinear.[6] I will refer to this sort of opposition resolution as "dual." Lévi-Strauss has made much of this dualism and has even argued that its apparent universality in culture and myth may be traced ultimately to the dual organization of the brain itself. I disagree with Lévi-Strauss on the source of such ubiquitous dualism, seeing cultural experience as a more powerful determinant.

The cultural source for dual syntagmatic structure in the West is our pre-Christian Indo-European mythology. To a large extent, however, dual structure is being displaced by a second type of syntagmatic structure which involves mediation of principles (such as action and spirit) which are not necessarily understood as opposites. The result of mediation or negation is a new state, which is not finite, and which belongs to an open field of experience. Usually the associated images or actions relate to a future time or eternity. The chronological frame or structure is linear (as is often suggested by use of an arrow) and historical. The pattern is triune rather than dual, in the sense that two qualities are mediated or changed by a third. The result of the mediation is a new entity which can itself enter into subsequent mediatory action. The triune syntagmatic structure is unique in that it possesses the potential to be endless and of being extended endlessly into the future or infinity. The dual syntagmatic structure does not easily allow this linear, forward, historical movement, since it includes no principle such as mediation or negation to link its oppositions together.

The cultural source of triune syntagmatic structure in the West finds its beginnings in the Hebrew struggle to achieve attunement with the acting will of a world-transcendent God who generates temporal history and, significantly, creates a future. Here is the source of our linear understanding of time. The incarnation and sacrifice of Christ, according to Christian theology, introduced the means to change in state from finite to infinite, from temporal to spiritual, and from static to dynamic. The mediation of Christ opened the way to spiritual eternity and perfection for Christians through the offering of grace and forgiveness of sin. Here is the source of the central element of mediation or negation in triune syntagmatic structure.

The principle that furnished Western mythology with its extensibility was the perception of God's moving will. The result was an open-ended structure which can be located in the overall movement in the Bible, a document understood by Christians as a lineally organized body, beginning with creation, moving through the fall, the first and second covenants, and the growth of the church. My colleagues and I have referred to this total movement as the megaparadigm.[7] Note that this usage differs from Lévi-Strauss' use of the word "paradigm."

The overall movement in the Bible can be contracted to the triune model, creation-mediation-spirit. This same model has undergone numerous transformations, in which structural relations have remained the same but the terms are changed. Thesis-antithesis-synthesis, or production-alienation-transcendence are examples of recent Western transforms. Borrowing from the model of the Biblical megaparadigm, consciously or unconsciously, Western thinkers such as G.W.F. Hegel, J. G. Fichte, and Friedrich von Schelling articulated transformed triune systems which have heavily influenced recent Western perception of time and myth.

Unlike most primitive myths which take place in a Great Time or Dream Time, most science fiction stories take place in the future. We take our general future orientation and linear time concepts for granted, but a survey of the ethnographic record shows that our Western concepts of time differ radically from those of most cultures. The megaparadigm as an organizing model is of critical importance in Western life. The structure is implicit in presidential election rhetoric, in advertising, in science fiction, and in many other aspects of Western life. The West continues to move toward a future with the megaparadigm as the key unlocking the bolt to time's door—and releasing the imagination from the bonds of static dualism. The Western triune spirit unfolds into the spatial and temporal infinity of the cosmos where once only the gods were thought to dwell.

PARADIGMATIC STRUCTURE AND ANIMAL SYMBOLISM

In terms of syntagmatic structure, the structure which involves episodic relationships or chronology, science fiction differs significantly from non-Western myth. What about the other level of structure Lévi-Strauss identifies, paradigmatic structure, which according to Hammel involves the "characteristics of participants and of the actions between them"?[8] Are there differences here?

Commonly, the participants in primitive stories are animals which often interact with humans. In fact, animals may transform themselves into humans, and vice versa; animal-human mixtures of form and capability occur frequently. The mélanges and transformation in primitive myth may appear bizarre sometimes, but since animal stories remain part of our inheritance, we are accustomed to pigs that talk and frogs that turn into princes. Less frequently, plants and objects such as rocks and rivers play a part in primitive mythology, but again, we occasionally hear of people turned into rocks and trees in our own mythology. In general, however, in most primitive myths, if active agents other than people are employed, animals are the likely choice.

Strikingly, and increasingly, in Western fiction, especially science fiction, machines interact with humans. Superficially, at least, machines perform or operate as animals did in primtive and Western myth. They may be transformed into humans, and vice versa, and they may exist as admixtures. If we think some primitive animal-human transformations are weird, what would the primitive think of our stories of flexible flying men of steel (*Superman*), carnivorous automobiles (*The Car*), or copulating robots (*Westworld*)? Such participants are not normally found in primitive mythology: material objects may be animated but the objects are rarely man-made, and they are not mechanical in the sense of possessing numerous moving parts. Paradigmatically, primitive myth and Western science fiction differ substantially in this respect.

Why are we telling stories about men and machines, and what kinds of meanings emerge from these stories? To begin the consideration of these questions, it is helpful to look at some of the analytical contributions of structural and symbolic anthropologists who have studied animal roles in myth and world view. Most of the examples in the anthropological literature deal with non-Western societies, which have interested anthropologists most. Few anthropologists have dealt with Western science fiction in which machines as active agents might occur. A review of animal symbolism in non-Western cultures will provide a comparative basis for examining the roles that machines may play in contemporary science fiction stories.

Totemism

One of the earliest focuses for anthropological interests involving animal symbolism was totemism. Early workers wondered why animals figured so prominently as emblematic devices. Several late nineteenth-century observers interpreted the animal totems as gods or fetishes which provided a basis for clan organization. As ethnographic data accumulated, it became clear that not all primitive societies possessed totems and, of those that did, that not all were of a religious or sacred nature. A universal explanation in evolutionary terms seemed to be out of the question by the early twentieth century. During the 1920s and 1930s, several anthropologists offered functional or psychological explanations. To Bronislaw Malinowski, an anthropologist who conducted pioneer field work in the Trobriand Islands, animals and plants were the focus of totemism because to primitive man, food is the central concern. Hence, "an animal only becomes 'totemic' because it is first 'good to eat.' "[9] Similarly, A. R. Radcliffe-Brown, a British social anthropologist, early in his career concluded it was a universal that aspects of the environment that bear heavily on healthy physical, social, or spiritual conditions tend to become the focus of a ritual attitude. Therefore, the ritual attitude influences the selections of species, a relationship just the reverse of what Émile Durkheim, the French sociologist, had stated.[10] In Durkheim's thinking, primitive men selected arbitrary signs out of an emotional urge to define their community symbolically. But psychological, emotional, and functional arguments often end up as circular ones, as Lévi-Strauss had pointed out.

Later in his work, Radcliffe-Brown recognized, as Lévi-Strauss put it, that the "animals in totemism cease to be solely or principally creatures which are feared, admired or envied: their perceptible reality permits the embodiment of ideas and relations conceived by speculative thought on the basis of empirical observations. We can understand, too, that natural species are chosen not because they are 'good to eat' but because they are 'good to think.' "[11]

Lévi-Strauss found that Henri Bergson and Jean Jacques Rousseau preceded Radcliffe-Brown in understanding important facets of totemism and primitive thought. Bergson had argued that animals lose their individuality in species, and that animals, unlike men, are distinguished by species. Animals, then, may be apprehended in terms of class or qualities. When it comes to totemic representations, different animals are used to portray different blood or clans. In Bergson's metaphysics, Lévi-Strauss saw an interpretation of totemism involving the operation of opposition and integration, "complementary perspectives" proceeding to "the same truth."[12] Rousseau, according to Lévi-Strauss, perceived that, in the "triple passage (which is really one) from animality to humanity, from nature to culture, from affectivity to intellectuality," in order to adjust to population growth and territorial expansion, man acquired the social differentiation he needed to succeed in this passage by employing differentiation perceived in the natural world. "The total apprehension of men and animals as sentient beings, in which identification consists, both governs and precedes the consciousness of oppositions, firstly, logical properties conceived as integral parts of the field, and then, within the field itself, between 'human' and 'non-human.' "[13] Man, at first an animal, thought himself out of the animal world.

Early man may have employed animal symbolism to think himself into existence in the sense of a creation or of an etiology, yet the question of creation is probably nowhere near as important for primitive societies as for us in our extremely teleological view of time. Primitive mythologies certainly do deal with creation but in a way foreign to us: in a primitive creation myth, the events and characters exist in what might be called simultaneity, the time of the myth. The dualistic assertions made and resolved in the creation myth continue to exert their influence in ritual as well as everyday life, as if they were not in the past. (We experience this in our own ritual.) More importantly, dualistic thinking about animals and other topics embraces the broader problems of man in nature or the cosmion (man's socially constructed view of the cosmos), of man as an individual in society, and of society as an entity. A series of dualistic assertions or oppositions may cluster to form a complex which interrelates many aspects of culture and of social relations.

Kujamaat Animal Symbolism

Such a complex exists among the Kujamaat Diola of Senegal, West Africa. The Kujamaat individual may possess a "totemic double," an animal which at some point in his life he may defecate in the bush. By means of complementarity and opposition embedded in a ritual act, animal doubles are conceived, generating a self with two personas. In terms of dyadic relationships, one individual with two personas may enter into four types of interaction. Changing the sex of ego and the double results in sixteen categories of social relationships, yielding a "native model that defines the major features of Kujamaat social organization."[14]

The source of the categories is based in an opposition of birth versus defecation, and according to J. David Sapir, the "progress of opposition" in respect to self is this: womb/anus; birth/defecation; human/animal; and inside/outside. A following series deals with own/other oppositions such as husband-wife/mother-son and wife-takers/wife-givers. The ramifications of a few oppositions employing animal doubles are clearly extensive. Sapir's formal analysis resembled Lévi-Straussian structuralism to this point, but Sapir went on to demonstrate that much of everyday Kujamaat life and behavior draws on the principles and symbols of the totemic doubles, especially in situations where something is out of order. Everyday events, acts, or occurences, interpreted in the symbols of the complex, in turn furnish "entitlement" or reinforcement for the native theory. With the word-sign table turned, "things are the signs for words."[15]

Thai Animal Symbolism

That animals are good to think need not only apply to totemic societies, as Lévi-Strauss himself illustrates with his analysis of French names for dogs, pet birds, cows, and racehorses. Others have profitably examined animal symbolism in non-totemic societies.[16] In a study of a Thai village's dietary restrictions, S. J. Tambiah was able to correlate dietary restrictions with marriage and sex rules, domestic architectural organization, and animal classification and symbolism.

In the human series involving marriage and sex rules, Tambiah encountered five categories: blood siblings, first cousins, classificatory siblings beyond second cousins, other people, and outsiders. I will outline behavior in two of the categories, with the goal of showing how pervasive animal symbolism may be, and thereby suggesting similar possibilities for machines as symbols. In the first category, blood siblings are covered by an incest taboo. Marriage between siblings is impossible and sex is forbidden. The sleeping room, the most sacred room of the house, ideally located to the north, is divided into two parts by an invisible partition. North is associated with the elephant, royalty, and Buddhist mythology (the village is influenced by Buddhist and non-Buddhist culture streams). The parents' room, entered by its own door, is located in the eastern division of the sleeping room. East is associated with the rising sun, the right hand, and the male sex. The western room is for the son-in-law and the married daughter. West is linked with the setting sun, the left hand, the female sex, death, and impurity. The male children sleep on the father's side and the female children sleep on the mother's side, with the father sleeping on the right. The positions are reversed for the son-in-law and married daughter. First cousins who are unmarriageable may enter the sleeping room but may not sleep there. Classificatory siblings (beyond second cousins) who are marriageable may not enter until married-in.

In terms of oppositions sacred/profane and own/other, the elephant (not a village animal) symbolizes the sacred, power, danger, size, strength, royalty, and foreignness, and the elephant is covered by a Buddhist food taboo. The marriage bond is sacred and is not intended to be entered by blood siblings who must marry other (elephant) rather than own. The dog and cat are also relatable to this category. The dog, an indoor animal, is regarded as an incestuous creature which is dirty because it eats feces, and therefore as food it is proscribed. While the dog may live in the house, villagers do not like the dog to enter the sleeping room. Unlike the elephant, the impure, incestuous dog exists in the imagination as a profane creature analogous to a "degraded human."[17] In fact, the dog suffers in this opposition, in that ritually the dog is manipulated to deceive the "moral agents" in cases of quasi-incestuous marriages between second cousins, who eat rice from a tortoise shell like dogs and thus "fool" the moral agents into thinking they are dogs, thus escaping punishment. Tortoise shell (*duang*) also means "vagina," and the normal marriage feast, *kin daung,* means literally "to eat the female organ." While dogs and second cousins are incestuous and inedible, ritual sleight of hand at the dog's expense helps to make matters in a morally ambiguous situation liveable. Unlike the elephant, the dog (in terms of the category being discussed) represents profane and own, that which marriage should not be—incestuous—and those whom it should not join: blood siblings (among others).

Discussion of one additional category, that of classificatory siblings beyond second cousins, will serve to underline the extensiveness of the interrelations. Sex and marriage are permitted and recommended by the villagers for this class of relatives. Members of this category may enter the guest room, located south of the sleeping room, but not the sleeping room itself, until married-in, and then a son-in-law, after ritually entering through the parents' door, the eastern, must thereafter use the western door and never cross over to the wife's parents' side.

Certain domestic animals living under the house, especially the buffalo, may not be eaten by the members of the house; instead, buffalo for ritual or nonritual purposes must come from another house, as is the case for appropriate marriage partners: classificatory siblings beyond second cousins. Therefore, incestuous/nonincestuous marriage practices parallel edible/inedible rules for buffalo. Unlike the dog, the buffalo is accorded respect in a ritual pertaining to crop success, and unlike all other animals, the buffalo is thought to possess a spiritual essence, like humans. Several Buddhist restrictions which cover humans are extended to buffalo. The buffalo, again, unlike the dog, is thought of positively in regard to marriage and the sacred. The buffalo pen, predictably perhaps, is located under the western portion, the marrying-out portion, so to speak, of the sleeping room.

Pigs, ducks, and chickens are penned underneath the guest room, but the fowl are not kept there at night. Ducks may be eaten as ordinary food, but not as food for gatherings or marriage feasts. It is thought that the duck, which lays eggs but abandons them, furnishes a poor model for guests, who would not come together again if they followed the way of the duck, and for husband and wife, who would separate. The symbolism for the duck is profane and negative but not as strongly as for the dog. The pig is comprehended in a more positive fashion, but less positive than the buffalo. Pork is a second choice as a ceremonial food; and actually pigs, like ducks, are raised mainly for sale. Pigs and ducks are edible but with restrictions. The guest/pig-duck-chicken housing areas seem less emotionally loaded than the sleeping room/buffalo areas, and the oppositions span lesser emotional distances, with the tone of the mildly profane with sacred potential. Classificatory siblings beyond second cousins align before marriage with the series guest room–pigs-ducks-chickens and are mildly profane but with sacred potential. The prospect of marriage causes a movement toward the sacred and the series sleeping room-buffalo-marriage exchange.

In relationships such as those sketched above, Tambiah saw no attempts to express or deny affinity with animals. Assertions and images of affinity and separation instead are counterposed, creating a "tension." The animals, Tambiah concluded, "are effective vehicles for embodying highly emotionally charged ideas in respect to which intellectuality and affectivity cannot be rigidly separated as representing human and animal modes of conduct."[18] In respect to myth and symbol, animals are "good to think"; in respect to ritual and action, "animals are good to prohibit because they are good to eat."

We learn from Lévi-Strauss, Sapir, and Tambiah, that thinking about animals is not restricted to totemic societies, nor is it a simple kind of thinking. Major questions concerning meaning in existence, order in society, and the quality of social relations are explored, employing animals as referents and symbols. The animals are comprehended as story tellers, theologians, philosophers; everyday listeners wish to perceive them: that is, empirical observation is relevant, but not determinative. People see what they want to see and use it. One implication of this process in which implicit or explicit human choice is central is that each society must be considered in terms of the symbol complex the society creates or embraces. No two complexes are alike. If we are looking for an answer to why people have a ritual attitude toward animals, we will have difficulty discovering any universal principle controlling this behavior—and we will need an explanation more satisfying than mere recourse to needs, instinct, or interest.

THREE STORIES

The next step in the analysis is to examine the paradigmatic relationships in three stories, one from native Eskimo culture and two from more modern cultures. The object will be to relate paradigmatics of the myths or stories to broader aspects of culture and society, somewhat after the fashion of Tambiah and Sapir. However, I will use myth as a main source of data, working on the assumption that myths are located at the heart of any social system. Major oppositions or mediations of symbols are found generated and reflected in myths, which in turn furnish models for thought and action, although often or usually in negative form: myths frequently do not directly reflect an image of social reality, but invert it. The inversion establishes parameters for social life by illustrating the consequences of unwise, unlikely, or absurd choices or actions in myth.

I selected "Sedna and the Fulmar," "Goldilocks and the Three Bears," and *The Stepford Wives* because they share several important attributes. First, all three stories are very popular, so their respective audiences should be familiar with them. "Sedna and the Fulmar," an Eskimo story, has been recorded from one end of the Arctic to the other. It would be difficult to find an American child who has not heard of Goldilocks, and millions of moviegoers, TV watchers, and novel readers viewed or read *The Stepford Wives*. Second, none of the stories is heavily religious in nature so they all may be enjoyed by nonritually oriented audiences. Third, all three stories involve a female, human protagonist. Fourth, all contain nonhumans as actors, the first two using animals, the last machines. Finally, all of the stories are fairly typical of the folklore in the societies in which they are found.

"Sedna and the Fulmar"

Since the first story is probably unknown to a Western audience, I have included Boas' recorded version of "Sedna and the Fulmar":

Once upon a time there lived on a solitary shore an Inung [*Inung* is Eskimo for "man"] with his daughter Sedna. His wife had been dead for some time and the two led a quiet life. Sedna grew up to be a handsome girl and the youths came from all around to sue for her hand, but none of them could touch her proud heart. Finally, at the breaking up of the ice in the spring a fulmar flew from over the ice and wooed Sedna with enticing song. "Come to me," it said; "come into the land of the birds, where there is never hunger, where my tent is made of the most beautiful skins. You shall rest on soft bearskins. My fellows, the fulmars, shall bring you all your heart may desire; their feathers shall clothe you; your lamp shall always be filled with oil, your pot with meat." Sedna could not long resist such wooing and they went together over the vast sea. When at last they reached the country of the fulmar, after a long and hard journey, Sedna discovered that her spouse had shamefully deceived her. Her new home was not built of beautiful pelts, but was covered with wretched fishskins, full of holes, that gave free entrance to wind and snow. Instead of soft reindeer skins her bed was made of hard walrus hides and she had to live on miserable fish, which the birds brought her. Too soon she discovered that she had thrown away her opportunities when in her foolish pride she had rejected the Inuit [an Eskimo man of this group] youth. In her woe she sang: "Aja [an exclamation possibly asking for help or support]. O father, if you knew how wretched I am you would come to me and we would hurry away in your boat over the waters. The birds look unkindly upon me the stranger; cold winds roar about my bed; they give me but miserable food. O come and take me back home. Aja."

When a year had passed and the sea was again stirred by warmer winds, the father left his country to visit Sedna. His daughter greeted him joyfully and besought him to take her back home. The father hearing of the outrages wrought upon his daughter determined upon revenge. He killed the fulmar, took Sedna into his boat, and they quickly left the country which had brought so much sorrow to Sedna. When the other fulmars came home and found their companion dead and his wife gone, they all flew away in search of the fugitives. There were very sad over the death of their poor murdered comrade and continue to mourn and cry until this day.

Having flown a short distance they discerned the boat and stirred up a heavy storm. The sea rose in immense waves that threatened the pair with destruction. In this mortal peril the father determined to offer Sedna to the birds and flung her overboard. She clung to the edge of the boat with a death grip. The cruel father then took a knife and cut off the first joints of her fingers. Falling into the sea they were transformed into whales, the nails turning into whalebone. Sedna holding on to the boat more tightly, the second finger joints fell under the sharp knife and swam away as seals (*Pagomys foetidus*); when the father cut off the stumps of the fingers they became ground seals (*Phoca barbata*). Meantime the storm subsided, for the fulmars thought Sedna was drowned. The father then allowed her to come into the boat again. But from that time she cherished a deadly hatred against him and swore bitter revenge. After they got ashore, she called her dogs and let them gnaw off the feet and hands of her father while he was asleep. Upon this he cursed himself, his daughter, and the dogs which had maimed him; whereupon the earth opened and swallowed the hut, the father, the daughter, and the dogs. They have since lived in the land of Adlivun [Boas glosses this word as "those beneath us"], of which Sedna is the mistress.[19]

Is this merely a "just so," etiological, story about the creation of sea mammals? What can we learn about the Eskimo from this story? Implicit in this story are a number of oppositions of great importance to the Eskimo. In Eskimo thought, these related oppositions can be abstracted by the analysis: land/sea, summer/winter, man/woman, and antler/ivory.[20] Two sets of associations can be obtained, one being woman, sea, winter, and ivory. In the Sedna story it is possible to perceive these relations. Sedna, a woman, falls into the sea, and from her hands derive all the sea mammals and whalebone (ivory). The linking of woman, sea mammals, and the sea is not difficult to grasp. The seasonality seems more difficult to figure out from the text, but when we consider that these Eskimo in winter live on the ice and hunt sea mammals, it becomes clear that in "Sedna and the Fulmar" an inversion of oppositions assists in making the story's point. The girl Sedna does everything backwards: at the end of spring she flies over the water when she should be moving over land with a man, her husband. Further, she flies over woman's realm at the wrong time with a sea bird, and sea birds like sea mammals are associated with the female principle, even though the bird is a male. In a sense, Sedna is about to marry a woman. Finally, the building materials are wrong. In summer, fish skins are inappropriate, being a product of the sea; caribou skins would be the correct material. In the story the oppositions are disharmonic; hence the reflection of society is not direct. With more stories and with ethnographic material, the correct oppositions are more easily elicitable, but, with or without distortion, all of the oppositions listed above are present in the Sedna story.

As in the case of the Kujamaat Diola or the Thai village described above, the symbolism can be seen to ramify extensively, penetrating the world of action as well as the world of thought. For example, in terms of taboo, some Eskimo groups proscribe the cooking of sea mammal and caribou meat in the same pot, the sewing of caribou skins while camped on the ice (the frozen sea where Eskimo live in winter), or the carrying of walrus skins inland. Perhaps even hunting implements had to be shaped from appropriate material, such as sea mammal bone or ivory for projectile points to kill sea mammals.[21] The story contains a guide to much of the Eskimo world view and life implicitly or explicitly in its paradigmatic structure.

More than this, the Sedna story treats a particular problem, a common one in Eskimo myth and society. The problem involves a real or mythical girl who is reaching maturity but who does not wish to marry. Socially and economically, marriage figures of utmost importance to Eskimo society. Environmental conditions are harsh, and Eskimo adaptation relies on the single family as a unit for much of the year. As in our society, which also emphasizes geographical mobility, the Eskimo family is the most important unit of organization, and most of the time it is heavily burdened emotionally and physically. The arctic environment supports, given traditional Eskimo technology, low population densities; the most effective and reliable mode of adaptation was to separate into family units and to disperse, at least for part of the year. Maintaining larger units full time was impractical. Given past social and technological choices, men hunted while women maintained the men's clothing and raised children. Without this division of labor in a trying climate, survival itself would be difficult. There is little room on the sled for someone who will not pull his or her weight.

In the Sedna story, a young girl learns that she must grow up, give up her individualistic, selfish, animal-like desires, and make a commitment to society, which, unlike the fulmar's fellow birds, will in turn provide her with meat, oil, caribou skins, and warmth: the contribution of the male principle. The female principle alone is insufficient, as the myth shows, by negative lesson. Humans ordered by society can cooperate to correct the deficiencies and the asymmetry of the single principles. The birds will only bring fish.

How does the use of animal symbols in such a story contribute to the effective power of a myth? Animals and other concrete referents can be thought of in terms of contiguity or metonym and of resemblance or metaphor, to borrow terms from Lévi-Strauss, and definitions from Tambiah. (Note that the use of these terms here departs somewhat from both colloquial usage and the technical usage in literary and rhetorical analysis.[22]) In the Thai instance, for example, dogs were intimately involved with the human order, and therefore were metonymical social entities. As such, dogs would be taboo as food, or inedible. Dogs, impure and incestuous, were victims of a metaphorical projection of human impurity onto them. By contrast, French pet birds, according to Lévi-Strauss, are thought of as leading a separate existence, but with their own order in parallel to the human social order. Hence, the imagined social order among birds is likened to human society and is metaphorical. Birds, however, are given Christian names and therefore the naming itself is metonymical; the names are taken as contiguous.[23] Thai dogs and French birds, then, are thought about in two ways, increasing the power and complexity of the imagery but perhaps more importantly, permitting important paradoxes to be considered without literal resolution. Difficult paradoxes must be thought around but not out, for their resolution leads to the experience of an impossible one-dimensional reality.

In the case of Sedna, the fulmar fellows constitute a metaphorically patterned society. They are not part of human society but can be imagined to possess their own parallel order as birds. Their social behavior is conceived of metonymically: the birds interact with Sedna as if the two social orders were contiguous. The metonymical process sets the stage for the action; the metaphorical process creates bizarre action, ruptures the normal oppositions, and casts the characters into mythic time: an outrageous bird seduces a woman, abuses her, and, as she tries to escape from the bird's companions, her father cuts off her fingers, parts which animals lack. The fingers, human parts which should have fashioned hides into clothes (the cooked, the cultural) become the sources of the hides (the raw, the natural), the sea animals. The imagined qualities of animals and the relationships with them supply powerful tools to deliberately intensify the potential difference between oppositions, while softening audience bias by employing nonhuman characters to instigate action. The Eskimo audience is efficiently socially conditioned while being entertained by a story dealing in explicitly, implicitly, and emotively understood oppositions set at a comfortable distance by the time of the myth and by mythical metaphorical-metonymical animals.

"Goldilocks and the Three Bears"

The second story, "Goldilocks and the Three Bears," is given in summary form below. I am employing the following text of a modern version (1961) paraphrased by Hammel, who feels that it is the most "resonant," in terms of structure, of the available versions:

Papa Bear, Mama Bear, and Baby Bear were eating breakfast. Papa Bear said, "My porridge is too hot." Mama Bear said, "My porridge is too hot, too." Baby Bear said, "My porridge is too hot and I burned my tongue." So they went into the woods to look for some honey and to let the porridge cool. Meanwhile, Goldilocks had been walking in the woods and found their house. She went in and saw the porridge and tasted it. Papa Bear's porridge was too hot. Mama Bear's porridge was too cold. Baby Bear's porridge was just right, and she ate it all up. Then Goldilocks sat in Papa Bear's chair, but it was too hard. Then she sat in Mama Bear's chair, but it was too soft. Then she sat in Baby Bear's chair and it was just right, but she broke it. Then Goldilocks was tired and wanted to rest. She tried Papa Bear's bed, but it was too hard. She tried Mama Bear's bed, but it was too soft. Then she tried Baby Bear's bed, and it was just right, and she fell fast asleep. When the three bears came home with the golden honey, Papa Bear said, "Someone has been eating my porridge." Mama Bear said, "Someone has been eating my porridge." Baby Bear said, "Someone ate my porridge all up." Then Papa Bear said, "Someone has been sitting in my chair." Mama Bear said, "Someone has been sitting in *my* chair." And Baby Bear said, "Someone sat in my chair and broke it." Then Papa Bear said, "Someone has been sleeping in my bed." Mama Bear said, "Someone has been sleeping in *my* bed." And Baby Bear said, "Someone *is* sleeping in my bed." The three bears looked at Goldilocks. Goldilocks woke up and saw the bears and ran away home. The bears went back to their breakfast of porridge, milk and honey.[24]

Syntagmatically, the Sedna story was dualistic: a series of oppositions were established in the time of the myth. The action ended and Sedna's role in the land of Adlivun became fixed. Goldilocks ran home, and the story line ended, but presumably, as she grows up, her role will change and expand as a result of her experience, although we hear nothing more. Episodically, Goldilocks is triune or triadic.[25]

Paradigmatically, both stories are remarkably similar. Both contain numerous highly important oppositions for their respective cultures, even though means of movement of the oppositions differ syntagmatically. In Goldilocks, the following oppositions are present: nature/culture, animal/human, raw (honey)/cooked (porridge), home/forest, large/small, young/old, and male/female. As in the Sedna story, when the oppositions are distorted, the consequences of the asymmetry are serious: the triune syntagmatic structure saves Goldilocks, but she has a close call with the bears. In everyday American life, people live in houses in cleared and settled environments, sit in chairs, sleep in beds, eat porridge—and bears do not; but bears do wander in the forest and eat raw honey, while little girls stay home and eat porridge. We can easily sort out and restore the oppositions if asked (not so easy with the Sedna story), but probably no one gives it serious thought, except the occasional analyst.

As with the Sedna story, the oppositions in Goldilocks can be found in the world of action as well as that of thought. In respect to the home/forest opposition, for example, Americans until very recently regarded the forest as predominantly alien, dangerous, and inhospitable. The best thing to do with a forest was to cut it down, then lay out fields and erect towns. Abe Lincoln, chopper of trees, splitter of rails, is still our hero, and George Washington, who applied the right model to the wrong tree (a domestic tree) emerged victorious in mythical truth by admitting his mistake. Goldilocks walked amongst the wrong trees and redeemed herself by running out of the forest and home, setting the world aright.

As in the Sedna story, there is something more than the manipulation of oppositions. There is a problem, and it involves a little girl who is having trouble growing up. Unlike Sedna, she is not of marriageable age, yet, like Sedna, she needs to adjust to new pressures. Goldilocks is caught between childhood and adulthood, as we can tell by what happens. She can no longer be a little girl with special furniture and special treatment: the furniture breaks under her weight. She is not ready yet to be a wife and mother: Mama Bear's furniture is a bit too big. She feels lost in between, but she will have to give up her animal-like desires of childhood (nature, animal, small) and become a participating member of society (culture, human, large) which is her home.[26] There is a place for Goldilocks, but to get there she must turn in the right direction. Her mother and father will look out for her a bit longer, and she will just have to suffer some of the slings and arrows of civilized life.

Bruno Bettelheim sees in this story a "voyage of self-discovery," "a search for sexual identity," and a "struggle with the oedipal predicaments."[27] He argues that this fairy tale, unlike many others, is unsatisfying because it does not supply a happy ending. Oedipal predicaments (and sibling rivalry) in his view are not settled by running away. The story kindles no hopes. The prominent structural occurrence of the number three, which Bettelheim has noted, should be a clue that the story does not end at all, and that in fact Goldilocks is not running from but to.[28] The state of the union, child with culture, is sound. There is no tragedy such as Sedna's consignment to the Sheol of Adlivun.

Again, how does the use of animal symbols contribute to the effectiveness of the myth? The same relationships obtain metaphorically and metonymically as in Sedna. The bears constitute a separate society and therefore are presented in the story as metaphorical social beings, but they are cast as living like humans, and, therefore, the bears lead a metonymical cultural and behavioral existence. As before, the metonymical process creates bizarre action when a little girl finds a house instead of a bear's den. As in the Sedna story, the employment of animal characters instead of all human ones increases the potential difference between oppositions, and softens emotional bias during the portrayal of serious problems. Although the oppositions and the problems are different in the American and Eskimo stories, both profit in the same general fashion from the use of animals as concrete referents.

But suppose we change the referents? Suppose we employed plants in the two stories to substitute for the birds and the bears? It is likely that both stories would be rendered dreadfully boring. The Eskimo do not tell any stories about plants that I know of—at least not ones in which plants are actors. Westerners tell some stories about plants, but often the plants are not so much actors as symbols of or for transformations, usually triune, for example as in "Jack and the Beanstalk" or Matthew 13:4-9. A metaphorical plant society strains the imagination, and metonymical action issuing forth would appear comical. "Sedna and the Arctic Willow" and "Goldilocks and the Three Bushes" would probably not succeed as tales.

"Goldilocks and the Three 'Borgs"

Suppose we substituted machines in both cases. Since the traditional Eskimo did not employ machines in the sense we do, there would not be much chance of such a substitution working. Machines would be irrelevant to Eskimo life and existential dilemmas. The situation in the Western case is different, of course. I will open the question on referents in the West by presenting a Goldilocks with a new cast of characters: Kentucky Jones's "Goldilocks and the Three 'Borgs," in which the nearly brainless, bloodless cyborgs are decidedly more on the robot than on the human side.

Papa 'Borg, Mama 'Borg, and Baby 'Borg were eating breakfast. Papa 'Borg said, "My porridge is too hot." Mama 'Borg said, "My porridge is too hot, too." Baby 'Borg said, "My porridge is too hot and I burned my tongue." So they stepped out onto the moonscape to look for some galactose and to let the porridge cool. Meanwhile, Goldilocks had been out for a spacewalk and found their house. She went in and saw the porridge and tasted it. Papa 'Borg's porridge was too hot. Mama 'Borg's porridge was too cold. Baby 'Borg's porridge was just right and she ate it all up. Then Goldilocks sat in Papa 'Borg's chair, but it was too hard. Then she sat in Mama 'Borg's chair, but it was too soft. Then she sat in Baby 'Borg's chair and it was just right, but she broke it. Then Goldilocks was tired and wanted to rest. She tried Papa 'Borg's bed, but it was too hard. She tried Mama 'Borg's bed, but it was too soft. Then she tried Baby 'Borg's bed, and it was just right, and she fell fast asleep. When the three 'Borgs came home with the crystalline galactose, Papa 'Borg said, "Someone has been eating my porridge." Mama 'Borg said, "Someone has been eating *my* porridge." Baby 'Borg said, "Someone ate my porridge all up." Then Papa 'Borg said, "Someone has been sitting in my chair." Mama 'Borg said, "Someone has been sitting in *my* chair." and Baby 'Borg said, "Someone sat in my chair and broke it." Then Papa 'Borg said, "Someone has been sleeping in my bed." And Mama 'Borg said, "Someone has been sleeping in *my* bed." And Baby 'Borg said, "Someone *is* sleeping in my bed." Goldilocks woke up and saw the three 'Borgs and ran away home. The 'Borgs went back to their breakfast of porridge, milk, and galactose.[29]

At first, the substitutions may appear comical, because we have heard the version with animals so many times; yet, when this initial effect wears off, this story is not only functional for a Western audience, but it also creates a mood which looms cold, distant, and menacing. Syntagmatically, all is the same, but paradigmatically, the characters and, fantastically, the oppositions have changed. The 'borgs, virtual robots in this story, are unlike bears, which can be thought of as possessing their own separate wild society analogous to human society, but are like our domestic dogs, which can be understood as forming part of the human social order. Dogs and robots generally depend on man for society, and lead individualistic existences as far as members of their own species are concerned. The 'borgs, then, constitute a metonymical society in the story.

The 'borgs are programmed, as dogs are trained, so that their behavior will be parallel to human behavior. As human extensions, 'borgs and other machines do not choose their own behavior, but, for the purposes of the story, they have a separate, self-generated cultural existence of their own. In this sense, the 'borgs constitute metaphorical human actors. Note that these social and cultural relations are just the reverse of those for the birds and the bears. The reason, of course, is that the social-cultural beings in the new story have not been chosen from the natural world but from man's world. A metonymical process includes the machines as social beings along with man. A metaphorical process takes the extensions of man and makes threatening willful actors of them in man's own image. Goldilocks can run from the bears to culture, but can she run from the products of labor to herself?

The oppositions of the original version of Goldilocks, "Goldilocks I," now must be different because the natural world is no longer involved. The nature/culture opposition now becomes works (products of labor)/self in the cyborg version, "Goldilocks II." Works represent the material world of machines and tools and so forth which man creates for himself. Culture may also be regarded as a nonmaterial product or work, the creation of man, which in turn may place culture in opposition to self. Self, by process of elimination, is all there is left for the other side of the opposition, since culture (learned behavior) has taken the self's vehicle, society, with it. The cyborgs, essentially inanimate things, by act of imagination become animate actors, possessors of culture by metaphorical projection. Metaphorical projection here implies a separation; that is to say, the cyborgs are like us, but are not a part of us. Symbolically, man has become separated from his works.

In everyday life, machines would be understood metonymically as actors, as extensions of men, put into action by men. To see them in the mythical imagination as metaphorical actors is to separate them and to give them a life of their own. Machines then become frightening symbolic projections of our own social and cultural being. To anyone familiar with the modern range of theories of alienation this should not sound surprising.

To continue with the oppositions, the animal/human pair translates to machine/human, and the raw/cooked pair to physical (mechanical)/biological. Space replaces forest to frame a space/home opposition. The meaning of home, however, is reduced to a lonely lean-to for the self, which, separated from the society and family of "Goldilocks I," must find contentment in self, or wait until society is reordered by court philosophers and history makers, who thereby cure alienation. The binaries male/female, large/small, and young/old remain the same: "Goldilocks II" must still grow up, but to do so she must find herself (now Bettelheim is right about the "voyage of self-discovery"), not her place in culture which is occupied by machine operatives (cyborgs). The task of finding self is a good deal more difficult than that of finding a nice warm place in human society. Will "Goldilocks II" succeed?

The Stepford Wives

With "Goldilocks and the Three 'Borgs" in mind, I will begin consideration of the final story, *The Stepford Wives* (1972), by Ira Levin.[30] For those unfamiliar with the plot, a brief summary follows. A suburban men's club composed of technological experts in everything from electronics to Disney animation tires of their restless, complaining, sloppy, fickle wives, and devises a way to construct doubles so lifelike that no one will be the wiser. (In the novel, the doubles are purely mechanical substitutes for the wives, and therefore might be classified as robots. In the film version of this story, something from the living human body is required to animate the duplicate, and therefore the term "cyborg" is, perhaps, more appropriate.) While they are at it, they provide their remanufactured wives with flawless figures and cheerful temperaments. The houses sparkle now, perfectly clean and orderly. The new wives smile perpetually, dress in chic flowery prints, and discuss the latest detergents with Madison Avenue inspired enthusiasm. Women's lib is just a hazy byte in a computer chip. There is a problem in constructing the double: all the Disneyland talent notwithstanding, the men fail to get the eyes "right" (movie version only). This is solved by removing the eyes from a human wife, which of course amounts to murder, but also, speaking in terms of doubles, of stealing the soul or spirit. This is quite symbolic since in Western imagery the eyes are often thought of as "the window to the soul."

The action in both the film and the novel involves an attractive, strong-willed, talented, and loveable wife-mother who gradually discovers what the men are up to. In the film, she is trapped before she can escape the club's theft of her eyes, by means of a trick employing the taped sound of her child moaning for her. The film ends with the mechanically sculpted Galatean community of soul-less women expanding to infinity. There is no hint that the evil will be checked. The men will continue to construct and then to enter into a novel clockwork sodomy with their mechanical brides of pliant plastic flesh concealing aluminum hexacomb, gears, and memory circuits. The men, too, will continue to live in a mechanical society of their own creation. Those who murder other humans and who copulate with rubber cyborgs or robots have already lost their own souls. Hope flickers only for the children, who may or may not assume the creation of their parents.

Syntagmatically, *The Stepford Wives* is triune. The movement has not stopped, as humans are still being eaten by the machine. The story could have further implications if we chose to generate them. (For example, in a sequel, the women could mount a countermovement to mechanize men, escalating the battle of the sexes and the souls.)[31] As with most science fiction stories, speculation about a future is involved. Here speculation deals with a possible near-future technology which could produce robots indistinguishable from humans. More important, speculation is concerned with notions of self and society and sex and role, in a world in which society has come to resemble a machine erected by mechanistic agents. *The Stepford Wives* shares the modern triune forward movement with "Goldilocks and the Three Bears," but the former's future orientation is much more emphatic. The dualistic Sedna story, unlike these two stories, establishes a permanent, enormous present which does not brook speculative questions about a changing social order, a shifting concept of self, or a developing member of society. Progress, development, and change are absent in Sedna's story, since passage involves not growth but switching within a static hierarchy of states or a series of alternations: the result of this absence is a quiet, comfortable, predictable Inuit world.

It is not the triune syntagmatic structure itself which introduces the disquiet experienced in many Western stories. In "Goldilocks and the Three Bears," Goldilocks escapes and continues to grow (we may safely assume) into a well-adjusted member of society; I sense little disquiet in "Goldilocks." In "Goldilocks and the Three 'Borgs," although home may be a cold, frightening place, Goldilocks manages to get there and to discover how her self must develop. Disquiet is moderate. In *The Stepford Wives,* perhaps because the protagonist Joanna is too old for fairy tale endings, the victim may not run home, even though she tries. Instead, she is consumed by the machine and the nightmare continues for others. Disquiet is intense. The feeling of disquiet is generated by the action imposed on the syntagmatic structure, and by the nature of the paradigmatics.

Paradigmatically, the central oppositions in *The Stepford Wives* resemble those named for "Goldilocks and the Three 'Borgs": works/self, machine/human, and physical (mechanical)/biological. The male/female opposition is probably of great significance, but I have chosen to avoid detailed examination of this opposition in all of the stories. In the case of the space/home binary, place, taken in the sense of stark Cartesian coordinates, supplants space. Joanna's home became a hell as her suspicion mounted that it would be the locus of her existence following her mechanomorphosis.[32] The home became a mere place, like a garage for a car. As Joanna's premonition of mechanomorphosis grew, she begged her husband to sell their place in Stepford, so they might reestablish a home in a community of normal people. Sensing the danger too late for action, Joanna was trapped and killed, her soul symbolically encased in the vinyl cocoon of her duplicate.

The female-like objects in *The Stepford Wives* (film) are cyborgs in the sense that they required something human in their makeup: the eyes. In all other respects, they are robots under the complete behavioral control of the men. Like the three 'borgs, the wife-doubles constitute a metonymical society, but unlike the three 'borgs and the Kujamaat doubles (except in unusual instances), these objects live in the same houses with knowing fathers and unknowing children, Goldilockses who have missed their cues to escape. The Stepford doubles, like the Kujamaat doubles, are metonymically linked to their alters, who are provided with social coordinates. In the Kujamaat case, the doubles represent the fabric of affinal, or "other" oriented kin relations.[33] In the Stepford story, the doubles represent the selves of wives, also affines, who were provided with names and personal histories translated into electronic memories. Culturally and behaviorally, the wife-robots or wife-cyborgs are programmed in the manner of futuristic mechanical pets. The mechanical wives do not really possess culture, but for the purposes of the story they are given a metaphorical culture: thus at the end of the film we see a supermarket full of beautiful grocery-cart wielding manikins, efficiently retrieving products, while exchanging rote pleasantries and ludicrous "pecuniary truths," the distorted truth of advertising.[34] They feed children, drive cars, clean house, buy clothes, just like human wives, but in a major sense, as in the three 'borgs, they form a separate realm, apart from culture and from the men. Where are the men? They are not with their wife-doubles, for of what interest are these soul-less, will-less, boring creatures to these latter-day Pygmalions, except as laboring sexual objects? They are off at the men's secret-society clubhouse engaged in the ritual acts of engendering mechanical doubles—producing the population for an emerging clockwork world.

CULTURAL PROBLEMS

What is the problem? In "Sedna and the Fulmar," and in "Goldilocks and the Three Bears," a young girl or woman must find her place in culture. By negative lesson a real girl learns what to do. Is the problem for Joanna that she did not learn in mid-life that she must bear the burden without complaining, while dutifully serving her husband and children? Has she suffered the penalty of the myth for her recalcitrance, as Sedna did? Could a real-life young woman learn by negative lesson that she must make the cultural commitment and enjoy its returns? Is the message "Shape up or ship out"?

In Sedna and Goldilocks I, culture is not something to be feared. It may demand sacrifice of animal wants and selfish desires, but in the end, maintaining the culture—and the cultural status quo—is worth the compromises. Growing up or getting married won't be all that bad, and it beats the alternatives. Joanna is a loving wife-mother and a reasonable housekeeper: does her independent streak and her talent as a part-time photographer really threaten cultural stability? The answer is no, as can be ascertained from the discussion of oppositions earlier. The problem involves the quality of culture itself: the protagonist is innocent! To the Eskimo, the postulation of a dangerous and evil culture would be as incredible as the idea of mechanical doubles for wives, but what Joanna suffers is the onslaught of a loveless, opportunistic, and mechanistic culture, whose actors, having lost their own souls, steal the souls of others. Joanna is not pitted against a metonymical animal culture but against a metaphorical, mechanical, inhuman culture, the kind of culture that throws self into an adversary relation to it. The self, rather than culture, now represents that which is human, sheltering, sustaining, and adaptive.

In the Kujamaat Diola and in the Thai village, the use of animal symbols provides imaginative frames of reference for many aspects of society and social relations. The Kujamaat animal symbols furnish a means of dealing emotionally with problems relating to paradoxical feelings experienced in respect to affines. The Thai animal symbols serve as effective vehicles for thinking about the meaning of marriage and exchange and about the conflicts between incestuous desires and the social need for alliance. The symbols in *The Stepford Wives* describe an evil society and the horror of meaningless social roles and relations. The play of symbols, unlike those in the Thai, Kujamaat, and Eskimo examples, calls for pragmatic action in the new territory of a changing social world, but no guide is given, only warnings. The range of action for a Joanna, however, might include (1) give up because the situation is hopeless, (2) ignore the situation because it does not matter, (3) start a revolution and replace the evil social machine with a better society, or (4) look out for number one.

In the non-Western cultural examples employed above, mythic and ritual symbols apply to everyday life. All three cultures, for example, practice food proscriptions in respect to their animal symbols. While food taboos may not apply to *The Stepford Wives'* machine symbols (machines are not good to eat), they may apply to additive stuffed, machine processed food, often referred to as junk food. Sexual taboos on machines presumably still would have some effect in the real world, but a glance through men's magazine advertisements might lead one to question this. The man-cum-machine coitus in *Westworld* and *The Stepford Wives* apparently fascinated the cinematic audience more than it offended it. In the world of whatever feels good for number one, mechanality (as in bestiality) along with sodomy, may be a dead issue. More broadly, everyday experience can be interpreted and acted out in terms of the symbols. Bettelheim, for example, has reported on the case of an autistic child who thought he was a machine.[35] In everyday conversation we can hear comments in the machine idiom: he has a photographic memory, a mind like a steel trap, a viselike grip, and a desire for input. Analyst Erich Fromm has noted correctly some of the more sinister implications of such figures of speech: "Today we can meet a person who acts and feels like an automaton: we find that he never experiences anything which is really his; that he experiences himself entirely as the person he thinks he is supposed to be. . . . " Fromm contends:

> that we have made ourselves into instruments for purposes outside ourselves, that we experience ourselves as commodities, and that our powers have become alienated from ourselves. We have become things and our neighbors have become things. The result is that we feel powerless and despise ourselves for our impotence. Since we do not trust our own power, we have no faith in man, no faith in ourselves or in what our own powers can create.[36]

As in the Eskimo case, many more examples could be cited to link the mythical imagination with everyday life, but Fromm's commentary on the feelings of real people stands as a nearly perfect duplication of the mythical, fictional experience in *The Stepford Wives*.

MODERN CULTURAL CONTEXT

At this point, the structural comparisons of the three stories have been carried out in parallel. The topic has only been partially sketched out, and the analysis is far from exhausted, but perhaps it has been sufficiently pursued to indicate that the presence of machine metaphor and metonym in *The Stepford Wives* and other works of science fiction indicates serious problems of alienation not encountered in "Sedna and the Fulmar" and in "Goldilocks and the Three Bears," and many other stories like them, Western and non-Western. There are many theories of alienation, and there are many proposed political and psychoanalytical cures which accompany them; all of these theories and proposed cures might be analyzed for their significance to machine imagery. Also, paradoxically, machines may figure as highly positive symbols, as in *Close Encounters of the Third Kind*, in which the shimmering mothership represents a "machine-messiah, an archetypal god-figure"[37] or as in *The Little Engine that Could*, in which a small locomotive points the way to an eschatology of works. These topics deserve extended discussion, but I shall depart from considerations of structure to conclude with some observations concerning the selection of animal and machine symbols.

If *The Stepford Wives* had been told one hundred years ago, Joanna might well have been transformed into a vampire or a vixen. That she was not is worth investigating. Animals, in part, are good to think because they are there. It is hard to think about what is rarely encountered, as Sapir has pointed out, and if animals become rare as objects, they may also become rare as symbols, which may be responsible for the decline in fecal animal symbolism among the Kujamaat.[38] Wild animals, as in Senegal, are definitely becoming rarer in our American environment. Perhaps now that nature is coming increasingly (we think) under mechanical, chemical, and architectural control, animals are not as good to think as they once were. But animals have been good to think because they move, react, give birth, cuddle, emote, form groups, and possibly even dream and think. Such attributes offer food for the imagination in a way plants do not. We can still appreciate animals in these ways, even if they are not so plentiful.

For the primitive, however, there is still something more than physical or even emotive affinity that renders animals appropriate as symbolic referents. In the Eskimo thought-world, for example, animals and humans all possess discrete souls. Animals may be thought of in class terms, as Lévi-Strauss argues, but nevertheless, each is animated by a soul, which is or is not separable from the body. When a seal is killed by an Eskimo, it is given a drink of fresh water by the hunter to appease its soul, and to apologize to it for its death, so that it will return to animate another seal. This is a necessary act, far different from our casual knocking on wood, which serves to maintain world stability.

To the Eskimo and many other non-Westerners, transcendence of the soul, as limited and undifferentiated as it may be in primitive speculations, is shared by man and animal. Animal species, because they appear to be immutable while human individuals come and go, provide rich analogy for transcendence in society.[39] Society, man writ large, participates in the mythic time, along with the souls of seals. It is temporal society that is of value to primitive people, who would rather not think about the shadows drifting in Adlivun. Better that the seal's soul return to the icy sea to spark the Inuit hunter's willing victim.

We can still understand this since in our Indo-European past, and even in our Greek intellectual inheritance, the souls of men and animals melded with the physical. To the early Greeks, men's souls were "thought of as a material substance consisting of the marrow of the spine and the head, and forming a sort of concentrated essence of male semen. At death, when the body was placed in the tomb this marrow coagulated into a live snake."[40] In Platonic philosophy, though animals do not figure importantly, the examination of the human soul provides the means to attunement with the divine measure, and, further, this human "spirit must manifest itself in the visible, finite form of an organized society."[41] Though we use the late Greek experience to manipulate the physical world as we understand it, for the classical Greeks a purely physical world did not exist. The soul, for the Greeks, as for many peoples, was the center of reality and the source of order. Until the Hebrew-Christian experience, animals could not be effectively excluded from this reality and order.

In the Hebrew experience, the soul oriented itself toward an acting will which, unlike the god sensed by Plato, is movable. The Hebrew God, though relevant for the political realm, exists beyond time and space. The recognition of a world-transcendent God, to the exclusion of all other gods and spirits, empties the world of all spiritual entities except the souls of men, which relate only to God. The temporal realm is separated from the spiritual realm as the world becomes increasingly dedivinized or emptied of gods and spirits. One of the implications of a dedivinized world is that a ritual attitude toward animals would gradually weaken, as this example from scripture illustrates:

> The Egyptians are men, not gods,
> their horses are flesh, not spirit.
>
> Isaiah 31:3

The result of this dedivination is a world increasingly perceived as a physical entity, to the point that we have difficulty seeing it any other way.

The Christian experience intensified the dedivination of the world to the extent that political representation became a major problem, only temporarily assuaged by the "double representation of man in society through church and empire" during the Middle Ages.[42] The problem arose as Christians oriented themselves away from the rewards of the Hebrew temporal world toward the rewards of the eternal spiritual world. The potential difference in the opposition physical/spiritual increased markedly, setting Christians apart from the primitive understanding of a unified spiritual-physical experience of existence.

Beginning with the model of temporal dedivination, Reformation and Enlightenment thinkers would take the additional steps of reducing soul to brain or mind, and of separating the resulting entity from the physical, thus making it possible for Westerners to think in terms of mind/body binaries. Nineteenth-century philosophers (actually philodoxers in the Platonic view) would create a parallel binary, that of culture/world, derived from the Christian Holy Spirit/temporal world dichotomy, with a trinitarian model supplying the transformational idiom. Culture, including ethics, would eventually be understood as a socially constructed reality to be taken in relative terms.

That which is cultural thus reduces to works or products of labor. Mind, the creator of culture, reduces to biological and chemical matter: neurons, enzymes, electrons. The Hebrew-Christian matter/spirit dichotomy has been broken as the superorganic and the subatomic have replaced spirit. The acting powers of the nineteenth-century universe are now Brownian motion, van der Waals forces, and gravity, which orchestrate the music of the spheres for the ballet of the orrery. Man, spawned from randomness, the new chaos, awakens to discover himself as the genitor of the social orrery, the most recent evolutionary extension of the physical universe. The social orrery, the divine machine, will be perfected by rational man, thereby generating a substitute for meaning in a redivinized temporal world which now, however, stands alone. Man, his products, and the world are one, united by Idealist philosophy's triune symbolism.

How do machine and animal referents relate to Christian and later world views? Animals in New Testament parables are rare: seeds, plants, and fruits more frequently provide the images of transformation. There are, however, some significant exceptions. In a symbolic act, Jesus freed a man possessed of evil spirits by sending the devils into a herd of pigs which rushed into a lake and perished (Matthew 8:28–32). The most powerful animal symbolism is probably vested in sheep, as in John 21:15–17, and in the pervasive Lamb symbolism as in Apocalypse 14 and in the liturgy (*Agnus Dei*, for example) of many churches. The Lamb symbolism effectively mediates between a stern father and sinful children.[43] Animals are still good to think, but now men form a series apart from animals. Men and animals are different just as God and man are different. As men may feed and tend sheep in the physical realm, so may God feed and tend men in the spiritual realm. In triune symbols, men are the sheep of Christ, and Christ, the mediator, is the Lamb of God. The Bride of Christ, the Church carried out into the world by Peter and Paul, functions as the mediator in the physical absence of Christ.

The Hebrew-Christian articulation placed animals in a series separate from man, because animals lack souls, but more recent articulations have put animals back into the classificatory world which includes humans, because neither have souls. (I am aware that in formal Christian theology animals may be understood as possessing souls, but souls of a different kind from human souls. For example, animal souls might be qualified as lacking the properties of immortality and reason.) If neither man nor animals possess souls, then what is the difference between men and animals? If the answer is that men possess culture, then a late nineteenth-century to mid-twentieth-century story like "Goldilocks and the Three Bears" with its oppositions nature/culture and animal/human will be able to gain currency. Note that although the oppositions seem to parallel the Eskimo ones, the contextual basis for separation differs, and so does the meaning carried.

What if the answer is that people and animals do not differ physically or culturally, which is easy to argue in a time when chimps make tools with their hands and gorillas talk in American Sign Language? If a storyteller wishes to bring up the outmoded, semiforbidden answer of transcendence, he may profit by employing frivolous, emotionally removed referents: animals. *Bambi* (deer, 1929) and *Watership Down* (rabbits, 1975) both found strong audiences while allegorically treating this topic, perhaps without audience recognition.[44] The animals are given metaphorical societies and metonymical cultures and souls. The souls would be taken for granted in most primitive tales, but to the Christian and other Westerners, animals only have souls in the imagination. When man has lost his sense of transcendence, he may turn to gentle imaginary animals to soothe his longing. But if he is lost in a world of physical matter and "biological and chemical machines" which build themselves, he may turn to the stark symbolism of the inanimate: robots, cyborgs, ray guns, and Death Stars.[45]

In the Christian experience, with its emphasis on things spiritual, products of man, social or mechanical, inspire only mild interest. From prophet or disciple one learned that the human spirit could stand apart from temporal society. In this alienation there was the comfort of the calling and Logos of a world-transcendent God. For the secularized, gnostic children of the Enlightenment, collective man would bravely stand by himself, comforted by his powers of reason and prepared to build the heavenly earthly city. As the Enlightenment child grew into the nineteenth-century superman, the self, a vessel as empty of spirit as the Christian temporal world, could rise like a Hebrew prophet to assail society and its evils. For the child, the machines were toys of messianic promise; for the superman in his fall from faith in God, society, and reason, the machines could become tools of diabolical annihilation. The myths of the twentieth century reveal the new Leviathan, not of flesh and blood, but of alloy and diode. But things have not come to stand for words. The Leviathan is only the symbol of what our imagination says we are in spirit. If machines are good to think, it is because they warn of a crisis of the soul. If machines are good to prohibit, it is because somewhere there is still hope.

NOTES

I would like to thank James Nickell, with whom I discussed many ideas presented in this essay, and John Hirschfield and Betty Knight for assisting with the typing and reproduction of the manuscript. Eugene Hammel and Addison-Wesley Modular Publications kindly granted permission to reprint the paraphrase of "Goldilocks and the Three Bears," and the University of Nebraska Press kindly granted permission to reproduce "Sedna and the Fulmar."

1. Robert Jewett and John Shelton Lawrence, "The Problem of Mythic Imperialism," *Journal of American Culture*, 2, No. 2 (1979), 309.

2. Ibid., p. 311; and Robert Jewett and John Shelton Lawrence, *The American Monomyth* (Garden City, NY: Doubleday, Anchor, 1977), p. 30.

3. D. W. Ingersoll, Jr., *"Close Encounters of the Third Kind:* A Hegelian Drama" (paper read at the annual meeting of the American Anthropological Association, Cincinnati, 30 November 1979).

4. Stephen J. Tonsor, "The Use and Abuse of Myth," *Intercollegiate Review*, 15, No. 2 (1980), 75.

5. Eugene A. Hammel, *The Myth of Structural Analysis: Lévi-Strauss and the Three Bears* (Reading, MA: Addison-Wesley Modular Publications, 1972), Module 25, p. 9. [This and further quotations from this source in this chapter reprinted by

permission from Eugene A. Hammel, THE MYTH OF STRUCTURAL ANAL-YSIS: LÉVI-STRAUSS AND THE THREE BEARS, © 1972, by the Benja-min/Cummings Publishing Co., Menlo Park, CA.]

6. Dorothy Lee, *Freedom and Culture* (Englewood Cliffs, NJ: Prentice-Hall, 1959), pp. 164-65. Lee's comments refer to the Trobrianders, but they could apply as well to many non-Westerners.

7. D. W. Ingersoll, Jr., J. M. Nickell, and C. D. Lewis, *"Star Wars,* the Future, and Christian Eschatology," *Philosophy Today,* 24, No. 4/4 (1980), 367.

8. Hammel, *Myth of Structural Analysis,* p. 9.

9. Claude Lévi-Strauss, *Totemism,* trans. Rodney Needham. (Boston: Beacon Press, 1963), p. 62.

10. Ibid., p. 61.

11. Ibid., p. 89.

12. Ibid., pp. 98-99.

13. Ibid., pp. 101-02.

14. J. David Sapir, "Fecal Animals: An Example of Complementary Totemism," *Man* (N.S.), 12 (1977), 5.

15. Ibid., p. 17.

16. Claude Lévi-Strauss, *The Savage Mind* (Chicago: University of Chicago Press, 1966), pp. 204-08.

17. S. J. Tambiah, "Animals are Good to Think and Good to Prohibit," *Ethnology,* 8, No. 4 (1969), 435.

18. Ibid., p. 457.

19. Text originally published in 1888 by the Smithsonian Institution; it also ap-pears in Franz Boas, *The Central Eskimo,* 3rd edn. (Lincoln, NB: University of Nebraska Press, 1970), pp. 175-77.

20. Robert McGhee, "Ivory for the Sea Woman: The Symbolic Attributes of a Prehistoric Technology," *Canadian Journal of Archaeology,* No. 1 (1977), 147.

21. Ibid., pp. 144-45.

22. Tambiah, "Animals," p. 454.

23. Lévi-Strauss, *Savage Mind,* pp. 205-06.

24. Hammel, *Myth of Structural Analysis,* pp. 8-9.

25. Ibid., p. 13.

26. Ibid., p. 14.

27. Bruno Bettelheim, *The Uses of Enchantment: The Meaning and Importance of Fairy Tales* (New York: Vintage Books, 1977), pp. 215, 220, 223.

28. Ibid., pp. 218-19.

29. Kentucky Jones, *Spaced Out Fairy Tales.* [Kentucky Jones is the pseudonym of Daniel W. Ingersoll, Jr., who transmits his *Tales* in the folk tradition.—Eds.]

30. Ira Levin, *The Stepford Wives* (New York: Dell, 1972). *The Stepford Wives* (film), directed by Bryan Forbes (USA: Columbia, 1975).

31. [After this essay was received, a sequel to *Stepford Wives* did appear on tele-vision; see comment in the entry on *Stepford Wives* in the Drama section of the "List of Works Useful . . . " that appears at the back of this volume.—Eds.]

32. Roger B. Rollin, "Deus in Machina: Popular Culture's Myth of the Machine," *Journal of American Culture,* 2, No. 2 (Summer 1979), 297-308. Rollin uses the term "mechanomorphosis."

33. Sapir, "Fecal Animals," p. 1.

34. Jules Henry, *Culture Against Man* (New York: Vintage Books, 1965), pp. 49-54.

35. Bruno Bettelheim, "Joey: a 'Mechanical Boy,' " *Scientific American,* 200, No. 3 (1959), 116-27.

36. Erich Fromm, *Man For Himself: An Inquiry Into the Psychology of Ethics* (New York: Holt, Rinehart and Winston, 1976), pp. 222-23.

37. Rollin, "Deus in Machina," p. 304.

38. Sapir, "Fecal Animals," p. 19.

39. Eric Voegelin, *Israel and Revelation* (Baton Rouge: Louisiana State University Press, 1956), p. 73.

40. E. R. Leach, *Rethinking Anthropology* (New York: Humanities Press, 1966), p. 127.

41. Eric Voegelin, *Plato and Aristotle* (Baton Rouge: Louisiana State University Press, 1957), p. 227.

42. Eric Voegelin, *The New Science of Politics* (Chicago: University of Chicago Press, 1952), p. 106.

43. W. Lloyd Warner, *The Family of God* (New Haven: Yale University Press, 1961; rpt. Westport, CT: Greenwood Press, 1975), p. 312.

44. Felix Salten, *Bambi* (New York: Grosset and Dunlap, 1929), p. 286; Richard Adams, *Watership Down* (New York: Avon Books, 1975), pp. 253, 285.

45. Jacques Monod, *Chance and Necessity* (New York: Vintage Books, 1971), pp. 45-46.

Richard D. Erlich and Thomas P. Dunn

LIST OF WORKS USEFUL FOR THE STUDY
OF MECHANIZED ENVIRONMENTS IN SF

Technically, this is an analytical, selected list, with comments, of works useful for the study of mechanized environments in SF. It will help users of our List if we review here briefly the key elements of this technical title.

Analytical. This List is divided into the following sections, with works arranged alphabetically within each section:

     I. Reference Works
    II. Anthologies and Collections
   III. Fiction (and Poetry)
   IV. Literary Criticism
    V. Stage, Film, and Television Drama
   VI. Stage, Film, and Television Drama Criticism
  VII. Music
 VIII. Background Reading

Where we think it will aid users to do so, we have cross-listed items.

Selected. Our List is extensive but by no means exhaustive. Users desiring additional titles should consult the reference works listed in our Acknowledgments, in Section I, and in the notes to the essays in this volume. Note well that our List for *Clockwork Worlds* will not ordinarily include citations to works dealing with relatively small machines: robots, cyborgs, and so forth. Citations to these works are collected in our List for *The Mechanical God: Machines in Science Fiction*, a companion volume in the Greenwood Press series, Contributions to the Study of Science Fiction and Fantasy.

List. Besides being a bibliography (a list of books and other writings), our List is also a filmography and discography. All of our contributors have aided us in compiling the bibliography, but we owe special thanks to Gary K. Wolfe (of *The Mechanical God*) for his aid with works featuring various kinds of barriers. The initial work on the filmography was done by John

Cooper; the initial work on the discography was done by Jeffrey R. Wilson; and much of the typing of the List was done by Karen Akers—all of whom have our thanks.

Comments. We will usually provide comments with citations. In particular, we often cite critical and reference works that summarize and discuss primary works.

Works Useful. Again, we provide only a selection of works. We have attempted to cover most of the classic SF works and a number of lesser-known works. We have also cited background materials that will familiarize beginning students with some of the social, political, and philosophical issues alluded to in the primary works using the theme of this volume.

Three final notes, of caution: (1) SF works often appear under variant titles or pseudonymously and/or in variant editions or translations. We have tried to alert the users of this List to the problems we know of, but we can guarantee only that there are undoubtedly additional problems we know not of. We have attempted to examine for content most of the works we cite. Where direct examination has not been possible, we have cross-checked references, and we have tried to provide indications of at least one source of the citation. Students of SF bibliography are referred to our Acknowledgments and to the references given below in Section I. (2) We have kept to a minimum number of citations our section on mechanical environments in music and have totally eliminated a proposed section on machines in the graphic and plastic arts. Note well that machines and mechanized environments have figured significantly in the graphic and plastic arts at least since the beginning of the Industrial Revolution and have been quite common in modern art. Users of the List who would like information on the machine and mechanized environments in relatively recent art would do well to consult "The Machine" in William S. Liebermann's *Art of the Twenties* and then move on to two works recommended by William M. Schuyler, Jr., and two recommended by Brian W. Aldiss: Joshua C. Taylor on *Futurism*, and K. G. P. Hulten on *The Machine . . . at the End of the Mechanical Age*, and Jasia Reichardt's *Robots: Fact, Fiction and Prediction,* and *Cybernetic Serendipity*. We have also severely limited in our List citations to "mainstream" works featuring mechanized environments and the theme of mechanization. Users of the List who would be interested in such themes and motifs in "mainstream" fiction would do well to begin their studies with the anthology *The Theme of the Machine,* cited in Section II of the List, and with Leo Marx's classic study *The Machine in the Garden,* cited in Section VIII. (3) The *MLA Handbook . . .* (1977) requires that citations to films include "the title (underlined), distributor, and date" (section 35c), and current usage, as we have observed it, encourages citing also the country of production. These requirements seem straightforward; given the complexities of the film industry, however, they are not. Our citations to films, then, will give title (italicized), director (or

major director), main country or countries of production, distributor
and/or production company, and date of completion (or copyright) and/or
of release—plus other information and warnings we think will be useful to
users of the List. Students of SF filmography should consult Walt Lee's
three-volume compilation, *Reference Guide to Fantastic Films: Science Fic-*
tion, Fantasy, & Horror (see below under Acknowledgments).

ABBREVIATIONS IN THE LIST

1. We have abbreviated the names of states of the United States, using
the standard abbreviations accepted by the United States Postal Service.

2. When we refer to the author of a work in the comments on that work,
we will give the author's initials in roman type; when we refer to the work
itself in a comment, we will abbreviate the work's title in italic type or place
the abbreviation within quotation marks.

3. We use the standard abbreviations and reference words as found in
The MLA Style Sheet, 2d edn. (1970; section 31, pp. 28-29), and the *MLA
Handbook* . . . (section 48, pp. 123-39). We give below additional abbreviations, our most usual abbreviations, and abbreviations and short titles
that might cause confusion.

Amazing	*Amazing Stories, Amazing Science Fiction, Amazing Science Fiction Stories* (vt)
Astounding	*Astounding Stories of Super-Science, Astounding Stories, Astounding Science Fiction* (vt); after 1960, *Analog* . . .
biblio.	bibliography, bibliographical
cf.	compare
coll.(s)	collection(s), collected
CW	*Clockwork Worlds: Mechanized Environments in SF*
dir.	director
ed(s).	editor(s)
edn.	edition
esp.	especially
F&SF	*The Magazine of Fantasy and Science Fiction*
If	*If, Worlds of Fantasy and Science Fiction; Worlds of IF* (vt)
introd.	introduction
n.d.	no date
passim	throughout the work, here and there
pseud.	pseudonym
q.v.	which see
rpt(s).	reprint(s), reprinted
SF	SF (an undefined term); "Speculative Fiction," includ- ing science fiction, utopias, eutopias, dystopias, and re-

lated subgenres; and "Structural Fabulation" as defined
by Robert Scholes in *Structural Fabulation (1975)*

S. F.	*science fiction*
S. F. Ency.	*The Science Fiction Encyclopedia*
SFS	*Science-Fiction Studies*
TMG	*The Mechanical God: Machines in Science Fiction*
trans.	translator(s), translation(s)
vol(s).	volume(s)
vt	variant title, variant titles

ACKNOWLEDGMENTS

In compiling our List, we depended a good deal on the works cited in
Section I (Reference Works) and immediately below; we refer back to these
works in the main body of our List.

John Baxter, compiler, "Selected Filmography," in his *Science Fiction in
the Cinema,* Peter Cowie, ed. (1970; rpt. New York: Paperback Library,
1970).

William Contento, *Index to Science Fiction Anthologies and Collections*
(Boston: G. K. Hall, 1978). Our primary source for information on magazines of initial publication and reprints for a number of short stories and
novellas; consult for additional places to find short stories and novellas,
beyond the locations we have cited.

L. W. Currey, *Science Fiction and Fantasy Authors: A Bibliography of
First Printings of Their Fiction and Selected Nonfiction* (Boston: G. K.
Hall, 1979). Our primary source for information on first printings of
novels.

William Johnson, ed. *Focus on The Science Fiction Film* (Englewood
Cliffs, NJ: Prentice-Hall, 1972). References in the List to Johnson refer to
the selected filmography in this work.

Walt Lee, compiler, *Reference Guide to Fantastic Films: Science Fiction,
Fantasy, & Horror,* 3 vols. (Los Angeles: Chelsea-Lee Books, 1972-74).

Frederik Pohl & Frederik Pohl IV, *Science Fiction: Studies in Film* (New
York: Ace, 1981). The filmographic information given passim in this work
is the source for a number of citations to science fiction films of the late
1970s.

Patricia S. Warrick, *The Cybernetic Imagination in Science Fiction*; full
citation below, under Literary Criticism. References in the List to Warrick
are to summaries and discussions in this work.

Gary K. Wolfe, *The Known and the Unknown;* full citation below, under Literary Criticism. References in the List to Wolfe are to the summaries and discussions in this work.

"The Year's Scholarship in Science Fiction and Fantasy," compiled 1976-1979 by Roger C. Schlobin and Marshall B. Tymn in the journal *Extrapolation.* For 1976, vol. 20, no. 1 (Spring 1979); for 1977, vol. 20, no. 3 (Fall 1979), for 1978, vol. 21, no. 1 (Spring 1980); for 1979, vol. 22, no. 1 (Spring 1981). "The Year's Scholarship" will be published by Kent State University Press as an annual monograph series beginning with the 1980 installment. For earlier years, we have consulted Tymn and Schlobin, *The Year's Scholarship in Science Fiction and Fantasy: 1972-1975* (Kent, OH: KSU Press, 1979), and Thomas Clareson, *Science Fiction Criticism: An Annotated Checklist* (Kent, OH: KSU Press, 1972).

I. REFERENCE WORKS

Brosnan, John. *Future Tense: The Cinema of Science Fiction.* New York: St. Martin's Press, 1978.

> History of SF films from 1900 to 1978, with criticism. Includes an Appendix, "SF on Television," giving a year-by-year chronology of SF shows on TV.

Cox, David M., and Gary L. Libby, compilers. "A Bibliography of Isaac Asimov's Major Science Fiction Works through 1976." In *Isaac Asimov.* Joseph D. Olander and Martin Harry Greenberg, eds. New York: Taplinger, 1977, pp. 217-33.

> Based in part on Marjorie Miller's *Isaac Asimov: A Checklist of Works Published in the United States* (Kent, OH: KSU Press, 1972). See Cox and Libby for works we have been unable to include in our List.

Gerrold, David, compiler. "First Season Episodes," "Second Season Episodes," "Third Season Episodes." In Gerrold, *The World of Star Trek.* New York: Ballantine, 1973, pp. 127-53.

> A list of *Star Trek* episodes for the show's entire three-season run; gives names of scriptwriters and cast lists of guest performers. We have consulted DG's list for our *Star Trek* citations.

Hughes, David Y. "Criticism in English of H. G. Wells's Science Fiction: A Select Annotated Bibliography." *SFS*, 6 (Nov. 1979), 309-19.

Divided into sections: "Bibliographies," "Collections of Critical Essays," "Overviews (after 1930) of the SF/Utopian Opus," and "Particular Studies of One Work or a Group of Works." Eighty-five entries in all.

Kagan, Norman, compiler. "Kubrick Filmography." In *The Cinema of Stanley Kubrick*. Norman Kagan, ed. 1972; rpt. New York: Grove Press, 1975.

A complete filmography for Kubrick's work through *A Clockwork Orange*. *CSK* also includes plot summaries and stills for *Dr. Strangelove, 2001*, and *Clockwork Orange* (as well as for Kubrick's other films from 1953 to 1971).

Klinkowitz, Jerome, compiler. "The Vonnegut Bibliography." In *Vonnegut in America: An Introduction to the Life and Works of Kurt Vonnegut*. Klinkowitz and David L. Lawler, eds. New York: Delacorte/Seymour Lawrence, 1977; rpt. New York: Dell (Delta), 1977, pt. 3.

Mullen, R. D. "Books, Stories, Essays [by Philip K. Dick]." *SFS*, #5 = vol. 2, pt. 1 (March 1975), 5-8. (The special Dick issue of *SFS*.)

Gives a brief list of standard S. F. reference works and a chronologically arranged Dick biblio. from 1955 to 1974. Based on the standard reference tools and "a list compiled by Robert Greenberg . . . for distribution at Westercon 1974."

The New Film Index: A Bibliography of Magazine Articles in English, 1930-1979. Richard Dyer MacCann and Edward S. Perry, compilers. New York: Dutton, 1975.

An annotated, analytical biblio. covering a wide range of topics important for film studies, and the source of several of our citations for film criticism.

Sargent, Lyman, Tower. *British and American Utopian Literature, 1516-1975*. Boston: G. K. Hall, 1979.

Includes a briefly annotated "Chronological List of Utopian Literature, 1516-1975" (including both utopian and dystopian works); a list of books, articles, and unpublished material dealing with utopian studies; and full author and title indexes to the chronological list. References below to Sargent are to this biblio.

The Science Fiction Encyclopedia. Peter Nicholls, general ed. Garden City, NY: Doubleday, 1979.

Esp. useful for film and S. F. themes, motifs, and sub genres. Includes entries on dystopias, generation starships, machines, technology, and utopias.

Survey of Science Fiction Literature. 5 vols. Frank N. Magill, ed. Englewood Cliffs, NJ: Salem Press, 1979.

Contains plot summaries, evaluations, and brief critiques of a wide variety of works ranging in quality and relevance from E. M. Forster's "Machine Stops" to D. F. Jones's *Colossus*, including Isaac Asimov's *Caves of Steel* and *Naked Sun*, Ray Bradbury's stories coll. in *Illustrated Man* and *Martian Chronicles*, Karel Čapek's *R. U. R.*, Arthur Clarke's *City and the Stars* and *2001*, Samuel Delany's *Nova,* Robert Heinlein's *The Moon Is a Harsh Mistress,* Stanislaw Lem's *Invincible*, George Orwell's *Nineteen Eighty-Four,* Kurt Vonnegut's *Player Piano, Sirens of Titan,* and *Slaughterhouse-Five,* H. G. Well's eutopian and dystopian fiction, Jack Williamson's Humanoids stories, and other works useful for the study of mechanized environments in SF.

Tymn, Marshall B., compiler. "Philip K. Dick: A Bibliography." In *Philip K. Dick.* Martin Harry Greenberg and Joseph D. Olander, eds. New York: Taplinger, 1983.

Biblio. of Dick's books and pamphlets, short fiction, articles and essays, and general writings. Also lists selected criticism of Dick's work.

———, compiler. "Ray Bradbury: A Bibliography." In *Ray Bradbury.* Martin Harry Greenberg and Joseph D. Olander, eds. New York: Taplinger, 1980.

Biblio. of Bradbury's books and pamphlets, short fiction, articles and essays, and general writings. Also lists selected criticism of Bradbury's work.

Whitfield, Stephen E., and Gene Roddenberry, compilers. *"Star Trek*

Shows." In Whitfield and Roddenberry, *The Making of Star Trek*. New York: Ballantine, 1968.

A list of *Star Trek* episodes, with dates of first transmissions and names for guest stars for *Star Trek's* first two seasons (through 29 March 1968). We have consulted this work for our *Star Trek* listings below.

II. ANTHOLOGIES AND COLLECTIONS

As Tomorrow Becomes Today. Charles Wm. Sullivan III, ed. Englewood Cliffs, NJ: Prentice-Hall, 1974.

Includes Harlan Ellison's "A Boy and His Dog" and "Repent, Harlequin . . . . "

Asimov, Isaac. *The Bicentennial Man and Other Stories.* Garden City, NY: Doubleday, 1976; Greenwich, CT: Fawcett, 1976.

The Best of John W. Campbell. Lester del Rey, ed. New York: Ballantine, 1976; rpt. Garden City, NY: Doubleday (S. F. "Book Club Edition"), n.d.

The Best of Philip K. Dick. John Brunner, ed. New York: Ballantine, 1977.

Includes Dick's "Second Variety," "Imposter," "Service Call," "Autofac," "Human Is," "If There Were No Benny Cemoli," "The Electric Ant," and other stories useful for an introduction to P. K. Dick.

Ellison, Harlan. *The Beast that Shouted Love at the Heart of the World.* New York: Avon, 1969, 1970 [Currey notes 1970 issue as the authorized text]; rpt. New York: New American Library, 1974; London: Millington, 1976.

Coll. includes "A Boy and His Dog," "Asleep: With Still Hands," and "Worlds to Kill."

Final Stage: The Ultimate Science Fiction Anthology. Edward L. Ferman and Barry N. Malzberg, eds. New York: Charterhouse, 1974 [cut and rewritten by publisher, according to Currey]. Harmondsworth and other cities: Penguin, 1975. ["Prints the original versions of the authors' stories," according to Currey].

See for Harlan Ellison's "Catman" and Malzberg's "All-Purpose Transmogrifier." Isaac Asimov's "That Thou Art Mindful of Him!" is also of interest as a kind of ultimate robot story; it may be found here and also in Asimov's coll., *The Bicentennial Man and other Stories*.

Of Men and Machines. Arthur O. Lewis, Jr., ed. New York: E. P. Dutton, 1963.

Includes Karel Čapek's *R. U. R.*, Lewis Mumford's "The Monastery and the Clock," Isaac Asimov's "Robbie," E. M. Forster's "Machine Stops," and other works of interest.

Science Fiction Thinking Machines: Robots, Androids, Computers. Groff Conklin, ed. New York: Vanguard, 1954. Also, *Science Fiction Thinking Machines (Selections From)*. New York: Bantam, 1955.

Anthology of relatively early stories on "thinking" machines. Vanguard edn. includes S. Fowler Wright's "Automata" (I-III), Karel Čapek's *R. U. R.*, Clifford Simak's "Skirmish," and Poul Anderson's "Sam Hall." Bantam edn. rpts. "Skirmish" and "Sam Hall."

Survival Printout. Leonard Allison et al., eds. New York: Random House (Vintage), 1973.

The "et al." includes Illiac 4, an ancestor of HAL 9000. Anthology includes Robert Silverberg's "A Happy Day in 2381" (1970), incorporated into *The World Inside*, and Harlan Ellison's "I Have No Mouth. . . " (q.v. below, under Fiction).

The Theme of the Machine. Allan Danzig, ed. Dubuque, IA: Brown, 1969.

Large number of selections from Ezekiel to Zelanzy and Pohl, mostly brief works and excerpts from "mainstream" drama, essays, fiction, and poetry. Includes Act III of *RUR* (sic), "The Book of the Machines" chapters from Samuel Butler's *Erewhon,* Henry Adam's "Dynamo and the Virgin," E. T. A. Hoffman's "Automata," H. G. Wells's "Lord of the Dynamos," Roger Zelazny's "For a Breath I Tarry," Frederik Pohl's "Day Million," and Stephen Vincent Benet's "Nightmare Number Three."

III. FICTION (AND POETRY)

Aldiss, Brian. *The Eighty-Minute Hour.* Garden City, NY: Doubleday, 1974; London: Jonathan Cape, 1974.

Post-World War III world taken over by "a massive computer complex whose robotic projections rule the socio-political system" (briefly discussed in introductory essay by BA in Dunn and Erlich, eds., *TMG*).

_____. "Neanderthal Planet." *Science Fiction Adventures,* Sept. 1960. Coll. in *Neanderthal Planet.* New York: Avon, 1970, pp. 9-57.

Includes future world in which intelligent machines preserve a colony of humans in a zoo.

_____. *New Arrivals, Old Encounters.* London: Jonathan Cape, 1979.

Coll. of stories organized around a theme. "Two stories feature technological and astronautic priesthoods, while in a third a United Earth prepares to switch on the Ultimate Machine . . . " (review by Colin Greenland in *Foundation*, No. 19 [June 1980], p. 90).

_____. *Non-Stop.* London: Faber and Faber, 1958. (US publication under vt *Starship*, New York: Criterion, 1959.)

Currey notes "textual differences" between US and UK edns. A spaceship-as-world story in the manner of Heinlein's "Universe" (q.v. below), but with a twist giving the novel political implications condemning the use of technology to control and manipulate people. See below under Literary Criticism the essay by Frederic Jameson.

Anderson, Poul. "Goat Song." *F&SF,* Feb. 1972.

"The narrator is a contemporary Orpheus, singing for his dead love in a technological world controlled by an underground computer who has the power to re-create and restore . . . [his] lost love to him" (Warrick, p. 146).

_____. "Sam Hall." *Astounding,* Aug. 1953. Rpt. in *Science Fiction Thinking Machines,* q.v. under Anthologies and Collections. Coll. in *The Best of Poul Anderson.* New York: Pocket Books, 1976.

Shows a computerized police state; cf. Crossen's *Year of Consent* (1954; q.v. below, this section). Discussed by Warrick, pp. 141-42.

Asimov, Isaac.

See above under Reference Works, David M. Cox and Gary R. Libby, compilers, "A Bibliography of Isaac Asimov's Major Science Fiction Works through 1976."

Asimov, Isaac. "The Caves of Steel." *Galaxy,* Oct., Nov., Dec. 1953. Rpt. as novel Garden City, NY: Doubleday, 1954. Frequently rpt., including Greenwich, CT: Fawcett, 1972.

A human protagonist partnered with a robot detective solves a murder. Note hive-cities (our term) inhabited by bureaucratized Earth-folk afraid of the open air and too timid to go to the stars to solve the problem of overpopulation. Discussed in ch. 5, "The Robot Novels," in James Gunn, *Isaac Asimov,* q.v. below, under Literary Criticism. See below, IA's "Naked Sun"; cf. E. M. Forster's "Machine Stops" and Arthur C. Clarke's *City and the Stars* (cited below, this section).

_____. The Foundation trilogy: *Foundation* (1951), *Foundation and Empire* (1952), *Second Foundation* (1953). Garden City, NY: Doubleday, 1961. Frequently rpt., including New York: Avon, 1964 (*Second Foundation*), 1966 (first two vols.). See Cox and Libby for other rpts. For magazine versions and vts see "Asimov" in *S. F. Ency.*

Presents a determinable and possibly determined universe in which mass human action may be as predictable as the behavior of the masses of molecules that make up a gas. See under Literary Criticism the essays by Charles Elkins and James Gunn. See below IA's *Foundation's Edge.*

_____. *Foundation's Edge.* Garden City, NY: Doubleday, 1982.

Fourth novel of what has become the Foundation series. *FE*'s climax explicitly raises questions of free will and the retention of humanity in a Galaxy to be run by the technological First Foundation, the "mentalic" Second Foundation, or Gaia (a planet-wide mentality comprising all the human *individuals* on that world, plus everything else down to rabbits and rocks). The novel's immediate resolution has Gaia pulling the strings in both the novel and the Galaxy; the Conclusion goes on to hint strongly that a small number of robots supervise the action of Gaia, and finally to suggest that some other force may be acting on the Galaxy raising question to be resolved, apparently, in further sequels.

_____. "The Last Question." *Science Fiction Quarterly,* Nov. 1956. Coll. in Asimov's *Nine Tomorrows: Tales of the Near Future.* Garden City, NY: Doubleday, 1959, 1970. Other rpts. listed in Cox and Libby.

Deals with the three-stage evolution of *H. sapiens sapiens* from (1) our current state, to (2) bodies with free-roaming minds, tended by machines and, finally, to (3) minds merged with the cosmic computer; parallel development of computers also handled. "The Last Question" is how to reverse entropy; the answer is, Creation by the ultimate computer-god.

_____. "The Life and Times of Multivac." *New York Times Magazine,* 5 Jan. 1975. Coll. in Asimov, *The Bicentennial Man and Other Stories,* q.v. above under Anthologies and Collections.

Deals with the relationship of humans and computers, specifically "*the* world-girding Computer . . . with millions of robots at its command," exercising a benevolent tyranny over a humankind growing to consider security under Multivac as slavery. An expert in math games "kills" this world-machine.

_____. "The Naked Sun." *Astounding,* Oct., Nov., Dec. 1956. Rpt. as novel Garden City, NY: Doubleday, 1957, and frequently thereafter; see Cox and Libby.

Sequel to "Caves of Steel" (q.v.). Again, a human and a robot detective work together to solve a murder, this time, however, not on Earth but on an Outer World with a robot-run economy. Discussed by Hazel Pierce in her essay cited below, under Literary Criticism, and by James Gunn in ch. 5 of his *Isaac Asimov* (also cited under Literary Criticism).

_____. "Profession." *Astounding,* July 1957. Coll. in Asimov, *Nine Tomorrows.* Garden City, NY: Doubleday, 1959, 1970.

See for people programmed and functioning like machines. Handled by Warrick, p. 56.

Auden, W. H. "The Unknown Citizen" (1940). In *The Collected Poetry of W. H. Auden*. New York: Random House, 1945. Frequently rpt., including in A. O. Lewis. *Of Men and Machines*, q.v. under Anthologies and Collections.

This poem ironically celebrates "the Modern Man" in a modern state: complacent, compliant, conforming, and unfree.

Barth, John. *Giles Goat-Boy*. Garden City, NY: Doubleday, 1966; rpt. New York: Fawcett, 1967.

An alternate-world story, but primarily SF in the sense of "Satura Fantastique": a particularly wild hodgepodge of elements that add up (more or less) to a satire, in the tradition of Jonathan Swift's *Tale of a Tub* and Laurence Sterne's *Tristram Shandy*. Significant for the study of mechanized environments for the hero's various descents into the Belly of WESCAC: a computer that may or may not be a "Troll," that may or may not be a kind of metonym for a mechanical universe, and that may or may not be the fictive main author of *GG-B* (vol. Two, Third Reel, ch. 5—p. 733 in Fawcett edn.; second paragraph of "Posttape," p. 755; second paragraph of "Publisher's Disclaimer," p. xi, and title page following "Cover-Letter"; and passim).

Bellamy, Edward. *Looking Backward: 2000-1887*. Boston: Ticknor and Company, 1888; rpt. New York: New American Library, 1960; and numerous other edns.

A highly influential utopian novel with some aspects many readers today find dystopian: esp. significant here is its uncritical acceptance of a thoroughly bureaucratized world. (See below under Literary Criticism the essays by Erich Fromm, and David Ketterer.) Discussed in *CW* by Reimer Jehmlich.

Benét, Stephen Vincent. "Nightmare Number Three." In *The Selected Works of Stephen Vincent Benet*. New York: Holt, Rinehart and Winston, 1935. Rpt. in *The Theme of the Machine*, q.v. under Anthologies and Collections.

A poem presenting a nightmare vision of a takeover by machines, with a strong hint that the takeover has already begun in the daylight world.

Bester, Alfred. *Computer Connection*. New York: Berkley, 1975; *Extro* (vt). London: Eyre Methuen, 1975.

Explores "the social and political implications of a computerized world" (Warrick, p. 89).

Bierce, Ambrose. "Moxon's Master." In *Can Such Things Be?*, 1893. Rpt. in *Science Fiction Thinking Machines*, q.v. under Anthologies and Collections.

An early examination of whether or not machines can think, the question leading to a more general consideration of the differences between machines and living things. Briefly summarized by Warrick, p. 40.

Bishop, Michael. *A Little Knowledge*. New York: Berkley, 1977.

See for the working out in the domed city of New Atlanta of "the sf trope of an enclosed society" (Ian Watson, "A Rhetoric of Recognition," q.v. below under Literary Criticism).

Blish, James. *Cities in Flight*. Tetralogy, 1955-62. Coll. in one vol. New York: Avon, 1970.

The "cities in flight" are literal cities flying off to the "cosmic frontier"; their usual form of government is "totalitarian technocracy," a form of government Blish seems to present neutrally (see Wolfe, pp. 122-23). In *The Triumph of Time*, the last vol. of the tetralogy, "The city is finally revealed as merely a machine . . . " (Wolfe, p. 124).

_____. "Common Time." *Science Fiction Quarterly*, Aug. 1953. Coll. in Blish, *Galactic Cluster*. New York: New American Library, 1959.

The environment of the spaceship in this story "becomes an integral part of the mind of its inhabitant" (Wolfe, p. 78). The protagonist of the story sees that environment as "perfectly rigid, still, unchanging, lifeless" (Blish, in *Galactic Cluster*, p. 56; quoted by Wolfe, p. 78).

_____, adapter. *Star Trek [1]-11*. New York and other cities: Bantam, 1967-75.

Relevant episodes are given below: *Star Trek*, under Stage, Film, and Television Drama. Blish's eleven vols. fictionalize most *Star Trek* episodes (the series may be completed by other adapters).

Bond, Nelson, S. "The Priestess Who Rebelled." *Amazing,* Oct. 1939. Rpt. in *When Women Rule.* Sam Moscowitz, ed. New York: Walker, 1972.

Discussed by Joanna Russ in "Amor Vincit Foeminam," *SFS,* 7 (March 1980), 5. Russ says that the "primitive matriarchy" of the future society of the story is "modeled on bees and termites (a common model for matriarchies in SF)."

Boorman, John. *Zardoz.* New York: New American Library, 1974.

See below under Stage, Film, and Television Drama, *Zardoz.* In his preface to this novelization, Boorman discusses the genesis of his film and the relationship of the film and this novel.

Bova, Ben. *THX-1138.* From the screenplay by George Lucas and Walter Murch. New York: Paperback Library, 1971; reissued New York: Warner, 1978. (1971 copyright held by Warner Brothers.)

Annotated in Stage, Film, and Television Drama section under *THX-1138.* BB's only significant departure from the Lucas film is to show us the man who is Control.

Boyd, John. *The Last Starship from Earth.* New York: Berkley, 1968.

Features a computer-run "hive" dystopia, but with a surprise twist which reveals that a mechanically rigid society is only part of the full reality of the novel's world. Discussed by Warrick, pp. 188-90; see under Literary Criticism the essay by Jane Hipolito.

Brackett, Leigh. *The Long Tomorrow.* Garden City, NY: Doubleday, 1955.

Postholocaust tale; note esp. Bartorstown, in Book Three, an underground research facility dominated by a computer and a nuclear reactor (Wolfe, p. 136). See "Holocaust and After," *S. F. Ency.,* pp. 290-92 and passim.

Bradbury, Ray.

See under Reference Works, Marshall B. Tymn, compiler, "Ray Bradbury: A Bibliography."

Bradbury, Ray. "The Lost City of Mars." *Playboy,* Jan. 1967. Coll. in

Bradbury, *I Sing the Body Electric!* New York: Knopf, 1969; rpt. New York: Bantam, 1971.

Features a "completely mechanized city, a kind of amusement park supreme" (Marvin Mengeling, p. 107 of "Machineries" essay, q.v. under Literary Criticism).

_____. "The Murderer." *Argosy* (England), June 1953. Coll. in *The Golden Apples of the Sun.* Garden City, NY: Doubleday, 1953; rpt. New York: Bantam, 1954.

The victim is the murder's mechanical house.

_____. "There Will Come Soft Rains." *Collier's,* 6 May 1950. Coll. in *The Martian Chronicles.* New York: Doubleday, 1950. *Chronicles* rpt. S. F. Book Club, Nov. 1952, and New York and other cities: Bantam, 1972. "TWCSR" frequently anthologized, including *The Vintage Anthology of Science Fantasy.* Christopher Cerf, ed. New York: Random House, 1966. See Contento, *Index* (cited under Acknowledgments) for other rpts.

A very important postholocaust story, showing the death of a mechanical house. See under Literary Criticism the essays by Edward Gallagher and Marvin Mengeling.

_____. "The World the Children Made." *Saturday Evening Post*, 23 Sept. 1950. Coll. as "The Veldt" (vt) in *The Illustrated Man.* Garden City, NY: Doubleday, 1951; New York: Bantam, 1952. Also coll. in *The Vintage Bradbury.* New York: Vintage, 1965. See Contento, *Index*, for rpts.

A mechanized nursery's artificial environment proves psychologically unhealthful for children. This story is included in the film *The Illustrated Man* (1968).

Brautigan, Richard. "All Watched Over by Machines of Loving Grace." In Brautigan, *The Pill Versus the Springhill Mine Disaster.* San Francisco: Four Seasons Foundation/City Lights Books (distributor), 1968, p. 1.

Poem. Apparently a nonironic celebration of a future Eden in which humans and other mammals live in peace and harmony with computers. The "cybernetic ecology" of this Eden is "watched over" by the machines.

Brown, Frederic. "Answer." New story in Brown, *Angels and Spaceships.* New York: Dutton, 1954. For rpts. see Contento, *Index.*

A very short story or medium-length joke, now a part of urban folklore. Question to supercomputer: Is there a God? Answer: "Now there is" (see Warrick, p. 112).

Brunner, John. "Bloodstream." *Vertex,* June 1974.

Features a positive presentation of an "entire city [that] is a self-regulating biological machine" (Edward Lamie and Joe De Bolt, "Computer and Man" essay, q.v. under Literary Criticism).

_____. "Judas." In *Dangerous Visions.* Harlan Ellison, ed. New York: New American Library, 1967.

In a world in which humankind has "made a machine our God," a Judas-figure who helped create the ruling robot (and whose megalomania was transferred to it) kills the god-machine. Unfortunately for human freedom, this Judas kills the machine on a Friday in spring, and the robot will be repaired in three days.

_____. *Stand on Zanzibar.* Garden City, NY: Doubleday, 1968; rpt. New York: Ballantine, 1969.

Shalmaneser, the computer, becomes "a sort of mechanical Messias," in many ways (mostly ironic) the ruler and savior of his world. See below under Literary Criticism the essay by Michael Stern.

_____. *Timescoop.* New York: Dell, 1969; London: Sidgwick & Jackson, 1972.

Edward Lamie and Joe De Bolt discuss the "benevolent domination" (their phrase) by the computer SPARCI and put this novel into the context of JB's canon; see Lamie and De Bolt, "Computer and Man" essay under Literary Criticism.

Bryant, Edward, and Harlan Ellison. *Phoenix without Ashes.* Greenwich, CT: Fawcett, 1975. A Novel of *The Starlost* #1.

Novelization by EB of HE's original version of the pilot script for *The Starlost* TV series (q.v. under Stage, Film, and Television Drama). A generation-starship story; see below, this section, Heinlein, "Universe." *PWA* includes an Introduction by HE giving his version of the genesis of *The Starlost* and comments on other matters of interest.

Burgess, Anthony (John Anthony Burgess Wilson). *A Clockwork Orange.* London: Heinemann, 1962; rpt. without final chapter, New York: Norton, 1963.

Features a totally amoral rebel in (anti)heroic rebellion against a mechanical society. Basis for Kubrick film, q.v. below, under Stage, Film, and Television Drama. See under Literary Criticism the essay by Rubin Rabinovitz.

Butler, Samuel. *Erewhon; or, Over the Range.* London: Trübner, 1872; rpt. New York: New American Library, 1960. Afterword by Kingsley Amis.

Described by Sargent as "*The* classic utopian satire." See esp. chs. 23-25, "The Book of the Machines," for organism vs. mechanism, machine takeover, humans as part of a mechanized system, and foreshadowings of Frank Herbert's *Hellstrom's Hive*, and John Sladek's *Reproductive System* (q.v. below, this section).

Campbell, John W. "The Last Evolution." *Amazing,* Aug. 1932. Coll. in *The Best of John W. Campbell,* q.v. above under Anthologies and Collections.

A meditation by the last machine, before it wears out and bequeaths our solar system and beyond to the entities of pure energy and intelligence which it created. Most of the meditation presents an Earth where humans and machines cooperate, each "race" recognizing the powers and limitations of the other; on balance, however, the machines are superior and run things—and survive long after the deaths of their human creators.

_____. "The Machine." *Astounding,* Feb. 1935. Coll. in Campbell, *Cloak of Aesir.* Chicago: Shasta, 1952. Also coll. in *The Best of John W. Campbell,* q.v. above.

Gaht, "the Machine who gave all things" to the future humanity in this story, departs the Earth (as it had departed the world of its makers), forcing the human race to fend for itself again. Very similar to E.M. Forster's "Machine Stops" (q.v. below, this section), but with a more positive ending.

_____. "Out of Night." *Astounding*, Oct. 1937. "Cloak of Aesir." *Astounding*, March 1939. Coll. in *Cloak of Aesir*. Chicago: Shasta, 1952. Also coll. in *The Best of John W. Campbell*, and in Campbell, *Who Goes There? And Other Stories*. New York: Dell, 1955.

One story in two parts. Important for Jungian and other archetypal approaches to the motif of mechanized environments: inverts many of the traditional oppositions between the Great Mother (and matri- archy) and her male opponents.

_____ (writing as John A. Stuart). "Twilight." *Astounding*, Nov. 1934. Coll. in *The Best of John W. Campbell*, q.v. above. Rpt. in *Man Unwept: Visions from the Inner Eye*. Stephen V. Whaley and Stanley J. Cook, eds. New York and other cities: McGraw-Hill, 1974. Also rpt. in *The Road to Science Fiction #2*. James Gunn, ed. New York: New American Library, 1979.

Features a city of the far future whose residents know nothing of the machines that run the city. Cf. E. M. Forster's "Machine Stops" and Robert Heinlein's "Universe," q.v. below, this section.

Clarke, Arthur C. *The City and the Stars*. New York: Harcourt, Brace, 1956; rpt. New York: New American Library, 1957.

A revision and expansion of *Against the Fall of Night* (listed below under *The Lion of Comarre*). The city of the title is controlled by a central computer, located in an "underground city, the city of machines." See for a mechanized womb-world and for contrasts of the city, a garden world, and the stars. Discussed by Eric Rabkin, *Arthur C. Clarke*, and in various places in the anthology of critical essays, *Arthur C. Clarke*, edited by Joseph Olander and Martin Greenberg (q.v. under Literary Criticism).

_____. *The Lion of Comarre & Against the Fall of Night*. New York: Harcourt, Brace & World, 1968.

Coll. of two stories. *Lion of Comarre* is a hackwork variation on the land of the lotus-eaters, significant here for the dream land's being replaced by a dream city, "a vast honey-comb of chambers" run by machines. *Against the Fall of Night* is the precursor of *City and the Stars*, q.v. above. In his "Preface" to *City and the Stars*, ACC says that *AFN* was written between 1937 and 1946; it appeared in *Startling Stories* in 1948. *TLC* first appeared in *Thrilling World Stories*, in 1949. For additional information, see "Clarke" entry in *S. F. Ency.*

_____. *Rendezvous with Rama*. London: Gollancz, 1973; New York: Harcourt Brace Jovanovich, 1973. Rpt. London: Pan Books, 1974; New York: Ballantine, 1974, 1976. Serialized in *Galaxy*, Sept., Oct. 1973.

Terran investigators explore the interior of a huge alien artifact discovered in our solar system.

_____. *2001: A Space Odyssey*. New York: New American Library, 1968. Based on the filmscript by Kubrick and Clarke.

The deep-space ship *Discovery* is run by the computer HAL 9000. See below under Stage, Film, and Television Drama, *2001*.

Compton, D. G. *The Steel Crocodile*. New York: Ace, 1970.

The Colindale Institute, home of the European Federation's central research computer, is a place of constant surveillance and heavy security—and of a conspiracy by the scientists who control the computer to control the direction of science by preventing new discoveries that may prove dangerous. Discussed by Warrick, pp. 143-44.

Cook, Robin. *Coma*. Boston: Little, Brown, 1977.

Medical "thriller" novel and source for the film. At the Jefferson Institute, brain-dead people are suspended by wires from the ceiling, hooked to computer-controlled machines, and used for spare body parts sold on the black market to wealthy recipients.

Cooper, Edmund. *Seed of Light*. London: Hutchinson, 1959; New York: Ballantine, 1959.

Generation-starship story featuring the development of a tribal culture on the spaceship. Discussed by Wolfe, pp. 71-73. See below, this section, Robert Heinlein, "Universe."

Crichton, Michael. *The Andromeda Strain*. New York: Dell, 1969; rpt. New York: Knopf, 1973. Canadian edn.: Toronto: Random House of Canada, 1973.

See for a mechanized "underworld" (our term): the underground Wildfire laboratory. Film version cited below under Stage, Film, and Television Drama. *TAS* is discussed in *TMG* by Peter Alterman.

Crossen, Kendell. *Year of Consent*. New York: Dell, 1954.

SOCIAC (nicknamed "Herbie" in honor of Herbert Hoover, "the first engineer to be elected president") monitors life functions of all citizens and occasionally prescribes lobotomy for misfits, that is, rebels.

Daley, Brian. *Tron*. New York: Ballantine, 1982. A Del Rey Book (S. F. Book Club Edition). Based on the screenplay by Steven Lisberger, story by Steven Lisberger and Bonnie MacBird.

Novelization of the Disney film *TRON*, q.v. below under Stage, Film and Television Drama.

Dante, Alighieri. *[Divina] Commedia (The Divine Comedy)*. Composed circa 1302. Printed Foligno, Italy: Johann Neumeister, 1472. Available in numerous edns. and trans.

"Archetype" for presentations of dystopian mechanized environments; see in *CW* the essay on Dante's Hell by Merritt Abrash.

Davidson, Michael. *The Karma Machine*. New York: Popular Library, 1975.

Described by Sargent as a "computer dystopia."

Delany, Samuel R. *The Fall of the Towers*. New York: Ace, 1970; Boston: Gregg Press, 1977.

Apparently SRD's final intention of a unified trilogy (based on a 1966 UK edn.—Wolfe, p. 106) collecting and revising *Captives of the Flame* (rev. edn. of *Out of the Dead City,* 1963) and *City of a Thousand Suns* (1965). See for rigidity of Toron vs. freer, communal life of the City of a Thousand Suns. Discussed by Wolfe, pp. 106-8.

_____. *Nova*. Garden City, NY: Doubleday, 1968. Rpt. with textual corrections Garden City, NY: Doubleday, S. F. Book Club, 1969 (Currey); and New York and other cities: Bantam, 1969.

Suggests the possibility of the reduction or elimination of the alienation from labor in technological societies by a "Man-Machine Symbiosis." Discussed by Warrick, pp. 176-78; discussed in *TMG* in the essay by Andrew Gordon.

Dick, Philip K.

See above under Reference Works, R. D. Mullen, "Books, Stories, Essays [by Philip K. Dick]," and Marshall B. Tymn, "Philip K. Dick: A Bibliography."

Dick, Philip K. "Autofac." *Galaxy,* Nov. 1955. Coll. in *The Best of Philip K. Dick,* q.v. above under Anthologies and Collections. See Contento, *Index,* for rpts.

Under a postholocaust wasteland, an automated factory still produces goods—and begins "to show the instinct for survival which organic living entities have" ("Afterthoughts by the Author," *Best of Philip K. Dick,* p. 449). At the end of the story the autofac network begins to seed the world, and possibly the universe, with automated factories. Discussed in *CW* by Merritt Abrash, in his essay on PKD. See Warrick, p. 119. Cf. Walter Miller, "Dumb Waiter" and cf. and contrast Ray Bradbury. "There Will Come Soft Rains," both in this section.

_____. "The Electric Ant." *F&SF,* Oct. 1969. Coll. in *The Best of Philip K. Dick*, q.v. See Contento, *Index,* for rpts.

After an accident, a man awakes to discover that he is not a man but a robot. Story set in a highly computerized world of complex economic manipulations.

_____. "Human Is." *Startling Stories,* Winter 1955. Coll. in *The Best of Philip K. Dick,* q.v.

Not a robot, android, or mechanized world story, but gives PKD's "early conclusions as to what is human," conclusions PKD held through 1977 ("Afterthoughts," *Best of Philip K. Dick,* p. 449).

_____. *Martian Time-Slip.* New York: Ballantine, 1964; rpt. London: New English Library, 1976.

Insanity as a struggle to be human rather than become adjusted to being a human mechanism, a cog in the social apparatus. Discussed by Warrick, pp. 219-20.

_____. *The Penultimate Truth.* New York: Belmont, 1964. Rpt. London: Jonathan Cape, 1967; New York: Dell, 1980.

Surface world in which robots—"leadies"—do all physical work, and an underground human environment of "ant tanks." (Very important for PKD's idea of the mendacity of ruling elites.) Discussed in *CW* by Merritt Abrash in his essay on PKD.

_____. "Second Variety." *Space Science Fiction,* May 1953. Coll. in *The Best of Philip K. Dick,* q.v. See Contento, *Index,* for other locations.

The world of the story is a future Earth that has become a desolate, mechanized, and computerized battlefield. The ultimate threat to humankind is very humanoid and humanlike robots.

_____. "Service Call." *Science Fiction Stories,* July 1955. Coll. in *The Best of Philip K. Dick,* q.v.

A small group of Americans in 1954 gets a glimpse of a future world controlled by swibbles: predatory organic machines that make sure everyone's ideology "is exactly congruent with that of everybody else in the world." Social deviants run the risk "that some passing swibble will feed on" them (*Best of Philip K. Dick,* p. 260).

_____. *The Simulacra.* New York: Ace, 1964.

Totalitarian dictatorship behind a figurehead, simulacrum president.

_____. *Vulcan's Hammer.* New York: Ace, 1960. (Mullen gives date of 1956 in addition to 1960—#10 of "Books, Stories, Essays," p. 6 in *SFS #5,* the special Dick issue.)

Total control of human society by the computer Vulcan III.

Elder, Michael. *Paradise Is Not Enough.* London: Robert Hale, 1970.

Described by Sargent as a "dystopia of mechanical perfection."

Ellison, Harlan. "Asleep: With Still Hands" (vt "The Sleeper with Still Hands"). *If,* July 1968. Coll. in Ellison, *Beast that Shouted Love,* q.v. under Anthologies and Collections.

A very hard-nosed, possibly militaristic, handling of the motif of gentle control—exercised in this story by a world-ruling man/machine being.

_____. "A Boy and His Dog." *New Worlds*, April 1969. Coll. in Ellison, *Beast that Shouted Love*; rpt. in *As Tomorrow Becomes Today*— see both under Anthologies and Collections. Other rpts. listed in Contento, *Index*.

See for the mechanized underworld of the "downunder" of Topeka. Source of film by L. Q. Jones, q.v. below, under Stage, Film, and Television Drama. See under Stage, Film, and Television Drama Criticism the essay by John Crow and Richard Erlich.

_____. "Catman." In *Final Stage: The Ultimate Science Fiction Anthology*, q.v. under Anthologies and Collections, pp. 134-70 in US issue of Penguin rpt.

See for the subterranean computer, called by the Narrator "the machine." The computer is served by once-human cyborgs.

_____. "I Have No Mouth, and I Must Scream." *If*, March 1967. Coll. in Ellison, *I Have No Mouth and I Must Scream*. New York: Pyramid, 1967. Frequently rpt., including *Man Unwept*. Stephen V. Whaley and Stanley J. Cook, eds. New York: McGraw-Hill, 1974; *The Road to Science Fiction #3: From Heinlein to Here*. James Gunn, ed. New York: New American Library, 1979. See Contento, *Index*, for other locations.

The interior monologue of the "last man," trapped inside the malevolent computer AM. An important work for the study of mechanized environments. See essay in *CW* by Charles W. Sullivan.

_____. " 'Repent, Harlequin!' Said the Ticktockman." *Galaxy*, Dec. 1965. Frequently rpt., including in *Nebula Award Stories*. Damon Knight, ed. Garden City, NY: Doubleday, 1966; *World's Best Science Fiction: 1966*. Donald A. Wollheim and Terry Carr, eds. New York: Ace, 1966; *The Hugo Winners*. Vol. 2. Isaac Asimov, ed. Garden City, NY: Doubleday, 1971; *Science Fiction: The Future*. Dick Allen, ed. 1st and 2d edns. New York and other cities: Harcourt Brace Jovanovich, 1971, 1983.

See for the Harlequin, a Trickster figure, in opposition to the Ticktockman and the mechanized, efficient, time-worshiping, *Taylorized* society he represents. (On Frederick W. Taylor, see Gorman Beauchamp, essay in *CW*, and the first essay cited for Carolyn Rhodes, below under Literary Criticism.)

_____. "Worlds to Kill." *If*, March 1968. Coll. in Ellison, *Beast that Shouted Love*, q.v. under Anthologies and Collections.

See for a wise computer and the city built around it.

Etzler, J[ohn] A[dolphus]. *The Paradise within Reach of All Men, without Labour, by Powers of Nature and Machinery.* 2 Parts. Pittsburgh, PA: Etzler and Reinhold, 1833.

Described by Sargent as "the basic work of Etzler's many depicting eutopia through technology."

Fairman, Paul W. *I, The Machine.* New York: Lancer (Lodestone), 1968.

In the domed world of Midamerica, the Machine has established a "Second Eden," a womb-world similar to that in E. M. Forster's "Machine Stops" (q.v., this section). See also for overprotective robots similar to Jack Williamson's humanoids (see below, this section, *The Humanoids*).

Farmer, Philip José. *Behind the Walls of Terra.* New York: Ace, 1970.

We learn in *The Magic Labyrinth* (q.v. below) that human souls (*wathans*) in the universe of Riverworld are created by machines; in *BWT* we learn that our universe itself was machine-made (pp. 88-93). PJF does little with this point, however, contenting himself with telling a story of heroic adventure.

_____. *The Magic Labyrinth.* New York: Berkley, 1980 (distributed by G. P. Putnam's Sons; S. F. Book Club).

See for the giant "protein computer" that helps run the Riverworld, and for the odd combination of mechanism and mysticism in what seems to be the underlying metaphysics for the Riverworld series (*TML,* possibly the concluding volume, together with *To Your Scattered Bodies Go, The Fabulous Riverboat,* and *The Dark Design*).

_____. "Queen of the Deep" (vt "Son"). *Argosy,* March 1954. Coll. in Farmer, *Strange Relations.* New York: Ballantine, 1960.

The birth of the "healthy, independent individual locked inside the neurotic, mother-dominated weakling" who is the story's protagonist. "Jonah-like, Jones is held prisoner in the guts of a cybernated submarine that looks like a whale and talks like a woman." See Russell Letson, "The Worlds of Philip José Farmer," *Extrapolation*, 18 (May 1977), 128-29 quoted here.

Forster, E. M. "The Machine Stops." *Oxford and Cambridge Review,* 8 (Michaelmas term 1909), 83-122. Frequently rpt., including in *Of Men and Machines,* q.v. under Anthologies and Collections; *The Science Fiction Hall of Fame,* IIB. Ben Bova, ed. New York: Avon, 1973; *Science Fiction: The Future.* Dick Allen, ed. 1st and 2d edns. New York and other cities: Harcourt Brace Jovanovich, 1971, 1983; *Man Unwept.* Stephen V. Whaley and Stanley J. Cook, eds. New York and other cities: McGraw-Hill, 1974.

The prototypical mechanical hive story. Brings together most of the relevant motifs developed by dystopian authors for the rest of the twentieth century. Discussed in *CW* by Charles Elkins.

Foster, Alan Dean. *Alien.* New York: Warner, 1979. From the screenplay by Dan O'Bannon, and story by Dan O'Bannon and Ronald Shusett.

Novelization of the film, q.v. below under Stage, Film, and Television Drama.

Frayn, Michael. *A Very Private Life.* London: Collins, 1968.

Described by Sargent as a dystopia in which technology "brings isolation of people."

Gardner, John. *Grendel.* New York: Knopf, 1972; rpt. New York: Ballantine, n.d.

The Beowulf story through the death of Grendel (with foreshadowings of later episodes) told from the point of view of the monster, Grendel, who knows "the mindless, mechanical bruteness of things" (Ballantine edn., p. 46)—including the mechanical nature of the universe, goats, men, and Grendel. See for a highly sophisticated "mainstream" use of the mechanization motif; cf. Ken Kesey's *One Flew Over the Cuckoo's Nest,* q.v. below, this section.

Gerrold, David. *When HARLIE Was One.* New York: Ballantine, 1972; rpt. Garden City, NY: Doubleday, S. F. Book Club, n.d.

HARLIE is a young, precocious, godlike computer who is very good at games. At the end of *WHWO*, HARLIE has taken over a major socioeconomic game and has "the capacity to take over all the *rest* of the games"—that is, human "civilization, culture, society." See copyright page of Doubleday edn. for other HARLIE stories.

Glut, Donald F. *The Empire Strikes Back*. New York: Ballantine, 1980. A Del Rey Book (S. F. Book Club Edition). Canadian edn.: Toronto: Random House of Canada, 1980.

See *The Empire Strikes Back* under Stage, Film, and Television Drama. See also the entries for James Kahn and George Lucas below, this section.

Haldeman, Joe. "Juryrigged." *Vertex*, Oct. 1974. Coll. in Haldeman, *Infinite Dreams*. New York: St. Martin's Press, 1978.

The hero is commandeered to serve as part of the city's computer nexus (his brain is wired into the system). Cf. William Hjortsberg's *Gray Matters*, q.v. below, this section.

Harrison, Harry. *Captive Universe*. New York: Berkley, 1969.

Generation-starship story featuring two primitive cultures. See below in this section Robert Heinlein's "Universe."

_____. "I Always Do What Teddy Says." *Ellery Queen's Mystery Magazine,* June 1965. Rpt. in *The New Improved Sun*. Thomas M. Disch, ed. New York and other cities: Harper & Row, 1975.

Electronically sophisticated teddy bears condition children into standard morality.

Harrison, William. "Roller Ball Murder." *Esquire,* Sept. 1973. Coll. in Harrison, *Roller Ball Murder*. New York: Warner, 1975. Rpt. in *Science Fiction: The Future*. Dick Allen, ed. 2d edn. New York and other cities: Harcourt Brace Jovanovich, 1983.

Corporation-run dystopia; source of film *Rollerball*, q.v. below, under Stage, Film, and Television Drama.

Heinlein, Robert A. *The Moon Is a Harsh Mistress*. New York: G. P. Putnam's Sons, 1966; rpt. New York: Berkley, 1968. (Shorter version published in *If*, 1965-66.)

The mechanized "warrens" (RAH's term) on the Moon are presented quite positively; they are contrasted with the negative hive-world (our term) on Earth. See esp. pp. 87 and 211 in Berkley edn. Discussed in *CW* by Charles Sullivan. See also H. Bruce Franklin's excellent discussion in *Robert A. Heinlein*, pp. 162-70 (q.v. below, under Literary Criticism).

————. *Orphans of the Sky*. See below, "Universe."

————. *Starship Troopers*. New York: G. P. Putnam's Sons, 1959; rpt. New York: Berkley, 1968, 1975.

Inadvertent dystopia of a future Terran federation ruled by service veterans and defended by a rigidly hierarchical, elite military establishment. The war against the "Bugs" in this novel is an allegory of the resistance of free men against "hive-communism." Discussed by H. Bruce Franklin, *Robert A. Heinlein*, pp. 110-24 (q.v. below, under Literary Criticism).

————. "Universe." *Astounding*, May 1941. Rpt. as book New York: Dell, 1951. Rpt. in *The Science Fiction Hall of Fame*. Vol. IIA. Ben Bova, ed. Garden City, NY: Doubleday, 1973; rpt. New York: Avon, 1974. Rpt. with its sequel "Common Sense" as *Orphans of the Sky*. London: Gollancz, 1963; New York: Berkley, 1970.

Possibly the definitive story about a generation starship, that is, a ship whose passengers and/or crew are "men and women, whose families breed, and whose remote descendants eventually reach the destination" (*S. F. Ency.*, "Generation Starships"). As in this story, the people have often forgotten that they are on a spaceship and mistake the spaceship for a world. See in this section Edward Bryant's *Phoenix Without Ashes*, Harry Martinson's *Aniara*, Kevin O'Donnell's *Mayflies*, Murray Leinster's "Proxima Centauri," and E. C. Tubb's *The Space-born;* see under Stage, Film, and Television Drama, Karl-Birger Blomdahl, *Aniara*, the TV series *Starlost*, and the *Star Trek* episode "For the World Is Hollow." "Universe" is discussed by Wolfe, esp. pp. 61-65, and by H. Bruce Franklin in *Robert A. Heinlein*, pp. 43-44, q.v. below under Literary Criticism.

Herbert, Frank. *Destination: Void*. New York: Berkley, 1966. Rev. edn. New York: Berkley, 1978. Based on Herbert, "Do I Sleep or Wake," *Galaxy*, 1965.

Both edns. relevant. The spaceship *Earthling* is run by an Organic Mental Core: an isolated human brain managing a computer. When the Core and its backup fail, the few awake crew members must deal with the feasibility, safety, and morality of creating true machine intelligence and putting it in control of their ship—and of the lives of the unconscious passengers. They finally construct a machine intelligence that turns out to have godlike powers and demands "WorShip" from the crew. Discussed by Warrick, pp. 181-88, and by Wolfe, pp. 79-80.

_____. *Hellstrom's Hive.* Garden City, NY: Doubleday, 1973; rpt. New York: Bantam, 1974. Originally published as "Project 40," *Galaxy*, Nov./Dec. 1972-March/April 1973.

The Hive is an underground world of machines and people: a society intentionally striving to imitate the social insects. The opposition outside the Hive is a nasty espionage bureaucracy called only "the Agency."

_____, and Bill Ransom. *The Jesus Incident.* New York: Berkley-Putnam, 1979; London: Gollancz, 1979. Rpt. New York: Berkley, 1980.

A sequel to FH's *Destination: Void* (q.v. above). The computer-god, Ship, teaches his people the meaning of true "WorShip": to find their "own humanity and live up to it" (p. 412 of Berkley rpt.). Reviewed by Brian Stableford in *Foundation*, No. 19 (June 1980), pp. 68-69, with a useful reference to the "hive intelligence" dominating the Ship-created planet of Pandora (Stableford, p. 68).

Herrick, Robert. *Sometime.* New York: Farrar & Rinehart, 1933.

According to Sargent, deals with technology and a "labor army." Cf. Edward Bellamy's *Looking Backward*, cited above, this section.

Hjortsberg, William. *Gray Matters.* New York: Simon and Schuster, 1971.

In WH's future world, humankind have given up their bodies to live as brains in a huge hivelike complex. Here they go through a process of emotional purgation and perfection intended to prepare them for "Nirvana," when they will be granted use of perfect bodies grown to receive their perfected brains.

Horton, Forest W., Jr. *The Technocrats.* New York: Nordon, 1980. A Leisure Book.

The world of *Nineteen Eighty-Four* brought to us by computer take-over, with the computers operating through the android president of the United States and his android chief assistant. *TT* is significant neither for its analysis of technocracy nor for its literary quality (both minimal), but for its presentation of the motifs of robotization and machine-takeover in a book marketed for a general audience.

Hughes, Monica. *The Tomorrow City.* London: Hamish Hamilton, 1978.

Computer-takeover novel for children. The City Central Computer for Thomasville logically but unfeelingly attempts to make Thomas-ville into a perfect city by eliminating useless people, controlling behavior through surveillance and subliminal suggestion, and engag-ing in other standard acts of gentle but total control. Two children save the city. Reviewed by Pamela Cleaver in *Foundation*, No. 15 (Jan. 1979), pp. 100-102.

Huxley, Aldous. *Brave New World.* Garden City, NY: Doubleday, 1932; rpt. New York: Bantam, 1958. Frequently reissued.

Presents a world-state of gentle but total control. People in the "Brave New World" are conceived in bottles and, in a sense, never leave their bottle-wombs. The literal womb-bottles move through a literal machine; the figurative womb-bottles, after one is decanted, are themselves within the apparatus of the World State.

_____. *Island.* New York: Harper & Row, 1962; rpt. New York and other cities: Bantam, 1963.

Discussed in *CW* in the essay by Reimer Jehmlich. A dystopian ele-ment in AH's utopia is of immediate relevance: the combination of Hitler's Brownshirts, insects, and machines in the unpleasant por-tion of the protagonist's drug-induced vision near the end of the story (ch. 15).

Jarrell, Randall. "The Death of the Ball Turret Gunner." 1945. Included in Jarrell, *The Complete Poems.* Frequently rpt. Rpt. with Jarrell's useful explanatory note in *Literature: An Introduction to Fiction, Poetry, and Drama.* X. J. Kennedy, ed. Boston & Toronto: Little, Brown, 1976.

Poem. See for motifs of a mechanical womb and the state as machine.

Johannesson, Olof (pseud. of Hannes Alfven). *Sagan om den stora data-*

maskinin, 1966. Trans. as *The Tale of the Big Computer.* New York: Award Books, 1968. Vts *The Great Computer, a Vision,* and *The End of Man?*

A future-history written (it claims) by a computer who sees humankind as a step in the evolution of machines. See Warrick, p. 152, and Wolfe, pp. 174-75.

Jones, D[ennis] F. *Colossus.* London: Rupert Hart-Davis, 1966; rpt. New York: Berkley, 1976.

The first book of the *Colossus* trilogy (with *The Fall of Colossus* and *Colossus and the Crab*). *Colossus* presents the computer-takeover theme, with a significant variation on the containment motif usual in dystopias: the world of this novel becomes a prison for the protagonist; he is only free when in the nuturing containment of his bedroom. See under Stage, Film, and Television Drama, *Colossus: The Forbin Project;* see under Literary Criticism, Richard Erlich, "D. F. Jones's *Colossus.*"

Kahn, James. *Return of the Jedi.* New York: Ballantine, 1983. A Del Rey Book.

See *Return of the Jedi* under Stage, Film, and Television Drama. See also the entries for Donald F. Glut and George Lucas, this section. The novelization is rather more explicit than the film in its handling of the philosophical implications of the Force and the opposition between the Empire and the Rebel Alliance; it is also an intriguing book for searchers for allusions and "sources and analogues" in SF.

Kesey, Ken. *One Flew Over the Cuckoo's Nest.* New York: Viking, 1962; rpt. New York: New American Library, n.d.

A "total Institution," an asylum, becomes a microcosm and metaphor for a world in danger of succumbing to mechanizing and castrating influences represented in the Narrator's mind as "the Combine." Features a Terrible Mother (Big Nurse) opposed to a clownish rebel (R. P. McMurphy).

Kirchner, Paul. "Hive." *Heavy Metal,* Jan. 1980, pp. 89-95.

The opening sentence of the text informs us that "THE HIVE IS A SUBTERRANEAN WORLD WHERE MAN AND MACHINE ARE ONE." Some of the artwork gets across this idea.

Koontz, Dean R. *Demon Seed*. New York: Bantam, 1973.

> Proteus, a giant computer, takes over a house computer and servo-mechanisms, traps a woman, and attempts to impregnate her to create a race of computer-men. See *Demon Seed* under Stage, Film, and Television Drama.

Kornbluth, C. M., and Frederik Pohl. *Wolfbane*. New York: Ballantine, 1959; London: Gollancz, 1960. Shorter version published in two parts in *Galaxy*, Oct., Nov. 1957.

> Baroque variations on the theme of the relationship between persons (both human and nonhuman) and machines, with much use of the motif of mechanized environments. See for machine-takeover and a group mind, mechanical "wombs," and an ultimately dangerous "womb-world" (our locution)—and for the possible mechanization and deification of persons and machines.

Lafferty, R. A. *Past Master*. New York: Ace, 1968.

> A dual dystopia set in the mechanically dead golden cities of Astrobe and in the seeming "cancers" on Astrobe: the vast slum cities of Cathead and the Barrio. See for "programmed people" and for a rather idiosyncratic reading of Sir Thomas More's *Utopia*. Discussed in *CW* by William Hardesty.

Lee, Tanith. *Electric Forest*. New York: DAW, 1979; rpt. Garden City, NY: Doubleday, S. F. Book Club, n.d.

> The ugly Magdala trades freedom for a beautiful body, but that body is in reality a "waldo," a cybernetic extension. Cf. James Tiptree's "Girl Who Was Plugged In," q.v. below, this section. (See in *S. F. Ency.*, "Waldo.")

Le Guin, Urusla K. "The Lathe of Heaven." *Amazing*. March, May 1971. Rpt. as novel, New York: Charles Scribner's Sons, 1971; New York: Avon, 1973.

> See for Dr. Haber's "dream machine" and his use of it to control the world. (See below, under Stage, Film, and Television Drama, the PBS film of *LoH*.)

Leinster, Murray (pseud. of William F. Jenkins). "A Logic Named Joe." *Astounding,* March 1946. Rpt. in *Modern Masterpieces in Science*

Fiction. Sam Moskowitz, ed. Cleveland and New York: World, 1965. Also rpt. *Souls in Metal.* Mike Ashley, compiler. New York: St. Martin's Press, 1977; rpt. New York: Jove/HBJ, 1978.

A "logic" (what we would call a computer terminal) becomes a self-conscious individual because of a minor mistake on the assembly line. Joe gets the other logics to give people all the data they might want, with amusing results for the readers but rather great trouble for the human characters: logics are central to the civilization in the story, and the system can't be disconnected.

_____. "Proxima Centauri." *Astounding*, March 1935. Rpt. in *The Road to Science Fiction #2: From Wells to Heinlein.* James Gunn, ed. New York: New American Library, 1979.

Features a spaceship as "a self-contained, self-sustaining world" (Gunn). Cf. Robert Heinlein's "Universe" (q.v. above under Fiction), *Starlost,* and the *Star Trek* episode "For the World is Hollow" (q.v. below under Stage, Film, and Television Drama).

Lem, Stanislaw.

See below under Literary Criticism, Jerzy Jarzębski, "Stanislaw Lem Rationalist and Visionary."

Lem, Stanislaw. *The Cyberiad: Fables for the Cybernetic Age.* Michael Kandel, trans. New York: Seabury, 1974.

Translation of selected fiction by Lem. See Warrick, pp. 193-98.

_____. "The Experiment (A Review of 'Non Serviam,' by James Dobb)." Michael Kandel, trans. *The New Yorker,* 24 July 1979, pp. 26 f.

The nonexistent "Non Serviam" presents the life and philosophy of "personoids," mathematical analogs to humans; the personoids are contained in computers. SL may see the "personoid" condition as similar to the human condition.

_____. "In Hot Pursuit of Happiness." 1971. Rpt. in *View from Another Shore: European Science Fiction.* Franz Rottensteiner, ed. New York: Seabury, 1973.

A satiric tale of a robot's attempt to build utopia.

_____. *The Invincible.* 1964. Wendayne Ackerman, trans. (from the German). New York: Seabury, 1973.

Machine evolution produces "a black cloud consisting of myriads of minuscule robots"; the cloud threatens a Terran expedition. One character "discovers beauty in the horrible empire of the black 'insects' " (Jarzębski, "Stanislaw Lem," p. 115, q.v. under Literary Criticism).

_____. *Memoirs Found in a Bathtub.* 1961. Michael Kandel and Christine Rose, trans. New York: Seabury, 1973.

In the same way that Ahab and Ishmael in *Moby Dick* strive to determine the meaning of the White Whale, the Narrator of *MFB* tries to find the meaning of a labyrinthian building that seems to determine the lives of the people inside. See pp. 118-19 of Jarzębski article cited below under Literary Criticism.

_____. "The Seventh Sally." In Lem, *The Cyberiad,* q.v. above.

The creation by a robot of a miniature cybernetic kingdom whose citizens are abused by a tyrant; stresses the criminality of abandoning to suffering any creatures capable of suffering. Summarized by Warrick, p. 196.

Levin, Ira. *This Perfect Day.* New York: Random House, 1970.

Machine-like behavior is enforced by computerized surveillance.

Lewis, C. S. *The Screwtape Letters & Screwtape Proposes a Toast.* New York: Macmillan, 1961; London: Geoffrey Bles, 1961. Expansion, as indicated, of *The Screwtape Letters* (1942).

Significant in presenting the Devil as not only a gentleman but also a bureaucrat, and in presenting the Underworld as a perversely ordered bureaucracy. See Lewis' Preface, esp. pp. ix-x; see in *CW* Merritt Abrash's essay on Dante's Hell.

_____. *That Hideous Strength.* London: John Lane The Bodley Head, 1945. Most readily available US rpt.: New York: Macmillan, 1965 (bears copyright notice of 1946).

See for the technologically preserved head of Alcasan, the computer-like "Pragmatometer," and the thoroughly nasty bureaucracy of N.I.C.E. *THS* discussed in *TMG* by Rudy Spraycar.

Lucas, George. *Star Wars: From the Adventures of Luke Skywalker.* New York: Ballantine, 1976.

See *Star Wars* under Stage, Film, and Television Drama. Book includes filmographic information about *Star Wars* and color photographs from the film, plus some comments by Lucas and others involved with the production of the film. See entries for Donald F. Glut and James Kahn above, this section.

McCaffrey, Anne. *The Ship Who Sang.* New York: Walker and Company, 1969; rpt. New York: Ballantine, 1969. Also see title story, "The Ship Who Sang." *F&SF*, April 1961. Rpt. in *Women of Wonder.* Pamela Sargent, ed. New York: Random House, 1975. See Contento, *Index*, for other rpts.

Coll. of AM's Helva stories. Isolated human brains are used to run spaceships. (See below, this section, Joseph McElroy's *Plus,* and Kevin O'Donnell's *Mayflies*).

McElroy, Joseph. *Plus.* New York: Knopf, 1977.

SF in the sense of "cybernetic fiction," *Plus* presents "the story of a human brain excised from its body" and placed into orbit around Earth in a "computerized capsule. The brain is hitched to various machines for control and communication. At first a sheerly mechanical device," the brain "slowly regains consciousness of itself as human and retrieves some of its human memories" (quoting David Porush, abstract for "The Imp in the Machine: McElroy's *Plus* and Cybernetics," paper delivered at the session on Writing as a Self-Reflexive Technology, Conference on Science, Technology, and Literature, Brooklyn, NY, 24 Feb. 1983). See in this section the citations for Anne McCaffrey's *Ship Who Sang*, and Kevin O'Donnell's *Mayflies.*

Malzberg, Barry N. "The Men Inside." In *New Dimensions [1].* Robert Silverberg, ed. Garden City, NY: Doubleday, 1971.

See for a literal "Diminution" of the men who serve as servants to technology and deal with "machinery and technique" as soldiers in a medical bureaucracy in the war against cancer. Esp. interesting in using the "cave" of the human body as a place of threatening and—in a surprise ending—joyous confinement: the cancer-ridden body is both literal setting and *perhaps* a variation on the machine/hive/organism metaphor of less problematic stories.

_____. "The Wonderful, All-Purpose Transmogrifier." In *Final Stage*. Edward L. Ferman and Barry N. Mazlberg, eds. (q.v. under Anthologies and Collections).

The ultimate pleasure machine keeps people spaced out but inside their little apartments and out of trouble, while the world degenerates.

Martinson, Harry. *Aniara: A Review of Man in Time and Space*. Swedish, 1956. Hugh Macdiarmid and Elspeth Harley Schubert, trans. New York: Knopf, 1963; rpt. New York: Avon, 1976, as #24 in Equinox SF Rediscovery Series.

Epic poem in 103 cantos. Title page of Avon edn. claims only that their English version was "Adapted from the Swedish," but on p. 54 we learn that canto *"42 was omitted, in agreement with the author, as untranslatable"*—which augurs well for close, authorized trans. elsewhere.   In his brief introd., Tord Hall calls *Aniara* "a symbolic poem about our own age, and the symbols have been taken from modern science" (p. vii); the poem gives to S. F. a highly original version of the motif of the generation starship. See above, this section, citation for Robert Heinlein, "Universe"; see below, under Stage, Film, and Television Drama, entry for Karl-Birger Blomdahl.

Maxim, Hudson. "Man's Machine-Made Millenium." *Cosmopolitan,* 45 (Nov. 1908), 569-76.

According to Sargent, describes a "technological eutopia."

Merritt, A[braham]. "The Metal Monster." *Argosy*, 1920. Rpt. as novel, New York: Avon, 1946; Westport, CT: Hyperion, 1974.

Lost-world story featuring an Asian city that is a unified, conscious, "living Thing" (quoted in Wolfe, p. 190). The inhabitants of the city resemble robots; travelers who enter the Metal Monster's kingdom "are affected by the mechanical being and begin to experience the harmonies of the geometric consciousness" (Leonard Heldreth in *TMG,* p. 139).

Miller, Walter M., Jr. "Dumb Waiter." *Astounding*, April 1952. Rpt. in *Science Fiction Thinking Machines,*   q.v. under Anthologies and Collections.

See for computer-run city, with robot police but no people. Cf. Philip K. Dick's "Autofac," q.v. this section. "DW" briefly discussed by Warrick, p. 119.

O'Donnell, Kevin, Jr. *Mayflies.* New York: Berkley, 1979.

Science in the twenty-third century preserves the hero's brain for use as a starship computer. Cf. Anne McCaffrey's *Ship Who Sang,* Joseph McElroy's *Plus,* and William Hjortsberg's *Gray Matters,* all of which see above, this section. Also uses the generation-starship motif; cf. Robert Heinlein's "Universe," q.v. above, this section.

Oliver, Chad (pseud. of C. Oliver Symmes). "Stardust" (vt "First to the Stars"). *Astounding,* July 1952.

A generation-starship story; cf. Robert Heinlein's "Universe," q.v. this section, above. See Wolfe, p. 67.

Orwell, George (pseud. of Eric Blair). *Nineteen Eighty-Four.* London: Secker & Warburg, 1949; rpt. as *1984* New York: New American Library, 1961. "Casebook" edition: *Orwell's Nineteen Eighty-Four: Text, Sources, Criticism.* Irving Howe, ed. 2d edn. New York and other cities: Harcourt Brace Jovanovich, 1982. [An enlarged version of the 1963 1st edn., adding Orwell's "The Prevention of Literature," excerpts from Orwell's correspondence, a critical essay by John Wain, initial reviews of the novel, an essay by Michael Harrington, and some additional apparatus to aid users of the volume.]

Shows a totalitarian policestate run by the oligarchs of the "Inner Party." See for a womb-world in which the Terrible Mother shows her teeth. Along with Yevgeny Zamiatin's *We* and Aldous Huxley's *Brave New World,* one of the greatest of the book-length dystopias.

Piercy, Marge. *Woman on the Edge of Time.* New York: Knopf, 1976; rpt. New York: Fawcett, 1976. Also, "Woman on the Edge of Time." In *Aurora: Beyond Equality.* Susan I. Anderson and Vonda N. McIntyre, eds. Greenwich, CT: Fawcett, 1976.

The protagonist is trapped in the repressive bureaucracy of a contemporary mental health institution. Literal machinery in the story, though, is both good and bad: the technology in the eutopian section of the novel is "appropriate." Reviewed by Colin Greenland in

Foundation, No. 19 (June 1980), pp. 81-82. Discussed in *CW* by Phyllis Day. Cf. Ken Kesey's *One Flew Over the Cuckoo's Nest,* cited above, this section.

Pohl, Frederik. *Man Plus.* New York: Random House, 1976.

Relevant here for its narration by computers who have attempted, with a good deal of success, to manipulate human history.

————. "The Midas Plague." *Galaxy,* April 1954. Coll. in *The Best of Frederik Pohl.* Introd. Lester del Rey. New York: Ballantine, 1975. Frequently rpt., including *The Science Fiction Hall of Fame.* Vol. IIB. Ben Bova, ed. New York: Avon, 1974.

Comic handling of how to deal with the plague of affluence in a world where "Everything is mechanized," and "Too many robots make too much of everything."

————. "The Tunnel Under the World." *Galaxy,* Jan. 1955. Coll. in *The Best of Frederik Pohl*; see immediately above. (Acknowledgments page lists date for "TUW" as Jan. 1954.) Frequently rpt. including *More Penguin Science Fiction.* Brian W. Aldiss, ed. Harmondsworth, England: Penguin, 1963.

A town destroyed by an explosion is reconstructed in miniature, as are its dead inhabitants. The reconstructed humans/robots are the subject of controlled experiments in advertising, wherein they continually relive the same day.

————, and Jack Williamson. *The Reefs of Space* (1963), and *Starchild* (1965). In *The Starchild Trilogy.* Garden City, NY: Doubleday, 1977; rpt. New York: Pocket Books, 1977.

The third novel of the trilogy, *Rogue Star* (1969), is not immediately relevant. The first two novels, however, are quite important, featuring a world run by "the Machine," an underground computer that administers "the Plan of Man" and ruthlessly suppresses all "unplanned" activity.

Reynolds, Mack (pseud. of Dallas McCord Reynolds). *After Utopia.* New York: Ace, 1977.

The utopia in the title is that of Edward Bellamy in *Looking Backward* (q.v. above, this section). *AU* is set in 2050, some fifty years after the time of Bellamy's work, and shows the degeneration of utopia as people, lacking incentives, turn to "intuitive" computers: machines for escape into worlds of fantasy. *AU* is discussed by Brian Stableford in "The Utopian Dream Revisited: Socioeconomic Speculation in the SF of Mack Reynolds," *Foundation*, No. 16 (May 1976), p. 49.

Roddenberry, Gene. *Star Trek: The Motion Picture: A Novel.* Based on the screenplay by Harold Livingston and the story by Alan Dean Foster. New York: Pocket Books, 1979.

See *Star Trek: The Motion Picture,* below, under Stage, Film, and Television Drama.

Roshwald, Mordecai. *Level 7.* New York: McGraw-Hill, 1959; rpt. New York: New American Library, n.d.

Underground containment in a military *apparat.*

Roszak, Theodore. *Bugs.* Garden City, NY: Doubleday, 1981, rpt. S. F. Book Club edn., n.d.

A S. F./Fantasy-Horror story (with a strong hint of disaster novel) from the author of *Where the Wasteland Ends, The Making of a Counter Culture,* and other critiques of the "Technocratic Society" (see Roszak citations below, under Background Reading). Relevant here for its association of computers and insects and for its theoretical use of the conceit of human beings within computers, mechanical hives, and a war machine.

Saberhagen, Fred, and Roger Zelazny. *Coils.* Garden City, NY: Doubleday, S. F. Book Club, 1982. Illustrated.

The quest by a hero for his true name and identity and for his kidnapped lover, Cora, in a near-future world. The hero is able to "coil," descending into the data-net of computer programs; his former lover ends up as a computer program. At the end of the novel, the hero meets "the sentience which evolved within the data-net": a kind of very literal *deus ex machina* in terms of the plot and an Adam/Eve figure in an electronic Eden, to whom the hero will play serpent, giving instruction in good and evil (cf. Hal and his neurosis in Arthur Clarke's *2001,* q.v. above, this section). See entries for John Sladek's *Müller-Fokker Effect* and Brian Daley's *Tron,* this section. See also entry for *TRON* under Stage, Film, and Television Drama.

Sargent, Pamela. *Watchstar.* New York: Pocket Books, 1980.

> See for "communion" between human minds and "cybernetic minds" that are world-machines.

Serviss, Garret P. *A Columbus of Space.* New York and London: D. Appleton and Company, 1911; rpt. Westport, CT: Hyperion, 1974.

> Clublike (as in "gentlemen's club") interior in a spaceship. Discussed by Wolfe, pp. 57-58.

Sheckley, Robert. "Street of Dreams, Feet of Clay." *Galaxy,* Feb. 1968. Frequently rpt., including in *Wandering Stars: An Anthology of Jewish Science Fiction.* Jack Dann, ed. New York: Harper & Row, 1974; rpt. New York: Pocket Books, 1975. See Contento, *Index,* for other rpts.

> The model city of Bellwether is "a well-wrought machine for living," it thinks, coming equipped with "a voice and artificial consciousness." Bellwether's consciousness, however, is that of a stereotypically overprotective Jewish mother, making the city, as John Sladek notes, "the kind of concentration camp we are now building for the future" (review of *Wandering Stars* in *Foundation*, Nos. 11 and 12, p. 65). Cf. Williamson's humanoids stories (q.v. below, this section).

Silverberg, Robert. "A Happy Day in 2381." In *Nova 1.* Harry Harrison, ed. New York: Delacorte Press, 1970. Frequently rpt., including in *Science Fiction: The Future.* Dick Allen, ed. 2d. edn. New York and other cities: Harcourt Brace Jovanovich, 1983. *Survival Printout,* q.v. under Anthologies and Collections, and as ch. 1 of Silverberg, *The World Inside,* q.v. below. See Contento, *Index,* for other rpts.

> Introduction to the world of Urban Monad 116, the bureaucratized and mechanized environment for a large group of people who are still only a minute fraction of the human population of an overpopulated Earth.

_____. *The World Inside.* Garden City, NY: Doubleday, 1971.

> Features a world of three-kilometer high urban monads, whose citizens almost never leave. Characters suffering inchoate rebelliousness

are co-opted or "morally engineered"; those who cannot or will not adjust are killed. See below under Literary Criticism, Thomas Dunn and Richard Erlich, "The Mechanical Hive."

Simak, Clifford D. "Lulu." *Galaxy,* June 1957. Coll. in *The Worlds of Clifford Simak.* New York: Simon and Schuster, 1960; New York: Avon, 1961.

Lulu is an artificial intelligence running a spaceship whose crew play adolescent children to her nurturing mother. Discussed by Wolfe, pp. 80-81. Cf. and contrast Arthur Clarke's *2001,* Kevin O'Donnell's *Mayflies,* and Sheckley's "Street of Dreams" (all cited above, this section), and the films *Alien* and *2001* (q.v. below, under Stage, Film, and Television Drama).

_____. "Skirmish" (vt "Bathe Your Bearings in Blood"). *Amazing,* Dec. 1950. Rpts. include *Penguin Science Fiction.* Brian W. Aldiss, ed. Harmondsworth, England: Penguin, 1961 (included in *The Penguin Science Fiction Omnibus,* 1973); *Science Fiction Thinking Machines,* q.v. under Anthologies and Collections.

Strongly asserts that liberated machines will enslave humans (see Wolfe, p. 152).

_____. "Target Generation." In *Strangers in the Universe.* New York: Simon and Schuster, 1956; New York: Berkley, 1957; London: Faber and Faber, 1958.

Wolfe gives 1953 for original date of publication; Contento, *Index,* lists only the three printings of *Strangers in the Universe.* "TG" features a rather literal "mother" ship, serving as "a womb from which the [human] race could be renewed" (p. 52 of Berkley edn.; quoted and discussed by Wolfe, p. 65). Cf. Vernor Vinge's "Long Shot," and Jack Williamson's *Manseed,* cited below, this section.

Skinner, B. F. *Walden Two.* New York: Macmillan, 1948; rpt. New York: Macmillan, 1962, 1966, and subsequently, with alternate pagination.

BFS's Behaviorist utopia. See below under Background Reading, BFS's *Beyond Freedom and Dignity* and, this section, Aldous Huxley's *Brave New World.* If one were ignorant of the dates of publication, one might take Huxley's dystopia for a satire on *WT.*

Sladek, John T. *MECHASM.* See below, *The Reproductive System.*

_____. *The Müller-Fokker Effect.* London: Hutchinson, 1970; rpt. London: Granada, 1972; New York: Pocket Books, 1973.

A major character finds himself "digitalized" and trapped inside a computer. While "entombed" within the machine, he considers, among other things, the definition of the noun "man." Cf. Brian Daley's *Tron* and Fred Saberhagen and Roger Zelazny's *Coils*, q.v. above, this section; and *TRON* listed below, under Stage, Film, and Television Drama.

_____. *The Reproductive System.* London: Gollancz, 1968. Rpt. as *MECHASM*, New York: Ace, 1969; New York: Pocket Books, 1980.

A send-up of, among other things, the theme of machine-takeover.

Smith, Martin Cruz. *The Analog Bullet.* 1977; rpt. New York: Nordon, [1981]. A Leisure Book.

Computer tyranny in contemporary USA. The threat to civil liberties of data banks in the world of *TAB* was carefully extrapolated by MCS from public records of real-world abuses and potential for abuse of computers in the USA of the late 1960s and early 1970s. Nordon edn. of *TAB* includes a brief introd. by MCS.

Tevis, Walter. *Mockingbird.* Garden City, NY: Doubleday, 1980.

See for a wasteland world run—as much as it is run—by robots. Discussed in *TMG* in the essay by Donald Hassler.

Tiptree, James, Jr. (pseud. of Alice Sheldon). "The Girl Who Was Plugged In." In *New Dimensions 3.* Robert Silverberg, ed. New York: New American Library, 1973. Rpt. in *The Hugo Winners.* Vol. III. Isaac Asimov, ed. Garden City, NY: Doubleday, 1977.

An ugly woman accepts an offer to be made into the computer control of a beautiful female "waldo." Cf. Tanith Lee's *Electric Forest,* cited above, this section.

Tubb, E. C. *The Space-Born.* New York: Ace, 1956; rpt. New York: Avon, 1976.

Generation-starship story showing a static, rather dystopian womb-world society. Discussed by Wolfe, pp. 67-69. See above, this section, Robert Heinlein's "Universe."

Verne, Jules. *From the Earth to the Moon* (1865); *Around the Moon,* and *Twenty Thousand Leagues Under the Sea* (1870).

Wolfe calls attention to these and other works by JV—available in numerous edns. and trans.—in which JV presents ever more secure interior (more or less mechanical) environments as the featured crafts' external environments become increasingly threatening (Wolfe, pp. 55-56).

Vinge, Joan D. *The Snow Queen.* New York: Dial Press, 1980.

See for an unusual and highly sophisticated variation of the motif of secret manipulation of society by a sentient computer, in this case a kind of computer goddess who gives the possibility of true change and an end to stasis. Important also for Pollux, a friendly robot, and for a subtle and generally positive handling of technology.

Vinge, Vernor. "Long Shot." *Analog,* Aug. 1972. Rpt. in *Best Science Fiction Stories of the Year: Second Annual Collection* (1972). Lester del Rey, ed. New York: Dutton, 1973.

See for a conscious, computer-run spaceship carrying a fertilized human ovum; hence the ship is a literal mechanical womb (summary from Warrick, p. 180). Cf. Clifford Simak's "Target Generation," cited above, this section, and Jack Williamson's *Manseed,* cited below, this section.

Vonnegut, Kurt, Jr. *Player Piano* (vt *Utopia 14*). New York: Charles Scribner's Sons, 1952; rpt. New York: Dell, 1974.

The near-future world of *PP* is run by machines and a technocratic elite. Discussed in *CW* in the essays by Thomas Hoffman and Lawrence Broer.

_____. *The Sirens of Titan.* New York: Dell, 1959; Boston: Houghton Mifflin, 1961; New York: Dell, 1970 (new Dell edn.).

See esp. chs. 4-6, with the Army of Mars. Except for its real leaders, this army is totally "mechanized" (our word): that is, turned into obedient, radio-controlled human robots. In this way KV literalizes the common metaphor of an army (the prototypical bureaucracy) as a human machine. (See below under Background Reading, Lewis Mumford, "Utopia, The City and The Machine.")

_____. *Slaughterhouse-Five.* New York: Seymour Lawrence/Delacorte, 1969; rpt. New York: Dell, 1971.

Note the Tralfamadorian view of a determined universe and of people as machines. Discussed in *CW* by Lawrence Broer; see also the essay by Thomas Wymer in *TMG*, and his essay cited below under Literacy Criticism.

Wells, H. G. *The First Men in the Moon.* Indianapolis, IN: Bowen-Merrill, 1901; rpt. New York: Berkley, 1967. See Currey for additional biblio. data (cited above, under Acknowledgments).

Features a womblike spherical spaceship (see Wolfe, p. 56), and the Selenites: machine-using, sublunar "insects" with a rigid social order.

_____. "The Lord of the Dynamos." *Pall Mall Budget,* Sept. 1894. Frequently coll. and anthologized, including in *Best Science Fiction Stories of H. G. Wells.* New York: Dover, 1966; *Best Stories of H. G. Wells.* New York: Ballantine, 1960; *Stories from Science Fiction.* G. D. Doherty, ed. London: Nelson, 1966. See Contento, *Index,* for other colls.

Mainstream "mechanical god" story, set in the real-world mechanized environment of an electric railway power station. See entry for Henry Adams, below, under Background Reading.

_____. *A Modern Utopia.* London: Chapman & Hall, 1905; rpt. with introd. by Mark R. Hillegas, Lincoln, NE: University of Nebraska Press, 1967.

Presents a technocratic utopia ruled by holders of professional degrees (with lawyers and teachers supplementing the usual engineers and scientists). Possibly one of the works E. M. Forster satirizes in "Machine Stops." *AMU* is discussed by W. Warren Wagar in "The Steel-Gray Saviour" (q.v. under Literary Criticism), pp. 44-45.

_____. *The Time Machine.* New York: Henry Holt, 1895. Frequently rpt., including *H. G. Wells: The Time Machine [and] War of the Worlds:*

A Critical Edition. Frank D. McConnell, ed. New York: Oxford
University Press, 1977.

Possibly the first work with an inhabited, mechanized underworld—
contrasted with an apparently ideal green world on the surface. (The
Underworld, traditionally, is the womb of the Great Mother; mechanizing the Underworld is a radical displacement of a central archetype.)

_____. *When the Sleeper Wakes*. London and New York: Harper &
Brothers, 1899. Abridged version: *The Sleeper Wakes* (1910).

An almost totally "civilized"—that is, *urbanized*—world featuring
high technology and control by Capital. Discussed by Wolfe, pp.
99-104, and by Frank McConnell, *The Science Fiction of H. G.
Wells*, pp. 149-53 and passim (see under Literary Criticism).

Wilcox, Don. "The Voyage that Lasted Six Hundred Years." *Amazing*,
Oct. 1940. Rpt. in *Looking Forward*. Milton Lesser, ed. New York:
Beechhurst Press, 1953.

The *S. F. Ency.* entry for DW cites "VLSHY" as "a good GENERA-
TION-STARSHIP tale"; Edward Bryant and Harlan Ellison cite it
as the earliest such tale in S. F., "as best as we can trace it"
("Acknowledgment" of *Phoenix without Ashes*, q.v. above, this section, under Bryant). See entry above for Robert Heinlein's "Universe" for other cross-references.

Williamson, Jack. *The Humanoids*. New York: Avon, 1980. Expanded edn.
Contains an introd. (1980); "With Folded Hands" (1947); *The
Humanoids* (rev. of serial in *Astounding*, " . . . And Searching
Mind," 1948—ellipsis mark in original); and "Me and My Human-
oids" (1977, Suncon Program Book; rpt. *New Mexico Humanities
Review*, 1 [Jan. 1978], 37-42; this essay may have been revised to serve
as the afterword for the expanded edn. of *The Humanoids)*.

See below, JW's "With Folded Hands." *Humanoids* shows the complete victory of the "mechanicals" as the last human rebels are brain-
washed and integrated into the contented hive of the humanoid universe.

_____. *The Humanoid Touch*. New York: Holt, Rinehart and Winston,
1980.

Possibly the *Ten Trillion Wise Machines* sequel JW refers to in his
1980 introd. to *The Humanoids* (q.v. above). Certainly, in *The
Humanoid Touch* the humanoids "are still themselves"—perfect,
unbeatable machines—but JW offers "a more endurable alternative"
to total humanoid victory: coexistence of the humanoids with a race
of humans who are nontechnological and nonaggressive.

————. "Jamboree." *Galaxy*, Dec. 1969. Coll. in Williamson, *People
Machines*. New York: Ace, 1971. Rpt. with afterword by Williamson
in *Those Who Can*. Robin Scott Wilson, ed. New York: New American Library, 1973.

Presents a machine-ruled world complete with a robot Terrible Father
and mechanical Devouring Mother. "Mother" (JW's word) quite
literally devours her children when they are on the verge of puberty,
preventing them from becoming adults.

————. *Manseed*. New York: Ballantine, 1982. A Del Rey Book (S. F. Book
Club Edition).

Features "seedship[s]" that can produce cyborgs; the ships are designed to carry a genetically engineered humanity to the stars in
"electromechanical wombs" (quotations from dust jacket). See
above, this section, Clifford Simak, "Target Generation," Vernor
Vinge, "Long Shot," and the generation-starship stories cited in the
annotation for Robert Heinlein's "Universe."

————. "With Folded Hands." 1947. Rpt. (with 1954 copyright) in *The
Science Fiction Hall of Fame*. Vol. IIA. Ben Bova, ed. New York:
Avon, 1973. Also rpt. in expanded edn. of *The Humanoids* (q.v.
above). See Contento, *Index,* for other rpts.

Humanoid robots cripple humans by doing all their work for them
and protecting them from *all* possible dangers. These "mechanicals"
are mobile extensions of a central computer on the planet Wing IV.
See above, JW's *Humanoid Touch*, and *The Humanoids*.

Wolfe, Bernard. *Limbo* (vt *Limbo '90*). New York: Random House, 1952;
New York: Ace, 1952.

See for the mechanization of people through prosthetics, the com-
puter/military complex, and (if Warrick is correct) the necessity for
laughter and ironic flexibility against various kinds of rigidities. Dis-

cussed by Warrick, pp. 149-50, and by Gary K. Wolfe in his essay in *TMG*. See under Literary Criticism the article by David Samuelson.

Wolfe, Gene. "The Death of Dr. Island." in *Universe 3*. Terry Carr, ed. New York: Random House, 1973, pp. 1-60. Coll. in Wolfe, *The Island of Doctor Death and Other Stories and Other Stories* (sic). New York: Pocket Books, 1980.

Dr. Island is a machine and an island "in (not on) an artificial asteroid." His patients are three mad teenagers. Discussed in *TMG* by William Schuyler; coll. reviewed by Roz Kaveney in *Foundation*, No. 21 (Feb. 1981), p. 82 (the quotation above is from Schuyler).

Wright, S. Fowler. "Automata." *Weird Tales*, Sept. 1929. Rpt. in *Science Fiction Thinking Machines*, q.v. under Anthologies and Collections.

Superiority of machines, with their precision, to clumsily constructed organic beings: "in a universe where law and order rule," the machines are "in greater harmony with their environment" (*Science Fiction Thinking Machines*, p. 203; quoted in Wolfe, p. 156).

Zamiatin, Yevgeny (variously translated and transliterated). *We*. Written ca. 1920. Available in various trans., including Mirra Ginsburg, trans. New York and other cities: Bantam, 1972.

Shows a world in which the "Taylor system" of "scientific" industrial management has been applied to all aspects of life. Along with E. M. Forster's "Machine Stops," George Orwell's *Nineteen Eighty-Four*, and Aldous Huxley's *Brave New World* (all cited above, this section), one of the seminal dystopias. See under Background Reading the entry for Frederick Taylor. *We* is discussed in detail in *CW* by Gorman Beauchamp; also handled by Alexandra Aldridge, and passim in other essays (consult *CW* index). See under Literary Criticism the article on *We* by Carolyn Rhodes, "Machine" by Mark Rose, and the entries for D. Richards and Alex Shane.

Zelazny, Roger. "For a Breath I Tarry." *New Worlds,* March 1966; corrected version, *Fantastic*, Sept. 1966. Coll. in Zelazny, *The Last Defender of Camelot*. New York: Pocket Books, 1980. Frequently rpt., including in *Survival Printout,* and *The Theme of the Machine* —both cited above under Anthologies and Collections. See Contento, *Index,* for additional rpts.

On an Earth where only the machines remain and rule, a machine transforms itself into a man. Discussed in detail in three essays in *TMG*.

IV. LITERARY CRITICISM

Aldiss, Brian W. *Billion Year Spree: The History of Science Fiction.* London: Weidenfeld & Nicholson, 1973; Garden City, New York: Doubleday, 1973. Rpt. New York: Schocken, 1974. Subtitle on US edns., *The True History of Science Fiction.* (Information on UK edn. from Currey biblio. listed above under Acknowledgments.)

A major history of SF, including brief discussion of Edward Bulwer-Lytton's *The Coming Race* (urbanized underworld), Jules Verne's "satanic cities," E. M. Forster's "The Machine Stops," Aldous Huxley's *Brave New World*, Jack Williamson's *Legion of Time* (anthropoidal ants), and Frederik Pohl's and C. M. Kornbluth's *Wolfbane*.

Aldridge, Alexandra. "Myths of Origin and Destiny in Utopian Literature: Zamiatin's *We*." *Extrapolation*, 19 (Dec. 1977), 68-75.

Opposition in *We* of the "mechanized, dehumanized environment" of the city of the United State and the demonic, chaotic "life forces" outside the dystopian city's green wall.

————, and Gorman Beauchamp, guest eds. *Extrapolation,* 19, No. 1 (Dec. 1977).

Special Utopias Issue of *Extrapolation*. Of interest here are Howard P. Segal, "Young West: The Psyche of Technological Utopianism"; David Y. Hughes, "The Mood of *A Modern Utopia*"; A. Aldridge, "Myths of Origin and Destiny in Utopian Literature: Zamiatin's *We*"; David N. Samuelson, "*Limbo:* The Great American Dystopia"; and G. Beauchamp, "Cultural Primitivism as Norm in the Dystopian Novel." See above (Aldridge) and below (Beauchamp, Samuelson, Segal), this section.

Bailey, J[ames] O. *Pilgrims Through Space and Time: Trends and Patterns in Scientific and Utopian Fiction.* New York: Argus, 1947; rpt. Westport, CT: Greenwood Press, 1972.

Earliest full-length study of SF by an academic literary historian. Discusses, passim, a number of works showing "man's slavery to the Machine in a Machine age" (ch. 6, B, p. 148). Handles well-known works such as Aldous Huxley's *Brave New World* and lesser-known works such as Claude Ferrére's ⟨ (pseud.) *Useless Hands* (1920; trans. 1926).

Bailey, K. V. "Spaceships, Little Nell, and the Sinister Cardboard Man: A Study of Dickens as Fantasist and as a Precursor of Science Fiction." *Foundation,* No. 21 (Feb. 1981), pp. 34-47.

Demonstrates to KVB's satisfaction that there is in the works of Dickens "an early sounding of motifs which the literature of later technologies would develop"—including "a universe of technological conditioning" and the enslavement of human beings "by a technological 'system.' " Uses as a primary recent example of the "Ark" motif Brian Aldiss' *Non-Stop*, q.v. above, under Fiction.

Beauchamp, Gorman. "The Anti-Politics of Utopia." *Alternative Futures,* 2, No. 1 (Winter 1979), 49-59.

On the "closed society" totalitarianism implicit in *all* utopias. Cf. Lewis Mumford, "Utopia, The City and The Machine" (q.v. under Background Reading), cited by GB. See GB's p. 59, n.10, for other references.

_____. "Cultural Primitivism as Norm in the Dystopian Novel." *Extrapolation*, 19 (Dec. 1977), 88-96.

Includes discussions of E. M. Forster's "Machine Stops," Aldous Huxley's *Brave New World*, Kurt Vonnegut's *Player Piano*, and Yevgeny Zamiatin's *We* (all cited above, under Fiction). Opposed to nature, in much dystopian fiction, is "the Machine," which has come to stand for the technological world-view and which "daily comes closer to synonymity with civilization itself" (p. 90).

Berger, Harold L. *Science Fiction and the New Dark Age*. Bowling Green, OH: BGU Popular Press, 1976.

See esp. section II, "The New Tyrannies." Discusses Jack Williamson's *The Humanoids*, Harlan Ellison's "A Boy and His Dog," Kurt Vonnegut's *Player Piano*, Yevgeny Zamiatin's *We*, and other works relevant for the study of mechanized environments.

Berman, Jeffrey. "Forster's Other Cave: The Platonic Structure of 'The Machine Stops.' " *Extrapolation*, 17 (May 1976), 172-81.

E. M. Forster's use of the "cave" as a "setting for an entire underground universe, in which the basic living unit, expressed by the
ironic simile of the 'cell of a bee,' remains irreconcilably antithetical
to the organic . . . imagery evoked by the delicate insect . . . . "
Handles the story's "impassioned warnings against the growing
nightmare of technological dehumanization" (pp. 173, 172).

Biles, Jack I., ed. "Aspects of Utopian Fiction" issue of *Studies in the
Literary Imagination*, 6, No. 2 (Fall 1973).

David Ketterer's article (cited below, this section) is the most immediately relevant, but the issue as a whole is quite useful for putting
the motif of the mechanized environment into its context in dystopian and eutopian fiction. See esp. Biles's "Editor's Comment,"
pp. v-vii; Sylvia E. Bowman on "Utopian Views of Man and the
Machine," pp. 107-9, 111; Howard Fink on George Orwell and
H.G. Wells on "machine-civilization," pp. 54-55; Darko Suvin's
attempt at "Defining the Literary Genre of Utopia," pp. 132-34,
137, 144; and W. Warren Wagar on technology, technocracy, and
several relevant works by H. G. Wells.

Brady, Charles J. "The Computer as a Symbol of God: Ellison's Macabre
Exodus." *Journal of General Education*, 28 (Spring 1976), 55-62.

Concentrates on Ellison's "I Have No Mouth, and I Must Scream,"
with references to other God-like computers in recent SF.

Colmer, John. *E. M. Forster: The Personal Voice*. Boston: Routledge &
Kegan Paul, 1975.

Has a section on Forster's "Machine Stops."

Dean, John. "The Science Fiction City." *Foundation*, No. 23 (Oct. 1981),
pp. 64-72.

Useful survey of SF cities, both eutopian and dystopian (but mostly
dystopian) from the London of H. G. Wells's *When the Sleeper
Wakes* (1899), through the San Francisco of John Shirley's *City
Come A-Walkin'* (1980). Very good on Thea von Harbou's novel,
Metropolis, but slightly misleading in handling of Es Toch in Ursula K. Le Guin's *City of Illusions*. See JD's essay for the close
relationship of cities and machines.

De Bolt, Joe, ed. *The Happening Worlds of John Brunner*. Port Washington, New York, and London: Kennikat Press, 1975.

Includes "A Brunner Bibliography," two indexes, and several useful essays by various authors discussing Brunner's works. Most immediately relevant: Edward L. Lamie and Joe De Bolt, "The Computer and Man," q.v. below, this section, under Lamie.

Dick, Philip K. "Man, Android, and Machine." In *Science Fiction at Large*. Peter Nicholls, ed. New York: Harper & Row, 1976; London: Gollancz, 1976.

PKD on the contemporary trend toward the "reification" of living things and "a reciprocal entry into animation by the mechanical." See Warrick, pp. 223-29, esp. p. 223.

Dunn, Thomas [P.] "E. M. Forster's 'The Machine Stops.' " In *Survey of Science Fiction Literature*, q.v. above under Reference Works. Vol. 3, 1299-303.

Deals with "Machine Stops" as the prototypical mechanical-hive dystopia.

———, and Richard D. Erlich. "The Mechanical Hive: Urbmon 116 as the Villian-Hero of Silverberg's *The World Inside*." *Extrapolation*, 21 (Winter 1980), 338-47.

Urban Monad ("Urbmon") 116 is the three-kilometer-high building that is the setting for most of R. Silverberg's plot in what appears to be an episodic dystopian satire. TPD and RDE demonstrate that this book is a dystopian novel unified around the victories of Urbmon 116 over human characters and the human spirit.

———. "A Vision of Dystopia: Beehives and Mechanization." *Journal of General Education*, 33 (Spring 1981), 45-58.

The beehive and the machine as two symbols for individual helplessness and triviality in a number of dystopian works.

Eizykman, Boris. "Chance and Science Fiction: SF as Stochastic Fiction" (trans. by Will Straw of "S-F: Science Spéculative Stochastique Fiction" in *Traverses*, No. 24 [1981], pp. 115-24). *SFS*, 10 (March 1983), 24-34.

Argues that "the utopian inclination in the modern world has entered the political as well as the scientific domain, imparting, through its determinism, a mechanistic vision of man and nature." This determinism is opposed by Chance (Straw's trans. of *le hasard*), and a number of works of SF deal seriously with Chance. Handles briefly, Hugo Gernsback's *Ralph 124C41 + : A Romance of the Year 2660* (1911), Stanley Kubrick's *2001* (q.v. below, under Stage, Film, and Television Drama), Robert Silverberg's *The Stochastic Man* (1975), and a few other works of immediate or tangential interest for the study of mechanized environments in SF; usefully applies to SF some of the concepts of Marshall McLuhan and Henri Bergson.

Elkins, Charles. "Asimov's 'Foundation' Novels: Historical Materialism Distorted into Cyclical Psycho-History." *SFS*, 8 (March 1976), 16-36. Rpt. with expansions in *Isaac Asimov*. Joseph D. Olander and Martin Harry Greenberg, eds. New York: Taplinger, 1977, pp. 97-110.

See for the non-Marxist determinism of the Foundation trilogy: a determinism that reflects "the material and historical situation out of which these works arose: the alienation of men and women in modern bourgeois society" (*Isaac Asimov*, pp. 109-10).

Erlich, Richard D. "[D. F. Jones's] *Colossus*." In *Survey of Science Fiction Literature*, q.v. above, under Reference Works. Vol. 1, 409-13.

An introd. to *Colossus*, q.v. above, under Fiction.

_____. " 'Trapped in the Bureaucratic Pinball Machine': A Vision of Dystopia in the Twentieth Century." In *Selected Proceedings of the Science Fiction Research Association 1978 Convention*. Thomas J. Remington, ed. Cedar Falls, IA: University of Northern Iowa Press, 1979, pp. 30-44.

Treats mechanism and containment in a number of recent S. F., dystopian, and generally pessimistic works.

Extrapolation, Special Utopias Issue: see above, this section under Alexandra Aldridge and Gorman Beauchamp, guest eds.

Fekete, John. "*The Dispossessed* and *Triton*: Act and System in Utopian Science Fiction." *SFS*, 6 (July 1979), 129-43.

Crotchety, contentious, overly difficult, and occasionally wrong, JF's is still an important article on Ursula K. Le Guin's *Dispossessed* and Samuel R. Delany's *Triton*, with a provocative observation on Yevgeny Zamiatin's *We* (p. 141, n.5). See for Le Guin's presentation of "the decay of organic revolutionary culture into

mechanical conventionality" on Anarres, and for Delany's presen-
tation of "emptiness coordinated cybernetically in patterns" on
Triton. (Organism vs. mechanism is a subtle but important theme in
Dispossessed.)

Fogg, Walter E. "Technology and Dystopia." In *Utopia/Dystopia?* Peyton
E. Richter, ed. Cambridge, MA: Schenkman, 1975, pp. 59-73.

Cited by Sargent.

Frank, Frederick S. "The Gothic at Absolute Zero: Poe's *Narrative of
Arthur Gordon Pym*." *Extrapolation*, 21 (Spring 1980), 21-30.

Presents the final action of *Pym* as an escape from a "globalized
Gothic Castle" into a "lost Eden." (This escape pattern is highly
important for dystopian works featuring mechanized Gothic castles
on a global scale, sometimes contrasted with Garden worlds.)

Franklin, H. Bruce. *Robert A. Heinlein: America as Science Fiction*. New
York: Oxford University Press, 1980.

Esp. relevant for its discussions of *Starship Troopers* and *The Moon
Is a Harsh Mistress* (pp. 110-24 and 162-70)—and for putting these
works into the contexts of Heinlein's canon and of America in the
twentieth century. Includes an excellent chronological biblio. of
works by Heinlein through 1979 and an equally good, annotated
"Selected List of Works about Robert A. Heinlein." An indispensable work for the study of Heinlein's S. F.

Fromm, Erich. Foreword to Edward Bellamy, *Looking Backward* (1888).
New York: New American Library, 1960, pp. v-xx.

Excellent introd. to *Looking Backward*, esp. useful for its critique
of Bellamy's "managerial society," with its "hierarchical bureaucratic principle of administration" (section IV, pp. xi-xii).

Gaar, Alice Carol. "The Human as Machine Analog: The Big Daddy of
Interchangeable Parts in the Fiction of Robert A. Heinlein." In
Robert A. Heinlein. Joseph D. Olander and Martin Harry Green-
berg, eds. New York: Taplinger, 1980, pp. 64-82.

Deals with Heinlein's response to "a cosmos that might really be
just a giant computer" (ACG, p. 265).

Gallagher, Edward J. "From Folded Hands to Clenched Fist: Kesey and Science Fiction." In *Perspective on a Cuckoo's Nest: A Special Symposium Issue on Ken Kesey. Lex et Scientia,* 13, Nos. 1-2 (Jan.-June 1977), 46-50.

Argues that the worldview in Kesey's *Cuckoo's Nest* is "the world as machine, the cybernetic model, a world whose total service homogenizes humanity"; discusses that worldview as it appears in over a dozen stories.

_____. "The Thematic Structure of *The Martian Chronicles.*" In *Ray Bradbury.* Martin Harry Greenberg and Joseph D. Olander, eds. New York: Taplinger, 1980, pp. 55-82.

See pp. 79-80 for a brief but excellent analysis of "There Will Come Soft Rains" as a commentary on the relationship between humankind and technology.

Goodheart, Eugene. "The Romantic Critique of Industrial Civilization." In Technology and Pessimism special issue of *Alternative Futures,* pp. 126-38 (see below, under Marthalee Barton and Dwight W. Stevenson, guest co-eds., under Background Reading).

Concentrates on Thomas Carlyle, John Ruskin, William Morris, and D. H. Lawrence; see for the literary tradition of a radical "aversion to technological progress."

Greenberg, Martin Harry, and Joseph D. Olander, eds. *Philip K. Dick.* New York: Taplinger, 1983.

An anthology of original and rpt. essays on Philip K. Dick. Includes also Marshall Tymn, "Philip K. Dick: A Bibliography" (q.v. above, under Reference Works), an introd. by Barry N. Malzberg, a brief biographical note on Dick, and ("in slightly different form") Dick's introd. to *The Golden Man,* titled "Now Wait for This Year" (quoting from the acknowledgment on p. 215). See index to *PKD* for brief discussions (passim) of "The Electric Ant," *Martain Time Slip, Penultimate Truth,* and "Second Variety."

Gunn, James. *Isaac Asimov: The Foundations of Science Fiction.* Oxford, New York, and other cities: Oxford University Press, 1982.

Includes a chronology of Asimov's life to 1980, a "Checklist of Works by Isaac Asimov" through 1981, a brief "Select List of

Works about Isaac Asimov," and a useful index. Text handles in detail the Foundation trilogy and Asimov's robot stories and novels, and places Asimov and his work into the context of twentieth-century S. F.

_____. "On the Foundations of Science Fiction." *Isaac Asimov's Science Fiction Magazine*, 4 (April 1980), 64-84; rpt. with slight changes in Gunn's *Isaac Asimov*, q.v. above.

Significant here for seeing "the expansion of humanity into the galaxy" (as opposed to confinement) as, in Jack Williamson's words, "the central myth" of science fiction's view of the future. Also significant for finding the "spirit of the early stories" in Isaac Asimov's Foundation trilogy "determinedly anti-deterministic" —a reading that differs from that of Charles Elkins (q.v. above, this section).

The Happening Worlds of John Brunner. Joe De Bolt, ed. Listed above, this section, under De Bolt.

Hildebrand, Tim. "Two or Three Things I Know About Kurt Vonnegut's Imagination." Ch. 9 of *The Vonnegut Statement*, q.v. below, this section.

Brief, numbered comments on, and often longer quotations from, Vonnegut's works, with some use of other sources. These yield interesting insights into Vonnegut's work up to *Slaughterhouse-Five*, and, indirectly, *Breakfast of Champions.*

Hillegas, Mark R. *The Future as Nightmare: H.G. Wells and the Anti-utopians.* New York: Oxford University Press, 1967; rpt. Carbondale, IL: SIU Press, Arcturus Books, 1974.

Occasionally inaccurate but still indispensable. Deals with Wells's utopian and antiutopian works and their influence on Zamiatin, Huxley, Orwell, Čapek, and others; quite good on Forster's "Machine Stops."

Hipolito, Jane. "*The Last* and First *Starship From Earth.*" In *SF: The Other Side of Realism* . . . . Thomas D. Clareson, ed. Bowling Green, OH: BGU Popular Press, 1971, pp. 186-92.

An analysis of John Boyd's *The Last Starship from Earth*, q.v. above, under Fiction.

Jameson, Fredric. "Generic Discontinuities in SF: Brian Aldiss' *Starship*." *SFS*, 1 (Fall 1973), 57-68.

Briefly compares *Starship* (vt *Non-Stop*) with Robert Heinlein's *Orphans of the Sky*. Notes the "political character" of *Starship*, given its surprise ending: "the problem of the manipulation of men by other men," using the tools of technology. See above under Fiction, Brian Aldiss, *Non-Stop*, and Robert Heinlein, "Universe."

Jarzębski. Jerzy. "Stanislaw Lem, Rationalist and Visionary." Franz Rottensteiner, trans. *SFS*, 4 (July 1977), 110-26.

A survey of Lem's works, most immediately useful for its aid with bibliography. Note 1, pp. 124-25, is a brief list by *SFS* ed. R. D. Mullen of US edns. of Lem's work through 1976. The article's text refers to many relevant works by Lem that, in time, should appear in English.

Ketterer, David. *New Worlds for Old: The Apocalyptic Imagination, Science Fiction, and American Literature*. Garden City, NY: Doubleday, Anchor, 1974.

Ch. 12 deals usefully with Kurt Vonnegut's *Sirens of Titan*.

_____. "Utopian Fantasy as Millennial Motive and Science Fictional Motif." *Studies in the Literary Imagination*, 6, No. 2 (Fall 1973), 79-103.

Bellamy's *Looking Backward* as an inadvertent dystopia: "a conveyor-belt vision of hell." See for the ambiguity of technology and, even more, of the social (hyper)organization associated with industrial society: Bellamy's utopian "gigantic mill" appears to DK to resemble William Blake's "dark Satanic Mills."

Klinkowitz, Jerome, and John Somers, eds. *The Vonnegut Statement*.

Listed below, by title.

La Bossière, Camille R. "Zamiatin's 'We,' A Caricature of Utopian Symmetry." *Riverside Quarterly*, 6, No. 1 (August 1973), 40-43.

Cited by Sargent, *British and American Utopian Literature*, q.v. above, under Reference Works.

Lamie, Edward L., and Joe De Bolt. "The Computer and Man: The Human Uses of Non-Human Beings." In *The Happening Worlds of John Brunner.* Joe De Bolt, ed. (q.v. above, under De Bolt, this section).

On Brunner's "balanced insight" into the uses and abuses of computers (and other machines) in human society. Briefly discusses a wide range of Brunner's fiction up to the mid-1970s, with useful comments on Shalmaneser in *Stand on Zanzibar,* and on the city as organism and machine in "Bloodstream" (both cited above, under Fiction).

Lundquist, James. *Kurt Vonnegut.* New York: Ungar, 1977.

Cited by Schlobin and Tymn as "the most thoughtful study of Vonnegut to date." Includes a biblio. ("The Year's Scholarship in Science Fiction and Fantasy: 1977," q.v. above under Acknowledgments).

Lyngstad, Sverre. "Beyond the God-Machine: Towards a Naturalized Technology." In Technology and Pessimism special issue of *Alternative Futures*, pp. 92-110, q.v. below, under Marthalee Barton and Dwight W. Stevenson, guest co-eds., Background Reading.

Esp. useful for SF and related works in European languages other than English. Includes a substantial discussion of Harry Martinson's "space epic *Aniara* (1956)," pp. 104-7.

McConnell, Frank. *The Science Fiction of H. G. Wells.* New York: Oxford University Press, 1981.

Includes a checklist (only) of works by Wells and an annotated "Select List of Works about H. G. Wells"; limited citations (text only), no notes. The discussions contain a couple of errors and perhaps some overly ingenious readings but are superbly written and always stimulating. FM covers most of Wells's works important for the study of mechanized environments, with some esp. useful comments on *First Men in the Moon* and *Time Machine* and *Time Machine*'s relationships to Edward Bellamy's *Looking Backward,* and William Morris' *News from Nowhere* (McConnell, ch. 3).

Marx, Leo. "American Literary Culture and the Fatalistic View of Technology." In the Technology and Pessimism special issue of *Alternative Futures,* pp. 45-70 (see below, under Marthalee Barton and Dwight W. Stevenson, guest co-eds., Background Reading).

An updating of LM's *Machine in the Garden,* with esp. good comments on technology in classic American literature (including Henry Adams' "Dynamo and the Virgin," Benjamin Franklin's *Autobiography,* and Mark Twain's *Huckleberry Finn*).

_____. *The Machine in the Garden.*

Cited below, under Background Reading.

Mathews, Richard. *Aldiss Unbound: The Science Fiction of Brian Aldiss.* San Bernardino, CA: Borgo Press, 1977. Vol. 9 in The Milford Series: Popular Writers of Today.

Brief introduction to Aldiss' works. Includes a list of Aldiss' books through 1976.

_____. *The Clockwork Universe of Anthony Burgess.* San Bernardino, CA: Borgo Press, 1978. Vol. 19 in The Milford Series: Popular Writers of Today.

Section 4 is on *A Clockwork Orange.* Includes a list of Burgess' published works.

Mayo, Clark. *Kurt Vonnegut: The Gospel from Outer Space . . . .* San Bernardino, CA: Borgo Press, 1977. Vol. 7 in the Milford Series: Popular Writers of Today.

Includes a list of Vonnegut's published books through 1976, and discussions of *Player Piano, The Sirens of Titan, Slaughterhouse-Five, Breakfast of Champions,* and other works.

Meckier, Jerome. "Our Ford, Our Freud and the Behaviorist Conspiracy in Huxley's *Brave New World.*" *Thalia,* 1, No. 1 (1978), 35-39.

Cited by Schlobin and Tymn in the "Year's Scholarship in Science Fiction and Fantasy: 1979" (#D81), q.v. under Acknowledgments, as "An exhaustive examination of Huxley's use of psychology and reactions to psychological theories in *Brave New World.*" See the entries for B. F. Skinner under Fiction, and Background Reading, and the entry for John B. Watson under Background Reading.

Mellard, James M. "The Modes of Vonnegut's Fiction: Or, *Player Piano* Ousts *Mechanical Bride* and *The Sirens of Titan* Invade *The Gutenberg Galaxy.*" Ch. 12 of *The Vonnegut Statement* (q.v. below, this section).

Includes insightful comments on the humanization of machines and the mechanization of humans in *Player Piano, Sirens,* and contemporary industrial society. Intelligently relates *Player Piano* to the themes of "mechanics and sex" analyzed in Marshall McLuhan's *The Mechanical Bride.*

Mengeling, Marvin E. "The Machineries of Joy and Despair: Bradbury's Attitudes toward Science and Technology." In *Ray Bradbury.* Martin Harry Greenberg and Joseph D. Olander, eds. New York: Taplinger, 1980, pp. 83-109.

Includes discussions of Bradbury's "robot houses" and "robot cities." See for Bradbury's ambivalent and changing attitudes toward technology.

Mumford, Lewis. *The Story of Utopias.* 1922; rpt. with a new Preface by Mumford, New York: Viking (Compass), 1962.

Excellent introd. to utopian thought from Plato's *Republic* through H. G. Wells's *A Modern Utopia*; quite useful for Edward Bellamy's *Looking Backward* (q.v. under Fiction) and for its analysis of the great models of the Country House and Coketown (aristocratic vs. more modern, industrialized utopias). Relates literary utopias to social thought in the real world; see below, under Background Reading, citations for other works by LM.

Munson, Ronald. "The Clockwork Future: Dystopia, Social Planning, and Freedom." In *Ecology and Quality of Life.* Sylvan J. Kaplan and Elaine Kivy-Rosenbert, eds. Springfield, IL: Charles C. Thomas, 1974, pp. 26-38.

Cited by Sargent.

Myers, Alan. "Some Developments in Soviet SF Since 1966." *Foundation,* No. 19 (June 1980), pp. 38-47.

Also includes a few comments on Russian SF prior to 1966. Survey handles some works relevant to the study of mechanized environments: S. Snegov's *Men Like Gods,* and the stories set in the "repressive society of machine slavery" of Donomaga, by I. Varshavskiy.

Olander, Joseph D., and Martin Harry Greenberg, eds. *Arthur C. Clarke.* New York: Taplinger, 1977.

An anthology of original and rpt. critical essays on Clarke. See index for discussions (passim) of material relevant for *City and the Stars, Rendezvous with Rama*, and *2001*.

Orwell's Nineteen Eighty-Four: Text, Sources, Criticism. Irving Howe, ed. New York and other cities: Harcourt, Brace & World, 1963, 1982.

Includes selections from Yevgeny Zamiatin's *We*, Aldous Huxley's *Brave New World*, and less well-known sources for *Nineteen Eighty-Four*. The "Criticism" section includes Erich Fromm's excellent Afterword to the 1961 New American Library edn. of Orwell's novel, two of Howe's critical essays, and the works of a number of other critics and reviewers—plus two items on "The Politics of Totalitarianism," giving the political background for *Nineteen Eighty-Four*: Richard Lowenthal's essay "Our Peculiar Hell," and from Hannah Arendt's *Origins of Totalitarianism* the chapter on "Ideology and Terror: A Novel Form of Government."

Palumbo, Donald. "William Burroughs' Quartet of Science Fiction Novels as Dystopian Social Satire." *Extrapolation*, 20 (Winter 1979), 321-29.

Deals with *Naked Lunch, Soft Machine, Nova Express,* and *Ticket that Exploded*. Notes how *Ticket* presents contemporary life "as a film that is rerun again and again, trapping the human in amber, negating any possibility of real freedom." This repetition is associated by Burroughs with Hell.

Philip K. Dick: Electric Shepherd (Best of SF Commentary Number 1). Bruce Gillespie, ed. Melbourne, Australia: Norstrilia Press, 1975.

Includes text of Dick's lecture "The Android and the Human" and critical items by others.

Pierce, Hazel. " 'Elementary, My Dear . . . ': Asimov's Science Fiction Mysteries." In *Isaac Asimov*. Joseph D. Olander and Martin Harry Greenberg, eds. New York: Taplinger, 1977, pp. 32-58.

Includes a discussion of *Caves of Steel* and *Naked Sun*. Esp. good comments on *Naked Sun* (pp. 44-49).

Pitcher, Edward W. R. "That Web of Symbols in Zamyatin's *We*." *Extrapolation*, 22 (Fall 1981), 252-61.

An interesting and helpful attempt to use a close reading of the symbolism of *We* to elucidate that work's basic oppositions and thematic upshot. Concludes that the essential choice offered in *We* "is not between the Natural World and the One State, the Garden and the City," but between opting—wrongly—for "one or the other . . . of the polarized positions in the novel" and retaining "the wisdom . . . to live with . . . the ambiguous and the irrational" (p. 260). Many readers will disagree with this article's elucidation of at least some of *We*'s symbol's and may question as well the interpretation of some action in *We*'s plot; its author notes that his conclusions oppose those of most critics, esp. Alexandra Aldridge in "Myths of Origin and Destiny" (q.v., above, this section).

Rabinovitz, Rubin. "Mechanism vs. Organism: Anthony Burgess' *A Clockwork Orange*." *Modern Fiction Studies*, 24 (Winter 1978-79), 538-41.

Does little with the mechanism/organism antithesis but useful for summarizing and discussing the significance of the final chapter of *Clockwork Orange* in the unshortened form of the novel published in the UK (London: Heinemann, 1962): "Alex concludes that there is a cycle of recurring phases in which each young man undergoes a period of existence as a violent, mechanical man; then he matures, gets greater freedom of choice, and his violence subsides. . . . The determined progress of the clockwork man, who must move in a straight line, is thus contrasted with the circular shape and movement of God's orange, symbol of life and organic growth" (p. 539).

Rabkin, Eric S. *Arthur C. Clarke*. West Linn, OR: Starmont House, 1979. Starmont Reader's Guide 1.

Includes chapters on *City and the Stars, Rendezvous with Rama*, and *2001*.

Rhodes, Carolyn H. "Frederick Winslow Taylor's System of Scientific Management in Zamiatin's *We*." *Journal of General Education*, 28 (Spring 1976), 31-42.

See for Zamiatin's recognition of the dehumanizing effect when all of life is "Taylorized." (See in *CW* the essay by Gorman Beauchamp.)

_____. "Tyranny by Computer: Automated Data Processing and Oppressive Government in Science Fiction." In *Many Futures, Many*

Worlds: Theme and Form in Science Fiction. Thomas D. Clareson, ed. Kent, OH: Kent State University Press, 1977, pp. 66-93.

Esp. useful for Vonnegut's *Player Piano*, and Crossen's *Year of Consent.*

Richards, D. J. *Zamyatin: A Soviet Heretic.* Studies in Modern European Literature and Thought. New York: Hillary House, 1962.

A brief, popular introduction to Zamiatin. Uses Erich Fromm's ideas on "positive freedom" for comments on *We* and other works by Zamiatin attacking "social conformity and the mechanisation of life" (pp. 58-59, 87). See below, this section, the entry for Alex Shane.

Richter, Peyton E., ed. *Utopia/Dystopia?* Cambridge, MA: Schenkman, 1975.

Cited by Sargent. See for background and recent studies.

Rose, Mark. "Filling the Void: Verne, Wells, and Lem." *SFS,* 8 (July 1981), 121-42.

Includes comments on the Martians' association with an indifferent cosmos and as a "metaphorical projection of the capitalistic industrial system of the late 19th century . . . conceived as a social machine" in H. G. Wells's *War of the Worlds* and on the "closed and safe spaces," necessarily mechanical, in Jules Verne, and in Stanislaw Lem's *Solaris* (pp. 130 and 132; cf. Wolfe on positive views of enclosure).

———. "Machine." Ch. 6 of *Alien Encounters: An Anatomy of Science Fiction.* Cambridge, MA, and London: Harvard University Press, 1981.

Discusses Zamiatin's *We* and other dystopias, concentrating on "the metaphor of society as a kind of machine that has reduced the individual to the status of a robot." See pp. 166-75.

Samuelson, David N. "*Limbo*: The Great American Dystopia." *Extrapolation,* 19 (Dec. 1977), 76-84.

Limbo as an attack on "the utopian desire for perfect order."

Science-Fiction Studies, #5 = Vol. 2, Pt. 1 (March 1975).

The special issue of *SFS* on Philip K. Dick. Includes R. D. Mullen's biblio. of Dick's "Books, Stories, Essays" through 1974.

Segal, Howard P. "*Young West:* The Psyche of Technological Utopianism." *Extrapolation,* 19 (Dec. 1977), 50-58.

Young West as a representative technological utopia embodying a belief common in the USA from 1833 to 1933: "the belief in the inevitability of progress and in progress as technological progress"; pushed to an extreme this belief yields technocracy or at least "the equation of advanced technology . . . with utopia."

Shane, Alex M. *The Life and Works of Evgenij Zamjatin.* Berkeley and Los Angeles: University of California Press, 1968.

Includes an extensive biblio. of works by and about Zamiatin. Main discussion of *We* is in ch. 6, "Middle Period, 1917-1921," esp. pp. 137-61. Excellent on color imagery in *We*, the square root of minus one, and the relationship between *We* and Zamiatin's other works, esp. "*Ostrovitjane*" ("The Islanders"), and Zamiatin's essays. See for Zamiatin's own comments about *We* as "a warning against . . . the hypertrophic power of machines and the hypertrophic power of the State," and for cautions against taking for the norms of *We* irrationality and cultural primitivism, and against taking *We* as ultimately pessimistic. (*LWEZ* can be difficult reading for people without a knowledge of Russian; see above, this section, the entry for D. J. Richards. See also above, this section, the entry for Gorman Beauchamp, "Cultural Primitivism.")

Shippey, Tom. "A Modern View of Science Fiction." In *Beyond This Horizon: An Anthology of Science Fiction and Science Fact.* Christopher Carrell, ed. Sunderland, UK: Ceolith Press, 1973.

Cited by David Ketterer (*SFS*, #21, p. 230) for its discussion of the generation-starship of the "Universe" sort. See esp. pp. 8-9. (See above, under Fiction, Robert Heinlein, "Universe.")

Slusser, George Edgar. *The Classic Years Of Robert A. Heinlein.* San Bernardino, CA: Borgo Press, 1977. Vol. 11 in The Milford Series: Popular Writers of Today.

Brief survey concentrating upon RAH's earlier works. Includes a selected biblio. GES discusses RAH's later novels in *Robert A. Heinlein: Stranger in His Own Land,* 2d edn., vol. 1 in The Milford Series.

_____. *The Delany Intersection: Samuel R. Delany* . . . . San Bernardino, CA: Borgo Press, 1977. Vol. 10 of The Milford Series: Popular Writers of Today.

Includes a brief biblio., a full section on *The Fall of the Towers,* and comments on *Nova*; few comments on Delany's work after 1970.

_____. *Harlan Ellison: Unrepentant Harlequin.* San Bernardino, CA: Borgo Press, 1977. Vol. 6 of The Milford Series: Popular Writers of Today.

Brief survey of Ellison's major works. Includes a list of Ellison's published books through 1975.

Stern, Michael. "From Technique to Critique: Knowledge and Human Interests in John Brunner's *Stand on Zanzibar, The Jagged Orbit,* and *The Sheep Look Up.*" *SFS*, 3 (July 1976), 112-30.

See discussion of Shalmaneser (the computer), General Technics, and Georgette Talon Buckfast (pp. 120-22). MS sees Shalmaneser as " 'environment forming' for everybody on earth," and as a machine that loses its godhead by becoming human.

Studies in the Literary Imagination, "Aspects of Utopian Fiction" issue: see above, this section, under Jack I. Biles, ed.

Sussman, Herbert L. *Victorians and the Machine: The Literary Response to Technology.* Cambridge, MA: Harvard University Press, 1968.

Includes a discussion of Samuel Butler's *Erewhon*; also includes HLS's "The Machine and the Future: H. G. Wells" (pp. 162-93, cited in David Y. Hughes, "Criticism in English of H. G. Wells's Science Fiction," q.v. above under Reference Works). Said by Warrick to deal with important aspects of the use of the machine as a metaphor for the conflict in Western philosophy between determinism and free will—a conflict aggravated by the rise of modern science, with its apparent support for determinism (see HLS, *VM,* p. 155, and Warrick, p. 43).

Suvin, Darko. "P.K. Dick's Opus: Artifice as Refuge and World View (Introductory Reflections)." *SFS* 2 (March 1975), 8-22.

For those familiar with the work of Philip K. Dick, these "Opening Reflections" in the special Dick issue of *SFS* provide an excellent survey of the philosophical (social, political) implications of Dick's opus. See for androids and totalitarian organizations and societies.

Utter, Glen H. "The Individual in Technological Society: Walker Percy's *Lancelot.*" *Journal of Popular Culture*, 16, No. 3 (Winter 1982), 116-27.

On Percy's Lancelot Lamar as an individual attempting "to awaken from a somnambulistic life" in American technological society. The first four and one half pages of GHU's article provide an elegant "sketch of technological society" (p. 120), and the notes provide an excellent bibliography for an introduction to the sociological literature on technology. See for an intriguing analysis of the use in a mainstream work of the motif of being trapped in a metaphorical clockwork world—and see GHU's notes for some useful works we have been unable to include in our section on Background Reading.

The Vonnegut Statement. Jerome Klinkowitz and John Somer, eds. New York: Delacorte Press/Seymour Lawrence, 1973; rpt. New York: Dell, Delta, [1973].

Anthology of essays on Vonnegut's life and work; esp. relevant: the essays on "The Literary Art" by Tim Hildebrand, Karen and Charles Wood, and James Mellard (q.v., below, this section). Includes an index and an excellent analytical biblio. of works by and about Vonnegut, through 1972.

Wagar, W. Warren. "The Steel-Gray Saviour: Technocracy as Utopia and Ideology." *Alternative Futures*, 2, No. 2 (Spring 1979), 38-54.

Discusses technocracy as a living ideology—indeed, the controlling ideology in the twentieth century—and as a motif in literature and film.

Walsh, Chad. *From Utopia to Nightmare.* New York and Evanston, IL: Harper & Row, 1962; rpt. Westport, CT: Greenwood Press, 1962; London: Geoffrey Bles, 1962 (Sargent).

A concise, sensible, and beautifully written survey of the utopian vision from the Hebrew prophets and Plato's *Republic* through B. F. Skinner's *Walden Two* and Aldous Huxley's *Island*—and of the dystopian vision from Dante's Hell and Feodor Dostoevsky's Grand Inquisitor (in *The Brothers Karamazov*) through the great dystopias of the twentieth century. Handles the mechanization motif passim. Most immediately relevent: chs. 6-8, on dystopias, and chs. 10-11, on "Recurrent Themes." An excellent place to begin a study of utopian and dystopian literature, placing as it does the mechanization motif into its context in literary history.

Warrick, Patricia S. *The Cybernetic Imagination in Science Fiction.* Cambridge, MA, and London: MIT Press, 1980.

A study of some 225 works of fiction from 1930 to 1977. Includes a very useful biblio. of nonfiction works. Rpts. with some variations PSW, "Images of the Man-Machine Intelligence Relationship," q.v. below; "A Science Fiction Aesthetic," *Pacific Quarterly,* 4, No. 3 (July 1979); and two essays on P. K. Dick. Helpfully brings together PSW's work on Isaac Asimov and Dick, adding some comments on Stanislaw Lem. For warnings on *TCI*'s limitations, see the review by Dagmar Barnouw, *SFS*, 8 (July 1981), 215-17.

————. "Images of the Man-Machine Intelligence Relationship in Science Fiction." In *Many Futures, Many Worlds.* Thomas D. Clareson, ed. Kent, OH: Kent State University Press, 1977, pp. 182-223.

Included in Warrick, *Cybernetic Imagination* (q.v. above; see esp. chs. 2, 6, 7). Surveys a large number of works briefly but competently. Esp. useful in differentiating between the presentation of artificial intelligence in (dystopian) extrapolative works, and in speculative works (the "closed-" and "open-system" models in *Cybernetic Imagination*).

Watson, Ian. "A Rhetoric of Recognition: The Science Fiction of Michael Bishop." *Foundation*, No. 19 (June 1980), pp. 5-14.

Surveys Bishop's SF through 1980, providing useful plot summaries and some highly provocative comments on Bishop's use of motifs important for the study of mechanized environments. See esp. IW's comments on "the domed secular infernos of the North American Urban Federation," pp. 10-12.

West, Anthony, "H. G. Wells." In West, *Principles and Persuasions.* New York: Harcourt Brace, 1957. Rpt. in *H. G. Wells: A Collection of Critical Essays.* Bernard Bergonzi, ed. Englewood Cliffs, NJ: Prentice-Hall, 1976, pp. 8-24.

Includes useful comments on Wells's *War of the Worlds, First Men in the Moon,* and *When the Sleeper Wakes*, stressing the dystopian aspects of these works (pp. 14-17 in Bergonzi rpt.)

White, Michael D. "Ellison's Harlequin: Irrational Moral Action in Static Time." *SFS*, 4 (July 1977), 161-65.

A Marxist critique of "Repent, Harlequin." Recognizes the stasis of the "ticktock" society and that Ellison "has written this story to protest a rigid bureaucracy ruled by a social elite."

Wolfe, Gary K. *The Known and the Unknown: The Iconography of Science Fiction*. Kent, OH: Kent State University Press, 1979.

For mechanized environments, see Part 2: "Images of Environment," esp. "The Technological City," in ch. 4. The wide scope of issues covered in this excellent book is indicated in our annotations using it, passim in our List.

Wolk, Anthony. "The Sunstruck Forest: A Guide to the Short Fiction of Philip K. Dick." *Foundation*, No. 18 (Jan. 1980), pp. 19-34.

A thematic approach to Dick's short fiction, dealing with several works of interest for the study of mechanized environments.

Wood, Karen, and Charles Wood. "The Vonnegut Effect." Ch. 10 of *The Vonnegut Statement*. (q.v. above, this section).

On Vonnegut as a writer of S.F. (of sorts), writing both S.F. and a "literature of experience" exploring the human condition in a "technology-dominated" society—ours. Includes some excellent comments on *Player Piano* and other works by Vonnegut through *Slaughterhouse-Five*.

Wymer, Thomas L. "The Swiftian Satire of Kurt Vonnegut, Jr." In *Voices for the Future: Essays on Major Science Fiction Writers*. Vol. 1. Thomas D. Clareson, ed. Bowling Green, OH: BGU Popular Press, 1976, pp. 238-62.

Argues that Vonnegut satirizes Billy Pilgrim's acceptance of the Tralfamadorian view of humans as machines without free will, trapped in a determined, mechanistic universe (an argument that TLW extends in his essay on Vonnegut in *TMG*).

Zanger, Jules. "Goblins, Morlocks, and Weasels: Classic Fantasy and the Industrial Revolution." *Children's Literature in Education*, 8 (Winter 1977), 154-62.

Applies to Wells's *Times Machine* and other works the premise that "late-Victorian and Edwardian fantasy was a struggle against the changes of the Industrial Revolution" (R. Schlobin and M. Tymn in "The Year's Scholarship in Science Fiction and Fantasy: 1977," p. 256, q.v. under Acknowledgments).

V. STAGE, FILM, AND TELEVISION DRAMA

Alien. Ridley Scott, dir. USA: 20th Century-Fox, 1979. Dan O'Bannon, script. Dan O'Bannon and Ronald Shusett, story.

Threatening containment within a spaceship that is in large part controlled by a computer programmed by the Company owning the ship to accomplish a morally perverse mission, even at the cost of the lives of the crew. Novelized by Alan D. Foster, q.v. above, under Fiction.

Alphaville. Jean-Luc Godard, dir. France: Pathécontemporary/Chaumiane-Film, 1965.

Computer-domination story that *S. F. Ency.* describes as "an ambiguous allegory of contemporary technology-dominated society." Godard, it is said, wanted to call this film *Tarzan vs. IBM* (see below, under Stage, Film, and Television Drama Criticism, Richard Roud's article on this film).

The Andromeda Strain. Robert Wise, dir. USA: Universal, 1971. Based on the novel by Michael Crichton (q.v. above, under Fiction).

Closely follows the novel, nicely emphasizing the brightness and sterility of the underground labs. (See in *TMG* the essay by Peter Alterman.)

Blomdahl, Karl-Birger, composer. *Aniara.* Opera, 1959.

Libretto based on Harry Martinson's *Aniara*, q.v. above, under Fiction.

A Boy and His Dog. L. Q. Jones, dir. USA: LQJaf, 1975. Based on the novella by Harlan Ellison.

Improves upon Ellison's excellent story (q.v. above, under Fiction). Features a mechanized Underworld. Discussed by John Crow and

Richard Erlich in the article cited below under Stage, Film, and Television Drama Criticism; discussed in *CW* by Leonard Heldreth.

Brave New World. Burt Brinckerhoff, dir. USA: Universal, 1980. Made for TV; first shown, NBC, 7 March 1980.

Closely follows Aldous Huxley novel of the same title (q.v. under Fiction), but with less emphasis on "bottles" and conditioning. Originally planned as a miniseries, so version shown on 7 March 1980 may lack important footage.

Čapek, Karel. *R. U. R.* 1921 (Czech). First English edn., Oxford University Press, 1923. Frequently rpt., including in *Of Men and Machines*, q.v. above, under Anthologies and Collections. Also, P. Selver, trans. Adapted for English stage by Nigel Playfair. Harry Shefter, ed. New York: Washington Square Press (Pocket Books), 1973 ("enriched" edn.).

Play. Rossum's robots—"androids" in current terminology—take over because they are, in many ways, superior to humans. This play gave us the word "robot."

A Clockwork Orange. Stanley Kubrick, dir. UK: Hawk (production)/ Warner (US release), 1971.

Closely follows US version of Anthony Burgess' novel of the same title (q.v. above, under Fiction). Discussed in *CW* by Leonard Heldreth.

Close Encounters of the Third Kind. Steven Spielberg, dir., script. USA: Columbia/EMI, 1977. 135 min. in original theatrical release.

The mechanized environment of the alien mothership at the end of the film is a highly positive, almost mystical, experience for the flim's hero, and for the audience, esp. in the "Special Edition" rerelease and in the version shown on television. *CETK* is discussed in *TMG* in the essay by Donald Palumbo.

Colossus: The Forbin Project (variously punctuated; vt *The Forbin Project*, UK). Joseph Sargent, dir. USA: Universal, 1969 (completion), 1970 (US release). Walt Lee lists additional vts for this film before and during its production.

Closely follows the novel by D. F. Jones (q.v. under Fiction); changes are minor, necessary, and usually improvements. Discussed in *CW* by Leonard Heldreth.

Dark Star. John Carpenter, dir. USA: Bryanston Pictures, 1974.

See for character Pinback trapped in the spaceship *Dark Star*'s elevator shaft, the female computer that runs the *Dark Star,* and the computer-bomb that eventually develops delusions of godhead. *S. F. Ency.* cites a novelization by Alan Dean Foster (1974).

Demon Seed. Donald Cammell, dir. USA: United Artists (*S. F. Ency.*: MGM), 1977. Based on the novel by Dean R. Koontz.

See Koontz under Fiction. The film's end improves upon the novel's, but otherwise the film tells the same story.

Dr. Strangelove: Or How I Learned to Stop Worrying and Love the Bomb (variously capitalized and punctuated). Stanley Kubrick, dir. UK: Hawk/Columbia, 1963 (completion), 1964 (US release).

Features mechanized humans (primarily Peter Sellers' Dr. Strangelove), humanized machines, men in a B-52, and humanity "trapped" in a doomsday machine. Important for Kubrick's later work in *2001* and *Clockwork Orange,* q.v. above, this section.

The Empire Strikes Back. Irvin Kershner, dir. USA: Lucasfilm (production)/20th Century-Fox (release), 1980. Leigh Brackett and Lawrence Kasdan, script; story by George Lucas. George Lucas, executive producer.

Sequel to *Star Wars,* q.v. below, this section. Many images of containment within machinery are contrasted with the open, snow-covered plains of Hoth (the base for the Rebel Alliance in the opening sequence) and the swamp of the planet where Yoda trains Luke Skywalker. Usually, the containment within machinery is immediately or potentially dangerous for the good characters in the film; the shots of Darth Vader's exits from his meditation chamber suggest the demonic. (Lucas' story has been novelized by Donald F. Glut; see Glut entry above under Fiction.)

Fahrenheit 451. François Truffaut, dir. UK: Anglo-Enterprise and Vineyard/Universal, 1966. Script by Truffaut and Jean-Lewis Richard, from the novel by Ray Bradbury.

The hero escapes a highly mechanized, urban world, where books are burned, to join a rural community where books are memorized and thereby preserved. Perhaps most interesting for the ambiguity in its presentation of the standard opposition of the wicked city and purer countryside: the "book people" at the end of the film memorize the words of the texts "while plodding about the snow-covered landscape like zombies" (*S. F. Ency.*).

Futureworld. Richard T. Heffron, dir. USA: American International Pictures, 1976.

Sequel to *Westworld*, q.v. below, this section. Robots try to take over the world by replacing human leaders with robot look-alikes. The setting for most of the film is the robot-run resort of Delos (with the robots, as things turn out, in complete charge). Discussed in *CW* by Leonard Heldreth.

Ikaria XB-1 (variously spelled and hyphenated; vt *Voyage to the End of the Universe*). Jindřich Polak, dir. Czechoslovakia: Film Export/American International Pictures, 1963 (completion), 1964 (release).

Features a subtly alien culture inside a huge spaceship.

The Lathe of Heaven. David Loxton and Fred Barzyk, dirs. USA: Educational Broadcasting Corporation, 1979. Produced for the Public Broadcasting Service; first shown 9 Jan. 1980. Based on the novel by Ursula K. Le Guin, q.v. above, under Fiction.

Closely follows the novel in all matters important for the study of mechanized environments.

Logan's Run. Michael Anderson, dir. USA: MGM/United Artists, 1976. Based on the novel by William F. Nolan and George Clayton Johnson.

Humanity in the future has sealed itself into a domed pleasure-city, a city managed in large part by a computer (which we see and hear at key moments in the plot). Cf. and contrast Arthur Clarke, *City and the Stars*, and Robert Silverberg, *World Inside*, and the generation-starship works cross-referenced under Robert Heinlein, "Universe" (all cited above, under Fiction).

Metropolis. Fritz Lang, dir. Germany: Ufa, 1926.

Silent film showing a pleasure city for the elite and a mechanized underground portion of the Metropolis, where mechanized workers tend the city's machines. A very important work for the motif of mechanized Underworlds; cf. *THX 1138,* and *A Boy and His Dog,* this section, and see above, under Fiction, E. M. Forster, "Machine Stops," and H. G. Wells, *Time Machine* and *First Men in the Moon. Metropolis* is discussed in *CW* by Leonard Heldreth.

Modern Times. Charles Chaplin, chief dir. USA: Charles Chaplin Corp. (production)/United Artists (US release), 1936.

Note esp. Chaplin's clown, Charlie, on the assembly line, trapped in the feeding machine, and being pushed through the gears of a gigantic mechanism. These sequences add up to a cogent, if symbolic and grotesque, commentary on the condition of workers in industrialized society.

A New Hope. Cited and annotated below, this section, as *Star Wars.*

1984. Michael Anderson, dir. UK: Holiday Films (production)/Columbia, 1955 (completion), 1956 (US release). Based on the novel by George Orwell, q.v.

Recreates the totalitarian society of the novel. Esp. powerful in evoking the constant surveillance by telescreens in the Ministry of Love. (See *1984* entries in *S. F. Ency.* and Walt Lee, *Reference Guide,* for different endings of prints released in UK and USA: UK version differs greatly from end of the novel. Note that a remake of *1984* is planned.)

North Dallas Forty. Frank Yablans, dir. USA: Paramount, 1979. Based on the novel by Peter Gent. Nick Nolte, star.

Mainstream film. Note computerized football management, and players as parts of a professional football athletic machine. Cf. *Rollerball,* q.v. below, this section.

The Phantom Empire (advertised as *Gene Autry and the Phantom Empire*). USA: Mascot, 1935. Gene Autry and Smiley Burnette, stars. Serial in twelve episodes. Later released as feature films under titles *Radio Ranch* and *Men with Steel Faces* (Walt Lee).

Combines "four or five" cinematic traditions by Baxter's count (p. 71; see Acknowledgments, above), including the Western, and the SF motifs of the lost world and the subterranean city. Significant for presenting a mechanized Underworld like that of *Metropolis* (q.v. above) in the film equivalent of pulp fiction.

The President's Analyst. Theodore J. Flicker, dir. USA: Panpiper (production)/Paramount (US release), 1967. James Coburn and Godfrey Cambridge, stars.

   Mainstream satire. Robots running TPC (The Phone Company) may have us all under surveillance, and may seek total control over us.

The Prisoner. Patrick McGoohan, creator, star, occasional writer and dir. UK: ITC (Independent Television), 1967. Seventeen episodes; available on videotape.

   TV series showing one man (McGoohan) against a bureaucratic spy agency and a prison-camp, "The Village," disguised as a resort. Note constant surveillance, attempts at mind control through technology, relatively gentle entrapment—and the ultimate threat of a huge beachball that pursues, traps, and smothers its victims (a crude but effective symbol). *S. F. Ency.* cites two novels based on the series: Thomas M. Disch, *The Prisoner* (1969), and David McDaniel, *The Prisoner No. 2* (1969).

Return of the Jedi. Richard Marquand, dir. USA: Lucasfilm (production)/ 20th Century-Fox (release), 1983. Lawrence Kasdan and George Lucas, script; story by George Lucas. George Lucas, executive producer.

   Last film in the first *Star Wars* trilogy (see in this section, *Star Wars* and *The Empire Strikes Back*). Note explicit contrast of the Empire's Death Star and other evilly-employed technology and the forest world of the Ewoks. (See entry for James Kahn, above, under Fiction.)

Road Warrior. George Miller, dir. Australia: Warner (US release), 1982.

   Sequel to Miller's *Mad Max* (which we have not seen). Postholocaust world in which gasoline-driven vehicles are central to what little human culture remains.

Rollerball. Norman Jewison, dir. USA: United Artists, 1975. William Harrison, script, from his "Roller Ball Murder," q.v. above, under Fiction.

   The highly mechanized game of Rollerball is used by the ruling corporate *apparat* as an outlet for the violent emotions of the masses and as a way to teach them that individual effort is futile. Note sequence in which the film's hero goes to consult his world's central computer, where the human past is, theoretically, preserved. *Rollerball* is discussed in *CW* by Elizabeth A. Hull.

Slaughterhouse-Five (sometimes spelled without hyphen). George Roy Hill, dir. USA: Universal, 1971 (completion), 1972 (US release). Based on Kurt Vonnegut, Jr., *Slaughterhouse-Five*, q.v. above, under Fiction.

    Retains in attenuated form a question raised in Vonnegut's novel: Do humans have free will, or are we merely machines, doomed to do what we do because "the moment is structured that way"? Also retains Billy Pilgrim's cage in the Tralfamadorian zoo as a very homey sort of mechanical womb.

The Starlost. TV series from Canada's CTV, shown in syndication in the USA, 1974. Original idea credited to "Cordwainer Bird," pseud. of Harlan Ellison when he wishes to dissociate himself from a project.

    Features a generation starship with different Terran cultures in various "biospheres"; the crew of the starship are dead, and the passengers have forgotten the mission of the starship and mistake it for a world. See above, under Fiction, Robert Heinlein, "Universe"; see also in that section Edward Bryant and Harlan Ellison, *Phoenix Without Ashes*, based on Ellison's original intention for *The Starlost* series.

Star Trek Episodes—Television

"The Apple." *Star Trek,* 13 Oct. 1967. Max Ehrlich with Gene L. Coon, script.

    Vaal, a kind of deified, immobile, mechanical dragon, preserves in a stagnant paradise a society of gentle humanoids. Fictionalized by James Blish in *Star Trek 6,* 1972 (q.v. above, under Fiction); discussed by Karen Blair in "The Garden in the Machine," esp. pp. 312-13 (listed below under Stage, Film, and Television Drama Criticism).

"For the World Is Hollow and I Have Touched the Sky." *Star Trek*, 3d season (1968-69). Rik Vollaerts, script.

    Combines the motifs of the generation starship and mechanical—or electronic—"possession" (our term). See above, under Fiction, Robert Heinlein, "Universe," and Kurt Vonnegut, *Sirens of Titan.* This episode was fictionalized by James Blish in *Star Trek 8,* 1972 (q.v. above, under Fiction).

"The Return of the Archons." *Star Trek*, 9 Feb. 1967. Boris Sobelman, script, from a story by Gene Roddenberry.

A society has achieved unity and stasis by merging individual consciousnesses with what turns out to be a machine. Fictionalized by James Blish in *Star Trek 9*, 1973 (q.v. above, under Fiction).

Star Trek: The Motion Picture. Robert Wise, dir. USA: Paramount, 1979. Harold Livingston and Alan Dean Foster, script.

For most of the film the characters are inside the starship *Enterprise*, which is itself inside a gigantic machine. See for a positive view of human/machine merger. (Discussed in *TMG* by Donald Palumbo.)

Star Wars (retitled, *A New Hope*). George Lucas, dir. and script. USA: Lucasfilm (production)/20th Century-Fox (US release), 1977.

See for the malevolent technology of the Empire, esp. the labyrinthian mechanical world of the Death Star, and the limitations of technology in a galaxy where the ultimate force is the Force. Novelization by Lucas cited above under Fiction (but see also the last sentence of the *SW* entry in *S. F. Ency.*). Discussed in *TMG* by Leonard Heldreth and passim. See above, this section, the entries for *The Empire Strikes Back* and *Return of the Jedi*.

The Stepford Wives. Bryan Forbes, dir. USA: Columbia, 1975. Based on the novel by Ira Levin.

The husbands of Stepford, CT, replace their wives with robot duplicates. Discussed in *CW* by Daniel Ingersoll. Also note the 1980 TV film by Brian Wiltse, *The Revenge of the Stepford Wives*; the climatic sequence of this sequel is a kind of updating of the catastrophe of Euripides' *The Bacchae* (11. 1050-1150), with the malfunctioning roboticized wives of Stepford playing Maenads to the Pentheus of Diz (Arthur Hill), the male chauvinist leader of the Stepford Men's Association.

Terry, Megan. *Megan Terry's Home, or Future Soap*. New York: Samuel French, 1967. A playable version of the 1967 Public Broadcasting Service telecast.

One day in the life of one "home" (a cubicle in a huge building) in which nine people of the future live out their entire lives. Together

List of Works

with the people of billions of similar homes, all governed by Control, they carry out the mission of the human race: "We Will Populate Space!" Cf. Robert Silverberg, *The World Inside*, listed above under Fiction. MT's *Home* is discussed briefly in Thomas Dunn and Richard Erlich, "Vision of Dystopia," q.v. above, under Literary Criticism.

Things to Come. William Cameron Menzies, dir. UK: London Films (production)/United Artists (US release), 1936. H. G. Wells, script, from his *The Shape of Things to Come* (preproduction working title for the film). Alexander Korda, producer.

Positive presentation of technocratic takeover after a horrible war. Discussed by W. Warren Wagar in "Steel-Gray Saviour," q.v. above under Literary Criticism.

THX 1138. George Lucas, dir. USA: Warner (Johnson, and Pohl and Pohl) /American Zoetrope (Walt Lee, *S. F. Ency.*, and *Twyman 1977 Film Rental Catalogue*), 1969 (completion), 1971 (US release). Based on Lucas' student film, *THX-1138-4EB* (rental title, *Electronic Labyrinth* [Walt Lee]). George Lucas and Walter Murch, script; story by George Lucas. Francis Ford Coppola, executive producer.

Probably produced by American Zoetrope and initially distributed by Warner. *THX* is a very important film, featuring a technocratic, computerized, underground culture. Note esp. the sequence in which THX (Robert Duvall) is trapped and tortured by machines and machinelike men. *THX* has been novelized by Ben Bova (see entry above, under Fiction). For the place of *THX* in the tradition of mechanized underworlds, cf. *Metropolis* and *A Boy and His Dog* (listed in this section) and E. M. Forster, "Machine Stops" (listed above, under Fiction). *THX* is discussed in *CW* by Leonard Heldreth.

Time Bandits. Terry Gilliam, dir. UK: Handmade Films, 1981.

A fantasy film with live actors which could be subtitled "Monty Python and the Royal Shakespeare Meet the Problem of Evil." Significant here for associating mechanization with mythic evil (as Ralph Bakshi had done in his animated fantasy *Wizards*) and having that association work in a serious comedy: the Satan-figure is both a proponent and embodiment of things mechanical and cybernetic, while the great tradition (from medieval drama through *Dr. Strangelove*) is maintained of having incarnate evil both frightening and funny. At the end of the climactic battle, the devil's lair is littered with artifacts of human military technology from ancient Greece through the twenty-first century, and the Adversary has only barely been stopped, by direct intervention by God, from computerizing his operation.

The Time Machine. George Pal, dir. USA: Galaxy Films (production) /MGM (US release), 1960. Based on the novel by H. G. Wells (1895), q.v. above, under Fiction.

The film version of *TM* retains the mechanized Underworld of the Morlocks in Wells's novel.

TRON (also *Tron*). Steven Lisberger, dir. USA: Disney 1982.

MCP, the Master Control Program of the computer used by a high-technology corporation, rules as a god the microscopic world of the computer "he" is in and has large ambitions in the macroscopic world: our world in the very near future. He is opposed by TRON (a personified security program) and TRON's few allies among the programs run by MCP. Flynn, a human user of the computer, helps TRON destroy MCP after Flynn is "digitalized" by MCP and taken into the microscopic world to die in gladiatorial video games. Note the implied theme of computer takeover and the more explicit theme of the computer as god. Cf. Stanislaw Lem, "The Experiment," and John Sladek, *The Müller-Fokker Effect* (both cited above under Fiction). The use of computers in the production of *TRON* is discussed under both "Entertainment" and "Technology" in *Newsweek*, 5 July 1982 (pp. 58-62, 64-68).

2001: A Space Odyssey. Stanley Kubrick, dir. UK/USA: Stanley Kubrick Productions/MGM, 1968. Kubrick and Arthur C. Clarke, script. 160 minutes, cut to 141 minutes.

See for helpful machines, encompassing machines, the behavior of men and machines merging—and for HAL 9000. See above, under Fiction, Clarke, *2001*. See below, under Stage, Film, and Television Drama Criticism, the citations for Jerome Agel, Carolyn Geduld, and Mark Rose. For the complex history of the writing of *2001*, see Arthur C. Clarke, *The Lost Worlds of 2001* (New York: New American Library, 1972).

Wargames. John Badham, dir. USA: MGM/United Artists, 1983.

Combines motifs of the computer tyrant and the Strangelovian doomsday concept, largely set in the NORAD missile command enclave. See for detailed computer operation sequences, and listen for hacker jargon.

Westworld. Michael Crichton, dir. USA: MGM, 1973.

The robots of the Westworld section of the plush resort of Delos run amok. See above, this section, *Futureworld.*

Zardoz. John Boorman, dir. USA: John Boorman Productions/20th Century-Fox, 1973.

Zed (Sean Connery) brings love and death to a static, computer-run "utopia" appropriately called a Vortex. Includes some shots of huge mechanical wombs and a sequence with Zed in the computer (a mysterious crystal). See above, under Fiction, Boorman's novelization of *Zardoz.* Cf. and contrast *Zardoz,* as both novel and film, with Arthur C. Clarke, *City and the Stars* (q.v. under Fiction).

VI. STAGE, FILM, AND TELEVISION DRAMA CRITICISM

Agel, Jerome, ed. *The Making of Kubrick's 2001.* New York: New American Library, 1970.

Includes a ninety-six-page photo insert from the film, Arthur C. Clarke's "The Sentinel," and at least excerpts from every major handling of *2001* through 1970. An indispensable work for the study of *2001.* (See below, this section, the entry for Carolyn Geduld.)

Baxter, John. *Science Fiction in the Cinema.* Full citation above, under Acknowledgments.

A survey and "critical review of SF films from *A Trip to the Moon* (1902) to *2001: A Space Odyssey*" (front-cover blurb).

Blair, Karen. "The Garden in the Machine: The Why of *Star Trek.*" *Journal of Popular Culture,* 13 (Fall 1979), 310-20.

Focuses on the *Star Trek* episodes "The Apple" (q.v. under Stage, Film, and Television Drama) and "The Way to Eden." Most esp., the "Machine" in KB's title is the *Enterprise,* and the "Garden" is "the human community . . . on board the *Enterprise*" (p. 318). See below, under Background Reading, the entry for Leo Marx.

Brosnan, John. *Future Tense: The Cinema of Science Fiction.* Full citation above, under Reference Works.

Primarily useful for its plot summaries and its unabashed judgments of cinematic quality, but with some interesting critical comments (passim) on *2001, THX 1138,* and a number of films too minor for inclusion in our section, Stage, Film, and Television Drama.

Crow, John [H.], and Richard [D.] Erlich. "Mythic Patterns in Ellison's [and Jones's] *A Boy and His Dog.*" *Extrapolation,* 18 (May 1977), 162-66.

Deals with both Ellison's novella and L. Q. Jones's film (listed under Fiction, and Stage, Film, and Television Drama, respectively). Briefly handles the mechanization of the Underworld in both works. Also deals with the potentially fatal containment of the protagonist in the "marriage" sequence of the film.

Elkins, Charles, ed. "Symposium on *Alien.*" *SFS,* 7 (Nov. 1980), 278-304.

A Marxist analysis of the ideological implications of *Alien* (q.v. above, under Stage, Film, and Television Drama). Includes useful comments (passim) on the humanoid robot, Ash; the ship's computer, "Mother"; the Company; and the "biological-mechanical" derelict alien spaceship seen early in the film.

Franklin, H. Bruce. "Don't Look Where We're Going: Visions of the Future in Science-Fiction Films, 1970-82." *SFS,* 10 (March 1983), 70-80.

Concentrates on two "great archetypal image[s] of the future" in SF films, "THE WONDER CITY OF THE FUTURE and THE MARVELOUS FLYING MACHINE," from *Metropolis* (1926) to *Blade Runner* (1982), with most of the discussion on the more important of the fifty-two Anglo-American films "set wholly or in part in some distinctly future time which were released for general distribution from 1970 through . . . summer 1982" (p. 71). See for contrast of the celebration of the "technocratic order" in *Things to Come* with an attack on that order—seen as a "totalitarian apparatus"—in such films as *THX 1138, Ice,* and *A Clockwork Orange* (p. 72); see also for films we were not able to cover above under Stage, Film, and Television Drama (*Ice* and *Blade Runner* of those listed here).

Geduld, Carolyn. *Filmguide to 2001: A Space Odyssey.* Bloomington, IN, and London: Indiana University Press, 1973.

Includes the credits for and an outline of *2001*, a Kubrick filmography through 1971, and an extensive biblio. on the film. CG's analysis of *2001* is occasionally polemical and flawed but far more often very sound. (See above, this section, the citation for Jerome Agel.)

Isaacs, Neil D. "Unstuck in Time: *Clockwork Orange* and *Slaughterhouse-Five.*" *Literature/Film Quarterly*, 1 (1973), 122-31.

Cited by Jerome Klinkowitz in "The Vonnegut Bibliography," q.v. above under Reference Works.

Jensen, Paul. "*Metropolis.*" *Film Heritage*, 3, No. 2 (Winter 1967-68), 22-28.

Cited in *New Film Index* (q.v. above, under Reference Works) as an "Extended Analysis" of *Metropolis* (dated 1927 in the *New Film Index*); see *Metropolis* above, under Stage, Film, and Television Drama.

Johnson, William, ed. *Focus on The Science Fiction Film.* Full citation above, under Acknowledgments.

Includes essays on *Things to Come* and *2001*.

Moskowitz, Sam. *Explorers of the Infinite: Shapers of Science Fiction.* Cleveland, OH: World, 1963; rpt. Westport, CT: Hyperion, 1974.

Includes a discussion of *R. U. R.*: ch. 13, "Karel Čapek: The Man Who Invented Robots."

Newhouse, Edward. "Charlie's Critics." *Partisan Review,* 3 (April 1936), 25-26.

Described in *New Film Index* (q.v. above, under Reference Works) as "An attack on critics who do not see *Modern Times* as a film of social consciousness." See *Modern Times* above, under Stage, Film, and Television Drama.

Pohl, Frederik, and Frederik Pohl IV. *Science Fiction: Studies in Film.* Full citation above, under Acknowledgments.

Includes summaries and discussions of *Metropolis, Things to Come,* Stanley Kubrick's SF through *A Clockwork Orange* (see ch. 4, "Dr. Kubrick's Clockwork Odyssey"), *Rollerball,* and other films useful for the study of mechanized environments in SF. Illustrated with stills from the films discussed.

"Rollerbrawl." Stan Hart, writer; Angelo Torres, artist. *Mad,* No. 181 (March 1976), pp. 4-[11].

Mad presents *Rollerball* as a commentary on contemporary society. Note opening words of the parody, among the spectators at a "Rollerbrawl" game: they explicitly relate violence in sports, rule by "the large corporations," and the destruction of individuality (three of the central themes of *Rollerball*) to 1976 America.

Rollin, Roger B. *"Deus in Machina:* Popular Culture's Myth of the Machine." *Journal of American Culture,* 2 (Summer 1979), 297-308.

Argues that (Western, esp. American) "popular culture has begun to transform machines into archetypal heroes, villains, even gods, and gods, heroes, and villains into machines." Gives many examples from film and TV; esp. useful for lesser-known works such as *Breaking the Sound Barrier,* and *Future Cop* and for its discussion of how "The Cars Are the Stars" in recent films.

Rose, Mark. "Machine." Ch. 6 of *Alien Encounters.* Full citation above, under Literary Criticism.

Includes an excellent discussion of "the opposition between man and machine" in the "narrative foreground" of *2001,* and of the resolution of that opposition in the conclusion of *2001* (see pp. 142-52).

Roth, Lane. "The Rejection of Rationalism in Recent Science Fiction Films." *Philosophy in Context,* 11 (1981), "Philosophy and Science Fiction," 3d essay, no pagination.

On *Star Wars, Star Trek: The Motion Picture,* and *The Empire Strikes Back* (all cited above, under Stage, Film, and Television Drama). Relates these films to Romantic rebellion: the spaceship "as a marvelous machine could aptly symbolize the material culmination of the Age of Reason . . . . In the context of the science fiction film, however, the spaceship signifies a denial of this philosophy." In the films he discusses, LR finds spaceships as obstacles or limitations, to be eliminated or transcended. See LR's notes for further reading.

Roud, Richard. "Anguish: *Alphaville*." *Sight and Sound*, 34 (Autumn 1965), 164-66.

In praise of Jean-Luc Godard's *Alphaville*; includes comment about *Tarzan vs. IBM* as the title Godard wanted. Cited in *New Film Index*. See above, under Stage, Film, and Television Drama, *Alphaville*.

Shaheen, Jack G., ed. *Nuclear War Films*. Carbondale and Edwardsville, IL: Southern Illinois University Press; London and Amsterdam: Feffer & Simons, 1978.

Includes an essay by George W. Linden on *Dr. Strangelove*, q.v. above, under Stage, Film, and Television Drama.

Sobchack, Vivian Carol. *The Limits of Infinity: The American Science Fiction Film, 1950-75*. South Brunswick, NJ, and New York: A. S. Barnes and Company; London: Thomas Yoseloff Ltd., 1980.

Includes a selected biblio. of books, articles, and unpublished material; over 140 film stills; and a good index. Makes useful comments (mostly passim) about many films important for the study of mechanized environments, esp. films featuring secure or dangerous containment in spaceships (see pp. 68-77).

Sontag, Susan. "The Imagination of Disaster." In Sontag, *Against Interpretation*. New York: Farrar, Straus & Giroux, 1965/66; rpt. Farrar, Straus & Giroux, Octagon Books, 1978. "Imagination" rpt. in *Science Fiction: The Future*. Dick Allen ed. New York: Harcourt, Brace, Jovanovich, 1971, 1983. Also rpt. in *Science Fiction: A Collection of Critical Essays*. Mark Rose, ed. Englewood Cliffs, NJ: Prentice-Hall, 1976.

See this highly influential essay for a general introd. to SF films of the 1950s and 1960s and for some brief but excellent comments on "technological man" and the theme of mechanization.

Strick, Philip. "Philip K. Dick and the Movies." *Foundation*, No. 26 (Oct. 1982), pp. 15-21.

Primarily on Ridley Scott's film, *Blade Runner* (1982)—a translation into cinema of P. K. Dick's *Do Androids Dream of Electric*

Sheep?—but with useful references to other works important for the study of mechanized environments in SF. The essay also passes on news of other films "said to be in preparation" of works by Dick (pp. 17-18). Sees *Blade Runner* as the first serious effort in film to deal with the motif of humans struggling against more or less mechanical "human facsimiles" (p. 16).

Zukofsky, Louis. *"Modern Times." Kulchur,* 1, No. 4 (Winter 1961), 75-82.

Cited in *New Film Index* (q.v. above, under Reference Works) as an "Extended Analysis" of *Modern Times* (q.v. above, under Stage, Film, and Television Drama).

VII. MUSIC

The Alan Parsons Project. *I Robot.* Arista, 7002, 1977.

"The story of the rise of the machine and the decline of man. Which paradoxically coincided with his discovery of the wheel . . . and a warning that his brief dominance of this planet will probably end, because he tried to create robot in his own image" (liner note).

Downes, Geoff et al. Yes. "Machine Messiah." On *Drama.* Atlantic, SD 16019, 1980.

Lyrics for the three parts of this song given on liner. Ironic or ambivalent celebration of the "Machine, machine Messiah," with an explicit allusion to William Blake's "satanic mills" (quoting Yes quoting Blake).

Edge, Graeme. "In the Beginning." 1969. Coll. on *This Is the Moody Blues.* London, XZAL 13344 TH, 1974, record 1, side 2.

A brief cut featuring a dialogue between a contemporary Cartesian Man and a computer that tries to convince him that he is magnetic ink.

Kraftwerk. *Die Mensch•Maschine* [*The Man•Machine*]. Electrola, ICO58-32843, 1978.

Includes "Die Roboter," "Spacelab," "Metropolis," and "Die Mensch • Maschine." Album described legitimately in Blue Angel, Inc., catalog as "Teutonic Techno-Rock." In addition to the "mechanical" aspects to the music, note the album cover and the pictures on the record jacket and labels. The cover gives the album's title in German, Russian, English, and French; the last is both a famous phrase in French and the title of a 1748 work by Julien Offroy de la Mettrie arguing the rigorously materialistic thesis that human beings are machines. The pictures suggest both Susan Sontag's "technocratic" men (see Sontag entry under Stage, Film, and Television Drama Criticism) and a combined alumni of Hitler Youth and the more decadent cabarets of the Weimar Republic.

Moraz, Patrick. *I.* Atlantic, SD 18175, 1976.

A " 'hotel' offering," according to the liner notes. The guests in the hotel are united "in search of the ultimate experience"; the hotel building "is controlled by a sphere hovering overhead, within which is stored all information on the emotions, sentiments and sensations of all the people in the various rooms."

The Police. *Ghost in the Machine.* A&M, SP-3730, 1981.

Note esp. "Spirits in the Material World" (side 1, first cut) and "Rehumanize Yourself" (side 2, second cut). One reviewer comments that "Rehumanize Yourself" describes "a totally mechanized society in which violence has become a 'social norm' " (Jeff Callan, "Unabridged" supplement to *The Miami Student* [Miami University, Oxford, OH], 16 Oct. 1981, p. 2).

Reynolds, Malvina. "Little Boxes." On *Pete Seeger's Greatest Hits.* Columbia, CS 9416, n.d., side 1, first cut.

"You see, the machine says to all of us . . . 'If you want it cheap, take it like I make it—rectangular.' The song is an especial favorite with university students and teachers" (Seeger's comments on record jacket).

Slick, Grace (lyrics), and Jorma Kaukonen (music). The Jefferson Airplane. "Eat Starch Mom." On *Long John Silver.* Grunt, FTR-1007, 1972.

Lyrics on inner sleeve. Deals with America's love of things mechanical and lesser regard for things natural and human.

The Tubes. *Remote Control.* A&M, SP-4715, 1979.

Album cover depicts a baby in front of a TV set; the set has a nipple attached, apparently signifying TV as the "nurturer" of the child.

The music on the album deals primarily with television, including such songs as "TV Is King" and "Telecide."

VIII. BACKGROUND READING

Adams, Henry. "The Dynamo and the Virgin (1900)." Ch. XXV of *The Education of Henry Adams: An Autobiography.* Henry Cabot Lodge, ed. Boston and New York: Houghton Mifflin, 1918; rpt. in *Theme of the Machine,* q.v. above under Anthologies and Collections.

In the Gallery of Machines at the Great Exposition of 1900, HA begins a meditation on force—force expressed spiritually, sexually, physically. Asserts that "the nearest approach to the revolution of 1900 [the scientific and technological revolution] was that of 310, when Constantine set up the Cross" (pp. 382-83). Implies that in the new world after 1900, esp. in America, "the symbol of infinity," or of greatest force, would be neither Venus nor Virgin, fecundity nor deity, but the dynamo (pp. 380, 383-85). See H. G. Wells, "Lord of the Dynamos," above, under Fiction.

Arendt, Hannah. *On Violence.* New York: Harcourt, Brace & World, 1969, 1970.

Parts II and III relevant; see esp. pp. 38-39 for bureaucratic tyranny as "rule by Nobody," and pp. 81-87 for the rebellion of human beings using our "faculty of action" against "the huge party machines" and the apparatus of the state. Many of the world machines in dystopian fiction may be literalizations of such machine metaphors.

_____. *The Origins of Totalitarianism.* 2d enlarged edn., 1958; rpt. Cleveland and New York: World Publishing Co., Meridian, 1958.

Most relevant: Part Three: Totalitarianism, esp. ch. 11, part II ("Totalitarian Organization"), and ch. 12 ("Totalitarianism in Power"). A massive work documenting, among other things, the alienation of large groups of people from effective participation in political life. See for totalitarianism and for possible real-world referents for the motif of individual human helplessness before the machine of the state.

Barton, Marthalee and Dwight W. Stevenson, guest co-eds. Technology and Pessimism special issue of *Alternative Futures,* 3, No. 2 (Spring 1980).

Esp. useful articles by Eugene Goodheart, Sverre Lyngstad, and Leo Marx (all cited above, under Literary Criticism). The other articles, notably that by Richard Falk, provide useful real-world background.

Bergson, Henri. "Laughter." Ca. 1900. Available in various trans. Trans. by Presses Universitaires de France available in *Comedy*. Wylie Sypher, ed. Garden City, NY: Doubleday, Anchor, 1956.

Argues that the cause of laughter is the superimposition of the mechanical upon the organic, more specifically, upon the human. See for a simple introd. to HB on "vitalism" (a traditional antithesis to "mechanism").

Bettelheim, Bruno. "Joey: 'A Mechanical Boy.' " *Scientific American,* March 1959. Rpt. in *Man Alone,* q.v. below.

A case study of an autistic boy who was convinced that he was a machine. (See Lewis Yablonsky, *Robopaths*, this section.) Joey creates for himself an "artificial, mechanical womb," initially an "electrical papoose."

Bramson, Leon, and Michael S. Schudson. "Mass Society." *Encyclopædia Britannica: Macropædia.* 1974 edn.

Good introd. to the hypothesized effects of mass society that may be the real-world referents in much pessimistic SF using the theme of mechanized societies and individuals. Includes a briefly annotated, selected biblio. of works on mass society from Alexis de Tocqueville's *Democracy in America* (1835) through the work of contemporary scholars.

Braverman, Harry. *Labor and Monopoly Capital: the Degradation of Work in the Twentieth Century.* New York: Monthly Review Press, 1974.

Includes a Marxist critique of Taylorism. (See *CW* essay by Gorman Beauchamp, and entry below for Frederick W. Taylor.)

Carlyle, Thomas. "Signs of the Times." *Edinburgh Review*, No. 98 (1829). Coll. in *Thomas Carlyle: Critical and Miscellaneous Essays.* 5 vols. London: Chapman and Hall, 1899; rpt. New York: AMS Press, 1969 Centenary Edition of *The Works of Thomas Carlyle.* Vol. II (Vol. XXVII in the thirty-vol. *Works*).

A very influential essay contrasting the "outward" vision of the world, translated into attempts to control nature and humans through *"Mechanics,"* and the "inward" attempt of *"Dynamics"* to understand "the primary, unmodified forces and energies of man," which TC sees possessed of "a truly vital and *infinite* character" (pp. 66 and 68 f.). Argues that in "the Mechanical Age" of early nineteenth century Europe, people have "grown mechanical in head and in heart," with even philosophers organized into institutes that are "like so many . . . hives" (pp. 59, 63, 62). Deals with the metaphor of "the Machine of Society" and compares "Mechanism" to "some glass bell" that "encircles and imprisons us" (pp. 66, 81, and passim). Discussed by Leo Marx in ch. IV, sections 3 and 4, of *Machine in the Garden* (q.v. below).

Eaves, Morris. "Blake and the Artistic Machine: An Essay in Decorum and Technology." *PMLA*, 92 (Oct. 1977), 903-27.

On classic vs. Romantic aesthetics, and William Blake's idea of how "mechanical order becomes artistic order" (ME's abstract).

Eichner, Hans. "The Rise of Modern Science and the Genesis of Romanticism." *PMLA*, 97 (Jan. 1982), 8-30.

Argues that the temporary "replacement of the mechanical philosophy by an organic view of the cosmos is one of the most significant features of Romanticism." Explains "why the Romantics felt compelled to attack the mechanical philosophy" of the Scientific Age and "confirms [Morse] Peckham's findings that the new organicism accounts for a large part of Romantic theory" (quotations from EH's abstract). A very well written and important introd. to mechanism vs. organism: a debate of great significance for the motif of mechanized environments in the arts.

Eliade, Mircea. *The Myth of the Eternal Return (or, Cosmos and History).* France: 1949; English trans. 1954. Willard R. Trask, trans. Bollingen Series, No. XLVI. Princeton, NJ: Princeton University Press, 1971.

Summarizes EM's ideas on the social and psychological necessity for occasional or periodic return to the formless, the chaotic. See for the opposition of the living (vital and comic) against the mechanical. (See above, under Fiction, Harlan Ellison, "Repent, Harlequin!")

Ellul, Jacques. *The Technological Society. (La Technique ou l'enjeu du siècle,* 1954). John Wilkinson, trans. New York: Knopf, 1964. Rev.

American edn. New York: Knopf, 1967. Also, New York: Vintage Books, 1967.

Significant for its analysis of the replacement of "political man" by "the technician" (see Preface, p. vii of 1967 Knopf edn.). More significant for the analysis of contemporary industrial society which JE encapsulates in ch. 1: the machine is important because it "represents the ideal toward which technique strives. The machine is solely, exclusively, technique . . . . wherever a technical factor exists, it results, almost inevitably, in mechanization: technique transforms everything it touches into a machine" (p. 4)—and ours is a "technological society." JE's more recent works include *The Political Illusion* (New York: Random House, 1967), and *Le Système technicien* (Paris: Calmann-Levy, 1977). See Volkmar Lauber, "Efficiency and After," below.

Foucault, Michel. *Discipline and Punish: The Birth of the Prison.* Alan Sheridan, trans. New York: Pantheon, 1977.

MF cites Jeremy Bentham's plan for an ideal prison, the Panopticon, in which the prisoner is constantly subject to surveillance; the motif of constant surveillance is very important in dystopian fiction where the world, in a sense, becomes a prison.

Giedion, Siegfried. *Mechanization Takes Command.* New York: Oxford University Press, 1948.

According to Wolfe (p. 12), *MTC* recounts the effects of nineteenth-century technology on human behavior; GS reaches conclusions similar to those of Lewis Mumford in *The Pentagon of Power* (q.v. below).

Ihde, Don. "A Phenomenology of Man-Machine Relations." In *Work, Technology, and Education,* q.v. below, pp. 186-220.

Focuses upon "a descriptive psychology of man-machine relations," starting with the notion "that the machine . . . may be thought of as a 'means' of relating to the world"—one of our major means in everyday life in industrial societies.

Koestler, Arthur. *The Ghost in the Machine.* New York: Macmillan, 1968.

Includes a discussion of the hierarchical organization of life and an attack on the "pseudoscience called Behaviourism" (p. 5). Cf. and contrast Stanley Milgram's discussion of hierarchy in *Obedience to Authority*, q.v. below; see entries below for B. F. Skinner and John B. Watson.

Lasky, Melvin J. *Utopia and Revolution.* Chicago and London: University of Chicago Press, 1976.

Contains useful comments (mostly passim) on the metaphors and imagery of revolution and radical reform. Such metaphors for change—particularly the organic image of birth—should be contrasted with the images of mechanism often used to symbolize dystopian stasis. See below, citation for Giuseppa Saccaro-Battisti.

Lauber, Volkmar. "Efficiency and After: The Dilemma of the Technicized Society." *Alternative Futures*, 2, No. 4 (Fall 1979), 47-65.

Summarizes, places into its historical context, and extends the work of Jacques Ellul (q.v. above, this section). See VL's notes for further readings. Discusses the opposition of "technique" to political life, ideology, "spontaneity, creativity, [and] biological rhythms" (pp. 56-57).

Livingston, Dennis. "Science Fiction Models of Future Order Systems." *International Organization*, 25 (Spring 1971), 254-70.

Perhaps as much literary criticism as background, this essay handles the political aspects of John Brunner's *Stand on Zanzibar*, George Orwell's *Nineteen Eighty-Four* (both cited above, under Fiction), and a number of other works of immediate or secondary interest, including Poul Anderson, "Un-Man"; Fritz Leiber, *Gather Darkness!*" Andre Maurois, "The War against the Moon"; Frederik Pohl and C. M. Kornbluth, *The Space Merchants*; Mack Reynolds, "The Five Way Secret Agent"; and R. Theobald and J. M. Scott, *Teg's 1994: An Anticipation of the Near Future.* Refers briefly to other SF works, including "prophetic novels" by H. G. Wells and Robert A. Heinlein. Deals well with politically and socially significant technology.

Man Alone: Alienation in Modern Society. Eric and Mary Josephson, eds. New York: Dell, 1962.

A collection of essays and selections, "from Karl Marx to James Baldwin, from Dostoyevsky to Ignazio Silone," on alienation. Includes Bruno Bettelheim, "Joey" (q.v. above, this section) and selections from Lewis Mumford, C. Wright Mills, and William H. Whyte. An excellent introd. to the concept of alienation, an important theme in much dystopian fiction.

Mandel, Ernest, and George Novack. *The Marxist Theory of Alienation.* New York: Pathfinder, 1970.

An original introd. and rpts. of three essays by Mandel and Novack. Note the cover of *TMTA:* "Detail of a fresco by Digeo Rivera. This panel . . . was inspired by an actual punch press which was operated by manacled workers whose hands were automatically pulled back by the handcuffs each time the press descended" (cover note on copyright page). The essays develop systematically the causes of alienation symbolized by the picture on the cover.

Marx, Leo. *The Machine in the Garden: Technology and the Pastoral Ideal in America.* New York: Oxford University Press, 1964, 1970; rpt. A Galaxy Book, 1967, paperback.

The "garden" is America, the New World; the machine is urban culture in general and technology in particular. (An intelligent application of LM's seminal and indispensable work may be found in Karen Blair's analysis of *Star Trek*, q.v. above, under Stage, Film, and Television Drama Criticism.)

Merchant, Carolyn. *The Death of Nature: Women, Ecology and the Scientific Revolution.* San Francisco: Harper and Row, 1980.

Cited by Phyllis J. Day in her article "EarthMother/WitchMother: Feminism and Ecology Renewed" (*Extrapolation*, 23 [Spring 1982], 12-21). "According to Merchant, the new mechanistic ordering of the universe brought by the scientific revolution provided a new perspective on the place of humankind in nature" (Day, p. 18)—a place of dominion within a mechanism, rather than a cellular function in a cosmic organism.

Merton, Robert K. "Bureaucratic Structure and Personality." In Merton, *Social Theory and Social Structure.* Glencoe, IL: Free Press, 1957, ch. VI, pp. 195-206.

On bureaucracy, the *apparat* that may be the real-world referent of some of the imagery of machines in pessimistic SF.

Michels, Robert. *Political Parties: A Sociological Study of the Oligarchic Tendencies of Modern Bureaucracy.* 1915. Eden Paul and Cedar

Paul, trans. New York: Free Press, 1962, 1966; London and Toronto: Collier-Macmillan, 1962.

From his study of the bureaucratization of the German Social Democratic Party and other European socialist parties (the most democratic parties in Europe), RM inferred the "iron law of oligarchy." That is, all large organizations, however democratic in ideology, tend to fall under the control of a small group of knowledgeable, experienced, and energetic people who hold and seek to retain power. RM uses without apology mechanical metaphors for political phenomena in the bureaucratized state.

Milgram, Stanley. *Obedience to Authority.* New York and other cities: Harper & Row, 1974.

See esp. chs. 10, 11, and 15. SM opposes autonomy to being in "the agentic state" and holds groups in extreme agentic states to "consist not of individuals but automatons" (p. 181).

Mills, C. Wright. *The Power Elite.* New York: Oxford University Press, 1956.

See for powerlessness of individuals in real-world mass societies.

Mouzelis, Nicos P. *Organization and Bureaucracy: An Analysis of Modern Theories.* London: Routledge, 1967.

Summarizes many important recent theories on bureaucracy and how life in an *apparat* leads to alienation and feelings of helplessness. Notes that the "concentration of the means of administration" (of which the means of production is only a special case) leads to oligarchic control in which each individual "becomes a simple cog in a machine, a well disciplined and regulated automaton." See above, this section, Robert Michels, *Political Parties.*

Mumford, Lewis. *The Myth of the Machine.* Vol. 1, *Technics and Human Development,* 1966, 1967. Vol. 2, *The Pentagon of Power,* 1964, 1970. New York: Harcourt Brace Jovanovich, 1970.

Due to the application of mathematics and the physical sciences to technology, we have entered a new stage of human relationship to technics. "With this new 'megatechnics' the dominant minority will create a uniform, all-enveloping, super-planetary structure, designed for automatic operation. Instead of functioning actively as an autonomous personality, man will become a passive, purpose-

less, machine-conditioned animal whose proper functions, as technicians now interpret man's role, will either be fed into the machine
or strictly limited and controlled for the benefit of de-personalized,
collective organizations" (Vol. 1, ch. 1, p. 3). Cf. Jacques Ellul,
cited above, this section.

———. "Utopia, The City and The Machine." In *Utopias and Utopian
Thought*. Frank E. Manuel, ed. Cambridge and Boston: Riverside
& Houghton Mifflin, 1966, pp. 3-24. (Augmented rpt. of article in
Daedalus, Spring 1965).

Traces the "utopian" city's rise to the invention of the (labor) army:
"the collective human machine, the platonic model for all later
machines." Concludes that the price of the urban utopia was "total
submission to a central authority, forced labor, lifetime specialization, inflexible regimentation, one-way communication, and readiness for war" (pp. 15, 17).

Pirsig, Robert M. *Zen and the Art of Motorcycle Maintenance*. New York:
William Morrow and Company, 1974; rpt. Toronto, New York,
London: Bantam, 1975.

A best-selling attempt to show how a world split into "hip and
square, classic and romantic, technological and humanistic" can be
reunited through a proper appreciation of "Quality," a "real understanding" of which "*captures* the System, tames it, and puts it to
work for one's own personal use . . . " (Bantam, edn., p. 200). Since
"the System" is mostly technology and the intellectual approach to
the world underlying technology (pp. 14-15), the analysis offered
by this work is quite useful for an introd. to the philosophical oppositions RMP has indentified—even if Quality, thus far, has failed
to synthesize the oppositions and contradictions of Western culture.
(See below, the entries for Theodore Roszak.)

Randall, John Herman, Jr. *The Making of the Modern Mind: A Survey of
the Intellectual Background of the Present Age*. Boston and other
cities: Houghton Mifflin, 1926; rpt. New York: Columbia University
Press, 1976.

The survey starts in earnest in the medieval period (but with backward glances at the ancient world) and goes through World War I
to end with the internationalism and pacifism that seemed the reasonable responses to the particularly senseless carnage of the Great
War. Most immediately useful for telling well and simply the story
of the rise of "The mechanical interpretation of Nature" and the

subsequent vision of a "Newtonian World-Machine" in the seventeenth and eighteenth centuries, and of "The Romantic Protest Against the Age of Reason" and its mechanistic worldview in the nineteenth century: see esp. chs. X-XI, XVIII-XIX, XXI. The discussion of "Philosophic Reactions to the Growing World of Mechanism" (ch. XXI) includes generous quotations from Victorian and more recent poetry.

Riesman, David. *The Lonely Crowd.* New Haven: Yale University Press, 1950.

A study of alienation in mass society.

Roszak, Theodore. *The Making of a Counter Culture: Reflections on the Technocratic Society and Its Youthful Opposition.* Garden City, NY: Doubleday, 1969 (published simultaneously in hardcover and Anchor paperback edns.). "Portions of chapters I, II, IV, V and VI originally appeared in *The Nation* in March and April 1968 and have been revised for publication in this volume."

In Modern society, all are "locked into" a figurative "leviathan industrial apparatus" ruled by possessors of "technical expertise" who justify their rule by appeals to "Reason, material Progress, [and] the scientific world view." In a resurgence of the Romantic movement, "by way of a dialectic [Karl] Marx could never have imagined, technocratic America produces a potentially revolutionary element among its young": the counterculture of the 1960s and its opposition to technocracy (Anchor edn., pp. 21, 146, 34). See for real-world referents for fictional mechanized environments. (See entries above, for TR, under Fiction, and for Jacques Ellul, and Robert Pirsig, this section.)

_____. *Where the Wasteland Ends.* Garden City, NY: Doubleday, 1972.

The "wasteland" has been produced by the lack of discipline in our use and acceptance of technology; TR seeks to transcend, and thereby end, the wasteland (Wolfe, p. 12).

Saccaro-Battisti, Giuseppa (also, Giuseppa Saccaro Battisti). "Changing Metaphors of Political Structures." *Journal of the History of Ideas*, 44 (Jan.-March 1983), 31-54.

Originally scheduled to appear in revised and expanded form in *CW*, this essay includes a highly relevant and important discussion of metaphors "describing the socio-political structure as a machine" or "comparing this structure to the human body" (p. 33).

Sheckley, Robert. *Futuropolis: Impossible Cities of Science Fiction and Fantasy.* 1978; rpt. New York: A & W Publishers, 1978.

Pictures with explanatory text of many proposed (and sometimes built) or envisioned cities, ranging from a plan by Dinocrates, architect to Alexander the Great, to photographs of real cities to comic book art to SF illustration to illustrations for recent proposals for space colonies. Most of the imagined cities are highly mechanized and will be viewed by different people as eutopian, dystopian, hellish, heavenly, and most stops between.

Skinner, B. F. *Beyond Freedom and Dignity.* New York: Knopf, 1971.

BFS denies the existence of "autonomous man" and asserts the current existence of a "technology of behavior"—conditioning—which should be used rationally and systematically. BFS's opponents see him proposing a view of humans-as-automata and recommending for us a dystopia of totalitarian control. BFS and the whole school of Behaviorism are favorite targets in a fair amount of pessimistic S. F. and dystopian satire. (See entry below for John B. Watson.)

Soleri, Paolo. *Arcology: The City in the Image of Man.* Cambridge, MA, and London: MIT Press, 1970.

Presents PS's ideas for a real-world civilization based in "*a structure called an arcology, or ecological architecture.*" Allowing humankind to function in the physical universe ("*an immense megamachine*"), an arcology is a city viewed as a huge organism, preferably one including a computer brain as well as the interacting organic brains of its human inhabitants. (PS's idea of an arcology is modified and given fictional life in Larry Niven and Jerry Pournelle's novel, *Oath of Fealty* [1981], in which an arcology is an antibureaucratic environment.)

Taylor, Frederick W. *The Principles of Scientific Management.* 1911; rpt. New York: Norton, 1967.

To its enemies, "scientific management" meant reducing workers to automata doing their jobs in the manner their bosses' hired experts ruled most efficient. In mechanized industries, this meant fitting workers ever more perfectly to the rhythm of the machines. For further readings on FWT and Taylorism, see Carolyn H. Rhodes, "Frederick Winslow Taylor's System of Scientific Management," cited above, under Literary Criticism; see also the *CW* essay by Gorman Beauchamp.

Technocracy: Technological Social Design. Savannah, OH: Technocracy, Inc., 1975.

Literature on the Technocracy movement is available cheaply from Continental Headquarters, Technocracy, Inc., Savannah, OH 44874. This pamphlet provides a simple introd. to Technocracy and briefly outlines how the "Technate of North America" will be run after the technocrats take over. (See under Literary Criticism the entry for W. Warren Wagar.)

Technology and Pessimism. Special issue of *Alternative Futures*.

Listed above, this section, under Marthalee Barton and Dwight W. Stevenson, guest co-eds.

Turner, Victor. "Passages, Margins, and Poverty: Religious Symbols of Communitas." *Worship*, 46 (Aug.-Sept. 1972), 390-412; (Oct.), 432-94. Rpt. as ch. 6 of Turner, *Dramas, Fields, and Metaphors: Symbolic Action in Human Society*. Ithaca, NY, and London: Cornell University Press, 1974.

Turner's discussion of structure vs. *communitas* ("community"), may be significant for a study of clockwork societies: the rebels opposed to such machine-worlds are necessarily outsiders, "liminal" characters.

_____. *The Ritual Process: Structure and Anti-Structure.* 1969; rpt. Ithaca, NY: Cornell University Press, 1977.

See chs. 3-5 for structured, hierarchical society vs. *communitas* ("community"): society as an "essential We" (Martin Buber's phrase). Exaggerations and perversions of structure and *communitas* may be the real-world referents of mechanical and hive worlds in dystopian SF.

Wagar, W. Warren. "The Steel-Gray Saviour."

Cited and annotated above, under Literary Criticism.

"A War on French Computers." *Newsweek,* 28 April 1980, p. 56.

> Brief report including mention of the French underground organization CLODO: "the Committee for the Liquidation or Deterrence of Computers." This group sees real-world computers as "the favorite instrument of the powerful. . . . used to classify, control, and to repress."

Watson, John B. "Psychology as the Behaviorist Views It." *The Psychological Review*, 20 (March 1913), 158-77.

> Classic statement of the Behaviorist view that "the prediction and control of behavior" is "psychology's sole task." See also JBW, *Psychology from the Standpoint of a Behaviorist* (1919), and his work for lay readers, *Behaviorism* (1924, 1925; rev. edn. 1930). JBW's name is preserved and much of his philosophy followed in the World State of Aldous Huxley's *Brave New World* (q.v. above, under Fiction). See above, this section, the entry for B. F. Skinner.

Welsford, Enid. *The Fool: His Social and Literary History.* 1935; rpt. Garden City, NY: Doubleday, 1961.

> The fool, Harlequin, Trickster, and Lord of Misrule have often been used by wise societies as antidotes for the stagnation and oppression threatened or achieved by too much social order. EW's work is the classic investigation of the role of the fool. (Note the Jester in Arthur Clarke, *City and the Stars*, and Harlan Ellison's Harlequin hero in "Repent, Harlequin!"; both works cited above, under Fiction.)

Whyte, William H. *The Organization Man.* 1956; rpt. Garden City, NY: Doubleday, Anchor, n.d.

> A serious discussion of "Organization Man" as a new and significant variety of *H. sapiens sapiens*. WHW's book was highly influential in the later 1950s and early 1960s and is still quite useful for an analysis of the bureaucratization of real life and the idea of the "Organization Man" in fiction.

Willey, Basil. Ch. V, "The Philosophical Quest for Truth—Descartes," and ch. VI, "The Philosophical Quest for Truth—Hobbes." In Willey, *The Seventeenth Century Background.* New York: Columbia University Press, 1935; rpt. Garden City, NY: Doubleday, Anchor, 1953.

On the effects on "literary developments in England after the middle of the seventeenth century" of the methodical thinking of René Descartes and "the perfection of his mechanised universe" (pp. 94-95 of Doubleday rpt.). Also treats the influence of the militant materialism and determinism of Thomas Hobbes.

Wills, Gary. Part Two, "A Scientific Paper," ch. 7. In Wills, *Inventing America: Jefferson's Declaration of Independence*. Garden City, NY: Doubleday, 1978; rpt. Random House, Vintage Books, 1979, pp. [93]-110.

On the liberating aspects of the Newtonian vision of a clockwork universe. See for a relatively simple introd. to the literally revolutionary effect of a mechanistic vision of the universe, society, and human beings.

Winner, Langdon. *Autonomous Technology: Technics-Out-of-Control as a Theme in Political Thought*. Cambridge, MA, and London: MIT Press, 1977.

Wolfe cites this work as an excellent survey of the subject identified in its subtitle. Cf. Jacques Ellul and Lewis Mumford, works cited above, this section.

Work, Technology, and Education: Dissenting Essays in the Intellectual Foundations of American Education. Walter Feinberg and Henry Rosemont, Jr., eds. Urbana, IL. Chicago, London: University of Illinois Press, 1975.

Immediately relevant: Kenneth D. Benne, "Technology and Community: Conflicting Bases of Educational Authority"; Marx Wartofsky, "Art and Technology: Conflicting Models of Education? The Uses of a Cultural Myth"; Don Ihde, "A Phenomenology of Man-Machine Relations" (q.v. above, this section). Taken all together, these essays attack contemporary American schools as places where the human soul is just "another element to be shaped, molded, and conditioned to the requirements of machine production" (Introduction, p. 11).

Yablonsky, Lewis. *Robopaths: People as Machines*. 1972; rpt. Baltimore: Penguin, 1972, 1973.

Discusses, passim, the state as machine, and "social machines" like corporations and many schools and families. Such metaphors are literalized in much pessimistic SF.

INDEX

CONTRIBUTORS

MERRITT ABRASH, Professor of History in the Department of the Arts at Rensselaer Polytechnic Institute, has become involved in science fiction and utopian studies through RPI's Human Dimensions Center. He organized the first Conference on Utopian Studies, coedited the scholarly quarterly *Alternative Futures*, and has published articles on Thomas More, Leonardo da Vinci, and art history.

ALEXANDRA ALDRIDGE was cofounder and coeditor of *Alternative Futures*, a journal of utopian studies, from 1978-81. She is currently an Associate Professor of Interdisciplinary Technology, College of Technology, Eastern Michigan University, and the director of its graduate program in technology and culture. She has published extensively in the fields of future studies and technology and culture and is at work on a book on the philosophical dimensions of futurism.

GORMAN BEAUCHAMP is an Associate Professor of Humanities, College of Engineering, University of Michigan; he was cofounder and Associate Editor of *Alternative Futures*. He is author of *A Reader's Guide to Jack London* and some thirty articles on subjects ranging from Shakespeare to science fiction. At present he is working on a book entitled *The Case Against Utopia: Studies in Dystopian Fiction*.

VALERIE BROEGE was educated at Vassar College and Bryn Mawr College and has taught Classical Studies at the University of Western Ontario. Currently teaching Humanities at Vanier College in Montreal, she has published a number of articles on the classical tradition and the modern world, astrology, and Canadian literature.

LAWRENCE BROER, Professor of English at the University of South Florida, is the author of three books, one of which is *Hemingway's Spanish Tragedy* (University of Alabama Press, 1973); dozens of articles; papers and reviews on twentieth-century literature; and is presently working on a full-length critical study of the works of Kurt Vonnegut, Jr.

PHYLLIS J. DAY is an Assistant Professor of Sociology and Social Welfare at Purdue University. Her degrees, all from the University of Michigan, include A.B., 1956; M.S.W., 1969; M.A., Sociology, 1974; and Ph.D., Sociology and Social Work, 1976. Her areas of study include the origins of social policy, sexism and racism in public programs, and social welfare as social control. She has published articles in *Social Service Review* and the *Journal of Sociology and Social Welfare.*

CHARLES ELKINS is an Associate Professor in English and Associate Dean of the College of Arts and Sciences at Florida International University in Miami, Florida. He is a coeditor of *Science-Fiction Studies* and has written several articles on SF and the sociology of literature.

WILLIAM H. HARDESTY III is an Associate Professor of English at Miami University, Oxford, Ohio. A contributor to the *Survey of Science Fiction Literature* and the *Survey of Modern Fantasy Literature*, he has also written articles on Samuel R. Delany, alternate universe novels, and Victorian literature. He has served terms as the Secretary of the Science Fiction Research Association and the Area Coordinator for SF and Fantasy of the Popular Culture Association.

LEONARD HELDRETH holds a Ph.D. in English Language and Literature from the University of Illinois at Urbana-Champaign. He currently teaches at Northern Michigan University (Marquette) and has written numerous papers and articles on SF and on film. His essay on fighting machines in SF appeared in *The Mechanical God: Machines in Science Fiction*, the companion volume to *Clockwork Worlds.*

THOMAS P. HOFFMAN is currently teaching American Literature and Drama courses at Midwestern State University, Wichita Falls, Texas. He has presented papers on Kurt Vonnegut, Jr., Neil Simon, and Joseph Heller at seven national conferences of the American Culture Association, South Central Modern Language Association, and the Popular Culture Association.

ELIZABETH ANNE HULL teaches SF as well as other literature and writing courses at William Rainey Harper College, where she is an Associate Professor of English. She has published articles on Robert A. Heinlein, Isaac Asimov, Lloyd Biggle, Jr., Judith Merril, and teaching SF. She is editor of both the *SFRA Newsletter* and the *World SF Newsletter* and has been active for over ten years in the Midwest Modern Language Association and in the Popular Culture Association, regionally, nationally, and internationally.

DANIEL W. INGERSOLL, JR., received his Ph.D. in anthropology from Harvard University in 1971 and has taught at the University of Massachusetts, Amherst (1970-1973), and at St. Mary's College of Maryland (1975-present). With John Yellen and W. K. MackDonald, he edited *Experimental Archaeology.*

REIMER JEHMLICH is a Senior Lecturer in English Literature at Siegen University in the Federal Republic of Germany. His chief fields of interest are English love poetry and science fiction and related genres. He has published scholarly articles on the English poets John Donne, Sir Philip Sidney, and Michael Drayton, and on SF.

ARTHUR O. LEWIS, Professor of English and Associate Dean, College of the Liberal Arts, The Pennsylvania State University, has written widely on a number of subjects ranging from emblem books to future studies and has been editor or co-editor of nine books, as well as of the forty-one-volume *Utopian Literature* series. He has served as President of the Science Fiction Research Association, as Chairman of the Steering Committee of the Conference on (now Society for) Utopian Studies, and served on the Board of Editors of *Alternative Futures.*

CHARLES WM. SULLIVAN III teaches American Folklore and Northern European Mythology in the English Department of East Carolina University. He edited the science fiction textbook/anthology, *As Tomorrow Becomes Today*, and is currently the editor of the *Children's Folklore Newsletter*. His articles on science fiction, fantasy, folklore, and mythology have appeared in a variety of journals and anthologies.

ABOUT THE EDITORS

THOMAS P. DUNN is an Associate Professor of English at Miami University's Hamilton Campus. He is an Associate Editor of *The Year's Scholarship in Science Fiction, Fantasy & Horror Literature* and a frequent contributor to *Science Fiction & Fantasy Book Review*. In addition to his collaboration with Richard D. Erlich, he has published essay-reviews in the *Survey of Science Fiction Literature* and the *Survey of Modern Fantasy Literature*, has presented several papers on SF at academic conferences, and has given workshops on the teaching of poetry.

RICHARD D. ERLICH is an Associate Professor in English at the Oxford, Ohio, campus of Miami University, where he teaches courses in Shakespeare, composition, and science fiction. Alone and in collaboration, he has published essays on Alexander Pope, D. H. Lawrence, historical criticism of Renaissance and other early literature, Ursula K. Le Guin's science fiction and fantasy, and various science fiction works by Harlan Ellison, D. F. Jones, and Frederik Pohl and C. M. Kornbluth. With Thomas P. Dunn he has presented and published papers on the theme of mechanized environments in SF and has edited the first volume in the Greenwood Press series Contributions to the Study of Science Fiction and Fantasy, *The Mechanical God: Machines in Science Fiction.*